An Anthology of Neo-Latin Poetry by Classical Scholars

BLOOMSBURY NEO-LATIN SERIES

Series editors: William M. Barton, Stephen Harrison, Gesine Manuwald and Bobby Xinyue

Early Modern Texts and Anthologies
Edited by Stephen Harrison and Gesine Manuwald

Volume 9

The 'Early Modern Texts and Anthologies' strand of the *Bloomsbury Neo-Latin Series* presents editions of texts with English translations, introductions and notes. Volumes include complete editions of longer single texts and themed anthologies bringing together texts from particular genres, periods or countries and the like.

These editions are primarily aimed at students and scholars and intended to be suitable for use in university teaching, with introductions that give authoritative but not exhaustive accounts of the relevant texts and authors, and commentaries that provide sufficient help for the modern reader in noting links with classical Latin texts and bringing out the cultural context of writing.

Alongside the series' 'Studies in Early Modern Latin' strand, it is hoped that these editions will help to bring important and interesting Neo-Latin texts of the period from 1350 to 1800 to greater prominence in study and scholarship, and make them available for a wider range of academic disciplines as well as for the rapidly growing study of Neo-Latin itself.

Also available in this series

An Anthology of British Neo-Latin Literature, edited by L. B. T. Houghton, Gesine Manuwald and Lucy R. Nicholas
An Anthology of European Neo-Latin Literature, edited by Daniel Hadas, Gesine Manuwald and Lucy R. Nicholas
An Anthology of Neo-Latin Literature in British Universities, edited by Gesine Manuwald and Lucy R. Nicholas
De persecutione Anglicana by Robert Persons S.J.: A Critical Edition of the Latin Text with English Translation, Commentary and Introduction, edited by Victor Houliston and Marianne Dircksen (with the assistance of Koos Kritzinger)
Ermolao Barbaro's On Celibacy 1 and 2, edited by Gareth Williams
Ermolao Barbaro's On Celibacy 3 and 4 and On the Duty of the Ambassador, edited by Gareth Williams
Japan on the Jesuit Stage, edited by Akihiko Watanabe
Roger Ascham's Themata Theologica, edited by Lucy R. Nicholas

An Anthology of
Neo-Latin Poetry
by Classical Scholars

Edited by William M. Barton, Stephen Harrison,
Gesine Manuwald and Bobby Xinyue

BLOOMSBURY ACADEMIC
LONDON • NEW YORK • OXFORD • NEW DELHI • SYDNEY

BLOOMSBURY ACADEMIC
Bloomsbury Publishing Plc, 50 Bedford Square, London, WC1B 3DP, UK
Bloomsbury Publishing Inc, 1385 Broadway, New York, NY 10018, USA
Bloomsbury Publishing Ireland, 29 Earlsfort Terrace, Dublin 2, D02 AY28, Ireland

BLOOMSBURY, BLOOMSBURY ACADEMIC and the Diana logo
are trademarks of Bloomsbury Publishing Plc

First published in Great Britain 2024
Paperback edition published 2025

Copyright © William M. Barton, Stephen Harrison, Gesine Manuwald,
Bobby Xinyue and Contributors, 2024

William M. Barton, Stephen Harrison, Gesine Manuwald, Bobby Xinyue
and Contributors have asserted their right under the Copyright, Designs and
Patents Act, 1988, to be identified as Authors of this work.

Cover image: Biblioteca Medicea Laurenziana in Florence, Italy.
© Yuri Turkov/Alamy Stock Photo

All rights reserved. No part of this publication may be: i) reproduced or transmitted
in any form, electronic or mechanical, including photocopying, recording or by means
of any information storage or retrieval system without prior permission in writing from
the publishers; or ii) used or reproduced in any way for the training, development or
operation of artificial intelligence (AI) technologies, including generative AI technologies.
The rights holders expressly reserve this publication from the text and data mining
exception as per Article 4(3) of the Digital Single Market Directive (EU) 2019/790.

Bloomsbury Publishing Inc does not have any control over, or responsibility for,
any third-party websites referred to or in this book. All internet addresses given
in this book were correct at the time of going to press. The author and publisher
regret any inconvenience caused if addresses have changed or sites have
ceased to exist, but can accept no responsibility for any such changes.

A catalogue record for this book is available from the British Library.

Library of Congress Cataloging-in-Publication Data
Names: Barton, William M., editor. | Harrison, S. J., editor. |
Manuwald, Gesine, editor. | Xinyue, Bobby, editor.
Title: An anthology of Neo-Latin poetry by classical scholars / edited by
William M. Barton, Stephen Harrison, Gesine Manuwald, and Bobby Xinyue.
Description: New York: Bloomsbury Publishing Plc, 2024. |
Includes bibliographical references and index.
Identifiers: LCCN 2023028739 (print) | LCCN 2023028740 (ebook) |
ISBN 9781350379442 (hardback) | ISBN 9781350379459 (paperback) |
ISBN 9781350379466 (pdf) | ISBN 9781350379473 (ebook)
Subjects: LCSH: Latin poetry, Medieval and modern. |
Latin poetry, Medieval and modern–Translations into English. |
Latin poetry, Medieval and modern–History and criticism.
Classification: LCC PA8120 .A58 2024 (print) | LCC PA8120 (ebook) |
DDC 871/.03—dc23/eng/20230727
LC record available at https://lccn.loc.gov/2023028739
LC ebook record available at https://lccn.loc.gov/2023028740

ISBN: HB: 978-1-3503-7944-2
PB: 978-1-3503-7945-9
ePDF: 978-1-3503-7946-6
eBook: 978-1-3503-7947-3

Series: Bloomsbury Neo-Latin Series: Early Modern Texts and Anthologies

Typeset by RefineCatch Limited, Bungay, Suffolk

For product safety related questions contact productsafety@bloomsbury.com.

To find out more about our authors and books visit www.bloomsbury.com
and sign up for our newsletters.

Contents

List of Contributors	vii
Preface	x

Introduction: The Neo-Latin Poetry of European Classical Scholars
Stephen J. Harrison — 1

Texts

1. Poems on Printed Books: The Case of Niccolò Perotti's (1430–1480) *Cornu copiae*
   Marianne Pade — 9

2. The *Natalis* of Paolo Marsi (1440–1484)
   Raphael Schwitter — 39

3. The Verses of Antonio de Nebrija (1444–1522) on the Philologist's Work and the Place of Greek
   William M. Barton — 59

4. Aldus Manutius (c. 1450–1515), *Musarum panagyris* and Other Early Poems
   Oren Margolis — 81

5. An Elegiac Poem by Julius Caesar Scaliger (1484–1558) on Sickness and Healing
   Bobby Xinyue — 105

6. Two Poems by Piero Vettori (1499–1585)
   Agnese D'Angelo — 123

7. Jean Dorat (1508–1588): The Latin Lyrics of a Greek Professor
   Stephen J. Harrison — 139

8   Janus Dousa (1545–1604): The Satires of a Dutch Scholar
David Andrew Porter   163

9   Editing Cicero (and Translating Aratus) in Sixteenth-Century Europe: Jan Kochanowski (1579) and Hugo Grotius (1600)
Daniele Pellacani   189

10   John Barclay (1582–1621): The *Argenis* as a Statian Scholar's Novel
Ruth Parkes   211

11   Spare Muses: Epigrams by the Cambridge Don James Duport (1606–1679)
Thomas Matthew Vozar   233

12   Writing a Woman Scholar: Poems around Birgitte Thott (1610–1662)
Trine Arlund Hass   255

13   The Plinian Dolphin: Johann Matthias Gesner (1691–1761), *Carmina*
Gesine Manuwald   293

14   Giovanni Pascoli (1855–1912), *Reditus Augusti*, an Horatian Mime
Francesco Citti   311

Index of Names   331

Contributors

William M. Barton teaches at the Institute for Classical Philology and Neo-Latin Studies, University of Innsbruck, Austria. His latest book presented a commented edition and translation of Pascasius Turcq's 1561 medical treatise on gambling, *De alea* (2022). William's present work explores the concepts and uses of ancient Greek in Western Europe among humanists and scholars until the mid-nineteenth century. His current project, funded by the Austrian Science Fund (FWF), is dedicated to the secret diaries of Karl Benedikt Hase (1780–1864), which the scholar kept in ancient Greek throughout his life.

Francesco Citti is Professor of Latin at the University of Bologna. He works in particular on Horace, Lucretius, Seneca and Latin declamation as well as on classical reception. Publications on these topics include: *Seneca nel Novecento: sondaggi sulla fortuna di un classico*, Rome 2001 (co-authored with C. Neri); *Cura sui: studi sul lessico filosofico di Seneca*, Amsterdam 2012; *Ragione e furore. Lucrezio nell'Italia contemporanea* (co-edited with D. Pellacani), Bologna 2020; *Agamennone classico e contemporaneo* (co-edited with A. Iannucci and A. Ziosi), Venice 2022.

Agnese D'Angelo is a PhD student in the philology and history of the ancient world at Sapienza University of Rome. Her research focuses on Latin literature and its reception in the Renaissance, especially in sixteenth-century Italy.

Stephen J. Harrison is Senior Research Fellow of Corpus Christi College, Oxford, and Professor of Latin Literature in the University of Oxford. He is author and/or editor of many items on Latin literature and its modern reception, and is now working on various Neo-Latin projects, including an anthology of Neo-Latin poetry by Popes and an edition of George Buchanan's *Silvae*. He is a co-editor of the *Bloomsbury Neo-Latin Series* and co-editor of this volume.

Trine Arlund Hass is currently Junior Research Fellow at Linacre College and a visiting member of the Corpus Christi College Classics Centre at the University of Oxford, funded by the Carlsberg Foundation. She is a member of the board of the Centre for Danish Neo-Latin and works especially on Danish and bucolic Neo-Latin poetry. Her contribution functions as a pilot study for the project *Danish Identity and Identities in Denmark 1500–1700*, funded by the Augustinus Foundation (PI: Marianne Pade).

Gesine Manuwald is Professor of Latin at University College London (UCL) and President of the Society for Neo-Latin Studies (SNLS). She has published widely on classical Latin authors (including Cicero, Ennius and Valerius Flaccus) as well as on Neo-Latin literature. Publications in the latter field include several articles on Thomas Campion as well as the edited collection *Neo-Latin Poetry in the British Isles* (with L. B. T. Houghton; 2012). She is co-editor of the texts and anthologies strand of the *Bloomsbury Neo-Latin Series*.

Oren Margolis is Lecturer in Renaissance Studies in the School of History at the University of East Anglia. He is a historian of humanism, history-writing and antiquarianism, and the art and culture of the Renaissance book. He curated *Aldus Manutius: The Struggle and the Dream* (2015) at the Bodleian Library, Oxford, and is author of *Aldus Manutius: The Invention of the Publisher* (2023).

Marianne Pade is Professor at Aarhus University, Denmark, in the Department of History and Classical Studies. Her research interests focus on Neo-Latin language and literature, Italian Renaissance humanism, the reception of Greek historians in the Renaissance and early modern translation studies. Her most recent publications include 'Boccaccio and the Humanist Movement' in *Habent sua fata libelli* (2021) and 'Pico's Multilingual Pentateuch' in *Late Medieval and Early Modern Libraries as Knowledge Repositories* (2023).

Ruth Parkes is Senior Lecturer in Classics at the University of Wales Trinity Saint David, UK. Her research focuses upon the epic tradition and its reception in Latin literature, including Neo-Latin texts. She is particularly interested in the works of Statius and has published a commentary on Book 4 of his *Thebaid* (*Statius, Thebaid IV: Edited with a translation and commentary*, 2012).

Daniele Pellacani is Professor of Latin Language and Literature at the University of Bologna, in the Department of Classical Philology and Italian Studies. His research interests mainly focus on didactic poetry and philosophical and technical prose, with a particular interest in ancient astronomy. He has published on the Latin *Aratea* (especially Cicero) and the reception of Latin Classics. His most recent book is a commented edition of Cicero's *Pro Archia*.

David Andrew Porter is an associate professor at Hunan Normal University. His research focuses on late medieval and early modern poetry, philosophy and comparative literature.

Raphael Schwitter teaches Latin in the Department of Classics at the University of Bonn, Germany. His research focuses on Roman historical culture in the late Republic and early Roman Empire, the transmission of literary knowledge and minor literary forms from antiquity to the early modern era. He has published on the semantics of writing, late Roman epistolography and poetry. His most recent book is an edition of Martin Le Franc's (*c.* 1408–61) *Agreste otium* and *De bono mortis* (2018). His forthcoming monograph is *Antiquarianismus in Rom: Perspektiven – Formen – Funktionen (2. Jahrhundert v. Chr. – 3. Jahrhundert n. Chr.)*.

Thomas Matthew Vozar is an Excellence Strategy Postdoctoral Fellow in Early Modern Studies at the University of Hamburg and an Honorary Research Fellow in English at the University of Exeter. His first book, *Abstracted Sublimities: Milton, Longinus, and the Sublime in the Seventeenth Century*, is forthcoming in the series 'Classical Presences', and he is currently at work on a second book project entitled *Polemical Erudition: Scholarship and Politics in the English Revolution*.

Bobby Xinyue is Lecturer in Roman Culture at King's College London. He works on Latin literature of the Augustan age and its reception in the early modern period. He has published articles on Vergil, Horace and Propertius as well as on a number of Neo-Latin poets such as Mantovano Fracco and Morisot. His most recent publication is *Politics and Divinization in Augustan Poetry* (2022). His current research focuses on the reception of Ovid's *Fasti* in the Renaissance.

Preface

This book provides a varied selection of poetry in Latin written by classical scholars, which offers a fascinating insight into the interplay between poetry and scholarship through the medium of Latin.

    The editors of this volume have various obligations to record. Most of the contributions in this volume were generated in response to a call for papers for a hybrid workshop held at University College London in June 2022, organised by Gesine Manuwald. We are most grateful to all those who spoke and attended either in person or online, to those who helped with the day at UCL, and especially to Bloomsbury for accepting this volume in its Neo-Latin Series.

W. M. B. / S. J. H. / G. M / B. X.
Innsbruck / Oxford / London
April 2023

Introduction: The Neo-Latin Poetry of European Classical Scholars

Stephen J. Harrison

The interdependence and interaction of scholarship and poetry was a feature of the classical world, at least from the time of Hellenistic Alexandria from the end of the fourth century BCE.[1] There it was fully possible for intellectuals to combine literary activity with a professional scholarly and/or didactic role: the poet Philetas (*c.* 340–285 BCE) was tutor to the young Ptolemy II and teacher of the first great Homeric scholar Zenodotus as well as a key literary figure, and was famously called by Strabo, writing more than two centuries later in Greek in Augustan Rome, 'poet and scholar at the same time' (*Geography* 14.657). In Philetas' output, in the words of Rudolf Pfeiffer, 'the work of ... the poet was inseparably allied to the work of ... the scholar' (Pfeiffer 1968: 90): his poetic works (now lost apart from a few fragments) included learned mythological narratives and a collection of epigrams, while he was also the author of a treatise explaining the language of Homer.

The foundation of the Mouseion by Philetas' employer Ptolemy I Soter at the beginning of the third century BCE provided a further step in the same direction. This institution was a major cultural centre and home to a vast library that attracted scholars from all over the Greek world, many of whom were also poets, and some of whom seem to have combined research, teaching and literary activity. The most famous of these were Callimachus of Cyrene (*c.* 305 – *c.* 240 BCE) and Apollonius of Rhodes (*fl.* 270–245 BCE), both of whom wrote scholarly works (Callimachus authored a form of catalogue for the Alexandrian library, Apollonius a critical work on Homer) as well as the poems for which they are better known (Callimachus' hymns and epigrams, Apollonius' epic *Argonautica*). These poems clearly show their authors' scholarly character in their linguistic and antiquarian learning.

Another feature of the Hellenistic age was the popularity of paraphrastic hexameter didactic poetry, where scholarly information previously associated with prose was framed in verse: a prime example is Aratus' *Phaenomena* on astronomy (third century BCE, later adapted into Latin by Cicero, Germanicus and Avienus), which was followed under the Roman republic and empire by Lucretius' *De Rerum Natura* on the nature of the universe (first century BCE) and Manilius' *Astronomica* on astrology (first century CE). This form in which poetry was itself the vehicle of scholarship was popular throughout the Neo-Latin period (see below for the special form used by Poliziano in the fifteenth century CE).[2]

Under the Roman republic and empire we know of a number of writers who composed both learned prose works and poetry: the dramatist Accius (*c*. 170–80 BCE) also wrote a work of theatre history, while the scholarly polymath Varro (116–27 BCE) authored a prosimetric collection of satires; the orator and philosopher Cicero (106–43 BCE) composed a range of poems as well as scholarly works such as the *Brutus*, a history of Roman oratory. The considerable output of the younger Seneca (4 BCE–65 CE) under the emperors Claudius and Nero includes poetic tragedies as well as the scientific encyclopaedia *Natural Questions*, while the Neronian Caesius Bassus, addressee of Persius' sixth satire, which shows that he was the author of lyric poems, also wrote a work on metre; in the second century the polymath Apuleius (*c*. 125 – after 164 CE) wrote scientific and scholarly treatises and a collection of poems (all lost) as well as his famous novel *Metamorphoses / The Golden Ass*.

In later antiquity Boethius (*c*. 480–524 CE) wrote the prosimetric *Consolation of Philosophy* alongside works on arithmetic, music, philosophy and theology. Similarly, in the revival of learning at the court of Charlemagne in the later eighth century, Alcuin (*c*. 735–804) wrote a range of poems alongside works on grammar and spelling, and in the mini-renaissance of the twelfth century Alan of Lille (*c*. 1128–1202/3) wrote both prosimetric and hexameter works alongside treatises of biblical commentary and theology.

In the major period of the revival of classical learning and the development of Neo-Latin traditionally dated from Petrarch (1304–74), literary composition was at the centre of scholarly and didactic activity: teaching Latin was primarily a matter of teaching Latin composition, which included both prose and verse.[3] Major emphasis was now placed on the close imitation of classical models, in which Petrarch himself was a crucial influence.[4] His hexameter work *Africa* was the first epic poem to make a wholehearted attempt to reproduce the classical Latin style of the great Vergil, and he combined literary composition in Neo-Latin verse (adding the Vergilian pastoral of the *Bucolicum Carmen* to the Vergilian epic of the *Africa*) with equally classicising scholarly works such as his lives of great men (*De Viris Illustribus*); he was followed in both these tendencies by his friend and admirer Boccaccio (1313–75).[5]

In the Renaissance two factors particularly promoted the combination of poetry and scholarship: the increased rise and importance of universities throughout Europe, providing a platform for scholars to engage in both exegesis and composition of Latin texts,[6] and the new technology of the printed book, enabling mass dissemination of every type of writing.[7] The great publishing enterprise of Aldus Manutius (c. 1450–1515) in Venice produced a crucial range of classical editions, employing some of the best scholars, editions that often contained congratulatory liminary verse by other scholars as advance praise (still a feature of academic publishing).[8] Aldus himself was also a scholar and a poet, as Oren Margolis' chapter in this volume shows, and Neo-Latin liminary verse by other scholars became a frequent feature of early modern printed editions of every kind of scholarly work. Such liminary poems were often more than ornamental, providing guidance on and interpretation of the work they introduced and framing it effectively for a contemporary readership.[9] This is exemplified in this volume in Marianne Pade's chapter on the poems associated with Niccolò Perotti's *Cornu copiae* (printed in 1489), one of the foundational texts of Latin lexicography, and in Trine Haas' chapter on the liminary verse for Birgitte Thott's impressive 1658 translation of the works of Seneca into Danish.

Angelo Poliziano (Politian, 1454–94), outstanding as both poet and scholar,[10] achieved an extraordinary combination of the two skills in his *Silvae*. These are a set of Latin hexameter poems composed as preludes to lectures delivered at the University of Florence in the period 1482–91: the *Manto*, introducing a set of lectures on Vergil's *Eclogues*, the *Rusticus* (Hesiod and Vergil's *Georgics*), the *Ambra* (Homer) and the *Nutricia* (on poetics and poets). These works combine discussions of the ancient works and their subject matter with imaginative literary episodes, such as the scene in which Manto, the prophetess, foretells the future greatness of Vergil (*Manto* 64–80) or the passage in which the life of the shepherd is praised (*Rusticus* 283–332).

Poliziano's contemporary Paolo Marsi (1440–84) also closely combined the exegesis of ancient poetry with his own Neo-Latin composition: as Raphael Schwitter shows in his chapter, Marsi's learned edition of Ovid's *Fasti* (1482) added hundreds of lines from his own hexameter poem *Natalis* as supplements to the Ovidian original. Poliziano's pupil Pietro Crinito (1474–1507) wrote both the first large-scale history of Latin poetry (*Libri de poetis latinis*) and many Horatianising Latin poems;[11] and as we can see from Agnese D'Angelo's chapter, Piero Vettori (1499–1585), professor of Greek and Latin at Florence and one of the most prolific and important editors of classical texts in the sixteenth century, also wrote some attractive Latin verse which uses Catullan imitation to create a Catullus-style like-minded literary community among his friends.

Outside Italy the German-speaking Conrad Celtis (1459–1508) wrote a work on poetic technique, an edition of Seneca and material on the topography of Germany. As well as establishing learned societies at Kraków and in Hungary and rediscovering the poetic works of Hrosvitha of

Gandersheim, Celtis was the author of three major collections of elegiac and lyric poems and was made Poet Laureate by the Emperor Frederick III.[12] In Spain, as William M. Barton shows in his piece, Antonio de Nebrija (1444–1522) composed poems to accompany his important treatises on Latin and Greek grammar. Erasmus of Rotterdam (1466–1536), perhaps the greatest scholar of his generation, was also an accomplished Neo-Latin poet: his *Epigrammata* of 1518[13] included a 150-line poem in praise of Britain voiced by Britannia in a metre from Horace's *Epodes* and an ode to St Michael and All Angels in sixty-three Sapphic stanzas. In France the leading teacher and scholar Jean Dorat (1508–88) combined critical work on Homer and Greek tragedy with elegant Latin verse, as can be seen from Stephen Harrison's contribution,[14] while the great humanist Marc-Antoine Muret (1526–85), who edited Horace, Propertius, Tibullus and Catullus, also wrote an attractive range of Horatian odes as a young man.[15]

In the religious divisions of the Reformation and Counter-Reformation in the sixteenth century, both the Catholic and the Protestant traditions could show major figures who combined scholarship and poetry. Amongst Catholics, the Spanish scholar Benito Arias Montano (1527–98), chief editor of the great Antwerp Polyglot Bible of 1572 (with versions in Greek and Latin throughout) and a major scholar of biblical history, also wrote three collections of Horatianising lyric poetry on theological subjects,[16] while the versatile Franco-Scottish writer John Barclay (1582–1621) wrote two major Latin prosimetric novels alongside Latin poems and a commentary on Statius' *Thebaid*; Ruth Parkes' chapter looks at the interplay between his work on Statius and some verse sections of his 1621 *Argenis*. The Catholic Julius Caesar Scaliger (1484–1558) was the author of a wide range of Latin poems (such as the expressive elegiac poem on his own illness analysed by Bobby Xinyue in his chapter) as well as one of the most important early modern critical studies of classical literature (the posthumous *Poetices libri septem*, 1561),[17] while his son Joseph Justus Scaliger (1540–1609), who became a Protestant in his twenties, combined in his published output key editions of classical authors such as Manilius, epoch-making work on chronology, and extensive Neo-Latin verse.[18]

Joseph Justus Scaliger ended his days in Leiden, and the Calvinist Netherlands were a great nurse of poet/scholars in the late sixteenth and early seventeenth centuries. These included the great scholar and political theorist Hugo Grotius (1583–1645), who added his own verses to Cicero's fragmentary *Aratea* in editing the text in his precocious *Syntagma Arateorum* (1600), following the lead of the Polish poet and scholar Jan Kochanowski (1530–84), as detailed by Daniele Pellacani in his chapter. Another Netherlandish figure was Janus Dousa (1545–1604), the first librarian of the major university established at Leiden in 1575, who published a wide range of accomplished Latin verse alongside many editions of classical texts and a history of Holland; David Andrew Porter's chapter considers his lively and gossipy hexameter satires that revived the ancient genre. Perhaps most distinguished were Daniel Heinsius (1580–1655), Scaliger's student and Dousa's successor as Leiden librarian, and his son Nicolaas (1620–81), two of the most famous classical scholars of the Dutch Golden Age and two of its leading Neo-Latin poets; both edited a wide range of classical texts, and both closely reflected their scholarly work in their poetry; Daniel edited Seneca's tragedies and wrote a Senecan tragedy of his own on the death of William of Orange (*Auriacus*, 1602),[19] while Nicolaas edited Claudian and Ovid and wrote Ovid-style travel poems and a collection dedicated to his patron Queen Christina of Sweden, which included a Claudian-style panegyric.[20]

Our anthology ends with pieces from the second half of the seventeenth, the eighteenth and one from the nineteenth century, showing that the combination of Neo-Latin poetry and scholarship continued in this period. Trine Arlund Hass' study of the liminary poems for Birgitte Thott's 1658 Seneca translation into Danish has already been mentioned, while Thomas Matthew Vozar's chapter presents some stylish occasional poems, influenced by Martial's epigrams, by James Duport (1606–79), Regius Professor of Greek at Cambridge and Master of Magdalene College.[21] Johann Matthias Gesner (1691–1761), first J. S. Bach's headmaster and friend at the Thomasschule in Leipzig and then a professor at Göttingen, combined a distinguished record of scholarly publication (including a major Latin dictionary that was a model for the *Thesaurus Linguae Latinae*) with composing elegant occasional poems in Latin, as Gesine Manuwald's chapter shows. Finally, the major Italian poet Giovanni Pascoli (1855–1912) was a distinguished composer of Latin verse as well as a professor of Latin and Greek literature at Bologna, Messina and Pisa.[22] Francesco Citti's chapter analyses Pascoli's *Reditus Augusti* (1896), a remarkable hexameter poem in the form of Horace's *Satires* and the spirit of Theocritus' urban mime (*Idyll* 15) which dramatises the celebrations of the return of Augustus to Rome in 24 BCE, focussing on the figure of Horace and recreating the occasion of his composition of *Odes* 3.14.

This was one of a record thirteen Latin poems by Pascoli to win the gold medal of the *Certamen Poeticum Hoeufftianum*,[23] a prestigious international competition for Neo-Latin poetry sponsored by the national scholarly academy of the Netherlands, which ran for the years 1844 to 1978.[24] The winners of this award included several other professional classical scholars: J.J. Hartman (1854–1924), professor of Latin at Leiden, in 1898 and 1899,[25] P.H. Damsté (1860–1943), professor of Latin at Utrecht, in 1903,[26] and G.B. Pighi (1898–1978), professor of Latin at Bologna, in 1951.[27]

This anthology thus presents selections from a long and rich tradition in which professional scholars of Latin and Greek have engaged in Neo-Latin poetic compositions of their own, which cast a fascinating light on their scholarly interests and broader cultural contexts. This combination of poetry and scholarship has always been connected with educational practice, since verse composition in Latin was a central part of classical instruction at school and university level from the Renaissance until the 1960s, and most of the authors of the verse in this volume worked as classical teachers in some sense as well as receiving that instruction themselves. It is still a living tradition, though a rare one: while the composition of classical verse is now almost unknown in European high schools, there are still some prize competitions in it at some traditional European universities,[28] and some working classical scholars also publish their Neo-Latin verse compositions.[29]

Notes

1. See Pfeiffer 1968.
2. See e.g. Moul 2017.
3. See e.g. Mack 2014.
4. See e.g. Ascoli / Falkeid 2015.
5. See e.g. Armstrong / Daniels / Milner 2015.
6. See Nicholas 2022.
7. See Eisenstein 2012.
8. See Wilson 2016; Grant 2017.
9. See Van Dam 2015.
10. For the *Silvae* see Fantazzi 2004, for Poliziano's classical poems other than the *Silvae* see Knox 2018, and for his scholarship see Dyck and Cottrell 2020.
11. See Mastrogianni 2002.
12. See e.g. Manuwald 2000; Schäfer 2012.
13. Published along with the first edition of his friend Thomas More's *Utopia*.
14. See Demerson 1979 and 1983.
15. See Leroux 2009; 2020.
16. See Coroleu / Fouto 2015: 464; Cziepiel 2023.
17. For a modern edition see Deitz / Vogt-Spira 1994–2003.
18. See Grafton 1983 and 1993.
19. See Lefèvre / Schäfer 2008.
20. See Papy 2014.
21. See O'Day 2004.
22. See Perugi 1980: XXXVII–XL.
23. One more than the twelve of Hermann Weller (1878–1956), who became professor of Indo-European at Tübingen in 1930, and who won the gold medal with the subtly anti-Nazi poem 'Y' in 1938 (see further the analysis of

Uwe Dubielzig at http://www.phil-hum-ren.uni-muenchen.de/GermLat/Acta/Dubielzig.htm).
24 See https://it.wikipedia.org/wiki/Certamen_poeticum_Hoeufftianum.
25 The first scholar to suggest Ovid did not in fact go into exile – for this and his career see van der Velden 2019.
26 For his poems and scholarly career see Wagenwoort 1945.
27 For his career see https://www.treccani.it/enciclopedia/giovanni-battista-pighi/.
28 E.g. the annual Chancellor's Prize for Latin Verse at Oxford, open to undergraduate and graduate students: https://governance.admin.ox.ac.uk/legislation/the-chancellors-prizes.
29 See e.g. Radke 2005, which surveys contemporary Latin verse composition and presents the verses of a number of practising classical and Neo-Latin scholars.

Bibliography

Armstrong, G. / Daniels, R. / Milner, S. J. (2015), *The Cambridge Companion to Boccaccio*, Cambridge.
Ascoli, A. R. / Falkeid, U., eds (2015), *The Cambridge Companion to Petrarch*, Cambridge.
Coroleu, A. / Fouto, C. (2015), 'Iberian Peninsula', in: S. Tilg / S. Knight (eds), *The Oxford Handbook of Neo-Latin*, 461–76, Oxford / New York.
Cziepiel, M. (2023), *Humanism and the Bible in the Poetry of Benito Arias Montano (ca. 1525–1598)*, DPhil. thesis Oxford.
Deitz, L. / Vogt-Spira, G., eds (1994–2003), *Julius Caesar Scaliger, Poetices libri septem. Sieben Bücher über die Dichtkunst*, 6 vols, Stuttgart-Bad Cannstatt.
Demerson, G. (1979), *Jean Dorat: Les Odes latines*, Clermont-Ferrand.
Demerson, G. (1983), *Dorat en son temps: culture classique et présence au monde*, Clermont-Ferrand.
Dyck, A. / Cottrell, A. (2020), *Angelo Poliziano: Miscellanies* [2 vols], Cambridge, MA.
Eisenstein, E. L. (2012), *The Printing Revolution in Early Modern Europe*, 2nd edn, Cambridge.
Fantazzi, C. (2004), *Angelo Poliziano: Silvae*, Cambridge, MA.
Grafton, A. (1983), *Joseph Scaliger: A Study in the History of Classical Scholarship I. Textual Criticism and Exegesis*, Oxford.
Grafton, A. (1993), *Joseph Scaliger: A Study in the History of Classical Scholarship II: Historical Chronology*, Oxford.
Grant, J. N., ed. (2017), *Aldus Manutius: Humanism and the Latin Classics*, Cambridge, MA.
Knox, P. E. (2018), *Angelo Poliziano: Greek and Latin Poetry*, Cambridge, MA.
Lefèvre, E. / Schäfer, E., eds (2008), *Daniel Heinsius: Klassischer Philologe und Poet*, Tübingen (NeoLatina 13).

Leroux, V. (2009), *Marc-Antoine Muret: Juvenilia*, Geneva (Travaux d'Humanisme et Renaissance 450).

Leroux, V. (2020), 'Le modèle des Odes d'Horace dans les œuvres poétiques et philologiques de Marc-Antoine Muret', in: M. Laureys / N. Dauvois / D. Coppini (eds), *Non omnis moriar. Die Horaz-Rezeption in der neulateinischen Literatur vom 15. bis zum 17. Jahrhundert / La réception d'Horace dans la littérature néo-latine du XVe au XVIIe siècle / La ricezione di Orazio nella letteratura in latino dal XV al XVII secolo (Deutschland – France – Italia)*, 933–55, Hildesheim.

Mack, P. (2014), 'Neo-Latin and Renaissance Schools', in: P. Ford / J. Bloemendal / C. Fantazzi (eds), *Brill's Encyclopaedia of the Neo-Latin World*, 55–61, Leiden / Boston.

Manuwald, G. (2000), 'Celtis, Epode 12 und Horaz, Epistel 1,19. Zu Celtis', Selbstverständnis als Dichter', in: U. Auhagen / E. Lefèvre / E. Schäfer (eds), *Horaz und Celtis*, 263–73, Tübingen (NeoLatina 1).

Mastrogianni, A. (2002), *Die Poemata des Petrus Crinitus und ihre Horazimitation: Einleitung, Text, Übersetzung und Kommentar*, Münster.

Moul, V. (2017), 'Didactic Poetry', in: V. Moul (ed.), *A Guide to Neo-Latin Literature*, 180–99, Cambridge.

Nicholas, L. R. (2022), 'Introduction', in: G. Manuwald / L. R. Nicholas (eds), *An Anthology of Neo-Latin Literature in British Universities*, 1–30, London (Bloomsbury Neo-Latin Series, Early Modern Texts and Anthologies 3).

O'Day, R. (2004), 'Duport, James (1606–1679)', *ODNB* (https://doi.org/10.1093/ref:odnb/8301 2004).

Papy, J. (2014), 'Heinsius, Nicolaus', in: *Brill's New Pauly Supplements I – Volume 6: History of Classical Scholarship – A Biographical Dictionary*, 274–6, Leiden (https://referenceworks.brillonline.com/browse/brill-s-new-pauly).

Perugi, M., ed. (1980), *Opere di Giovanni Pascoli: Tomo I*, Milan / Naples.

Pfeiffer, R. (1968), *History of Classical Scholarship from the Beginnings to the End of the Hellenistic Age*, Oxford.

Radke, A. E. (2005), *Alaudae: Ephemeridis nova series, fasciculus primus*, Hildesheim / Zürich.

Schäfer, E. (2012), *Conrad Celtis: Oden / Epoden / Jahrhundertlied. Libri Odarum quattuor, cum Epodo et Saeculari Carmine (1513)*, Tübingen (NeoLatina 16).

Van Dam, H.-J. (2015), 'Poems on the Threshold: Neo-Latin Carmina liminaria', in: K. Enenkel and A. Steiner-Weber (eds), *Acta Conventus Neo-Latini Monasteriensis*, 50–81, Leiden / Boston.

Van der Velden, B. (2019), 'J. J. Hartman on Ovid's (Non-)Exile', *Mnemosyne*, 73: 336–42.

Wagenwoort, H. (1945), 'Pieter Helbert Damsté (Wilsum, August 10, 1860 – Utrecht, February 5, 1943)', *Jaarboek van de Maatschappij der Nederlandse Letterkunde* 1945: 78–97.

Wilson, N. G. (2016), *Aldus Manutius: The Greek Classics*, Cambridge, MA (I Tatti Renaissance Library).

1

Poems on Printed Books: The Case of Niccolò Perotti's (1430–1480) *Cornu copiae*

Marianne Pade

Introduction

Niccolò Perotti's *Cornu copiae seu linguae latinae Commentarii* ('*Horn of Plenty or Notes on the Latin Language*') is one of the most important fifteenth-century books on Latin and came to influence Latin lexicography for centuries.[1] With its focus on correct Latin usage, the *Cornu copiae* is also part of the effort to 'reconquer the Roman language', one of the core projects of Renaissance Humanism.[2] The work is the result of Perotti's life-long study of the language and culture of antiquity. Its material fortune and printing history are testimony to the struggle of early modern scholars to create reliable tools for the study of Latin. The poems in this chapter are printed as paratexts in the early editions of Perotti's work and offer interesting insights into early modern editorial practices. Contrary to what a modern reader might expect, they also show that among the lessons to be learned from a work such as the *Cornu copiae* was the ability to express oneself in good (if not necessarily ancient) Latin.

Born in the city of Sassoferrato in the Marche, Niccolò Perotti (1430–80) came to Rome when he was not yet twenty years old in the service of the English nobleman William Gray, later Bishop of Ely. He quickly made his mark in the Roman curia as a translator from Greek, dedicating several of his early works to the humanist pope, Nicholas V. Shortly after his arrival in the papal city, Perotti became part of the household of the Greek cardinal, Bessarion, and was for many years his trusted secretary or rather head of his chancellery. In 1464, at Bessarion's request, Perotti was made Archbishop of Siponto (hence his nickname, 'il sipontino') and embarked on a career as a curial diplomat, eventually retiring from his final administrative post as papal governor of Perugia in 1477. In spite of his many official obligations, Perotti had still found some time to pursue his scholarly interests, publishing, amongst other things, the highly successful *Rudimenta grammatices* ('*Elementary Grammar*').[3]

When in 1477 Perotti retired to his native town, Sassoferrato, to live in a country house appropriately called *Curifugia* ('Escape from Worry', or *Sans souci*),[4] he dedicated himself to the redaction of his *opus magnum*, the *Cornu copiae*. In form, the work is a commentary on Martial's *Liber spectaculorum* and the first book of the epigrams, but with its focus on the semantic *copia* of Martial's language, it had developed into an encyclopaedia of ancient Graeco-Roman culture and, albeit strangely organized, a Latin lexicon. Commentaries were often repositories or storehouses of all sorts of knowledge; and commenting upon an ancient author, especially one as lexically rich as Martial, could be a way of organizing huge amounts of information. That was certainly the case with Perotti's *Cornu copiae*, which integrates much of the material he had compiled for other works, amongst them his first commentary on Martial, contained in an autograph manuscript that he had annotated over a period of about twenty years.[5] Considering that he likewise wrote a commentary on Statius' *Silvae*, Perotti is definitely an exponent of the interest in Silver Age Latinity seen in Italy in the second half of the fifteenth century.[6]

The *Cornu copiae* is preserved in a single manuscript, *Urbinas latinus* 301, a large tome produced between 1477 and 1480 and now in the Vatican Library.[7] The manuscript consists of 671 folios, the writing material is paper, and the original stratum of the text is in a regular cursive hand that shows some influence from the writing style of the Roman Academy, at the time the epitome of chic when it came to the material aspects of manuscript production. The Academy was led by Pomponio Leto, with whom Perotti collaborated on several occasions.[8]

The text is surrounded on both sides by marginalia. In the inner margins these refer to persons mentioned in the text, most of them the authors of the text-examples quoted by Perotti. In the outer margins the notes signal the lemmata discussed in the main text. The entire apparatus of marginalia, as well as an abundance of corrections of and additions to the original text, are in the hand of Perotti himself. As Fabio Stok has pointed out, the manuscript was originally intended as a presentation copy for Federico da Montefeltro, from whom Perotti hoped to obtain financial support for the printing of the work. During a long and unfinished revision, the manuscript became Perotti's working copy, and he did not live to see the publication of the work.[9] For reasons still not quite clear to us, the *Cornu copiae* was only printed in 1489, in Venice; that is all of nine years after Perotti's death in 1480. Subsequently, at least thirty-six editions appeared during the fifteenth and sixteenth centuries.[10] The only modern edition was published in Sassoferrato in eight volumes during the last decade of the twentieth century.

The paratexts of the fifteenth- and sixteenth-century editions of the *Cornu copiae* show how the work was increasingly used as a dictionary of Latin, and editors tried to accommodate their readers' expectations in the way in which the text was presented.[11] In what follows I show how the growing corpus of poems that accompanied edition after edition reflects the various meanings the text was given in the course of its reception by successive communities of readers.

Notes

1. For the influence of Perotti on Latin lexicography, see Margolin 1981; Charlet 1997a, 2004–5a–b and 2008; and Stok 2002b.
2. The literature on this subject is vast. Suffice it here to refer to Charlet 2009, Regoliosi 2010 and Baker 2015.
3. For Perotti's life, see Mercati 1925, Charlet 1997b and d'Alessandro 2015.
4. Charlet 1995.
5. For Perotti's first commentary on Martial, see Ramminger 2001b and Pade 2021, 351–2. For the commentary as 'repository of knowledge', see Pade 2013.
6. Cp. Stok 2011 and Pade 2014b–c.
7. For a description of Urb. lat. 301 see Stok 2001.
8. For the style of writing and illumination of Urb. lat. 301, see Pade 2007 and 2008. For Perotti's connection with the Roman Academy, see also Ramminger 2008 and Pade 2011a, 2014b–c and 2015.
9. Stok 2002a.
10. Milde 1982.
11. I have discussed the material fortune of Perotti's *Cornu copiae*, from the first presentation of the work in the Urb. lat. 301 and through a number of fifteenth- and sixteenth-century prints in Pade 2011b, 2014a and 2020.

Bibliography

Primary sources

Calderinus, D. (1471), *Commentarii in Martialem*, Rome: Johannes Gensberg
Constantius, Antonius (1502), *Epigrammatum libellus*, [s.l.].
Giovio, Paolo (1551 / 1972), *Imagines clarorum virorum*, modern edition in: *Gli elogi degli uomini illustri (letterati – artisti – uomini d'arme)*, ed. R. Meregazzi, *Pauli Iovii opera VIII*, Rome.
Perotti, Niccolò, *Cornu copiae seu linguae Latinae commentarii*
  (1489) Venice: Paganinus de Paganinis, ed. Ludovico Odasio.
  (1490a) Venice: Bernardinus de Choris, de Cremona and Simon de Luere, 30 May, reprint of the *editio princeps*.

(1490b) Venice: Baptista de Tortis, 19 Oct.
(1492) Venice: Bernardinus de Choris, de Cremona, 25 May, reprint of the *editio princeps*.
(1494a) Venice: Philippus Pincius, 27 Mar.
(1494b) Venice: Dionysius Bertochus, 12 May, reprint of the *editio princeps* (text 1), but adds *commentariolus*.
(1496a) Paris: Ulrich Gering and Berthold Rembolt, 23 Apr.
(1496b) Venice: Johannes Tacuinus, de Tridino, 20 Dec.
(1504) Venice: Johannes Tacuinus, de Tridino.
modern edition: Perotti, N. (1989–2001), *Cornu copiae seu linguae Latinae commentarii* 1–8, ed. by J.-L. Charlet, G. Abbamonte, M. Furno, P. Harsting, M. Pade, J. Ramminger and F. Stok, Sassoferrato. The full text of the edition is now available on the website of the *Repertorium pomponianum* (https://www.repertoriumpomponianum.it/textus/perotti_cornu_copiae.htm).
Perotti, Niccolò (1473), *Rudimenta grammatices*, Rome: Conradus Sweynheym and Arnoldus Pannartz, 19 Mar.

Secondary literature

Baker, P. (2015), *Italian Renaissance Humanism in the Mirror*, Cambridge.
Campanelli, M. (1998), 'Alcuni aspetti dell'esegesi umanistica di 'Atlas cum compare gibbo' [Mart. VI 77 7–8]', *Res Publica Litterarum*, 21: 169–80.
Charlet, J.-L. (1988), 'Observations sur certaines éditions du *Cornu copiae* de Niccolò Perotti (1489–1500)', *Res publica litterarum*, 11: 83–96.
Charlet, J.-L. (1995), 'Curifugia, la villa Sanssouci: N. Perotti "locataire" de Pline le Jeune (Corn. C. 18,11 = Ald. C. 731732)', *Studi Umanistici Piceni*, 15: 37–44.
Charlet, J.-L. (1997a), 'Allegoria, fabula et mythos dans la lexicographie latine humaniste (Tortelli, Maio, Perotti, Nestor Denys, Calepino, R. Estienne)', in: H.-J. Hornand / H. Walter (eds), *Die Allegorese des antiken Mythos*, 125–46, Wiesbaden (Wolfenbütteler Forschungen 75).
Charlet, J.-L. (1997b), 'N. Perotti', in: C. Nativel (ed.), *Centuriae latinae. Cent une figures humanistes de la Renaissance aux Lumières offertes à Jacques Chomarat*, 601–5, Geneva.
Charlet, J.-L. (2003), *Deux pièces de la controverse humaniste sur Pline: N. Perotti, Lettre à Guarnieri. C. Vitelli, Lettre à Partenio di Salo*, Sassoferrato.
Charlet, Jean-Louis (2004–5a), 'La lexicographie latine de l'époque humaniste', *Acta classica universitatis scientiarum Debreceniensis*, 40–51: 401–27.
Charlet, Jean-Louis (2004–5b), 'L'encyclopédisme latin humaniste (XVe – début XVIe s.): de la lexicographie à l'encyclopédie', *Quaderni Moderni e Antichi del Centro sul Classicismo*, 2–3: 285–306.

Charlet, J.-L. (2008), 'Libertas dans la lexicographie latine humaniste: Valla, Perotti, Maio, Nestore Dionigi, Calepino, R. Estienne', in: L. Secchi-Tarugi (ed.), *Il concetto di libertà nel Rinascimento*, 13-23, Florence.
Charlet, J.-L. (2009), 'Lorenzo Valla, Giovanni Tortelli, Niccolò Perotti: la restauration du latin', in: D. Sacré / J. Papy (eds), *Syntagmatia: Essays on Neo-Latin Literature in Honour of Monique Mund-Dopchie and Gilbert Tournoy*, 47-60, Leuven (Supplementa Humanistica Lovaniensia XXVI).
Cosenza, M. E. (1962), *Biographical and Bibliographical Dictionary of the Italian Humanists and of the World of Classical Scholarship in Italy 1300-1500*, Boston.
D'Alessandro, P. (2015), 'Perotti, Niccolò', in: *Dizionario Biografico degli Italiani* 82 (https://www.treccani.it/enciclopedia/niccolo-perotti_%28Dizionario-Biografico%29/).
Fattori, D. (1998), 'L'avventurosa vita di Democrito da Terracina (fra libri e altro)', *RR. Roma nel rinascimento*, 1998: 305-16.
Fattori, D. (2003), 'Democrito da Terracina e la stampa delle "Enneades" di Marco Antonio Sabellico', *La Bibliofilía*, 105:1: 27-48.
Formichetti, G. (1984), 'Costanzi, Antonio', in: *Dizionario Biografico degli Italiani* 30 (https://www.treccani.it/enciclopedia/antonio-costanzi_(Dizionario-Biografico)).
Greco, A. (1979), 'L'Umanesimo in: Ciociaria', in: A. Greco (ed.), *L'Umanesimo in: Ciociaria e Domizio Palladio Sorano. Atti del seminario di studi, Sora 9-10 dicembre 1978*, 19-38, Sora.
Kristeller, P. O. (1965-97), *Iter Italicum*, Leiden (1, 1965; 2, 1967; 3, 1983; 4, 1989; 5, 1990; 6, 1994; Index 1997).
Lehmann, P. / Stroux, J. (1967-), *Mittellateinisches Wörterbuch bis zum ausgehenden 13. Jahrhundert*, Munich.
Lizier, A. (1893), *Marcello Filosseno poeta trevigiano dell'estremo Quattrocento*, Pisa.
Margolin, J.-C. (1981), 'La fonction pragmatique et l'influence culturelle de la Cornucopiae de Niccolò Perotti', *Res Publica Litterarum*, 4: 123-71.
Martini, M. (1969), *Domitius Palladius Soranus Poeta*, Casamari.
Martini, M. (1979), 'Domizio Palladio Sorano, un discepolo di Pomponio Leto', in: A. Greco (ed.), *L'Umanesimo in: Ciociaria e Domizio Palladio Sorano. Atti del seminario di studi, Sora 9-10 dicembre 1978*, 81-123, Sora.
Martini, M. (1998), *L'opera poetica di Domizio Palladio Sorano. Contributo alla storia dell'Umanesimo. Testo latino a fronte, traduzione, introduzioni e note esplicative*, Sora.
Mercati, G. (1925, repr. 1973), *Per la cronologia della vita e degli scritti di Niccolò Perotti, arcivescovo di Siponto*, Rome (Studi e testi 44).
Milde, W. (1982), 'Zur Druckhäufigkeit von N. Perottis *Cornucopiae* und *Rudimenta grammatices* im 15. und 16. Jahrhundert', *Studi Umanistici Piceni*, 2: 29-42 (= Res Publica Litterarum 5).

Monfasani, J. (1988), 'The First Call for Press Censorship: Niccolò Perotti, Giovanni Andrea Bussi, Antonio Moreto, and the Editing of Pliny's *Natural History*', *Renaissance Quarterly*, 41: 1–31.

Morgan, L. (2010), *Musa Pedestris*, Oxford.

Osmond, P. / Sandal, E. (2005–7), 'La bottega del libraio-editore Antonio Moreto: ditorial e commercio librario a Venezia, c. 1480–1518', in: L. Pon / C. Kallendorf (eds), *The Books of Venice / Il libro veneziano*, 231–50, New Castle / Venice.

Pade, M. (2007), 'Un nuovo codice pomponiano? Appunti sulle relazioni tra Niccolò Perotti e Pomponio Leto', in: C. Cassiani / M. Chiabò (eds), *Pomponio Leto e la Prima Accademia Romana. Giornata di studi, Roma 2 dicembre 2005*, 25–40, Rome (RR inedita, Saggi 37).

Pade, M. (2008), 'Commenti perottini a Marziale? Il Ms B 131 sup. della Biblioteca Ambrosiana di Milano', *Studi Umanistici Piceni*, 28: 79–95.

Pade, M. (2011a), 'Pomponio Leto e la lettura di Marziale nel Quattrocento', in: A. Modigliani / P. Osmond / M. Pade / J. Ramminger (eds), *Pomponio Leto tra identità locale e cultura internazionale*, 103–23, Rome (RR inedita, Saggi 48).

Pade, M. (2011b), 'The Urbinas latinus 301 and the Early Editions of Niccolò Perotti's Cornu copiae', in: O. Merisalo / C. Tristano (eds), *Dal libro manoscritto al libro stampato. Atti del Convegno Internazionale di Studio, Roma, 10–12 dicembre 2009*, 91–108 and tavv. I–ii, Spoleto.

Pade, M. (2013), 'Niccolò Perotti's *Cornu Copiae*: the Commentary as a Repository of Knowledge', in: K. Enenkel / H. Nellen (eds), *Neo-Latin Commentaries and the Management of Knowledge in the Late Middle Ages and the Early Modern Period (1400–1700)*, 241–62, Leuven (Supplementa Humanistica Lovaniensia XXXIII).

Pade, M. (2014a), 'The Material Fortune of Niccolò Perotti's *Cornu Copiae* in the Fifteenth and Early Sixteenth Centuries', in: M. van der Poel (ed.), *Neo-Latin Philology: Old Tradition, New Approaches*, 72–87, Leuven (Supplementa Humanistica Lovaniensia XXXV).

Pade, M. (2014b), '*P. Papinius Statius poeta Neapolitanus* . . . . La Vita Statii di Niccolò Perotti', *Studi umanistici piceni*, 33: 9–17.

Pade, M. (2014c), '*P. Papinii Statii vita*', *Repertorium pomponianum* (https://www.repertoriumpomponianum.it/textus/leto_vita_statii.htm).

Pade, M. (2015), 'The *Vitae Statii* of Niccolò Perotti and Pomponio Leto', in: M. Pade (ed.), *Vitae Pomponianae: Lives of Classical Writers in Fifteenth-Century Roman Humanism*, *Renæssanceforum*, 9: 139–55 (https://www.njrs.dk/9_2015/08_pade_leto_and_perotti_vitae_statii.pdf).

Pade, M. (2020), 'The Paratexts to the Printed Editions of Niccolò Perotti's *Cornu copiae*: Commissions, Patronage and Intended Readership', in: G. Abbamonte / M. Laureys / L. Miletti (eds), *I paratesti nelle stampe di commenti ed edizioni di scrittori classici greci e latini (1450–1700)*, 231–51, Pisa.

Pade, M. (2021), 'Niccolò Perotti', in: G. Claessens / F. Della Schiava (eds), *Reading De Civitate Dei in Italy between the Fourteenth and the Fifteenth Century*, 349–62, Gent.

Prete, S. (1993), 'Antonio Costanzi: la sua vita, le sue opere', *Umanesimo fanese nel '400. Atti del convegno di Studi nel V Centenario della morte di Antonio Costanzi – Fano 21 giugno 1991*, 45–67, Fano.

Ramminger, J. (2001a), 'Brotheus e Timon: il vocabolario della polemica tra Domizio Calderini e Niccolò Perotti', *Studi Umanistici Piceni*, 21: 147–55.

Ramminger, J. (2001b), 'Auf dem Weg zum *Cornu copiae*: Niccolò Perottis Martialkommentar im Vaticanus lat. 6848', *Neulateinisches Jahrbuch*, 3: 125–44.

Ramminger, J. (2003–), *Neulateinische Wortliste: Ein Wörterbuch des Lateinischen von Petrarca bis 1700* (available at www.neulatein.de).

Ramminger, J. (2008), 'Niccolò Perotti', *Repertorium pomponianum* (https://www.repertoriumpomponianum.it/pomponiani/perotti.htm).

Regoliosi, M., ed. (2010), *Le radici umanistiche dell'Europa, Lorenzo Valla, la riforma della lingua e della logica: Atti del convegno del Comitato Nazionale VI centenario della nascita di Lorenzo Valla, Prato, 4–7 giugno 2008*, Firenze.

Ricciardi, R. (1973), 'Caetani, Daniele', in: *Dizionario Biografico degli Italiani* 16 (https://www.treccani.it/enciclopedia/daniele-caetani_(Dizionario-Biografico).

Stok, F. (1994), 'Perotti esegeta', *Studi Umanistici Piceni*, 14: 27–37 (repr. in: F. Stok [2002], *Studi sul Cornu Copiae di Niccolò Perotti*, 123–41, Pisa).

Stok, F. (2001), 'Il manoscritto', in: J.-L. Charlet et al. (eds), *Niccolò Perotti, Cornu copiae seu linguae Latinae commentarii* 8, 5–10, Sassoferrato.

Stok, F. (2002a), 'La revisione del Cornu copiae', *Studi Umanistici Piceni*, 22: 29–46; revised version in: F. Stok (2002), *Studi sul Cornu Copiae di Niccolò Perotti*, 71–93, Pisa (Testi e studi di cultura classica 25).

Stok, F. (2002b), 'Perotti, Calepino, Forcellini e l'OLD', in: F. Stok (2002), *Studi sul Cornu Copiae di Niccolò Perotti*, 217–30, Pisa (Testi e studi di cultura classica 25).

Stok, F. (2011), 'Gli umanisti alla scopertà dell'età Flavia', in: A. Bonadeo et al. (eds), *Filellenismo e identità romana in: età Flavia. Atti dell VII Giornata ghisleriana di Filologia classica (Pavia, 10–11 novembre 2009)*, 155–68, Pavia.

Latin text

Text 1

When the *editio princeps* of the *Cornu copiae* appeared (1489), it had on its opening page a short poem in elegiac distichs in praise of the work by Giovan Francesco Superchi, nicknamed *il Filomuso*.[1]

IOANNIS FRANCISCI PHILOMVSI PISAVRENSIS
  TETRASTICHON
IN CORNV COPIAE PEROTTAEI LAVDEM

Varronis Nigidique olim monumenta latinam
  Ditarunt linguam Romuleosque patres,
Pro quibus ammissis Perotti copia raptas
  Omnifero e cornu plena refundit opes.

Text 2

Only a year after the *editio princeps*, the *Cornu copiae* was printed twice more in Venice. One edition is a reprint of the *princeps* (1490a), but the other (1490b), by Antonio Moreto, offered several novelties.[2] On the opening page the rubric claims that the text of the *Cornu copiae* had been corrected, and below that there is a new collection of poems praising the *Cornu copiae* and Moreto's edition: apart from Filomuso's tetrastichon (Text 1), they are by Antonio Costanzi, Marcellus Philoxenus, Ludovicus Ponticus and Daniel Caietanus (Texts 2–6).[3] The six poems are reprinted in the 1494 reprint of Moreto's edition (= 1494a) and in 1496a.

ANTONIUS CONSTANTIUS FANENSIS AD LECTOREM

Non cornu Aetolum, non hic bona copia Cretum,
  Diva novum fundit candida χρυσόκερας.
Illa dabant fruges perituraque munera ventri;
  Hoc animo ambrosium perpetuasque dapes.

---

[1] In my transcriptions of the poems I retain the original orthography, but to make the texts more easily understandable I use modern punctuation.

[2] On Moreto, see Osmond / Sandal 2005–7.

[3] At the end of the text of the *Cornu copiae* Moreto prints a letter to himself from Marcantonio Sabellico, praising his edition. Next follows another philological text by Perotti, namely the letter to Guarnieri, in which he criticises Andrea Bussi's 1470 edition of Pliny's *Natural History* (fol. 287r–291v). For this and the printing history of the so-called *Commentariolus*, see Monfasani 1988, Charlet 2003 and Pade 2019.

English translation

By Giovanni Francesco Filomuso of Pesaro,
a tetrastichon
in praise of Perotti's *Cornu copiae*.

Once the works of Varro and Nigidius enriched
the Latin language and the Romulean fathers.
Their works are lost, but instead Perotti's rich abundance
lets the vanished riches flow back, from the all-containing horn.[4]

Antonio Costanzi of Fano to the reader

Not here the Aetolian horn nor the fine abundance of the Cretans,
now the new χρυσόκερας ('golden horn') flows with brilliant riches.
The former used to give us passing delights of the stomach;
this gives us ambrosia for the mind and perpetual sustenance.

---

[4] On this and other poems that gradually found their way into editions of the *Cornu copiae*, see Charlet 1988.

Commentary Text 1

Very little is known about Filomuso; he was professor in Udine, not far from Venice, where the *Cornu copiae* was printed, and his name appears in humanist miscellanea of Latin poetry. He is mentioned by Paolo Giovio in the *Elogia Doctorum Virorum*, in the entry 'Ioannes Marius Catanaeus'.[5]

The poem compares Perotti to the two ancient grammarians, Varro and Nigidius, both of them quoted repeatedly in the *Cornu copiae* (cf. the *Index auctorum* in vol. 8 of the modern edition), thereby emphasizing that Perotti's work brought back the riches of the Latin language. The prefix *re-* in the verb *refundit* (v. 4) is important: it places the *Cornu copiae* in the context of the restoration of Latin (see Introduction, n. 2).

Filomuso's tetrastichon is full of references to ancient Latin authors, which serve differing purposes. Whereas the borrowings from Statius and Ovid's *Fasti* seem mainly there to suggest ancient, venerable Latinity, Filomuso almost certainly expected his readers to recall the passages in which Horace wrote about the 'Horn of Plenty'. In Horace's *Carmen saeculare* we hear of the new Golden Age, in which 'blessed plenty dares to appear again, now, with her flowing horn', and in the Epistle to Iccius Horace ends by describing the present state of Italy (Hor. *Epist.* 1.12.28–29): 'Golden plenty has poured wealth over Italy from her filled horn' (see comment on vv. 3–4). By invoking the Horatian hypotexts, Filomuso implies that Perotti's work will bring about a new Golden Latin Age.

1 *Nigidique*: P. Nigidius Figulus served as a praetor in the late Roman Republic in 58 and died in 45 BCE. He was a grammarian whose works have only been transmitted in fragments.

2 *Romuleos ... patres*: the expression occurs only in Statius. *meu Romulei venient ad carmina patres* (Stat. *Silv.* 5.2.161).

3–4 *raptas ... opes*: cf. Ov. *Fast.* 3.70: *nam raptas fratri victor habebat opes*, about Amulius, the uncle of Rhea Silvia, mother of Romulus and Remus.

copia ... e cornu plena: cf. Hor. *Carm. saec.* 59–60: *apparetque beata plena | copia cornu*; *Epist.* 1.12.29–30: *aurea fruges | Italiae pleno defudit Copia cornu.*

4 *Omnifero*: *omnifer* has been transmitted in Ov. *Met.* 2.275, but the reading is now doubted (cf. *TLL* IX 2.590). It is, however, not uncommon in Neo-Latin (cf. e.g. Poliziano, *el.* 12.1 and *syl.* 3 proh).[6]

---

[5] See Giovio 1551 / 1972: 103. Filomuso's name also appears in humanist *miscellanea* of Latin poetry, cf. Kristeller 1965–97, passim.

[6] Where possible, I use the sigla of Rammenger 2003– for references to Neo-Latin texts.

Commentary Text 2

Antonio Costanzi (Fano, 1436–1490), a pupil of Guarino Veronese, was a person of consequence in his native city. He translated some Greek poetry into Latin and published a commentary on Ovid's *Fasti*, dedicated to Federico da Montefeltro, also the first dedicatee of the *Cornu copiae*. Costanzi was, moreover, a friend of Ludovico Odasio, its first editor, and a frequent visitor at the court of Urbino.[7] In view of this, and of the fact that he died in April 1490, it seems likely that the two poems by him in Moreto's edition were in fact written for Odasio's *editio princeps*. They were later included in a collection of Costanzi's epigrams, published after his death in 1502.[8]

Although Costanzi refers to the *Cornu copiae* by a Greek name, χρυσόκερας, the first distich seems to contrast myths of Greek material wealth with this new Latin intellectual abundance. In the second distich this contrast is further developed: the Greek works gave only fleeting pleasure and of an aesthetic character, whereas the *Cornu copiae* offers the mind lasting nourishment. Notice the alliteration of the isosyllabic polar opposites *peritura* ('passing') and *perpetuas* ('lasting') in lines 3–4.

1 *cornu Aetolum*: Diodorus Siculus mentions some myths according to which Hercules, when he fought the river god Achelous in the form of a bull, broke off one of its horns and gave it to the Aetolians who had helped him (Diod. Sic. 4.35.3). Diodorus is one of several Greek authors often quoted by Costanzi;[9] his text was available also in the 1461 Latin translation by Poggio Bracciolini, first printed in Bologna in 1472, which made Diodorus' work far more accessible to a larger Western audience.

bona copia: alludes to the passage in Ovid's *Metamorphoses* where Hercules' fight with Achelous is described: *divesque meo Bona Copia cornu est* (Ov. Met. 9.88). The expression is here quite perplexingly combined with *Cretum* ('the Cretans'): is Costanzi here combining the story of Hercules with the common notion of Crete as an 'island of Plenty'?

2 *Diva ... candida*: cf. Catull. 68B.70: *candida diva*.

χρυσόκερας: apparently a new coinage by Costanzi, though Greek adjectives meaning 'gold-horned' exist.

4 *ambrosium*: a Graecizing wordplay with *perpetua*s (both evoking immortality).

---

[7] Formichetti 1984; Prete 1993.
[8] Constantius 1502: fol. aiiiir–v.
[9] Prete 1993: 55.

Latin text

Text 3

IDEM AD EUNDEM

Quisquis amas lepidi sensus haurire poetae,
    Quem tulit arguto Bilbilis ingenio,
Fonte Peroteo te prolue: certus abibis,
    Tuque alios haustus, credula turba, cave.
5 Ducunt, crede mihi, per devia, per labyrinthum
    Et monstrant Libyco pro Garamante Getas.

Text 4

MARCELLUS PHILOXENUS

Fluminis evicti sacrato divite cornu
    Ornarunt famam Naiades Herculeam.
Sed nunc Perotti cornu foecundius extat,
    Quod victor multis amnibus eripuit.
5 Illud et est pomis et odoro flore repletum,
    Hoc sed habet fructus Pallados eximiae.
Naiades Herculeum dant, hoc tibi copia Musae;
    Haec duo si sumas cornua, maior eris.
Mittit et in Latias te nunc Antonius oras,
10 Vt tanto possit munere quisque frui.

Niccolò Perotti (1430–1480)

English translation

The same to the same

Whoever you are who loves to drink in the elegant poet's words
– the one from Bilbilis with the sharp intellect –
just drink away from the fountain of Perotti; you will leave enlightened.
And beware of drinking from other sources, you credulous lot.
Believe me, they are leading you astray, confusing you,   5
and showing you the Getans as if they were the Libyan Garamantes.

Marcello Filosseno

By consecrating the rich horn of the vanquished river,
the Naiads embellished Herculean fame.
But now we have Perotti's horn which is even more abundant
because he wrestled it from many streams.
The former is full of fruit and fragrant flower;   5
but the other has the fruits of exquisite Athena.
The Naiads give the Herculean horn, the abundance of the Muse provides
    you with this one.
If you take both these horns, you will be the winner.
Now Antonio sends you out also to the Roman shores,
so that all may profit from this great work.   10

Commentary Text 3

The poet from Bilbilis is Martial, and the 'other sources' Costanzi refers to must be the commentary on Martial by Domizio Calderini (1474). Perotti and Calderini conducted a heated polemic about the interpretation of Martial for several years.[10] Perotti treats the Garamantes in *Cornu copiae* 3.77.

4 *credula turba*: the same phrase is found in the same position at Ov. *Rem.* 687. The collocation was popular in Neo-Latin, cf. e.g. Petrarch, *fam.* 12.8.3 (gamma): *credula cristianorum turba*; Phialtes, C. *Philephum* 192: *Te tandem noscet credula turba rudem*; Baptista Mantuanus, *Calam.* 1.1166: *Ite procul iuvenes, simplex et credula turba*.

5 *Ducunt... per devia*: cf. Ov. *Fast.* 2.370–1: *per devia rura iuvencos,* | *Romule, praedones, et Reme... agunt*; *Met.* 1.676–7: *per devia rura capellas* | *dum venit abductas.*

---

[10] On this, see Campanelli 1998, Stok 1994 and Ramminger 2001.

Commentary Text 4

Marcello Filosseno (c. 1450–1520) from Treviso is a little-known poet from the late fifteenth century. He became a priest in 1488 and is the author of the vernacular *Sylve*, dedicated to Lucrezia Borgia and published in Venice in 1507.[11] Like Text 2, Filosseno's poem is composed around the contrast between the material abundance that came from the Horn of Plenty in the story about Achelous, and the intellectual profit to be had from Perotti's work.

1–5 cf. Ov. *Met.* 9.85–8 and the commentary on Text 2.

1 *Fluminis*: the river god Achelous whom Hercules fought.

divite cornu: cf. Ov. *Met.* 9.91: *praedivite cornu*.

7 *dant*: the 1496 edition has a semicolon after *Herculeum*, implying that *dant* would go with the next sentence and have *Musae* as subject. This, however, is metrically impossible as it would leave no place for *copia* with a short -*a*, i.e. in the nominative.

9–10 In the last two verses Filosseno addresses the new edition itself.

9 *in Latias... oras*: cf. Lucan 3.93 and Silius Italicus 5.10.

Antonius: Antonio Moreto, the editor.

---

[11] Lizier 1893.

Latin text

Text 5

L. Ponticus Tarvisanus

   Praemia debentur solerti magna Perotto,
      Dum pandit nodos, Bilbilitane, tuos.
   Praesul Amalthias solum κέρας attulit; ecce,
      Milia pro solo multa Moretus habet.
5 Auctori grates igitur debentur utrique,
      Quod prior ingenium, quod dedit alter opus.

Text 6

Daniel Caietanvs

   Hactenus quisquis sibi comparavit
   Copiae cornu, laterem lavasse
   Et sciat nunquam facili dedisse
      Semen arenae.

5 Quod fidem nullam faciat legenti
   Ordo confusus tabulae, nec ullum
   Stat sua verbum serie notatum
      Nec bene iunctum.

   Obvius tanto vicio Moretus
10 Et gravem certe ratus esse culpam,
   Consulens lautis animis benigna
      Mente reponit.

   Inde iam tersum, nitidum, politum
   Et carens menda madidisque nugis
15 Iam libens quaeso facilisque lector
      Accipe cornu.

English translation

L. Ponticus of Treviso

The clever Perotti is owed a lot,
as he unravels your knots, poet of Bilbilis.
The bishop brought just one κέρας ('horn') of Amalthea. Look,
Moreto has many thousands instead of one.
Thanks is due to both authors,   5
the first for his genius, the other for his work.

Daniele Caetani

Whoever bought himself a *Cornu copiae* until now, let him know that he
   wasted his time and threw seeds into the unyielding sand.

[5] The index was a mess, which should not inspire faith in the reader, and
   no word stands in the right order, nor is it referring to the correct
   passage.

[9] Moreto saw this great fault and, believing it to be a grave defect, he
   kindly restored it, providing for refined minds.

[13] Neat, in order, elegant, without blemish and drunken nonsense, now, I
   ask you, favourable reader, please enjoy the horn!

Commentary Text 5

I have not been able to identify Ludovicus Ponticus, but his poem is the first of the series that address the actual edition rather than Perotti's work: whereas Perotti produced just one horn of Amalthea – his manuscript, supposedly –, Moreto was now able to produce thousands of printed copies.

2 *Bilbilitane*: Martial was a native of Bilbilis in Spain.

3 *Praesul*: Perotti was archbishop of Siponto.

Amalthias ... κέρας: Quoting Gellius (1.8.1), Perotti recalls how the Aristotelian philosopher Phocion wrote a book of very mixed content and named it κέρας ᾽Αμαλθείας, which is almost the same as *cornu copiae* (cf. *Cornu copiae* 1.116).

Commentary Text 6

Daniele Caetani (1450–1528) was a humanist teacher, amongst other places in Udine in the 1490s. He was befriended by many Venetian humanists, among them Marcantonio Sabellico. The poem is by and large a praise of the new *index verborum* found in Moreto's edition. This may seem strange to modern readers, but the index to the work plays a prominent role, both in Perotti's presentation of the *mise-en-page* of the presentation copy and in the later printed editions. It was, after all, the entry to the work.[12] Caetani's use of the sapphic stanza may point back to the way in which both Horace and Statius used the metre writing on more humble subjects.[13] Caetani's criticism of the earlier editions of the *Cornu copiae* is quite harsh, but is probably still just a more colourful variant of the topos found in so many publications from the period, namely that the editor had corrected the 'innumerable errors' of his predecessors.

2 *laterem lavasse*: cf. Ter. *Phorm.* 186; Sen. *Contr.* 10 pr. 11.

4 *Semen arenae*: cf. Ov. *Her.* 5.115: *quid arenae semina mandas?*

---

[12] Pade 2014 and 2020.
[13] Morgan 2010: ch. 3.3: '"Narrower Circuits": The Sapphic Stanza', 181–283, esp. 272–3.

Latin text

Text 7

The next important development in the textual history of the *Cornu copiae* took place in 1496, when Polidoro Virgilio found two folia containing a handwritten addendum by Perotti to the original stratum of text in the Urbino manuscript (now *Cornu copiae* 2.736.10–2.746, i.e. fol. 185 *bis et ter* of the *Urbinas*). The missing folia were found in the ducal library at Urbino. Polidoro's new edition, made together with Giovanni Pompeo Corniano, announced the find immediately on the title page. It was clearly a selling point, and the edition could also boast a new way of presenting the text, in two columns, so that each lemma became the first word in a line, as well as a fuller, more accurate index, making the use of the *Cornu copiae* as a reference work much more efficient.

The reinserted pages also became the subject of a poem.

DOMICUS PALLADIUS SORANUS

Membra Pelops obtruncus erat; tamen ille deorum
    Dicitur iratus consuluisse pater.
Sic operi Polydorus opem tulit ante reciso,
    Quod nunc infirmo non pede carpit iter (sig. aa1v).

English translation

Domizio Palladio Sorano

Pelops was dismembered; but angered, the father of the gods
is said to have taken care of him.
Likewise, Polidoro came to the aid of a previously mutilated work;
it is now on its way on secure footing.

Commentary Text 7

Domic(i)us Palladius Soranus, Domenico Farina of Sora (c. 1460–c. 1533), a poet, was a member of the Roman Academy and a friend of Marcantonio Sabellico.[14] The poem is reprinted in the 1998 edition of Sorano's work, where, however, the editor claims that it was sent to Polidoro Virgilio to celebrate the publication of the latter's *Proverbiorum libellus*, dedicated to Guidobaldo da Montefeltro in 1498.[15] Obviously, its original setting is the 1496 *Cornu copiae* edition. Sorano's poem is followed by Texts 1–4.

1 *obtruncus*: the adjective *obtruncus* is found in Medieval Latin (cf. *Mittellateinisches Wörterbuch* s.v.), but very rare in Neo-Latin. Apart from in this poem it is only found in the *Bellum Parthicum* of the Sicilian humanist Tommaso Chaula (c. 1429): *fratrem ... hostibus obtruncum* (Chaula, *Parth.* 2.393–4) and *mundum ensibus obtruncum* (*ibid.* 5.271–72). The collocation *membra obtruncare* is found in Cic. *Nat. Deor.* 3.67, about Medea cutting up her children.

---

[14] Cf. Martini 1969, 1979 and https://www.repertoriumpomponianum.it/textus/palladio.htm.
[15] Martini 1998: 234.

Latin text

Text 8

After Perotti's *vita Martialis* and before the beginning of the *Cornu copiae* itself, there is a letter from Johannes Pompeius Cornianus of Brescia (Giovanni Pompeo Corniano), the other editor, to Sebastianus Badoarius, a Venetian patrician, followed by two poems by Cornianus.

IOANNIS POMPEII CORNIANI BRIXIANI AD AVRELIVM BACINETVM
    IVRISCONSVLTVM OPTIMVM CARMEN

O nove Moecenas, studiorum maxime fautor,
    Caesaris alterius qui mihi cura subis.
Quam tibi pro natis cuperem modo tradere, venit
    Fructifero cornu copia larga suo,
5 Quae plerisque locis prius incorrecta manebat,
    Nec fuerat series ulla magistra sui.
Ecce novo constans nunc ordine cultior ibit;
    Ad quodcumque voles et magis aptus eris.
Nec pete, patronum cur te properarit adire:
10   Haec laribus tutam se putat esse tuis.
        Vale.

English translation

A great poem by Giovanni Pompeo Corniano from Brescia to the lawyer
   Aurelio Bacineto

Oh, new Maecenas, great patron of learning,
who occupies my mind like a second Caesar.
I desire to give you, as if it were my offspring,
this overwhelming abundance which comes in its fruitful horn.
It was long incorrect in many places,   5
and there had been no passage where it was in control of itself.
But, look, now it will proceed more elegantly, steady with its new order;
and whatever you might want it for, you will be better able to do.
And do not ask why it hastened to approach you as a patron:
it thinks itself safe in your house.   10
Farewell.

Commentary Text 8

Very little is known about Polidoro Virgilio's co-editor, Giovanni Pompeo Corniano,[16] and even less about Aurelio Bacineto, whom Corniano calls a lawyer.[17] Corniano's poem, like that of Caetani (Text 6), praises the usefulness of the new edition: the text is more correct, and it is 'ordered' or organized, so as to be more easily consulted. The poem is yet another indication that editions of the *Cornu copiae* were increasingly produced to facilitate the work's use as a Latin lexicon.

1 *Moecenas*: Gaius Cilnius Maecenas (*c.* 70–8 BCE) was a friend and ally of Augustus and an important patron of several Roman poets, including Horace and Vergil. His name has become a synonym for 'patron of the arts'.

2 *Caesaris*: *Caesar* was the official title of the Roman emperors; here it probably refers to Augustus, with whom Maecenas was closely associated.

7 *novo . . . ordine*: could refer both to the index and to the new layout of the text itself.

---

[16] Cosenza 1962 s.v., has collected a few notices. He assumes that Corniano is from Brescia, though Latin *Brixia* is also used of Bressanone/ Brixen in South Tyrol.
[17] Fattori 2003: n. 18.

Latin text

Text 9

EIUSDEM SAPHICUM AD LECTOREM

Plaude nunc multum, studiose lector,
Copiae cornu qui habes politum,
Quum sit haec libro series reperta
   Lumine fuso.

5 Non prius cuique facile dabatur
Posse, quod vellet, reperire nomen:
Dictio rectum caput et negabat
   Ordine mixto.

Ergo fac grates habeas utrique:
10 Alter est, qui Democritus vocatur,
Hic dedit causam, Tacuinus alter,
   Qui bene pressit.
      Vale.

English translation

A poem in sapphic stanzas by the same to the reader.

Now applaud, learned reader, you have an improved *Cornu copiae*, since the text is found in a book with clarity everywhere.

[5] Before, not everyone could easily find the word they wanted, and the word rejected its right chapter because of the lack of orderly arrangement.

[9] Therefore, make sure to be grateful to two people, one who is called Democritus and is the cause of it all, and the other Tacuinus who printed the book so well.

Farewell.

Commentary Text 9

4 *Lumine fuso*: literally means something like 'bathed in light'. Here *lumen* is translated with its transferred meaning 'clarity'.

5 *cuique*: the last syllable is short as at Catullus 51.10, where according to the stricter metrical rules of the Horatian Sapphic stanza, it should be long.

8 *Ordine mixto*: refers to the alphabetical order of the index of words that preceded the text of the *Cornu copiae* in all the printed editions and was constantly enlarged and reorganized.

10 *Democritus*: *Democritus Terracinensis*, alias Bernardo de' Massimi. In the 1504 edition of the *Cornu copiae*, in his letter to the reader, the printer Tacuinus recalls how this Democritus, a learned man and expert editor of texts, had carefully corrected every page of the edition until it was ready to be printed (Perotti 1504, fol. 1v). For Democritus, see also Fattori 1998 and 2003, where she prints Corniano's poem on p. 32.

12 *pressit*: the new meaning of the verb *premere* = 'to print' is an example of how the invention of printing brought about changes in the meaning of existing Latin words, i.e. semantic expansion as well as a spate of new coinages. For this, see the section 'Lemmagruppen' in Ramminger 2003– (http://nlw.renaessancestudier.org/words/startgr.htm).

2

The *Natalis* of Paolo Marsi (1440–1484)

Raphael Schwitter

Introduction

The *Natalis* is a hexameter birthday poem for the city of Rome written by the teacher, scholar and poet Paolo Marsi (1440–84). His life and work show some typical characteristics of an Italian Quattrocento humanist. Born in Pescina in the Abruzzo mountains, Marsi went to Rome at a young age, where he held the position of a papal abbreviator, met Pomponio Leto and later became a key figure in his *sodalitas literaria*, the Roman Academy. After having held teaching positions in Perugia and Venice, he was appointed Professor of Rhetoric in Rome in the late 1470s. His studies of classical literature culminated in several learned commentaries on Lucan's *Pharsalia*, the *Rhetorica ad Herennium* and Ovid's *Fasti*. The last was quite successful and widely disseminated. It was first printed in Venice in 1482 and reissued in the following years. From the 1490s to the late 1520s, it was published in composite editions alongside the commentary of his academic rival, Antonio Costanzi of Fano (1436–90).

Title and preface (lines 1–5) refer to a certain type of occasional poetry, the *genethliacon*, which was popular in Neo-Latin literature, but had few classical precedents (see Smeesters 2017). This poem appears to have been written for the celebration of the *Palilia* on 21 April, the founding festival of Rome revived by Pomponio Leto and his Academicians, but its length makes it unlikely to have been performed during the festivities. The circumstances of its transmission are rather peculiar. The poem has not survived independently, but over 330 verses are preserved in the body of the author's commentary on Ovid's *Fasti* (cited at 2.384, 2.405, 2.418, 3.11, 3.57, 3.204, 3.214, 4.31 and 4.811f.). The longest section at *Fasti* 4.31 (282 lines) deals with the Trojan genealogy of Romulus, but it seems to be only a fraction of the work, as the author claims to have extended the narrative to the time of Augustus (line 8, and in the prose gloss on *Fasti* 4.31). Marsi quoted the poem in his commentary on Lucan in 1469 (see Bianchi 1981: 76), but it remains unclear whether it was widely circulated. A partial manuscript transmission in Vindob. 3111, fol. 69v–73v, is based on a printed version of the commentary, but Lilio Gregorio Giraldi (*De poetis nostrorum temporum* 1.85) mentions the poem, and the self-evident manner of Marsi's auto-quotations suggests that his readership was familiar with it. Another *genethliacon urbis Romae* is preserved from the same literary circle, composed by the young *poeta laureatus* Domizio Palladio and performed during the society's solemn 1484 celebration of the *Palilia* in the church of S. Maria in Ara Coeli (text in Martini 1998, 272–83). It differs both in metre (elegiac couplets) and size (90 lines), but Palladio equally draws on Rome's foundation myth with clear allusions to Ovid's narrative in *Fasti* 4.806–856.

Like many scholars of his time, Marsi used the commentary genre as an open platform for personal remarks and autobiographical notes. Above all, however, and throughout the commentary, Marsi took care to shape and emphasize his poetic identity, relentlessly drawing the reader's attention to his literary talents. The modes of this self-fashioning are both implicit and explicit, paratextual and intratextual. Marsi's name, for example, always appears with the apposition *poeta clarissimus*. Moreover, half of the prefaces to the individual books of the *Fasti* are written in verse, and the commentary is concluded with a hexameter *propempticon* beginning with the famous Ovidian sphragis *iamque opus exegi* (*Met.* 15.871). The most fascinating element is the inclusion of this learned birthday poem in the main body of the commentary. By embedding large parts of the *Natalis*, Marsi not only disrupts the conventional layout of a commentary, but also decisively alters the receptive framework of the poem.

As a stand-alone piece, it could be read as a kind of genealogical epyllion; yet alongside Ovid's text, it becomes a poetic extension of the *Fasti*, supplying what the poet could (or should) have narrated. When its longest quotation (printed below) elaborates on Ovid's brief account of the Julian genealogy at *Fasti* 4.31–40, Classicists may think of the infamous Helen episode in Vergil's *Aeneid* (2.567–288), which does not appear in any late antique or medieval manuscript but was (re-)inserted into the Vergilian text from the commentary of Servius as early as the fifteenth century. The supplementary function of the poem is not limited to the Ovidian hypotext, but equally relates to the exegetical level of the commentary. Quotations are often introduced with remarks such as 'about all this I wrote in the *Natalis*', hinting at the text's generic ambiguity as an epic poem and poetic commentary. On those occasions Marsi's exegetical mode shifts from a passive role to a more active and creative one. He morphs himself into the *vates operosus* (*Fasti* 1.101), the inspired poet engaged in the arduous exploration of the past, which Ovid seemingly became in his work on the Roman calendar. The way in which Marsi shaped his professional identity as a scholar-poet must be seen in the light of the humanist conception of an antiquarian didactic poetry derived from Ovid's *Fasti*, which Quattrocento scholars read as a poetic continuation of Varro's learned work on Roman antiquities (Fritsen 2015). As a humanist steeped in the classical past, Marsi did not content himself with explaining Ovid's text, but pursued his own antiquarian endeavour, staking his claim to become part of the learned tradition.

Metre: dactylic hexameter

Bibliography

Bianchi, R. (1981), 'Il commento a Lucano e il *Natalis* di Paolo Marsi', in: R. Avesani / G. Billanovich (eds), *Miscellanea Augusto Campana* I, 71–100, Padua.

Fritsen, A. (2015), *Antiquarian Voices: The Roman Academy and the Commentary Tradition on Ovid's Fasti*, Columbus.

Martini, M. (1998), *L'opera poetica di Domizio Palladio Sorano: Contributo alla storia dell'Umanesimo. Testo latino a fronte, tradizione, introduzioni e note esplicative*, Sora.

Smeesters, A. (2017), 'Le *Genethliacon Salonini* et le *Genethliacon Lucani* comme modèles pratiques (et théoretiques?) du poème généthliaque néo-latin', in: G. Ems / M. Minet (eds), *Les arts poétiques du XIIIe au XVIIe siècle: Tensions et dialogue entre théorie et pratique*, 263–86, Turnhout.

della Torre, A. (1903), *Paolo Marsi da Pescina: Contributo alla storia dell'Accademia Pomponiana*, Rocca S. Casciano.

Source of Latin text

The printed segments of the poem are drawn from Marsi's extensive quotation in the gloss on Electra at the beginning of the fourth book of the *Fasti*. The Latin text is based on Bianchi's edition with minor changes in orthography and punctuation.

Latin text

    Roma, genethliacam tibi nunc libatur ad aram.
    Candida lux orta est, qua primum iacta parenti
    fundamenta tibi, totum passura per orbem
    bracchia, sidereo caput admotura tonanti,
5 quo maius nihil est. Tua te si gloria tangit
    et decus antiquum, faveas pulcherrima vati,
    Roma, tuo et prima referentem ab origine rerum
    fas sit in Augustos deducere carmina fasces.
    Fabula vana procul tantis modo rebus abesto;
10 vera canam. Archadicos Atlas servabat honores,
    cum furit Electrae magno Dycteus amore
    Iuppiter hancque gravem et geminata prole parentem
    reddidit: Iasius pater hinc et Dardanus orti.
    Alter agit primo vitam sine coniugis usu,
15 accipit at Chrysem, magno Pallante creatam,
    Dardanus uxorem; proles Idaeus ab illa
    nascitur et Dymas. Subiit postremus honori
    Archadico; cedit pater hinc et filius alter
    Iasiusque simul. Magna iam classe parata
20 armiferam in Thracem deventum et celsa tenetur
    insula, Mercurio genitus Samothracia nomen
    cui dedit. At Cererem sibi dum concumbere tentat,
    occidit Iasius rutilo confossus ab igne.
    Protinus in Phrygiam penetravit Dardanus oram
25 Helleumque sinum tenuit. Conscendit in altos
    Idaeus Phrygiae montes, Idaea vocavit
    nomine deque suo iuga celsa atque orgia Bacchi
    instituit. Phrygios tum cum frenaret alumnos
    Scamandri soboles Idaeaeque unica nymphae
30 Teucrus, Cecropio quamvis referatur ab antro
    advenisse, suo populos de nomine Teucros
    ex illo dixisse ferunt, cui nulla virilis
    progenies, tantum patrios Bathea penates
    nympha colit. Chryse extincta tibi, Dardane, iungit
35 connubio pater hanc pariterque recepit aviti
    in partem regni; et Teucro subeunte supremi
    fata rogi Phrygia solus dominaris in omni.
    Natus Erychthonius, quo fortunatior alter
    non fuit: ille auri atque equitum et ditissimus agri

English translation

Rome, a birthday gift is being offered to you at the altar.
Bright light appeared when the first foundation was laid for you, Mother,
about to stretch out your arms to embrace the whole world
and to move your head up to the star-studded sky, the highest possible
    point.   5
If the glory and splendour of ancient times mean anything to you,
most beautiful Rome, be kind to your poet and allow him to tell the tale
from your first beginnings to the high office of Augustus.
Stay away, empty myths, from this most significant subject!
I will sing of true things. Atlas was watching over his Arcadian kingdom,   10
when the Dictaean Jupiter fell madly in love with Electra
and impregnated her, making her the mother of two sons:
Father Iasius and Dardanus both descend from him.
The first lived unmarried for a time, but Dardanus took Chryse,   15
the daughter of mighty Pallas, as his wife; from her two sons were born,
Idaeus and Deimas. The latter eventually became king of Arcadia,
when his father, brother and uncle Iasius left the country together.
After assembling a large fleet, they sailed to armed Thrace and landed   20
on a mountainous island to which a son of Hermes had given the name
    Samothrace.
But when Iasius desired to have intercourse with Ceres,
he died after being struck by a blazing bolt of fire.
Dardanus advanced further to the coast of Phrygia and occupied
the shore of the Hellespont. Idaeus climbed the high mountains of
    Phrygia,   25
which he called Idaean after his own name, and introduced the
    mysteries
of Bacchus there. This happened at the time when Teucer, the only
    scion of Scamander
and an Idaean nymph, was ruling the Phrygian people.
Although it is said that he came from a cave of Cecrops,   30
the Teucrians are alleged to have been named after him.
Yet he had no male descendants, only the nymph Batheia inhabited
the parental home. After the death of Chryse, Batheia's father
married her to you, Dardanus, and accepted you as co-ruler   35
of his ancestral kingdom. And when Teucer met his final fate,
you became the sole ruler of all Phrygia.
Erichthonius was your son; he was the most fortunate of men,
he possessed riches in gold, horses, and land,

40 atque huic Calliroe, Scamandri filia, nupta.
    Natus ab his Tros est; hinc magnae nomina Troiae.
    Ex Troe et sobole Eumedis Callanide nati
    Ilus et Assaracus Ganymedis et inclyta forma.
    Incoluit campos Ilus; hinc Ilion altum,
45 quod male servavit periurus filius Ili
    Laomedon. Priamus de Laomedonte creatus
    et matutinum raptus Tytonus in ortum.
    Ingentem Priamus cum fratribus Hectora gignit,
    at sacer Assaracus, Clytodore coniuge felix,
50 fit pater atque Capim genuit, cui Naide iuncta
    nascitur Anchises. Venus huic Simoentis ad undas
    Aeneam peperit, Priami cui nupta Creusa est.
    Natus et Euryleon, generis spes maxima, dictus
    inque fuga Ascanius. Nam Troia ardente supremum
55 et Priami genere extincto miserabile magno
    collapso imperio aeternum penetralibus ignem
    magnorumque deum sacra Troianosque penates
    sustulit Aeneas et cum genitore petivit
    aerios montes. Cui formidantia lustrum
60 rursus bis geminum consumier agmina bello
    omnia Graiorum tribuere abscedere tuto,
    quocunque ire velit. Fato iam coniuge rapta
    e patria illachrymans comites natumque patremque
    secum agit. Et structis iam puppibus aequora verrens
65 Thraces adit primum Troiae e regione iacentis.

[*Lines 66–101 tell the story of Aeneas' journey to the shores of the Tiber and the founding of Lavinium.*]

Cum tamen a Rutulis Latii premerentur et ipse
afforet auxilio regi caderetque Latinus
atque hostis pugna Turnus raperetur eadem,
105 imperium accepit soceri, tutatur et auget.
Et quartum regno iam tandem exegerat annum,
cum cadit aut bello raptus fluctuve Numici.
Quaesitumque diu nulla tellure cadaver
inventum inque deos translatum credidit omnis
110 Ausonia: huic pubes posuit Lavinia templum
atque hoc candenti scripsere in marmore carmen:
'Terrestris divique patris fluctusque Numici

and received the hand of Callirrhoe, the daughter of Scamander. 40
Their son was Tros, from whom the name of great Troy is derived.
Of Tros and Acallaris, the daughter of Eumedes,
Ilus, Assaracus and beautiful Ganymede were born.
Ilus inhabited the open land, he founded great Ilion,
which was evilly preserved by Ilus' doomed son 45
Laomedon. From him Priamus and Tithonus descend,
who was taken up into the dawn.
Priamus begat the mighty Hector and his brothers,
but venerable Assaracus, fruitful with his wife Clytodora,
begat Capis, to whom Anchises was born after his marriage to a Naiad. 50
To him, on the banks of the Simois, Venus gave birth to Aeneas,
who married Creusa, the daughter of Priam.
Of them Euryleon was born, the great hope of his lineage,
who in the flight was renamed Ascanius. For when Troy was burning,
the house of Priamus miserably destroyed, and his great empire broken, 55
Aeneas kept the eternal flame alive in the sanctuary,
picked up (and carried) the Great Gods and the Trojan Penates,
and took refuge with his father in the lofty mountains. Fearing to be involved
in another ten-year long war, the Greeks allowed him to go safely 60
where he wished. Fate had just taken his wife from him.
With tears in his eyes, he left his home and took his companions,
his son and his father with him. The ships were prepared; they set sail and
reached Thrace, which lies across from Troy. 65

However, when the Rutulians oppressed the Latins, Aeneas
came to the king's aid. Latinus fell, and the foe Turnus
lost his life in the same battle. Thus, Aeneas succeeded to the kingdom
of his father-in-law, which he preserved and expanded. 105
At the end of the fourth year of his reign, he either died in battle
or was swept away by the flood of the river Numicus.
After a long search, no body was found,
and all Ausonia believed that he had been taken up among the gods.
The youth of Lavinium built a shrine for him, 110
and this poem was inscribed on the white marble:
'To the earthly God and Father, who with his divine power

numine perpetuo qui flumina sancta gubernat.'
Ascanius Latiae suscepit pondera molis.
115 Hunc quoque Tyrrenis urget Mezentius armis;
victa tamen Latio cesserunt robora Marti
Tyrrena extincto crudeli funere Lauso.
Hinc memor Ascanius repetens mandata parentis
egregii simul et servanda oracula divum
120 saepe animo volvens, celsis in collibus Albam
condidit et Latiae dicta est ea regia genti.
Et iam tres septem lustris adiecerat annos
a patris interitu, quo regnum acceperat ingens,
cum ruit in funus generosa prole relicta.
125 Imperium natu maior deposcit Iulus;
venit Iuleum genus unde decusque superbum
militiae atque omnis Romanae gloria gentis.
Parte alia petit Aenea generatus avitum
filius in regnum recipi, quem mater in altis
130 ediderat silvis. Nam cum Lavinia rapto
coniuge iamque gravis privignum moesta timeret,
cesserat in silvas natumque enixa fideles
pastores inter patrios in saltibus altis
educat, et puero tribuit sua nomina casus.

[*Lines 135–175 describe the succession of the Albanian kings to Numitor and Amulius.*]

Haec quoque sive proco geniove aut numine divum,
aut ipse insignis pressisset Amulius armis,
sacra lavaturas dum mane incedit ad undas
et viridi consedit humo correptaque somno,
180 fit gravida. Obscura tegitur calligine tellus
solque fidem fecit rutilo mutatus amictu
concepisse deo, sed quo conceperat orbi
incertum est. Redit illa domum iam languida virgo
remque aperit matri. Velantur crimina: morbus
185 fit causa, in templum cur non eat illa pudicum.
Mens tamen interea saevi seu conscia regis,
seu suspecta doli metuens, curare medentes
illam adhibet. Genitrix arcet morbumque virili
non ait hunc sexu prodendum. Turgidus ira
190 uxorem mittit custodem atque illa tyranno

rules over the holy waters of the river Numicus in eternity.'
Ascanius took over the burden of ruling Latium.
Mezentius besieged him too with Tyrrhenian troops,   115
but the Tyrrhenian army was defeated by the Latin force
and retreated when Lausus suffered a cruel death.
Thereupon Ascanius, who often thought in his heart of the need
to fulfil the divine oracles, continued his father's mission and founded Alba   120
in the high hills, which was declared the royal residence of Latium.
Thirty-eight years after his father's death, when he had
succeeded to the great kingdom, he died leaving noble progeny.
Iulus, the eldest, claimed the kingdom;   125
from him came the Julian house, the highest military
splendour and the fame of the entire Roman nation.
Yet another son of Aeneas aspired to succeed to his grandfather's kingdom.
His mother had given birth to him in the high forests. For after the death   130
of her husband, the pregnant Lavinia was sad and feared her stepson;
she went into the woods and raised her new-born son in the company
of her father's trusted herdsmen in the high woodland; this fate gave
    the boy his name.

One morning, when Rhea fetched water for sacral use,
she sat down on the moist ground, fell asleep, and became pregnant –
whether by a human suitor, a divine spirit or deity,
or by rape by Amulius distinguished for his armour.
A gloomy darkness spread over the land, and the sun was shrouded   180
in a red glow, giving credence to the belief that she had lain with a god,
but with which is uncertain. The maiden, already faint, returned home
and told her mother everything. The crime was concealed: an illness
was given as the reason why she could not enter the holy temple.   185
But in the meantime, the cruel king, either because he knew
what had happened or because he suspected fraud,
sent physicians to attend to her. Her mother held them away
claiming that this disease had to be kept secret from the other sex.
Enraged, he sent his wife to look after her, and soon she informed the tyrant 190

mox scelus omne refert. Furit ille insanior Euris,
cum rapere ingenti maria omnia turbine tentant,
et caesurus erat praegnantis viscera ferro.
Hinc instat Numitor, hinc Antho, filia regis,
195   inque deos referunt crimen: saevissimus iram
distulit. In decimae redeuntia cornua lunae
Silvia fit genitrix, heu, prolem enixa gemellam
et virgis caedi virgo miseranda iubetur
defodierque solo; poena haec vestalibus ipsis,
200   quae vetitum patiantur opus. Miserabilis Antho
ante patrem supplex tumidum procumbit et orat,
orat opem miserae; et precibus servata sororis
dicitur. At geminos deferri ad Tybridis amnem
immergique iubet fluvio. Mandata ministri
205   inviti peragunt. Tantum scelus unda refugit
et pueri in sicca miseri versantur arena.
Quid nisi pro miseris poterant vagire querelis?
Vagitus enixa tamen lupa sensit ad undas
sedatura sitim progressa. Accurrit et illos
210   deposita feritate videt, miserata iacentis
eripit e coeno; dehinc ubera plena gemellis
admovet. O superi quanta est claementia coeli!
Qui positurus erat populis ingentia magnis
moenia perpetuos terrae latura triumphos
215   pascitur infelix infantia lacte ferino
atque avis expositis suggessit Martia picus
saepe cibos. Non hoc vatum, non fabula vulgi,
sed fatale quidem: quos sors in magna vocabat
imperia, hos casus et mille pericula rerum
220   Parca subire dedit. Tot per discrimina pastum
quid repetam Astyagis muliebri e stirpe nepotem
nutritum quoque lacte canum miserantius inter
pastores? Quanto post imperitaverit orbi!
Gorgoris indigno coitu cui filia natum
225   edidit, exponi iussit sua viscera silvis.
Lac illi tribuisse feras visum; inde relatus
inque iter angustum iactus, qua armenta redibat,
ut miserum obruerent: etiam haec alimenta dederunt.
Obiicitur canibus ieiunis: hi quoque pascunt

of the whole crime. He raged more furiously than the east wind
when it wants to stir up the whole sea with a violent storm
and was going to stab the pregnant girl with a knife.
On one side Numitor, on another Antho, the king's daughter, then rose in objection
and referred the crime to the gods, prompting the overly angry king 195
to put aside his wrath. Thus, when the horn of the moon returned for the tenth time,
Silvia gave birth to twin boys, and, oh!,
it was ordered that the poor girl be scourged with rods
and buried in the ground. This was the punishment for a vestal virgin
who suffered the forbidden act. Miserable Antho 200
fell to her knees beseeching her father, who was swollen with rage, and pleaded
and begged for the unfortunate girl's life; and it is said that she was saved
by her sister's plea. But Amulius ordered the twins to be taken to the Tiber
and submerged in the water. His servants reluctantly
carried out the order, but the stream resisted such a crime, 205
and the poor infants remained on the dry sand.
Ah! What could they do but weep miserably?
But a she-wolf that had just whelped heard the whimpering
as she went to the river to quench her thirst. She approached,
had mercy, having lost her wildness, and lifted them out of the mud. 210
Then she gave the twins her full teats to suckle.
Oh, what grace from the gods!
He, who was to build the mighty walls for a great nation
that would bring endless victories over the earth,
fed in his childhood miserably on the milk of a wild beast. 215
And while they were exposed to the birds, the bird of Mars, the woodpecker,
often helped in feeding them. This is not just a story told by poets
or the common people, but truly an act of fate. Those whom destiny calls
to great power, Fate makes endure a thousand calamities and dangers. 220
Why should I recall the grandson of Astyages, the child of his daughter, who
was nurtured through countless hazards, even miserably fed with dog's milk when raised
among shepherds? What an empire he would later command!
Gorgor had ordered his son, born to him by his daughter
after shameful intercourse, to be abandoned in the forest. 225
Apparently, they found him being fed milk by wild animals. They then
brought him back and threw him on a narrow trail used by cattle
so that the unfortunate boy would be trampled to death; yet, also these animals
gave to him their milk. He was thrown before starved dogs; those fed him, too,

230 ubera dantque sues. Et demum immergitur undis
Oceani summaque infans levis innatat unda
servaturque deum manifesto numine. Litus
excipit, exceptum pavit quoque cerva iacentem.
Et tandem ad magni sullatus culmina regni.
235 Fatave quid referam Mosis crudelia nostri,
eiectum Phario gemuit quem moesta fluento
mater? Et hic domini servatus munere coeli,
esset ut ille dei populo qui moenia sancto
poneret et vera sub relligione foveret.
240 Numina sic miseros servarunt alta gemellos,
esset ut ille deis magnam qui conderet urbem.

[*Lines 242–260 narrate Faustulus' caring for young Romulus and Remus.*]

Et iam bis novies Cancer gestaverat axes
soliferos, totiens tulerat Capricornus eosdem,
cum tegerent teneras prima lanugine malas.
Inter pastores orta est contentio saepe
265 montis Aventini et Pallantia septa tuentes.
Saepe duo fratres Pallantia septa tuentur
et sub Aventino pulsant Numitoris ovile.
Res domino delata suo regique superbo;
mittitur infestus iuvenes qui comprimat hostis.
270 Lucebatque dies, magni quo festa Licaei
Panos erant, castoque deum dum indulget honori
Romulus, insidiis capitur germanus ab hoste.
Ad regem trahitur manibus post terga revinctis
Plectendum accepit Numitor, mox indole motus
275 obstupuit tacitum. Iuvene in penetralia ducto
quo genitus rogitat; pastoris sanguine cretum
sese ait. Ecce subit tectum laturus alumno
pastor opem: tutas aperit Numitoris in aures
fata gemellorum remque omnem ex ordine pandit.
280 Romulus interea turbam collegerat omnem
pastorum secumque Albana in moenia ducit.
Subereo insignes clypeo sudibusque preustis
inferiore urbis subierunt parte ruuntque
consulto Numitore tamen sub tecta tyranni
285 et regem obtruncant. Et celsa Romulus arce
vi potitur prolesque omnis deletur Amuli.

and also the pigs gave him their teats. Eventually he was drowned 230
in the sea, but the infant floated lightly on the waves.
He was saved by the manifest will of the gods.
Safely back on shore, a doe gave its milk to the infant.
Finally, he was raised to the summit of a great empire.
Or why should I tell of the cruel fate of our Moses, 235
abandoned on the waters of the Nile and mourned by his mother?
The lord of heaven saved him so that he might found and preserve
a city in true faith for God's holy people.
In the same way, the unfortunate twins were saved by divine power 240
so that one of them might found a great city for the gods.

When Cancer had turned twice nine times around
its sun-bearing axis and Capricorn had done the same,
the young men covered their cheeks with fine down.
Quarrels frequently arose between the herdsmen
who tended the pastures on the Aventine hill and of Pallanteum. 265
Often, when the two brothers were tending the pastures of Pallanteum,
they drove off Numitor's cattle grazing at the foot of the Aventine hill.
This the herdsmen reported to their master and the proud king.
A hostile man was sent to suppress the youths.
At dawn on the festive day of Pan Lycaeus, 270
when Romulus was offering a chaste sacrifice to the gods,
the enemy captured his brother in an ambush.
He was dragged before the king with his hands bound behind him.
He was handed over to Numitor for punishment, who was soon impressed
by his innate character and puzzled by his silence. 275
He led the young man to his home and asked him who his parents were.
He answered that he was the son of a shepherd. Suddenly, the shepherd
entered the house and brought help to his foster-son: he confided the fate of
    the twins
to Numitor's trusted ears and told him how it had all come about.
Meanwhile, Romulus had gathered all the herdsmen together 280
and led them with him to the walls of Alba.
With cork-oak shields and stakes whose tips were hardened with fire,
they came up from the lower city and, on Numitor's instructions, stormed
    up to the tyrant's
house and killed the king. Romulus took the lofty 285
citadel by force, and all of Amulius' children were slain.

Commentary

1–10 Proem, beginning with a reverential address to Mother Rome and ending with the poet's conventional appeal to the goddess to assist him in his endeavour to sketch the history of Rome from its beginnings to the time of Augustus.

1 *genethliacam*: γενεθλιακός, 'belonging to a birthday'. *libatur ad aram*: cf. Vergil, *Aen.* 7.245: *libabat ad aras*.

4 *tonanti*: 'thunderer', epithet of Jupiter, here metaphorically 'sky'.

9–10 a conventional claim in didactic poetry, cf. Ovid, *Ars.* 1.25–30, echoing Hesiod's prologue to *Works and Days*, 10.

10–52 Marsi develops a theme that Ovid only briefly addresses in *Fasti* 4.31–8. Aeneas' Trojan genealogy is for the most part an abbreviated version of Dion. Hal. 1.61.1–62.2. It makes the Trojans essentially a Greek people, whereas Roman legend, as presented by Vergil (*Aen.* 3.167–8 and 7.240), has Dardanus coming from Italy (cf. Servius on Vergil, *Aen.* 3.104 and 3.167).

10 *Archadicos*: Narratives about ancient Arcadia and its emigrant Evander occupy a prominent position in Ovid's *Fasti* (e.g. 1.469–542; 2.271–302; 5.91–102). *servabat honores*: cf. Vergil, *Aen.* 5.601: *servavit honorem*. *honor* here means 'kingdom' as in 17–18.

11 *Electrae*: Electra was the daughter of Atlas and Pleione. *Dycteus*: poetic for 'Cretan', from Dicte, a mountain in Crete where Jupiter was concealed from Saturn.

13 *Iasius pater ... orti*: rephrases Vergil, *Aen.* 3.167–8: *hinc Dardanus ortus | Iasiusque pater*. Since the Trojan origins of Rome are the theme of the *Aeneid*, frequent echoes of Vergil (mostly without the intention of an intertextual allusion) underscore the epic tone of the poem.

15 *magno Pallante*: a Titan, who also fathered Eos, the goddess of dawn.

19 *Iasiusque*: Vergil, *Aen.* 3.168.

20 *armiferam in Thracem*: cf. Ovid, *Her.* 2.84; the epithet is probably an Ovidian coinage. Ancient writers considered the Thracians to be a warlike and ferocious people. *celsa tenetur*: cf. Vergil, *Aen.* 8.653: *Capitolia celsa tenebat*.

21 *Mercurio genitus*: i.e. Samon, the son of Hermes and the nymph Rhene; hence *Samo-thrace*. Cf. Dion. Hal. 1.61.3.

25 *Helleumque sinum*: the Hellespont, named after Helle, who drowned in it, cf. Ovid, *Fasti* 3.853–76; here meaning 'the shores of the Hellespont'.

27 *orgia Bacchi*: Vergil, *Georg.* 4.521; according to Dion. Hal. 1.61.4 Idaeus instituted the mysteries of the Mother of the Gods in the Phrygian mountains.

29 *Scamandri*: a river in the Troad, not mentioned by Dionysius of Halicarnassus. Marsi is following a Roman tradition, according to which Scamander was a Cretan king, cf. Servius Danielis on Vergil, *Aen.* 3.108 and 3.167. *Idaeaeque*: all printed editions read *ideaeque*.

30 *Cecropio . . . ab antro*: poetic for 'from Attica'. Cecrops was the oldest king of Attica. Dion. Hal. 1.61.5 gives credence to the story that Teucer came from Attica.

31 *de nomine . . .*: a Vergilian formula, cf. e.g. *Aen.* 1.367; 1.533; 6.70, recurring in this position also in Ovid, *Fasti* 1.41 et al.

32-7 Marsi again draws on additional sources to complement Dion. Hal. 1.62.1, especially Servius Danielis on Vergil, *Aen.* 3.167.

36-7 *supremi . . . rogi*: cf. 136-7: *supremos . . . in cineres*.

39-40 poetic elaboration of Dion. Hal. 1.62.1 with climactic emphasis on Erichthonius' wife.

41 *nomina Troiae*: cf. Vergil, *Aen.* 12.828: *cum nomine Troia*.

42 *Callanide*: Dion. Hal. 1.62.1 calls the mother Acallaris; the reading is most likely a transmission error, cf. Ἀκαλλαρίδος.

45 *male servavit*: Laomedon refused to grant Poseidon, who built the city walls of Troy, the wages agreed upon for his service. The god sent a sea monster, which Hercules was willing to defeat. When Laomedon cheated him out of his reward as well, Hercules killed him.

47 *raptus*: Tithonus was abducted by Eos, who made him her lover.

49 *coniuge felix*: an Ovidian formula, recurring in this position in Ovid, *Met.* 6.681; 7.60 et al.

51-2 rephrases Dido's question in Vergil, *Aen.* 1.617: *tune ille Aeneas, quem . . . | alma Venus Phrygii genuit Simoentis ad undam?*

53 *Euryleon*: the renaming of Aeneas' son during the flight is mentioned in Dion. Hal. 1.65.1.

54-65 The epic account of the destruction of Troy and the preparation of Aeneas' departure follows Dion. Hal. 1.46–47.

56 *penetralibus ignem*: cf. Vergil, *Aen.* 2.297; 5.660.

59 *montes*: Mount Ida, cf. Dion. Hal. 1.46.3.

60 *bis geminum*: numerical duplication is a feature of high poetry found in both the *Metamorphoses* and the *Fasti* and used repeatedly by Marsi (see below 122; 261). *consumier*: poetic infinitive passive, the printed editions read *consumer*.

62 *coniuge*: Aeneas lost sight of Creusa during his flight from the city. When he returned, she appeared to him as a ghost, cf. Vergil, *Aen.* 2.737-95.

63 *natumque patremque*: cf. Vergil, *Aen.* 4.605.

64 *aequora verrens*: cf. Vergil, *Georg.* 3.201.

65 *regione iacentis*: cf. Ovid, *Tr.* 3.3.5: *dira regione iacenti*.

102-13 The reign and death of Aeneas, narrated according to Dion. Hal. 1.63-64.

110 *Ausonia*: poetic for Italy. *pubes... Lavinia*: cf. Vergil, *Aen.* 5.450: *Trinacria pubes*; *Aen.* 5.599: *Troia pubes*.

111 *in marmore carmen*: cf. Ovid, *Fasti* 3.547, referring to Dido's epitaph, which Ovid cites at *Her.* 7.197-8.

112-13 Marsi's Latin version of Dion. Hal. 1.64.5; *terrestris* is problematic: Dion. Hal. writes χθόνιος, probably to translate lat. *indiges*, cf. Vergil, *Aen.* 12.794: *indigetem Aenean* (cf. Servius ad loc.); Ovid, *Met.* 14.607-8: *quem turba Quirini | nuncupat Indigetem*.

114-24 The reign and death of Ascanius, narrated according to Dion. Hal. 1.65-66 in ostentatiously Vergilian language.

114 *pondera molis*: cf. Ovid, *Met.* 15.1, echoing Vergil, *Aen.* 1.33: *tantae molis erat Romanam condere gentem*.

115 *Mezentius armis*: cf. Vergil, *Aen.* 8.482; 10.768; Ovid, *Fasti* 4.881.

117 *crudeli funere Lauso*: cf. Vergil, *Aen.* 4.308: *crudeli funere Dido*.

118 *mandata parentis*: cf. Vergil, *Aen.* 10.840; Ovid, *Met.* 6.534.

119 *servanda oracula divum*: cf. Vergil, *Aen.* 8.131: *sancta oracula divum*. A deliberate allusion to Aeneas' initial words when he first meets Evander's Arcadians.

125-34 The conflict between Silvius and Iulus, narrated according to Dion. Hal. 1.70.

127 *Romanae gloria gentis*: cf. Vergil, *Aen.* 6.767: *Troianae gloria gentis*.

128-9 *avitum* . . . *regnum*: the kingdom of Latinus, Lavinia's father.

176-211 The story of Rhea Silvia and the twins closely follows Dion. Hal. 1.77-79, but is supplemented by other sources, esp. Ovid, *Fasti* 3.11-52.

176 *numine divum*: Vergil, *Aen.* 2.336 et al.

177 *insignis* . . . *armis*: cf. ὅπλοις ὡς ἐκπληκτικώτατος, Dion. Hal. 1.77.1; cf. Plutarch, *Rom.* 4.2.

178 *sacra lavaturas* . . . *ad undas*: rephrasing Ovid, *Fasti* 3.12: *sacra lavaturas mane petebat aquas*.

180-1 Cf. Dion. Hal. 1.77.2.

182 *deo*: Mars, according to Roman tradition, cf. Ovid, *Fasti* 3.21: *Mars videt hanc . . . potiturque capita*; *Fasti* 2.419: *Marte satos scires*.

183 *iam languida*: because she was pregnant, cf. Ovid, *Fasti* 3.25: *languida consurgit*.

184 *crimina*: as a vestal virgin, Rhea was forbidden to have sexual intercourse. See 198-200.

186-7 *seu* . . . *seu*: picks up εἴτε . . . εἴτε in Dion. Hal. 1.78.1. *conscia regis*: cf. Ovid, *Met.* 7.385.

191-2 The poem's only Vergilian-style simile. Similes drawn from natural phenomena are ubiquitous in epic poetry. For the comparison of a whirlwind with an enraged person, see e.g. Vergil, *Aen.* 10.603-4: *Dardanius, torrentis aquae vel turbinis atri | more furens*. Amulius' rage (189: *turgidus ira*; 195: *saevissimus*) and its possible effect (193: *caesurus*) are Marsi's invention to visually enhance the scene.

194 *Antho*: Amulius' daughter. Plutarch, *Rom.* 3.3, is the only ancient source stating her name. *filia regis*: Ovid, *Met.* 2.844.

196 *redeuntia cornua lunae*: cf. Ovid, *Met.* 10.479: *redeuntis cornua lunae*.

198 *virgis* . . . *virgo*: a striking wordplay.

200-1 Dion. Hal. 1.79.2, without mentioning Antho's name.

203-4 *amnem ... iubet*: rephrasing Ovid, *Fasti* 3.51: *amne iubet mergi geminos*.

205 *scelus unda refugit*: Ovid, *Fasti* 3.51.

206 *pueri in sicca*: rephrasing Ovid, *Fasti* 3.52: *in sicca pueri destituuntur humo*.

207 *pro*: interjection.

209-12 Cf. Dion. Hal. 1.79.6; Ovid, *Fasti* 2.413-418. *sedatura sitim*: a detail provided by Livy 1.4.6: *lupa sitientem*.

212-17 *O superi* ...: emphatic interjection, recalling the poem's festive occasion.

215 Note the alliteration and repeated f-sounds to enhance the emotional appeal. *lacte ferino*: Vergil, *Aen*. 11.571; Ovid, *Tr*. 3.11.3.

216 *Martia picus*: Ovid, *Fasti* 3.47, at a different position in the verse. The woodpecker helping the twins gives credence to the belief that Mars was their father, cf. Plutarch, *Rom*. 4.2.

217-41 An excursus in which Marsi interrupts the narrative to elaborate on three legendary examples of human infants who had to endure perils but later became leaders of their people: Cyrus, Habis and Moses.

218-20 The statement takes the form of an aphorism. *hos casus ... rerum* and *tot per discrimina* recall Vergil, *Aen*. 1.204: *per varios casus, per tot discrimina rerum*.

221-3 Cyrus, founder of the Persian empire. The tale is based on Justin 1.4.

224-34 Habis, legendary Tartessian king from Iberia. The tale is based on Justin 44.4.

231 *levis innatat unda*: cf. Verg. *Georg*. 2.451: *undam levis innatat alnus*; Ovid, *Tr*. 3.4a.11: *levis innatet unda*.

232 *manifesto numine*: Vergil, *Aen*. 11.232.

235-9 Moses, Israelite religious founder. The story of his birth is told in *Ex* 2.1-10.

235 *quid referam*: an Ovidian formula, cf. Ovid, *Am*. 1.5.23; 3.11.21; *Met*. 12.450 et al. *nostri*: the only reference to the Christian faith. Marsi is otherwise completely immersed in the persona of an ancient poet.

240-1 *sic ... esset ut*: concludes the excursus on other myths of child exposure and leads back to the main narrative.

241 *qui conderet urbem*: echoes Vergil, *Aen*. 1.5: *dum conderet urbem*.

261-86 The twins, now grown up, overthrow their great-uncle Amulius. The story is adapted from Dion. Hal. 1.79.12-83, but also draws on Livy 1.5-6.2 and Plutarch, *Rom*. 7-8.

261-2 *bis novies* ...: eighteen years. Cancer, the zodiac sign of the summer solstice, stands for summer, its opposite, Capricorn, for winter.

263 *lanugine malas*: cf. Lucretius 5.889; Vergil, *Aen*. 10.324; Ovid, *Met*. 9.398; 13.754.

265 *Pallantia*: Marsi picks up the Greek Παλλάντιος in Dion. Hal. 1.79.12. The Romans called the hill *Palatinus*, but traced the name back either to an Arcadian named Pallans (or Pallantia) or the Arcadian city Pallanteum (Servius on Vergil, *Aen*. 8.51; Varro, *Ling*. 5.53; Livy 1.5.1).

268 *domino*: Numitor. *regique superbo*: King Amulius.

270-2 The festival of Lupercalia. *Licaei Panos*: cf. Vergil, *Aen*. 8.344: *Panos de more Lycaei. castoque ... honori*: Marsi intermingles two different versions told by Dion. Hal. 1.79.13 (Remus is captured while Romulus is sacrificing) and 1.80.1-2 (Remus is ambushed during the ceremonial run). Cf. Livy 1.5.1-3 and Plutarch, *Rom*. 7.

275 *obstupuit tacitum*: cf. Ovid, *Fasti* 6.398: *obstipui tacitus*. For Remus keeping his calm even in peril, see Dion. Hal. 1.81.3; Plutarch, *Rom*. 7.3-4.

276 *sanguine cretum*: cf. Vergil, *Aen*. 4.191; Ovid, *Met*. 5.85.

277-8 *subit ... pastor*: Faustulus. In Dion. Hal. 1.81.4-6 Numitor discovers the truth by himself. Plutarch, *Rom*. 8.2, relates that Faustulus tried to inform Numitor, but was intercepted by the royal guard.

281 *in moenia ducit*: cf. Vergil, *Aen*. 1.645: *ad moenia ducat*.

282 *Subereo ... clypeo*: 'a shield made of cork-tree wood'. *subereo* is a conjecture by Bianchi; the printed editions read *sub aereo* or *sub aerio*. The 'pastoral' armament of Romulus and his band of herdsmen is Marsi's invention to visually enhance the scene.

283-6 The polysyndeton *-que ... et ... et* reflects the swiftness with which the city is stormed and the king and his offspring are killed.

3

The Verses of Antonio de Nebrija (1444–1522) on the Philologist's Work and the Place of Greek

William M. Barton*

Introduction

Elio Antonio de Nebrija (1444–1522) was born in Lebrija in the province of Seville, Spain. The humanist used the town's Roman name, *Nebrissa Veneria*, for his Latin *cognomen*. Born into an affluent agricultural family,[1] Nebrija was educated in his hometown before he left for Salamanca.[2] After four years at the city's university, Nebrija continued on to Italy in search of further education.[3] He would spend around ten years at the Spanish College of San Clemente in Bologna, where he studied theology at first, but later moved his attention to philology.[4] Nebrija's exposure to Italian humanism left a lasting impression on his approach towards Latin language and literature.[5]

On returning to Spain in 1470, Nebrija found employment with Alonso de Fonseca y Ulloa, Archbishop of Seville (died 1473), who employed the humanist as secretary and tutor to his nephew Juan Rodríguez. On the death of his employer, Nebrija returned to Salamanca, where he lectured in Latin grammar, beginning in July 1475.[6] Nebrija's experience as an instructor of Latin formed the basis for his first grammatical work, the *Introductiones Latinae*.[7] After its initial publication in 1481, the work saw widespread success and was soon reprinted (in 1482 and 1483) and edited (1485), with expanded reprints of the second edition across Spain (1493 and 1494) as well as in Venice (1491) before the end of the fifteenth century.[8] The popularity of this work drew the attention of Queen Isabella I of Castile, who requested a translation of the Latin grammar into Castilian, in order that religious women could have access to Latin without having to rely on a (male) instructor.[9] The result was Nebrija's facing translation of the Latin grammar printed as *Introducciones latinas contrapuesto el romance al latín* (1488).[10]

Nebrija's productivity in the final years of the fifteenth century was facilitated by a new Maecenas – Cardinal Juan de Zúñiga y Pimentel (1459–

1504), Archbishop of Seville – whose support for the humanist relieved him from his teaching duties from 1487 onwards. Nebrija was now able to complete the final step of his 'new method' for Latin instruction, the *Gramática castellana* (1492),[11] designed to allow Spanish-speaking students to become acquainted with the concepts of grammar in their own language before moving on to the final goal of Latin. This made the primary innovation of Nebrija's vernacular grammar – the first to be printed in Europe (though not the first composed)[12] – his 'transposition of the descriptive frame of Latin' to a new linguistic context.[13] In the same year Nebrija's Latin-Spanish dictionary appeared, followed closely by the Spanish-Latin vocabulary in 1494 or 1495.[14] This lexicographical work was expanded in later editions by lexica of geographical names, medical terms and a dictionary of classical authors.[15] Further results included an account of Spain's antiquities in 1491, an introduction to cosmography in 1498, a study of ecclesiastical hymns in 1501 and a commentary on Persius' *Satires* in 1503.[16]

Following the death of Zúñiga y Pimentel, Nebrija returned to the University of Salamanca, where he took up a Chair in Latin language and literature from 1505 to 1513. This return to an environment of teaching and language instruction brought Nebrija back to his grammatical work. Alongside numerous updated editions of his *Introductiones Latinae,* Nebrija now produced a dictionary focussed on legal terminology[17] as well as a short treatise on Greek and its usefulness for Latin learners, among other learning tools, in the following year.[18] Now nearly seventy, Nebrija met with disappointment at his *alma mater* when his attempt to win the first Chair in Latin grammar in 1513 was unsuccessful. He left the university embroiled in a series of disagreements – both personal and professional – with colleagues.[19]

On leaving Salamanca, Nebrija went first to the University of Seville before being offered the Chair of Rhetoric in 1514 at the newly established University of Alcalá de Henares. Here, Nebrija's latest patron and the university's founder, Cardinal Francisco Jiménez de Cisneros (1436–1517), gave the humanist almost free rein over his working style and material.[20] Aside from his collaboration on Cisneros' ambitious and ground-breaking Complutensian Polyglot Bible (1514–17),[21] Nebrija's renewed freedom saw a final flurry of scholarly output. He now produced, for example, an edition and notes on a set of *Libri minores*, including Latin translations of Aesop's fables and the *De contemptu mundi* (attributed to Bernard of Cluny) (1514),[22] and a series of commentaries on Scriptural passages, the *Tertia quinquagena* in 1516.[23] Nebrija died at his home in front of the Renaissance portal to the University of Alcalá de Henares in June 1522. The scholar's enormous influence across scholarly disciplines and national borders is evidenced by the 422 works published under his name before 1600 recorded by Esparza Torres and Niederehe in 1999.

Alongside his enormous output of works in the fields of grammar, rhetoric, language learning, history, geography, cosmography, textual scholarship and religious writing, Nebrija's poetic production throughout his career was also considerable. Published as part of the paratextual material to his prose works, or occasionally in separate volumes, these poems belonged very much to Nebrija's output as a scholar in the eyes of contemporary readers. Already by 1491 Nebrija had instructed a student to compile and edit a selection of his *Carmina*, which appeared in Salamanca.[24] The poems included an epithalamium on the marriage of Princess Isabella with Alfonso I of Portugal, a poem addressed to the ancient ruins in Mérida and a poem in praise of the scholar's home country, the *Salutatio ad patriam*. The two poems treated here reveal the extent to which Nebrija's ideas as a classical philologist found common expression in his scholarly works and his poetry.

Notes

* The author would like to thank Professors A. Alavar Esquerra, T. Jiménez Calvente and G. Alvar Nuño for their invitation to participate in the international conference 'Nebrija en Alcalá de Henares (1513–1522) y su legado' (30.11–02.12.2022, Universidad de Alcalá de Henares, Spain). Discussion with the organisers and participants at this event has enriched this chapter in numerous aspects.
1 Martín Baños 2019: 63–4.
2 Esparza Torres / Niederehe 1999: 12.
3 Nebrija included an account of this period of his life in the *Vocabulario de romance en latín*, Salamanca: [s.n.], 1495, fol. aiiv. In line with the accepted practice of scholarship on Nebrija, designed to facilitate navigation of his vast and varied written production in the world of late fifteenth- and early sixteenth-century publishing, original works are additionally referenced with their number in Esparza Torres and Niederehe's 1999 bibliography. In this case, the *Vocabulario de romance* [= Esparza Torres / Niederehe 1999: 24].
4 The precise duration of Nebrija's stay in Bologna remains an open question for historians.
5 Gil Fernández 1965: 347–9.
6 Olmedo 1942: 22–3.
7 *Introductiones Latinae*, Salamanca: [s.n.], 1481 [= Esparza Torres / Niederehe 1999: 1]. Nebrija addresses his reasons for composing the grammar in the work's prefatory material (fol. ir).
8 Esparza Torres / Niederehe 1999: 14. The bibliographic numbers of the respective works are: [Esparza Torres / Niederehe 1999: 2; 3; 5; 19; 20; 13].
9 On the Queen's letter and her request to Nebrija see Baldischwieler 2004: 9–10.
10 *Introducciones latinas contrapuesto el romance al latín* [s.l.]: [s.n.], 1488 [= Esparza Torres / Niederehe 1999: 8]. The text of the dedicatory letter to this

work, in which Nebrija responds explicitly to the request of Queen Isabella, is edited in Martín Baños 2014: 254-7.
11 *Gramática de la lengua castella*, Salamanca: [s.n.], 1492 [= Esparza Torres / Niederehe 1999: 18].
12 For Nebrija's work in the context of the grammaticalization of the European vernaculars see Linn 2013. For an overview of the *Gramática castellana* within Nebrija's grammatical project, see Niederehe 2004. Rodrigo 2014 sets Nebrija's vernacular grammar in the context of an Italian forebear.
13 Calvo Fernández / Esparza Torres 1993: 161-80.
14 Esparza Torres / Niederehe 1999: 24 and 26.
15 Esparza Torres / Niederehe 1999: 20-1.
16 The respective bibliographic numbers are: Esparza Torres / Niederehe 1999: 14; 37; 49; 55.
17 Esparza Torres / Niederehe 1999: 65.
18 *De litteris graecis*, Logroño: Arnao Guillén de Brocar 1507[?] [= Esparza Torres / Niederehe 1999: 71].
19 Esparza Torres / Niederehe 1999: 30.
20 See Olmedo 1942: 22.
21 On this edition, its numerous collaborators, their fractious working relationship and the project's place in the newly founded university at Alcalá, see the recent collection edited by Alvar Ezquerra 2016.
22 *Libri minores de novo correcti*, Burgos: Fadrique de Basilea, 1514 [= Esparza Torres / Niederehe 1999: 116].
23 Esparza Torres / Niederehe 1999: 152.
24 The title page says only that the poems were collected by a certain 'Bachelor P. Vivanco' (bacharlarius P. Vibanco) [Esparza Torres / Niederehe 1999: 15].

Bibliography

Alvar Ezquerra, A., ed. (2016), *La Biblia Políglota Complutense en su contexto*, Alcalá de Henares.
Baldischwieler, T. (2004), *Antonio de Nebrija: Las Introducciones latinas contrapuesto el romance al latín (1488). Wege zur Gramática de la lengua Castellana (1492) und eine kritische Edition des Textes*, PhD Diss., Heinrich-Heine-Universität Düsseldorf.
Barnard, J. A. (2017), 'The "Erasmian" Pronunciation of Greek: Whose Error Is It?', *Erasmus Studies*, 37.1: 109-32.
Bywater, I. (1908), *The Erasmian Pronunciation of Greek and Its Precursors, Jerome Aleander, Aldus Manutius, Antonio of Lebrixa*, London.
Calvo Fernández, V. / Esparza Torres, M. A. (1993), 'Una interpretación de la *Gramática Castellana* de Nebrija a la luz de la tradición gramatical escolar', *Cuadernos de Filología Clásica. Estudios latinos*, 5: 149-80.

Enenkel, K. (2013), 'Kommentare als multivalente Wissenssammlungen', in: K. Enenkel / H. Nellen (eds), *Neo-Latin Commentaries and the Management of Knowledge in the Late Middle Ages and the Early Modern Period (1400- 1700)*, 79–138, Leuven.

Esparza Torres, M. A. / Niederehe, H.-J. (1999), *Bibliografía Nebrisense: Las obras completas del humanista Antonio de Nebrija desde 1481 hasta nuestros días*, Amsterdam / Philadelphia.

Gil Fernández, J. (1965), 'Nebrija en el Colegio de los españoles en Bolonia', *Emerita*, 33: 347–9.

Gonzalez Vega, F. (2011), '*Non esse parva sine quibus magna constare non possunt*: la pequeña grandeza de la gramática según Antonio de Nebrija y Erasmo', *Studia Philologica Valentina*, 13: 281–95.

Herrero de Jauregui, M. (2019), 'De un rebusco, gran bodega: Nebrija helenista', in: M. J. Rodrigo Mora (ed.), *Nebrija en Bolonia: V Centenario de la Reglas de orthographía en la lengua castellana (1517)*, 111–36, Bologna.

Linn, A. (2013), 'Vernaculars and the Idea of a Standard Language', in: K. Allan (ed.), *The Oxford Handbook of the History of Linguistics*, 359–74, Oxford.

Martín Baños, P. (2014), *Repertorio bibliográfico de las Introductiones latinae de Antonio de Nebrija (1481–1599): o Hilo de Ariadna para el Teseo perdido en el laberinto de la gramática latina nebrisense*, Vigo.

Martín Baños, P. (2019), *La pasión de saber. Vida de Antonio de Nebrija*, con un prólogo de Francisco Rico, Huelva.

Niederehe, H.-J. (2004), 'La *Gramática de la Lengua castellana* (1492) de Antonio de Nebrija', *Boletín de la Sociedad Española de la Historiografía Lingüística*, 4: 41–52.

Olmedo, F. G. (1942), *Nebrija (1441–1522): Debelador de la barbarie, comentador eclesiástico, pedagogo-poeta*, Madrid.

Rodrigo, M. (2014), 'Nebrija e Italia: Un precedente toscano de la primera gramática romance', *Boletín de la Sociedad Española de la Historiografía Lingüística*, 9: 5–27.

Venturi, F. (2019), 'Introduction', in: F. Venturi (ed.), *Self-Commentary in Early Modern European Literature, 1400–1700*, 1–27, Leiden.

Source of Latin text

Text 1: Antonio de Nebrija, *Ars litteraria cum commento* [*Introductiones Latinae*], Salamanca: [Juan de Porras], 1499, fol. aiv–aiir [= Esparza Torres / Niederehe 1999: 40].

Text 2: Antonio de Nebrija, *De litteris graecis*, in: *Introductiones in Latinam grammaticen cum longioribus glossematis* (*Commentaria introductionum in grammaticam Latinam*). Logroño: Arnao Guillén de Brocar, 1508, fol. air [= Esparza Torres / Niederehe 1999: 76].

Text 1: AD ARTEM SUAM AUCTOR

This poem and the accompanying self-commentary appeared as the first part of the prologue to Nebrija's second edition of the *Introductiones Latinae*. The remainder of the prologue continues in prose, similarly accompanied by explanatory notes. In the original editions, the commentary was arranged around the text on three sides. The text of the poem first appeared alone in 1495.[1] Nebrija then added the commentary, and the two texts were published together in 1499.[2] This combined format was maintained in most later editions of the *Introductiones*.[3] This grammar appeared under numerous titles throughout its history. By the 1499 Salamanca edition, the work was also known under the title *Ars litteraria*.[4] Hence also the author's name for his work in this poem.

The piece opens with the author bidding farewell to his *Ars* for the last time (*tempus in omne vale!*, 'farewell forever!'). Nebrija calls on Ovid's opening address to the *Tristia* (1.1), in which the ancient poet sends his work off to Rome without him. Ovid was exiled to Tomis on the Black Sea in 8 CE after the publication of his *Ars amatoria* had caused offence to Emperor Augustus and his circle. Nebrija echoes Ovid's description of his work and its place in the world by giving comparable instructions on how the book should behave and sending the work to address its ruler (Queen Isabella of Castile) as does Ovid to Caesar Augustus. The Spanish humanist, however, turns Ovid's despondent and apologetic tone in the *Tristia* on its head by sending out his *Ars* proudly as an honoured daughter, accompanied by the commentary, to greet readers and rulers in his name.

The commentary was composed by Nebrija himself. It offers a five-line summary of the text's central idea, followed by explicative and interpretative comments on items of vocabulary, idiom and sources. The co-composition – with a gap of four years – of the poem and notes is emphasised by the reference to the notes as attendants of the *Ars* in the verse's lines 9–10. This type of self-commentary is a regular feature of Renaissance and early modern literature, with origins stretching back to Dante's *Vita nuova* (*c.* 1295).[5] It could function as a means to reveal a poem's philosophical and literary underpinning, a means to defend a given text from poor (or damaging)

---

[1] Esparza Torres / Niederehe 1999: 27.
[2] Esparza Torres / Niederehe 1999: 40.
[3] Martín Baños 2014: 249.
[4] Esparza Torres / Niederehe 1999: 40.
[5] For a useful summary of self-commentary in early modern literature see Venturi 2019: 1–27. Venturi addresses Dante's founding role in this tradition on pp. 2–3. The edited volume brings together a series of case studies that put the variety of uses for self-commentary in the period's literature on display. The brief overview offered here brings together insights from several chapters.

interpretation, as statement of authorial authority (or apology), and could even offer a means to re-analyse a work for new contexts. The practice of auto-commentary spanned the breadth of early modern literary production. Particularly relevant for Nebrija's self-commentary is the classroom context. As a professor of Latin language and literature, the tradition of textual exegesis and the ordering of scholarly knowledge in contemporary commentaries was the natural mode for Nebrija's self-annotation.[6] The book's core goal of instruction and pedagogy is thus clear from its first page onwards.

---

[6] An overview of the Neo-Latin commentary as a space for collecting and transmitting scholarly knowledge in early modern publication is offered in Enenkel 2013.

Latin text

O mihi per multos caste nutrita labores,
    Ars mea, quam genui, tempus in omne vale.
Tempus in omne vale, neque enim tuus addere quicquam,
    sed neque quod genitor demere possit, habet.
5 Quem sua nunc aetas opera ad maiora remittit,
    quaeque sibi fuerint invidiosa minus.
Et te iam grandem latebras exire paterni
    liminis, et media vivere luce decet.
Sed ne sola domo vadas, glossemata iunxi,
10   quae te circumstent quolibet ire velis.
His comitata (metu posito) contemnere vulgus,
    et detractorum verba maligna potes,
qui non agnoscant cum te, mera somnia fingunt,
    qui nihili versus supposuere meis.
15 Ito bonis avibus; tamen impartire salute
    multa, discipuli sint ubicumque mei,
sive ego quos docui, vel si quis doctus ab illis:
    Nam licet, et fas est dicere utrosque meos,
at si forte roges, quo primum vertere cursus,
20   quamque tibi iubeam protinus ire viam,
te prius ad nostrae hinc Augustae limina perfer:
    Nusquam tota tibi est ianua aperta magis,
invenies illic ab eadem stirpe sorores,
    quae te subcollocent excipiantque sinu.
25 Altera, qua nostro mutatur sermo latinus,
    altera, quae Hispane nectere verba docet.
Praeterea fratres alia sed matre gemellos
    invenies, quos tu non aliena petes.
Alter enim Latio sermonem reddit Iberum,
30   alter ab Hispanis verba latina refert.
Si regina tuos repetet volvetque libellos,
    utque solet, vultus forte serenus erit,
pauca tui referes memor haec mandata parentis:
    'Temporibus vestris non nihil iste dedit.
35 Quod si tu nobis foelicia tempora donas,
    et meus illustrat saecula vestra parens.'

English translation

O my *Ars*, brought up decorously with a good deal of work,
    I bid you, who I have created, farewell for ever!
Farewell for ever! Your parent has nothing more to give,
    nor has he anything he can take away.
His age now sends him on to greater works,   5
    which (he wishes) might be less troublesome.
Now is the right time for you now fully grown to leave the hiding place
    of your father's threshold and to show yourself to the world.
But lest you leave your home alone, I have added some comments,
    which should escort you wherever you want to go.   10
Accompanied by these (and your fear put aside) you can forget
    the common crowd and the harsh words of your critics,
who, since they do not know you, they imagine mere fantasies,
    and who have added worthless verses to mine.
Farewell and good luck! And give many greetings   15
    with affection, wherever my disciples may be,
whether they are those that I taught, or someone instructed by them,
    for it is allowed, and indeed right, that I regard them all as my own.
And if you ask where you might take yourself first,
    I tell you which road to take straightaway: 20
Get yourself first to the doorstep of our venerable Queen,
    nowhere else are the doors so completely open to you.
There you will find your two sisters of the same line,
    who are there in order to support you and take you into their lap:
the one in which Latin is turned into our language,   25
    and the other who teaches you to weave words in Spanish.
There you will find your twin brothers from a different
    mother, who you will not seek as a stranger,
for the one renders the Iberian language into Latin
    and the other Latin words into Spanish.   30
If the Queen asks you to show her your books and scrolls through them,
    and if, as usual, her face happens to be cheerful,
please remember to tell her these few words as instructed by your father:
    'He has given no little to your reign.
But if you give us happy times,   35
    my father also enlightens your rule.'

O mihi] Alloquitur Artem suam Antonius quasi filiam quandam ex se genitam, quae cum sit multo iam tempore domi caste integreque ab illo educata, iubet ipsam valere, atque ex latebris domesticis in lucem emittit. Quod tamen virgo est aetasque ludibrio exposita, addit illi glossemata, quasi comites stipatoresque, quae illam deducant atque ab invidorum iniuria defendant asserantque. Dat illi praeterea mandata ut suo nomine salutet discipulos quoscunque aut ubicunque nacta sit. Imperat quoque illi ut in primis regiam domum reverenter adeat, ubi non omnino erit hospes quippe quae illic sit inventura sorores fratresque ad quos divertat. Deinde praecipit ut suis verbis pauca reginae ipsi dicat.

O, inquit, *Ars mea, quam genui.*] Translatio frequens est, nam eo modo poetas opera sua dicuntur gignere atque amare, quo parentes filios. Auctor est Aristoteles in libro *Ethicorum* ix.

Tempus in omne] Id est in aeternum. Sic Ovidius 'Effice me meritis tempus in omne tuum.' Et Vergilius: 'Salve mihi, maxime Palla, aeternumque vale.'

Tempus in omne] Iucunda repetitio, Sappho poetisseae frequentissima.

Tuus genitor] Id est auctor; perstat in allegoria.

Habet quod possit addere aut demere] Nam in recte factis, ut ait Aristoteles ii. *Ethicorum*, nec addi nec detrahi quicquam potest.

Et te iam grandem] Ac si dicat nubilem ac viro maturam.

Exire latebras] Ubi ante hac latuisti.

Et vivere in media luce] Id est versari in oculis hominum ac frequentia.

Sed ne sola] Quod in virgine periculosum est.

Glossemata] Id est glossulas, sic enim Graeci appellant quas auctorum lectioni enarratores de suo addunt viva, ut aiunt, voce.

Quae te circumstent] Id est satellitio quodam stipent; eodem namque modo glossulae apponuntur lectioni, quo stipatores cingunt latus, atque circumstant eum quem comitantur.

Quolibet] Id est in quamcunque partem.

Comitata his] Scilicet glossematis.

O mihi] Antonio addresses his *Ars* as his own daughter, who, since she has already been brought up at home by him for a long time chastely and virtuously, he now bids her farewell and brings her out of her domestic hiding-place into the light. However, since she is a young woman and her age is open to mockery, he adds glosses to her to act like companions and attendants, who are to lead her away, preserving and protecting her from the malice of the envious. He further commands her to greet the disciples in his name, whomsoever they are or wherever she may stumble across them. He also instructs her to go first respectfully to the royal house, where she will find herself in no way a foreigner, since she will find sisters and brothers there to whom she can turn. He next tells her to address the Queen briefly in his words.

O, he says, *Ars mea, quam genui*] The metaphor is frequent, for poets are said to beget and love their works in the same way as parents do their children. The authority for this is Aristotle in his *Nicomachean Ethics* IX.

Tempus in omne] That is, 'forever'. Thus, Ovid writes, 'Make me yours for all time with your services'. And Vergil: 'Hail forever, great Pallas, farewell forever.'

Tempus in omne] A pleasant repetition, very frequent in the poetess Sappho.

Tuus genitor] This is the author; he continues in his allegory.

Habet quod possit addere aut demere] In the case of things done rightly, as Aristotle says in book II of his *Nicomachean Ethics*, nothing can be added or subtracted.

Et te iam grandem] As if he were to say that she was ready for marriage and for a husband.

Exire latebras] Where you were hiding beforehand.

Et vivere in media luce] That is to dwell in the eyes of mankind and with their attendance.

Sed ne sola] That is dangerous for a young woman.

Glossemata] That is, 'the glosses', for this is what Greeks call the notes which interpreters add to their readings of the authors 'out loud', as they say.

Quae te circumstent] That is, they stand around as a sort of guard; for in the same way glosses are attached to the lesson, as attendants keep close to one's side, and stay around the one they are accompanying.

Quolibet] That is, in any direction.

Comitata his] Understand: by the glosses.

Vulgus] Id est multitudinem imperitam.

Verba maligna] Ab invidia detractorum nascentia.

Qui] Scilicet homines imperiti et detractores.

Cum non agnoscant te] Id est intelligant quid contineas.

Mera somnia] Id est pura et quae nihil significent; nam sunt etiam aliquid significantia illa, quae sunt, videlicet, pituita purgatissima. Martialis: 'Semper mane mihi de me mera somnia narras.' Vergilius in *Bucolicis*, 'An qui amant ipsi sibi somnia fingunt?'

Versus nihili] Otiosos et nullius momenti.

Supposuere meis] Id est quasi supposititios inseruerunt.

Ito bonis avibus] Id est auspiciis felicibus; antiqui enim sine augurio nihil incipiebant.

Imprtire a salute multa] Id est saluta meis verbis discipulos meos. Sic Terentius in *Eunucho*: 'Plurima salute Parmenonem summum impertit Gnato', utroque enim modo declinatur impertior et impartio.

Utrosque] Scilicet discipulos et discipulos discipulorum.

At si forte] Quia permittit auctor artem suam libere vagari, suadet illi ut domum regiam imprimis adeat.

Augustae limina] Id est Reginae, nam uxores Caesarum Augustae appellantur. Vergilius in *Aeneide*: 'Perge modo atque hinc te reginae ad limina perfer.'

Nusquam] Id est nullo loco.

Tota ianua] Sic Martialis, 'Nulli tota magis ianua poste patet.'

Sorores] Duas artes grammatices: alteram, quam ipsius Reginae imperio e regione versuum Hispaniensem fecimus, alteram in qua sermonen Hispanum sub regulas atque artis praecepta contraximus, opus eiusdem Reginae auspiciis editum.

Quae te subcollocent] Humero et collo ferant. Varro in ii. *De re rustica* de apibus 'regem, inquit, suum sequuntur et fessum sublevant, et si nequit volare, subcollocant'. Suetonius *in Othone*: 'Donec omissa meta subcollocatus'.

Praeterea fratres] Id est duo vocabularia.

Vulgus] That is, the uneducated crowd.

Verba maligna] Born from the envy of detractors.

Qui] Understand: uneducated people and critics.

Cum non agnoscant te] That is, [since they do not] understand what you contain.

Mera somnia] That is, unmixed things that mean nothing; because there is something else also significant, which are, of course, very purified humours. Martial: 'In the morning you always tell me mere dreams about myself.' Vergil in his *Eclogues*, 'Do those who love themselves imagine dreams for themselves?'

Versus nihili] Idle and of no importance.

Supposuere meis] It is as if they inserted substitutions.

Ito bonis avibus] That is, with favourable auspices; for the ancients did not begin anything without an augury.

Impartire salute multa] That is, 'greet my students with my words'. Thus, Terence in his *Eunuch*: 'Gnato greets his Parmenon with best wishes', for *impartio* and *impertior* are conjugated in both ways.

Utrosque] Understand: his students and the students of his students.

At si forte] Since the author allows his *Ars* to roam freely, he advises her to go first to the royal house.

Augustae limina] That is [to the door] 'of the Queen', for the wives of the Caesars are called *Augustae*. Thus, Vergil in the *Aeneid*, 'Just go on and get yourself from here to the queen's threshold.'

Nusquam] That is, 'nowhere'.

Tota ianua] So Martial, 'The whole door is more open to no one.'

Sorores] Two grammatical works: one, which I prepared as a Spanish version for the empire and country of the Queen herself, the other in which we submitted Spanish speech to the rules and precepts of [grammatical] art, a work published under the auspices of the same Queen.

Quae te subcollocent] They carry you on their neck and shoulders. Varro says of bees in his *De re rustica* II, 'they follow the king and lift him when he is tired, and if he cannot fly, they put him down'. And Suetonius in his *Otho*: 'Until he left the goal, he was put down.'

Praeterea fratres] That is, two vocabularies.

Alia matre] Id est ex diversa vocabulorum materia; nam alterum ex sermone latino in hispanum; alterum ex hispano in latinas conversum dictiones. Forma vero est quam Ars inducit, nomina et verba aliasque partes orationis quadrans ad sermonis structuram; unde signanter dixit alia matre, alludens ad materiam vocabulorum.

Gemellos] Quia simul geniti atque editi sunt.

Latio] Id est latino sermoni.

Iberum] Id est Hispanum.

Si regina] Quid ipsi regina dicat ostendit.

Non nihil] Aliquid, et modeste de se loquitur. Atque ex Martiale sumptum est.

Quod si dicis o Regina te dare nobis tempora felicia et meus parens sua doctrina facit saecula vestra illustriora.

Alia matre] That is, from separate vocabulary material; for one of them is from Latin speech into Spanish; the other from Spanish into Latin expressions. The form, however, is that which the *Ars* introduces: the names and words and other parts of the speech make up the structure of speech; for this reason, he has clearly said 'from another mother', alluding to vocabulary material.

Gemellos] Because they were born and raised at the same time.

Latio] That is the Latin speech.

Iberum] That is Spanish.

Si regina] He shows what she should say to the Queen.

Non nihil] 'Something'; he speaks modestly of himself. This was also taken from Martial.

And if you say, O Queen, that you give us a blessed era, my father also makes your era more distinguished with his teaching.

Commentary

1 *caste nutrita*: The first line of the poem describes the circumstances of the book as imagined by its author. In beginning in this way, Nebrija echoes the arrangement of Ovid's *Tristia* 1.1, which opens (1–14) with a farewell to the work that situates the poem in the context of its production and contemporary reception. Whilst Nebrija's *Introductiones* are the result of his work on Latin grammar, Ovid's *Tristia* 1 is the result of composition during the poet's voyage to exile on the Black Sea. Thus, whilst the *Introductiones* has been 'brought up decorously with a good deal of work', Ovid's *Tristia* 1 is *incultus, qualem decet exulis esse*, 'unkempt, as befits an exile'. For another comparable address to the book imagined as child in ancient literature, see Hor. *Epist*.1.20.5.

2 *Ars mea*: In line with Nebrija's use of this word for both the title of the book and the name of his 'daughter' within this poetic conceit (again imitating Ovid's references in the exile poetry), *Ars* is capitalised throughout in the present text and translation.

Tempus in omne vale: Nebrija comments on the emphatic repetition of this phrase and compares it with Sappho's poetic diction.[7] Well-known examples of repetition in Sappho include *Fr*. 1.22–23 and 114.1.

4 *genitor*: Nebrija makes it clear in the commentary that he refers to himself in the third person as the 'creator' of the work, inside the Ovidian metaphor of the book as his daughter (*cf. Ars mea, quam genui*, line 2).

7–8 *te iam ... latebras exire ... decet*: An accusative and infinitive construction.

9 *glossemata*: Nebrija clarifies the use of the Greek word for 'comments' with the Latin *glossulas*. Here the author signals the important place of Greek in a complete Latin education. This was the principal motivation for adding the short tract *De litteris graecis* in later editions of the *Introductiones latinae*. The introductory poem for this tract follows here.

15 *Ito*: Future active imperative of *eo, ire*, 'to go'.

impartire salute: Nebrija uses the deponent *impartior*, a later alternative for *impertior*, here in the second person imperative. In directing his *Ars* to greet an audience on his behalf, Nebrija echoes Ovid's instructions to his *Tristia* 1

---

[7] For a recent study on Sappho's repetition see P. A. O'Connell, 'Repetition and the Creation of "Sappho"', in D. Beck (ed.), *Repetition, Communication, and Meaning in the Ancient World*, Leiden 2021, 156–86.

at e.g. 1.1.15–22. Whilst the humanist's audience should be hailed affectionately on his behalf, the context of Ovid's imagined greetings is somewhat cooler: *Ne, quae non opus est, forte loquare, cave!*, 'Take care lest you perhaps say more than necessary!' (Ov. *Tr.* 1.1.22).

21 *nostrae ... Augustae*: The commentary specifies that Nebrija is referring to Queen Isabella I of Castile (1451–1504), the humanist's parallel for Caesar Augustus. In sending his work to the Queen's doorstep, Nebrija echoes Ovid's vision of the *Tristia* arriving at the Palatine Hill to visit Caesar (Ov. *Tr.* 1.1.70–104). In contrast to the cold treatment of Ovid's work, the next line foresees a very different reception for Nebrija's *Introductiones*: *tota tibi est ianua aperta*, 'the doors are completely open to you'.

27 *fratres ... gemellos*: Nebrija explains the identity of these 'twin brothers' as his Latin-Spanish and Spanish-Latin vocabularies in the commentary to this line. He borrows the idea of an author's works as siblings from Ovid (*Tr.* 1.1.105–8), where the *Tristia* 1 meets *fratres* at the poet's home in Rome.

suo nomine salutet: Nebrija instructs his daughter (the *Ars*) to greet his readers on his behalf.

Translatio: Nebrija uses the term in the sense of a 'transfer of meaning' or metaphor. This sense is also frequently found among ancient authors (cf. e.g. Cic. *De or.* 3.38.156; Quint. *Inst.* 8.6.4).

Auctor est Aristoteles: The passage appears in *Nic. Eth.* 9.7, 1167b–8a, where Aristotle discusses the imbalance of affection between benefactors (who display greater love) and those who receive benefits (who reflect this love to a lesser degree). On artists and poets, the ancient author writes, 'the same thing happens with artists: every artist loves his own work more than he would be loved by that work were it to come to life. This is perhaps especially true about poets, for these love their own poems to an extraordinary degree, showing them almost parental love as towards children.'

Tempus in omne: For an example of the poetic use of this phrase and the idea of saying farewell forever, Nebrija cites Ovid, *Her.* 12.83 and Verg. *Aen.* 11.97–8.

Habet quod possit addere aut demere: Nebrija's explanation could be taken as a summary of the message of *Nicomachean Ethics* 2 as a whole. He was perhaps thinking more specifically of Aristotle's first general observation at *Nic. Eth.* 2.2, 1104a.

enarratores ... viva ... voce: The comment reveals the classroom-centred and oral engagement with classical authorities in Nebrija's humanist Europe.

pura: Plural of *pus, puris*, n. Nebrija emphasises that the *mera somnia* of critics are the product of destructive gall.

pituita purgatissima: Nebrija references Persius, Saturae 2.56–7 (*nam fratres inter aenos | somnia pituita qui purgatissima mittunt*, 'for there are those among the bronze brothers [*sc*. the Gods] who send highly purified humours as dreams') for an alternative (albeit ironic) image of healthy mental images.

mera somnia: Nebrija gives Mart. 7.54.1 and Verg. *Ecl*. 8.108 for poetic use of *somnia*, 'dreams', as destructive figments.

antiqui enim: This comment reveals, on the one hand, the importance for humanists of imitating accurately classical language use and, on the other, their acknowledgement of the occasional distance between the classical world and their own.

Plurima salute Parmenonem: Nebrija references Ter. *Eun*. 270 for this note on the meaning, usage and forms of *impertio/impertior*, 'I bestow, impart (greetings)'. Note that modern editions frequently read *suum* alongside or instead of the early modern *summum* (cf. e.g. Barsby 1999).

Perge modo: Nebrija cites Verg. *Aen*. 1.389 for the use of the phrase *limina Reginae*. Note also his explanation of the Roman tradition of naming Caesar's spouses *Augusta*. Fifteenth- and sixteenth-century readers of Latin also needed clarification of this custom.

Sic Martialis: Mart. 1.70.14. Nebrija references this line for the poetic use of the phrase *tota ianua*. The version of Martial's verse quoted in Nebrija's text supports this usage. Note that modern editions vary considerably in their readings of Martial's verse line (cf. e.g. Shackleton Bailey 1990).

Duas artes grammatices: By the time of adding this poem and the accompanying commentary to the *Introductiones latinae*, Nebrija's grammatical project had extended to include an edition of the *Introductiones* with a Spanish translation (under the title *Introducciones latinas contrapuesto el romance al latin* [Esparza Torres / Niederehe 1999: 8], 1488[8]) and then the famous *Gramática Castellana*. The first of these two later grammatical works was prepared at the command of Queen Isabella of Castile so that religious women could learn Latin without a (male) teacher. The second was dedicated to the same monarch in 1492. Nebrija uses the genitive of the noun

---

[8] There has been discussion over this work's precise date of publication, which is given as either 1486 or 1488. For a summary of this discussion and the arguments for 1488 see Martin Baños 2019: 260.

grammatice, *-ces*, f., 'grammar, philology', a Graecism based on the phrase γραμματική (sc. τέχνη).

collo ferant: For *subcollocare* with the meaning of 'to carry, bear', Nebrija quotes Varro, *Rust.* 3.16.8 and Suet. *Otho* 6.3.

duo vocabularia: Nebrija's scholarship produced a series of dictionaries over the course of his career. These included a Latin-Castilian dictionary [Esparza Torres / Niederehe 1999: 16] followed by a Castilian-Latin one [Esparza Torres / Niederehe 1999: 24]. These are the two *fratres*, 'brothers', of his Latin grammar referred to at line 27 of the poem. He would go on to add geographical and medical dictionaries to combined editions of these dictionaries [e.g. Esparza Torres / Niederehe 1999: 123; 1999: 180]. The dictionaries became especially popular in their later translations into Catalan (Barcelona, 1507) [Esparza Torres / Niederehe 1999: 68] French (Lyon, 1511) [Esparza Torres / Niederehe 1999: 91] and Sicilian (Venice, 1520) [Esparza Torres / Niederehe 1999: 174], for example.

ex sermone latino in hispanum: Nebrija identifies the vocabularies (Latin-Castilian / Castilian-Latin) to which he refers.

Atque ex Martiale: Martial uses the phrase *non nihil* with a similar emphatic force at e.g. 12.74.9.

Text 2: ANTONIUS AD LECTOREM, DE LITTERIS GRAECIS

This poem accompanied Nebrija's fifteen-page tract on ancient Greek, first published independently at Logroño in 1507. It then appeared as an appendix to the *Introductiones Latinae* from 1508 onwards. As the poem's final couplet clarifies, the principal goal of Nebrija's tract on Greek was a complete grasp of the Latin language. The work opens with a detailed introduction to the Greek alphabet and phonetics, in which Nebrija proposes a 'reformed' approach to pronunciation similar to that famously recommended by Erasmus in his *De recta Latini Graecique sermonis pronuntiatione* (1528). Nebrija's early formulation of this idea was acknowledged already in Ingram Bywater's lecture at Exeter College, Oxford in 1908.[9]

Latin text

Litterulas graecas fluxerunt unde latinae
    si qui nosse cupit, longa terenda via est.
Ut culmen teneas, subeundi mille labores:
    rara quidem res est, at preciosa tamen.
5 Maiores maiora petant; mihi parva secuto
    sufficiat pueris prima elementa dare.
Illa modo sine queis non constat sermo latinus,
    et quae si spernas mox habeare rudis.

---

[9] On Nebrija's acquaintance with Greek (another result of his time in Italy) and his early consideration of ancient pronunciation, see Barnard 2017 and Herrero de Jauregui 2019.

English translation

The beloved Greek letters from which the Latin letters sprang,
    if anyone wishes to know them, there's a long road to be trodden,
To reach their summit, a thousand labours must be undertaken:
    indeed, it is a curious, but valuable subject.
Let great men seek great things; for me let it be enough to have pursued
       small things   5
    and offered young men the basic components:
those without which the Latin language does not hang together,
    and if you snub them, you will soon be considered ignorant.

Commentary

1 *Litterulas graecas*: The diminutive of *littera*, 'letter', *litterae*, 'literature' (lit. 'letters'), is used here, on the one hand, to distinguish the letters of the alphabet, and on the other to express the affection the scholar-poet feels for the Greek literary world.

2 *si qui nosse cupit*: Cf. Ov. *Ars am.* 1.1. The echoes of Ovid's poem of amatory instruction in this line are intended to emphasise that learning Greek ought to be considered a labour of love.

longa terenda via est: Nebrija borrows the second half of this pentameter from Ov. *Ars am.* 1.52.

6 *pueris prima elementa dare*: Nebrija echoes Hor. *Sat.* 1.1.25–6: . . . *ut pueris olim dant crustula blandi | doctores, elementa velint ut discere prima*, '. . . just as gentle teachers give cakes to their boys at first, so that they are willing to learn the basic components'. Whilst, then, Nebrija makes merely the modest claim that he is only able to offer the basics, contemporary readers with the Horace passage in mind were invited implicitly to count Nebrija among the good-natured *blandi doctores*.

7 *queis*: An alternative form for *quibus* or *quīs*.

non constat sermo latinus: The central place of Greek learning in a complete knowledge of Latin is emphasised by Nebrija in the introductory paragraph to Greek noun declension (*De litteris graecis*, 1508, fol. aiiiv). Here the Spanish humanist cites his countryman Quintilian (Quint. *Inst.* 1.5.63) on the preference among some of the ancient orator's contemporaries for using Greek declensions for Greek words in Latin. This issue aside – Nebrija continues (fol. aiiir) – a grasp of Greek declensions for understanding the names of mythological and epic heroes in Latin remains essential. He declines the forms of the names Aeneas and Anchises from Vergil's epic as prominent examples of the first declension.

8 *habeare*: This is the second-person singular present passive subjunctive of *habeo*, used here with the meaning 'to consider, regard' (lit. 'to hold as').

4

Aldus Manutius (*c.* 1450–1515), *Musarum panagyris* and Other Early Poems

Oren Margolis

Introduction

All the poems presented here were written in very late 1483 or early 1484, shortly after Aldus Manutius (*c.* 1450–1515) arrived in Carpi to serve as tutor to the young prince Alberto III Pio (1475–1531), the verses' dedicatee. That is the first context. The second context is that of 1489 or possibly 1490, shortly after Aldus, having left Carpi, arrived in Venice. Here they were printed by the press of Battista de Tortis in a single-quire pamphlet together with a letter written, also in 1484, to Alberto's widowed mother Caterina Pico (1454–1501). Caterina was the sister of the philosopher-prince Giovanni Pico della Mirandola (1463–94), who had met Aldus in Ferrara and selected him for the job. In this letter Aldus set out clear views on the importance of the study of Greek. In early 1495 he would issue his first publication. Over the next two decades, the Aldine Press would become the most celebrated publishing house in Renaissance Europe, with Aldus' fame and reputation earned primarily through his printing of ancient Greek texts: more first editions than anyone before or since.

In his well-known study of Aldus and the Aldine Press, Martin Lowry gave no explanation when he characterized these poems as 'trite [and] lumbering elegiacs'.[1] The mature Aldus – Aldus the publisher – was not a frequent poet, and the most characteristic mode in which we encounter his voice is the dedicatory (prose) epistle.[2] This must partly be why, of the materials printed together, the letter to Caterina Pico has received the bulk of attention.[3] Carlo Dionisotti described the 'poetic element' found at the beginning and end of the volume as 'decorative and subordinate to the central part in prose, where the teacher expounds with exceptional clarity and force his pedagogical doctrine'.[4] But this is irrelevant to 1484, and the letter (which identifies a number of now-lost grammatical works by Aldus written around the same time) makes clear that the publication as we have it was not originally intended as a unit. The 'centrality' of the letter to the pamphlet is questionable too: with text running continuously from the top of the second recto until the bottom of the eighth verso, the most relevant factor for inclusion must have been what would fit a single quire (thus Battista de Tortis printed separately an exhortation to Alberto's brother Leonello II). A unifying thread is Aldus' relationship with the Pio-Pico family, his link to the social and intellectual elite. Given the significance of those connections and the relative paucity of sources for Aldus' Carpi period, the pamphlet's poetic contents in fact represent a critical body of evidence.[5]

The pamphlet is generally called by the name *Musarum panagyris* ('The Celebration of the Muses'), but that is only the title of the first of the poems (elegiac, 78 lines = 9 verses of 8 lines plus preceding hexastich, sig. a2r–a3v). It is followed by a *Paraenesis*, or exhortation, attached to that work (elegiac, 38 lines, sig. a3v–a4r); three lines from Hesiod's *Theogony* (77–9) on the names of the Muses, in Greek and in Latin translation (sig. a4r); the letter to Caterina Pico (a4r–a8r); and finally another poem for Alberto presented on New Year's Day (1 January) 1484 and inspired by Martial's *Xenia* (*Epigrams* 13) or 'book of gifts' (elegiac, 28 lines, a8rv). This last was written first and originally accompanied a book written by Aldus on Greek and Latin accents. Its placing at the end here gives the publication as a whole the sense of being a gift-book.

The *Musarum panagyris* has often been linked to the letter's concern for the importance of learning Greek. One after the other, the nine Muses named by Hesiod appear to the young Alberto to sing his praises or, alternatively, to prophesy dire punishments for any of his future enemies (as well as eternal fortune for him and eternal rewards for his friends). These punishments are inspired by some of the most lurid episodes in Greek mythology. Tityus, Hippolytus, Medea and Pasiphaë are just some of those whose suffering or sinning Aldus puts to use. Further references to the Furies and the Fates, Cerberus, the Stymphalian birds and other figures contribute to this sense, as does the Hesiod reference – though of course we cannot know for certain whether it accompanied the *Panagyris* when presented.[6] There are occasional Greek forms: *Cerberon, Pasiphaes*. But, as the commentary below shows, the poem has no Greek literary sources.[7] By contrast, the composition draws extensively on the 'major' authors of Latin literature, Vergil and Ovid above all (and its prophetic character and celebration of a young boy of great expectations certainly bring to mind the fourth *Eclogue*). There is a good reason for this: these were the authors through whom students gained the knowledge necessary for their own compositions in poetry and oratory, as well as their familiarity with such essential matters as Latin prosody and literary usage. What Aldus has done is create for the eight-year-old Alberto a model as well as a challenge: to identify the objects of the many allusions; to recognize Greek forms encountered in Latin poetry; perhaps even to stimulate discussion of historical trivia, debating points or epistolary themes. This manner of teaching and learning would seem to agree with the advice found in such treatises as those of Battista Guarini, with whose school in Ferrara Aldus had previously been associated, and of Erasmus of Rotterdam, who would come to work in Aldus' shop in Venice in 1508.[8] The schoolroom context, and this deep immersion in the Latin of the grammar curriculum, is precisely why the *Panagyris* cannot be judged by superficial aesthetic standards.

Alberto Pio did in fact go on to develop a significant interest in Greek – but in philosophy (where Aristotle, albeit in Latin, had anyway reigned supreme in the medieval university) rather than literature. This was mirrored too in the intellectual priorities of the Aldine Press.[9] In 1484, besides, still more urgent for Aldus than teaching Greek was providing his charge with the foundation of Latin.[10] A proper reading of the *Musarum panagyris* therefore helps us to a more textured understanding of Aldus' evolving concerns. It also contributes to our knowledge of reading culture in the Quattrocento humanist world of the Po Plain and the Italian Northeast. While Vergil and Ovid are paramount and the Augustan love elegists feature, the poem reveals engagement with late antique writers like Ausonius and Claudian and offers an example of a locally characteristic and philologically clever deployment of Ennodius and the Lombard-Carolingian intellectual Paul the Deacon.[11] In the background, too, are Boccaccio and perhaps also Dante. The *Paraenesis* and the *Xenia*, moreover, can be read as sources for the history of Northern Italian court life.

Metre: elegiac distich

Notes

1 Lowry 1979: 56.
2 Dedicatory prefaces published in Orlandi 1975, now with English translation in Wilson 2016 and Grant 2017.
3 Letter in Orlandi 1975: 160–4; for text, translation and commentary, see https://latlab.org/letter-4/.
4 In Orlandi 1975: 'Introduzione', xii.
5 The most important study of this period is now Pagliaroli 2021.
6 *Works and Days* is quoted in the separate *paraenesis* to Leonello Pio, but these moral exhortations joined by Latin paraphrases – one (289–92) presumably chosen for its similar use in Cicero, *Ad familiares* 6.18 – are more clearly integrated.
7 *Pace* Mollo 2018: 21–3.

8 E.g., Erasmus 1971: 119–29, 231–6; Kallendorf 2002: 286–8. On Latin education, see Black 2001.
9 For a cultural-intellectual history of Aldus as publisher, see Margolis 2023.
10 Though on Aldus as a Greek educator in this period, see Tomè 2019.
11 See Commentary on 'Clio' 4 (below) and Lapidge 1977: 256–8.

Bibliography

Aldus [Manutius] ([1489]), [*Musarum panagyris*], Venice.
Aldus [Manutius] ([1489]), *ad Leonellum Pium . . . paraenesis*, Venice.
Black, R. (2001), *Humanism and Education in Medieval and Renaissance Italy: Tradition and Innovation in Latin Schools from the Twelfth to the Fifteenth Century*, Cambridge.
Buettner, B. (2001), 'Past Presents: New Year's Gifts at the Valois Courts, ca. 1400', *The Art Bulletin*, 83: 598–625.
Bühler, C. F. (1948), 'The First Aldine', *The Papers of the Bibliographical Society of America*, 42: 269–80.
Erasmus of Rotterdam (1971), *Opera omnia . . .*, I-2, Amsterdam: *De ratione studii* (ed. J.-C. Margolin), 79–151; *De conscribendis epistolis* (ed. J.-C. Margolin), 153–579.
Grant, J. N., ed. and trans. (2017), *Aldus Manutius: Humanism and the Latin Classics*, Cambridge (MA).
Kallendorf, C. W., ed. (2002), *Humanist Educational Treatises*, Cambridge (MA).
Lapidge, M. (1977), 'The Authorship of the Adonic Verses "ad Fidolium" Attributed to Columbanus', *Studi medievali*, 18: 249–314.
Lowry, M. (1979), *The World of Aldus Manutius: Business and Scholarship in Renaissance Venice*, Oxford.
Margolis, O. (2023), *Aldus Manutius: The Invention of the Publisher*, London.
Mollo, P. (2018), 'Sul *Musarum Panagyris* di Aldo Manuzio. Fonti letterarie e traduzione italiana', in: A. Scarsella / M. Menato (eds), *Ancora per Aldo Manuzio*, special issue of *Studi Goriziani*, 111: 19–29.
Morelli, J., ed. (1806), *Aldi Pii Manutii scripta tria longe rarissima*, Bassano del Grappa.
Orlandi, G., ed. (1975), *Aldo Manuzio editore. Dediche, prefazioni, note ai testi*, Milan; with 'Introduzione' by C. Dionisotti.
Pagliaroli, S. (2021), *Per la biografia di Aldo Manuzio (1482–1496)*, Messina.
Renouard, A.-A. (1834), *Annales de l'imprimerie des Alde*, 3rd edn, Paris.
Tomè, P. (2019), 'Testi elementari di esercizio per l'apprendimento del greco. Il caso dell'*Appendix Aldina*', in: G. Comiati (ed.), *Aldo Manuzio editore, umanista e filologo*, 75–117, Milan.
Wilson, N. G., ed. and trans. (2016), *Aldus Manutius: The Greek Classics*, Cambridge (MA).

Source of Latin text

Only seven copies of the 1489 pamphlet are known to survive; I have used the Berlin copy (8° Inc 4640) available at https://digital.staatsbibliothek-berlin. de/. The Latin text has previously been printed by Morelli (1806), Renouard (1834), Orlandi (1975) and with Italian translation by Mollo (2018) (*Musarum panagyris* and *Paraenesis* only). *sic* in the footnotes to the Latin text refers to modern corrections of the 1489 text.

Latin text

Musarum Panagyris per Aldum Mannuccium Bassianatem
Latinum cum exasticho et paraenesis eiusdem ad Albertum
Pium Magnificum atque inclytum[1] Carpi principem.

Exastichon.

Carmina delectant pueros: en carmina, princeps,
    Dant ad te faciles ex Helicone deae.
Nanque tuis etiam resonat Parnasia rupes
    Laudibus, et nomen fertur ad astra tuum.
5 Prima arguta canit Clio, Cliusque sorores
    Alternis recinunt te super ista sonis.

Panagyris Musarum.
Clio.

O fortunati quam maxima gloria Carpi!
    Gloria per nullos emoritura dies!
Dive puer, carae spes et fidissima matris;
    Dive puer, gentis spesque decusque Piae:
5 Cresce, quia expectant ornent tua tempora lauri,
    Quas tibi servatas utraque Pallas habet;
Cresce, tibi quoniam magni debentur honores,
    Quos tibi victori parta trophea dabunt.

Melpomene.

Cresce tuis populis et carae, Alberte, parenti,
    Fortuna, heu, semper cui peracerba fuit.
Ex quo dilecti flevit sic fata mariti,
    Esse ut crudeles diceret illa deos,
5 Crudelesque deos crudeliaque astra vocaret,
    Tam cito delicias quod rapuere suas;
Quodque suam potius voluisset fundere vitam,
    Cernere quam funus coniugis aegra sui.

Polymnia.

Cresce, virum populis nam cum te fecerit aetas
    Tutor eris, gentis praesidiumque tuae;

---

[1] Alternative spelling of *inclutum* (very common in the Renaissance).

English translation

The Celebration of the Muses by Aldus Mannuccius of Bassiano in Lazio, with a six-line poem and an exhortation of the same author to Alberto Pio, magnificent and illustrious prince of Carpi.

Six verses.

Songs are a source of delight for boys: behold, Prince, the songs
    The friendly goddesses from Helicon bestow upon you.
For even Parnassus' rocky precipice resounds
    With your praise, while your renown ascends towards the stars.
Bright Clio is first to sing; then Clio's sisters   5
    Up on high alternately echo your sung celebration.

The Celebration of the Muses.

Clio.

O greatest-ever glory of fortunate Carpi!
    Glory undying for all time!
Divine boy and surest hope of a loving mother;
    Divine boy both hope and ornament of the house of Pio:
Grow to manhood, for to adorn each temple the laurels   5
    Pallas keeps safe for you await;
Grow to manhood, since to you are owed great honours,
    Which acquired trophies will bestow on you as conqueror.

Melpomene.

Grow to manhood for your people's sake, Alberto, and for the loving mother
    To whom Fortune, alas, was ever so harsh.
From the time when she bewailed a darling husband's fate
    To the extent of declaring the gods cruel,
Cruel gods, she called them, and cruel stars,   5
    For so quickly did they snatch away her heart's delight;
And she thought it better had she poured out her life
    Than beheld in sorrow her spouse's body.

Polymnia.

Grow to manhood, for when age has made a man of you,
    A guardian for the people and fortress of your family you shall be;

Tu quoque solamen, tu spes, tu gloria solus,
  Optimus et princeps. Quare age, cresce puer,
5 Optimus heroum quot sunt, quotcunque fuerunt,
  Et quot venturos fata severa trahent:
Nam tibi recte equidem nascenti, Alberte, recordor
  Sic fore concordes tris cecinisse deas.

                    Urania.

Ergo tuum nomen cum fama obscura recondet,
  Atque erit obscurus cum tuus altus honos,
Nec tibi perpetuum laudes nec facta manebunt,
  Unda dabit segetes, sydera[2] terra ferret,
5 Omnia tunc retro convertent flumina cursum,
  Lucis egens aer, lucis Olympus erit,
Enceladusque iterum supponet Pelion Ossae,
  Sed dabitur magnos vincere posse deos.

                    Euterpe.

Postquam te talem Parcae cecinere futurum,
  Qui te non coleret ferreus ille foret,
Ferreus ille quidem; sed qui te odisse valeret,
  Esset montanis saevior ille feris,
5 Atque foret multo calcato immanior angue,
  Nec non vorticibus, dira Charybdi, tuis.
Stymphalidasque truces et Cerberon ille trifaucem
  Saevitia, et Stygias vinceret ille canes.

                    Terpsichore.

Esset et ille idem dignus sine fine renatis
  Visceribus Tityi, quod satiaret aves;
Sorte vel illius qui se sequiturque fugitque,
  Versatur celeri dum levis orbe rotae;
5 Quodve ut tu, esuriens esset tua, Tantale, poma,
  Atque sitiret aquas, nec biberentur aquae;
Cervice aut misera ruiturum, Sisyphe, ferret,
  Quod petis aut urges irrequietus, onus.

[2] Alternative spelling of *sidera*.

The consolation too, the hope, you alone the glory,
    'Best prince' as well. So, onwards! Grow to manhood, boy –
Best of the heroes that are, of however many there have been,   5
    And of those the dreadful Fates shall cause to be:
For truly, Alberto, I remember how at your birth
    Together the three goddesses foretold it so.

Urania.

Thus when Fame conceals your name in darkness,
    And darkness even overtakes your great repute,
And neither your praises nor your deeds lastingly endure,
    The waves shall yield up wheatfields, the earth support the stars,
Every river shall then reverse its course,   5
    The mist without light shall be a luminous Olympus,
And Enceladus shall once again pile Pelion on top of Ossa,
    But this time he will be allowed to defeat the great gods.

Euterpe.

Since the Fates have foretold what is to befall you,
    He who would not revere you must be a man hard as iron –
Hard as iron, indeed; but he who had it in him to hate you
    Would be a man more savage than mountain beasts,
Much more monstrous even than the serpent trodden underfoot,   5
    And likewise, dread Charybdis, than your whirlpools.
And the fierce Stymphalian birds and three-throated Cerberus
    Would that man surpass in savagery, and even the Stygian she-hounds.

Terpsichore.

May that same man merit the endlessly regrown
    Entrails of Tityus, to satiate the birds;
Or the lot of he who both pursues and flees himself
    As he is turned around by the swift circle of the light wheel;
Or may he like you, Tantalus, try in hunger to eat your fruits,   5
    And thirst after water that yet cannot be drunk;
Or else may he bear with wretched neck the tumbling burden
    That tirelessly you, Sisyphus, chase down or push up.

Thalia.

Si mulier, miserum natorum digna cruore
    Esset crudeles commaculare manus;
Sive quod infando tauri poteretur amore
    Altera Minoae machina Pasiphaes.
5 Si puer, a caro donum exitiale parente
    Ferret, ut insanis obrueretur aquis;
Quodve foret turpis sceleratae flamma novercae,
    Cui maris exitium monstra timenda darent.

Erato.

Inclyte, seu posset, princeps, te odisse puella,
    Cui staret medio pectore dura silex,
Digna quidem fato Phryxi foret illa sororis,
    Quae Hellespontiacis nomina fecit aquis.
5 Sive quod irati manes placaret amantis
    Mactata; aut caderet quod patris illa manu,
Fataque, post urnas iterumque iterumque repletas,
    Ferret[3] apud manes Tartareumque Iovem.

Calliope.

Qui te amat et qui te posthac, puer inclyte, amabit,
    Et sanctos mores ingeniumque tuum,
Foelix[4] ille suos vel dextra computet annos,
    Mortuus aetereas[5] incolat ille domos.
5 At tu, qui flava caput accingeris oliva,
    Virtute et facies qui tibi ad astra viam,
Sis foelix, volitaque hominum cum laude per ora[6]
    Vel caeleste cibus cum tibi nectar erit.

Finis Musarum Panagyreos.

Paraenesis Aldi Mannuccii ad eundem principem

Te super ista solent cantare alterna Camenae,
    Haec de te Aonides carmina culta sonant.

---

[3] *sic*: Eerret
[4] Alternative spelling of *felix*.
[5] *sic* (for *aethereas*).
[6] *sic*: hora

Thalia.

If perchance it be a woman, may she merit that her cruel hands
    Be defiled with the blood of her wretched children;
Or may she receive a bull's unnatural love
    Through another contraption of Minoan Pasiphaë.
If it be a boy, may he take a fatal gift from a loving father   5
    To be drowned in the raging waters;
Or may he be a sinful stepmother's shameful passion,
    To whom fearsome sea monsters bring destruction.

Erato.

Or if, illustrious prince, the one able to hate you were a girl,
    With unfeeling flint standing in the middle of her chest,
Truly would that one merit the fate of Phrixus' sister,
    Who gave her name to the waters of Hellespont.
Or she could appease the shade of an angry lover   5
    As a sacrifice; or else die at the hand of her father,
Or endure her fate, having over and over her urns refilled,
    In the house of the shades and Jove's Tartarean brother.

Calliope.

He who loves you, and he who shall, illustrious boy, love you yet,
    Your divine conduct also and your character as well,
Happy may that man surely count his years,
    In death may he dwell in ethereal abodes.
But you, who will gird your head with the golden olive branch,   5
    And who with virtue will make your way towards the stars,
Be happy and fly with praise through the lips of men,
    Even when you have celestial nectar for food.

The End of *The Celebration of the Muses*

Exhortation of Aldus Mannuccius to the Same Prince

About you the Muses sing those alternating verses,
    These polished songs the Aonians pronounce in your praise.

Quae tibi quandoquidem nobis iussere daremus,
  En dedimus: cantus perlege Pierios,
5 Et cum carminibus nostrum, puer inclyte, librum
  Accipe, multa tibi qui pretiosa dabit.
Perlege, disce: tuae sic te praebere parenti
  Mirandum poteris; sic tibi crescet honos.
Sic etiam divo semper[7], puer optime, Marco
10 Carus eris, natum te velut ille fovet
Atque amat, et iusta tecum ditione gubernat
  Carpum, qui gentis firma columna Piae est.
Marcus hic ille Pius, nulli pietate secundus,
  Eloquio priscos qui bene vincit avos;
15 Marcus hic ille Pius, quo non praestantior alter
  Horrida Martigenas ducere ad arma viros.
Huic multum ut placeas studeas noctesque diesque:
  Hunc mihi ceu patrem tu face semper ames.
Ut patruo placeas, virtutem amplectere totis
20 Viribus, interea quae damus usque legas.
Nec tantum nostros libeat legisse libellos,
  Nec tantum chartis incubuisse meis:
Perlege, disce etiam Pallas tibi docta legendos
  Quos Romana dedit, quosque Pelasga dedit.
25 Et vigila, atque almae virtuti incumbe; labores
  Perfer, ut accedat laurea bina tibi.
Sic sublime tuum tolles ad sydera nomen,
  Mistus[8] eris magnis magnus et ipse viris.
Interea Graios, divina volumina, libros,
30 Et cum Romanis haec mea scripta lege;
Nanque ubi grammaticen pueros docuere Latinam,
  Instituunt cultos dicere posse modos.
Dehinc tibi nos dabimus geminae praecepta Minervae,
  Quae Romana, puto, Graecaque turba leget;
35 Assiduis quae nunc castigo scripta lituris,
  Ut valeant doctas non metuisse manus.
Te modo, quos dedimus, iuvet hos legisse libellos,
  Doctior ut posthac caetera[9] nostra legas.

                    Finis Paraeneseos.

---

[7] *sic*: sempter
[8] Alternative spelling of *mixtus*.
[9] Alternative spelling of *cetera*.

Since they ordered us to give them to you,
    See here, we have: read through the outpourings of Pierian song,
And with the songs, illustrious boy, accept
    Our book, which has much of value to offer you.
Read through and learn: that way will you show yourself admirable to
    Your mother; that way will your reputation grow.
And that way, best of boys, will you be forever dear
    To the divine Marco, the one who cherishes and loves you
Like a son, and by right rule together with you governs
    Carpi; he who is the sturdy column of the house of Pio.
This is the famous Marco Pio, second to none in piety,
    Who soundly bests the old ancestors in eloquence;
The famous Marco Pio whom none surpass
    In leading Mars-born men to fearsome battle.
Aim to be most pleasing to him, both day and night:
    Take care I say always to love this man like a father.
To please your uncle, embrace virtue
    With all your strength, while you read what we are giving you.
And yet may it be your pleasure to read not only these our little works,
    And to pore over not only these my pages:
Read through and learn as well from what learned Pallas has for reading
    Offered you in her Roman and Pelasgian guises.
Be alert and lean into the virtue that sustains;
    Endure labours, that the double laurel may be yours.
Thus shall you raise to the stars your sublime name,
    And, mixed among the great, great yourself shall be.
Meanwhile, read Greek books (volumes divine!),
    And these my own along with Roman writings;
For when they taught boys Latin grammar,
    They instilled cultured ways of speaking.
Hence we present you with the precepts of twofold Minerva,
    For the Roman throng and (I believe) the Greek to read;
Writings I now emend with constant corrections,
    That they have nought to fear from learned hands.
But may you find delight in reading these little works we've given you,
    So, once more learned, in future you may read the rest of ours.

            The End of the Exhortation.

Aldus Mannuccius Bassianas Latinus Alberto
Pio principi Carpensi. S.P.D.

Cum xenia, o Princeps, Romani, Alberte, quotannis
    Hospitibus brumae tempore rite dabant,
Reddideras et tu, sanctissime Iane, Calendas,
    Anni qui finem principiumque vides,
5 Hic mittebat aprum, qualis Diomedis in agro
    Occidit; hic foetae[10] pignora parva suis.
Ille dabat capreas, lepores, damasque[11] fugaces,
    Laetas, cum pingui sumine, cortis[12] aves.
Mitti et consuerat ventri lactuca movendo,
10   Rapaque brumali grandia facta gelu.
Dulcia mittebant alii farcimina: laetos
    Sic ducebat avos ebria bruma meos.
Sic te, magne puer, Carpumque Novumque salutet,
    Oppida quotque tuo sunt tibi cum patruo.
15 Mons tibi boletos mittat fungosque suillos,
    Saturnalitios[13] det tibi villa capos.
Nos tibi non dabimus quae pascant dona palatum,
    Mandentur ventri quae peritura tuo.
Mittemus potius pascentia munera mentem,
20   Quaeque docent mores, ingeniumque iuvant.
Accipe nunc igitur parvum, mea munera, librum,
    Conscriptum nuper compositumque mihi.
Hic dabit accentus, geminae moderamina linguae,
    Addictos facili sub brevitate tibi.
25 Qui si gratus erit, tribuam quae condita servo,
    Et sunt temporibus quae tibi danda suis.
Hunc ubi tu scieris, longe maiora dabuntur
    Dona tibi, pro te quae tuus Aldus habet.

FINIS.

---

[10] Alternative spelling of *fetae*.
[11] Alternative spelling of *dammas*.
[12] Alternative spelling of *chortis* (*cohortis*).
[13] Alternative spelling of *saturnalicios*.

Aldus Manutius (c. 1450–1515)

Aldus Mannuccius of Bassiano in Lazio to Alberto
Pio, prince of Carpi, greetings.

At that time when the Romans, O Prince Alberto, would every year
    Midwinter make (as religious custom had it) gifts to their guests,
And you, most holy Janus, who look on the year's beginning and its end,
    Had proclaimed the Kalends of the new month,
One would send a boar such as in the field of Diomedes   5
    Fell; one, the little offspring of the hog only just delivered.
The other one would present mountain goats, hare, and flighty does,
    Delightful poultry-birds together with a plump sow udder.
It had become tradition, too, to be sent lettuce for whetting the appetite,
    And turnips grown large in the winter chill.   10
Others would send sweet-seasoned sausages:
    Thus boozy winterfest used to incite my merry forefathers.
Thus, noble boy, let both Carpi and Novi come pay you their respects,
    And as many towns as are subject to you along with your uncle.
Let the mountain send you porcini and pinaroli,   15
    Let the farm give you the capons for the Saturnalian festivities.
We ourselves shall not give you gifts to gratify the palate,
    To be chewed up and disappear in your belly.
Rather we shall send offerings to gratify the mind,
    Which teach character and assist talent.   20
Accept now, therefore, my offerings: a little book,
    Newly transcribed and written by me.
It will provide the accents, the means of moderating the twin tongues,
    Delivered in easy short form for your benefit.
If this is welcome, I shall hand over the things I keep in store,   25
    And which are to be given to you when the time is right.
Once you have become skilled in this, you will be given
    The far greater gifts your Aldus has for you.

                  THE END.

Commentary

Title

Aldum Mannuccium: A much more Italianate spelling than the familiar 'Aldus Manutius Romanus'. *Manuccius* (and Μανούκιος) appear in some colophons of 1495/6, replaced by *Manutius* (and Μανούτιος) by 1497. In his Latin grammar (*Institutiones grammaticae*), published in Venice in 1493, Aldus identifies as *Bassianas Romanus*, associating himself and his hometown with Rome rather than its region of Lazio (ancient Latium).

Exastichon

2 *Helicone*: a mountain of Boeotia in Greece, sacred to the Muses.

3 *Parnasia rupes*: Verg. *Ecl.* 6.29, and common in the Quattrocento, e.g., Matteo Maria Boiardo, *Pastoralia* (Ferrara, *c.* 1462–74) 5.79. Parnassus: Another mountain sacred to the Muses and to Apollo, whose oracle was located on its southwestern slope at Delphi.

4 recalls Ov. *Fast.* 4.328: *fertur ad astra sonus*, in the same position.

Clio

Clio: Muse of history.

2 Cf. Prop. 4.6.64: *iusso non moritura die*, in the same position but with a very different sense (not 'undying', but '[Cleopatra fleeing Actium so as] not to die on an appointed day').

3 *matris*: Caterina Pico della Mirandola (1454–1501).

4 *spesque decusque* appears not infrequently in humanists of Ferrara and the NE, e.g., Tito Vespasiano Strozzi, *Erotica* 5.1 (1459): *Borsius* [d'Este], *Ausonii ... soli*; Bartolomeo Paganelli 3.5 (*c.* 1460): [Gaspare Tribraco] *Pierii ... chori*; Raffaele Zovenzoni, *Istrias* (*c.* 1474) 1.9.6: [Pietro Loredan] *Venetae ... togae*; Ermolao Barbaro, epitaph of Rudolph Agricola (1485): *Frisii spemque decusque soli*; then common widely. The words occur together in Lucan 7.588: *o decus imperii, spes o suprema senatus* (referring to Brutus), but the phrase itself is not classical. It originates rather in an adonic verse epistle of Ennodius, *Carmina* 1.7.69–70: *lux mea, Fauste | spesque salusque*, recalled by Paul the Deacon in adoneans transmitted with his Homiliary and written in praise of Charlemagne, *luxque decusque*, with the second substitution surely suggested by the Lucanic pairing. The importance of the Ennodian corpus for the *ars dictaminis* must explain the first version's later medieval success, e.g., in the

epitaph of Hector in Guido delle Colonne, *Historia destructionis Troiae* (*c.* 1287): *Occubuere simul spesque salusque Frigum*; and in Petrarch's epitaph for Jacopo II da Carrara, still visible in the Eremitani, Padua (1351): *En pater hic patrie spesque salusque iacent*. The humanists' elegant combination suggests that at least initially they recognised the relationship between the three sources. An open question is whether Aldus, who was likely recommended to Pico by Strozzi (whose son Ercole he had tutored in Ferrara) and who praised Barbaro effusively in the letter to Caterina, did.

5   recalls Verg. *Aen.* 5.246 and 539: *tempora lauro*, in the same position. The insistent *cresce* here and elsewhere brings to mind Verg. *Ecl.* 4, a key model, specifically lines 60 and 62: *incipe*.

6   *Pallas*: a name, or epithet, of Athena (and so of her Roman equivalent Minerva).

8   *parta trophea*: from Ov. *Her.* 17.242: *parta ... bina tropaea*, referring to Venus.

Melpomene

This stanza acknowledges Caterina Pico's conjugal devotion and care for her children's education, topics addressed around the same time in a poem for Giovanni Pico by Tito Vespasiano Strozzi, which Aldus published in *Strozii poetae pater et filius* (1513/14), sig. o7r–p1v. His own emphasis on Caterina's love, constancy, and extreme grief nevertheless resembles the exemplary treatment of Artemisia II of Caria from Valerius Maximus, 4.6.ext.1, and Boccaccio, *De mulieribus claris*. Vergilian representations of death of sons and the resulting pain are variously repurposed.

Melpomene: Muse of tragedy.

3   *mariti*: Leonello I Pio (d. 1477).

4–5   The symploce (*crudeles diceret ... deos, | Crudelesque deos ... vocaret*) will be a feature familiar from Vergil's *Eclogues*, e.g., 8.47–50, a passage recalled in 'Thalia'.

5   Cf. Verg. *Ecl.* 5.23: *atque deos atque astra vocat crudelia mater*, in the shepherd-poets' lament for Daphnis.

7–8   Cf. Verg. *Aen.* 2.531-2: *ante ... ora parentum | ... multo vitam cum sanguine fudit*, where the dying subject (unlike Caterina) is Polites, son of Priam and Hecuba, and 2.538-9: *nati coram me cernere letum | fecisti et patrios foedasti funere vultus*, where he is the *funus*.

Polymnia

Polymnia: Muse of sacred poetry (common Neo-Latin spelling of the classical 'Polyhymnia').

1 *virum . . . te fecerit aetas*: Verg. *Ecl.* 4.37.

2 *gentis praesidiumque tuae*: cf. Alberto as *praesidium meum* in Aldus' dedication of (pseudo-)Proclus, *De sphaera* with Thomas Linacre's translation (1499).

3 recalls Stat. *Silv.* 1.2.261: *dulcisque solo tu gloria nostro*.

4 *Optimus . . . princeps*: a title granted to Trajan by the Roman Senate (Plin. *Pan.* 2 and passim).

7–8 draws on Ov. *Pont.* 1.8.63–4: *at tibi nascenti. . . | nerunt fatales fortia fila deae*; Verg. *Ecl.* 4.47: *concordes . . . Parcae*; Hor. *Carm. saec.* 25: *veraces cecinisse Parcae*, referring in all cases to the Fates.

Urania

Urania: Muse of astronomy.

1 From Verg. *Aen.* 5.302: *quos fama obscura recondit*.

5 Cf. Claudian, *Gigantomachia* (*Carmina minora* 53) 65: *quot antiquas mutarunt flumina ripas*; but the specific recollection of Propertius (1.15.29): *alta prius retro labentur flumina ponto*, in the same metre and with *retro . . . flumina* in the same position, reinforces the sense that this will never happen (because, just as the poet's love will never change despite Cynthia's betrayals, Alberto's renown will never be obscured despite the ravages of time).

The stanza ends by recalling memorable phrases from Ovid's account of the origins of the world.

6 *Lucis egens aer*: Ov. *Met.* 1.17.

7 Cf. Ov. *Met.* 1.155: *subiecto Pelion Ossae*; but also Ov. *Pont.* 2.2.9: *si Pelion Ossa tulisset*, a condition that could never be.

Enceladus: One of the giants who sought to challenge the gods by stacking mountains on mountains to reach the heavens, defeated by Jupiter.

Euterpe

Euterpe: Muse of music.

1 recalls [Tibullus] 3.11.3: *te nascente novum Parcae cecinere puellis*.

6 *Charybdi*: Charybdis, a sea monster associated with a dangerous whirlpool, paired with Scylla (a hazardous rock).

7 *Stymphalidas*: a flock of man-eating birds, slain by Hercules for his Sixth Labour.

Cerberon: the multiheaded guard dog of the Underworld, whose capture was the Twelfth (and final) Labour of Hercules. *Cerberon*: Greek accusative; *trifaucem* from Verg. *Aen*. 6.417, Cerberus with *latratu trifauci*. The barking of 'three-throated Cerberus' is more Dantean: *Inferno* 6.13–14: *Cerbero ... con tre gole caninamente latra*; cf. Ov. *Met*. 4.450–1: *tria ... ora | et tres latratus*, in the passage on which the next stanza draws.

8 *Stygias ... canes*: i.e., the Furies, from Lucan 6.733: *Stygiasque canes*.

Terpsichore

Terpsichore: Muse of dance.

All of the figures here (Tityus, Ixion, Tantalus, Sisyphus, as well as the Danaids/Belides of the allusion in 'Erato' 7) are found in Ov. *Met*. 4.457–63, Juno's descent to the infernal regions; there, like here, the poet addresses Tantalus and Sisyphus directly, viz. in the vocative, with the names in the same position as in 5 and 7. The same figures are listed again at *Metamorphoses* 10.41–4, stopping to listen to Orpheus' song, and in Ov. *Ib*. 175–82, on which work the elaborate curses of this and the following two stanzas are partly modelled.

1–2 draw on the (other) great account of Tartarus in Verg. *Aen*. 6, here lines 598–600: *fecundaque ... viscera* and *fibris ... renatis*.

2 *Tityi*: Tityus, giant, punished by Zeus (Jupiter) to be tied down and undergo a torture whereby his liver, regrown daily, was devoured by vultures anew.

3 *illius qui*: Ixion, bound to a wheel of fire; from Ov. *Met*. 4.461: *volvitur Ixion et se sequiturque fugitque*, though withholding the name for the reader to provide.

4 repurposes as a description of torture what is a prophetic warning for Delia's wealthy new lover in Tib. 1.5.70: *versatur celeri Fors levis orbe rotae*, and similarly in Ov. *Ib*. 176: *quique agitur rapidae vinctus ab orbe rotae*, and 192: *versabunt celeres nunc nova membra rotae*.

5 *Tantale*: Tantalus, punished to stand in a pool of water receding whenever he bent to drink and under low-hanging fruits forever rising out of reach.

6–7 recall, along with *Met.* 4.458, also Ov. *Am.* 2.2.43–4: *quaerit aquas in aquis et poma fugacia captat | Tantalus*.

7 *Sisyphe*: Sisyphus, condemned for eternity to roll up a hill a boulder that would roll back down whenever it neared the top.

7–8 split over two lines Ov. *Met.* 4.460: *aut petis aut urges ruiturum, Sisyphe, saxum*, though retaining the position of the name in the hexameter.

Thalia

Thalia: Muse of comedy.

This stanza draws mainly on the cluster of myths surrounding the house of Minos (including Medea, who becomes stepmother to Phaedra's husband Theseus: she is invoked as an antitype twice in Sen. *Phaed.* 564 and 697).

1–2 From Verg. *Ecl.* 8.47–8: *natorum sanguine matrem | commaculare manus*, referring to Medea, who killed her own children by Jason to punish their unfaithful father.

4 *Minoae machina Pasiphaes*: Auson. *Epigrams* 69.2, though Aldus would have found the Latin ending *pasiphae* in the Venice 1472 *editio princeps*, sig. c1r (*Pasiphaae* in modern editions); the Greek ending is found occasionally in Latin, especially Ovid: *Remedia amoris* 453, *Ib.* 90. Pasiphaë, wife of Minos of Crete, conceived an unnatural love for a bull her husband had been meant to sacrifice to Poseidon (Neptune). Daedalus constructed for her a hollow cow. This fooled the bull and, when Pasiphaë climbed in, it mated with her. Their offspring was the Minotaur.

5 *donum exitiale*: Verg. *Aen.* 2.31, in the same position, referring to the Trojan horse.

6 An allusion to Icarus, whose wings fashioned from wax by his father Daedalus melted in the sun, leading him to plunge to his death in the sea. The passage recalls Ov. *Her.* 1.6: *obrutus insanis esset adulter* (= Paris) *aquis*, without assisting the identification.

7–8 draw on Ovid's account of Hippolytus' death by a monstrous bull produced from the sea by Poseidon, and specifically on *Met.* 15.498: *sceleratae fraude novercae*, for the false claim of his stepmother Phaedra, daughter of Minos and Pasiphaë, that he had tried to rape her; *flamma* is ubiquitous in Seneca, *Phaedra* (though for Phaedra's passion rather than its object: her stepson).

Erato

Erato: Muse of lyric poetry.

2 Cf. Tibull. 1.1.64: *neque in tenero stat tibi corde silex*, and Ov. *Met.* 9.614: *nec rigidas silices solidumve in pectore ferrum*.

3 *sororis*: Helle, who fell off and drowned in the strait also known as the Dardanelles when she and her twin brother Phrixus were fleeing across the sea on the back of a ram with golden wool (the famous Golden Fleece).

4 From Ov. *Fast.* 3.870: *de se nomina fecit aquae*.

5–6 draw jointly on accounts of the sacrifices of Polyxena, at Sen. *Troades* 196: *Pyrrhi manu mactetur*, and Iphigenia, at Lucr. 1.99: *hostia concideret mactatu maesta parentis*, as well as on Lucr. 6.759: *manibus . . . divis mactata*.

6 *Mactata*: Polyxena, daughter of Priam and Hecuba, sacrificed on the tomb of Achilles: though the sacrifice itself occurs in Euripides (*Hecuba* and *Trojan Women*) as well as in Seneca (*Troades*), where she is said to have been betrothed to him, the notion that an enamoured Achilles was lured to seek her and treacherously killed would have come from later Latin and romance traditions, e.g. Servius (commentary on *Aeneid* 3.321), Dictys Cretensis, Dares Phrygius, Benoît de Sainte-Maure, Guido delle Colonne, Dante (*Inferno* 5.65–6) and Boccaccio (*De mulieribus claris*).

caderet . . . manu: Iphigenia, slain by her father Agamemnon to appease Artemis, who had quieted the winds to ground the Greek fleet bound for Troy. In other versions of the myth (e.g., Euripides, *Iphigenia among the Taurians* and *Iphigenia at Aulis*) she is saved by the goddess at the last minute and spirited away.

7 draws on Ov. *Met.* 4.463 and 10.43–4; see note on 'Terpsichore'.

urnas . . . repletas: an allusion to the punishment of the Danaids (or Belides), fifty sisters of whom the forty-nine who killed their husbands on their wedding nights were condemned endlessly to refill with water urns that always leaked.

8 *Tartareumque Iovem*: literally, 'Tartarean Jove', i.e., Pluto, lord of the Underworld (where Tartarus is the place of punishment).

Calliope

Calliope: Muse of epic poetry.

3 repurposes Juv. 10.248–9: *felix nimirum* ... | ... *suos iam dextra conputat annos* (not the case for Nestor), but for positive ends.

5 *oliva*: the wild olive wreath, reward of victors in the Olympic Games.

7 recalls Verg. *Georg.* 3.9: *virum volitare per ora*, itself recalling Ennius' *volito vivos per ora virum*, cited and available in Cic. *Tusc.* 1.15.34.

Paraenesis

1 recalls *alternis* ... *sonis* of the opening hexastich as well as Verg. *Ecl.* 3.59: *amant alterna Camenae*, referring to verses sung in turn (as in the letter to Caterina, *de Alberti laudibus alternis concinunt*); but also Ov. *Fast.* 2.121: *canimus* ... *alterno carmine*, *Her.* 15.5–6: *alterna requiras | carmina*, and most expansively *Trist.* 3.1.11–12: *clauda quod alterno subsidunt carmina versu, | vel pedis hoc ratio*, referring to verses *in alternis*, i.e. in elegiac couplets, alternating between hexameter and pentameter. Both senses are relevant here, especially in an educational context where the fundamentals of prosody would be discussed.

2 *Aonides*: from Aonia, a region or another name of Boeotia, and thus applied to Mt Helicon and by Ovid to the Muses.

2 *carmina culta*: Ov. *Ars am.* 3.341–2.

4 *Pierios*: another reference to the Muses, who defeated the Pierides in a song contest, after which the Pierian Spring and the name itself became associated with them.

5 *librum*: one of those works mentioned in the letter to Caterina.

9 *Marco*: Marco II Pio (d. 1494), Alberto's father's brother and co-ruler of Carpi.

13 *Pius*: the family name, but also Aeneas' Vergilian epithet.

nulli pietate secundus: from the ancient verse *argumentum* to *Aeneid* 1, referring to Aeneas.

16 *arma viros*: echoing *arma virumque* of Verg. *Aen.* 1.1.

24 *Pelasga*: from the name for the most ancient inhabitants of Greece: thus the 'Roman Pallas' offers Latin reading and the 'Pelasgian Pallas' offers Greek.

26 *laurea bina*: the laurel crown of Apollo, poets and triumphant commanders; 'double' because it was made with two branches bound together at the back.

27 From Lucan 7.11: *attollique suum . . . ad sidera nomen*.

31 *grammaticen*: a Greek form often used in Latin, especially Quintilian, and then in the Renaissance.

docuere: the implied subject from 30 is [*Romana*] *scripta* ('Roman writings'), standing in for their authors (often the other way around).

33 *geminae*: 'twofold' in the sense of her 'Roman and Pelasgian guises'.

35 *castigo*: standard in the vocabulary of printing for proofreading.

Xenia

The main source for this poem is Mart. *Epigrams* 13, the 'book of gifts'.

1-2 *xenia . . . dabant*: Although it was also one of the main rituals of the Saturnalia (17-23 December), in the imperial period the giving of gifts, called *xenia* or specifically *strenae*, became primarily associated with the Kalends of January. Absorbed as the Feast of the Circumcision into the Christmas festivities that stretched until Epiphany (6 January) – a period corresponding to Aldus' Saturnalia in line 16 –, nevertheless, 1 January retained this association at late medieval and Renaissance courts, yielding to 25 December only later (see Buettner 2001).

3 *Calendas*: in the same position as [*Aurea porrigitur Iani caryota*] *Kalendis*, Martial 13.27.1.

5-6 rework 13.93: [*Aper*] *Diomedeis . . . agris . . . cecidit*.

5 *aprum*: the Calydonian boar, slain during a famous hunt by Meleager (uncle of Diomedes, Trojan War hero).

7 *capreas*, 13.98; *lepores*, 13.92; *damas*, 13.94.

8 *sumine*, 13.44; *cortis aves*, 13.45.

9 *lactuca*, 13.14, recalls Martial's question of why meals used to end with lettuce but now begin with it.

10 *rapa*, 13.16, likewise drawing on *brumali gaudentia frigore rapa* (line 1).

12 *ebria bruma*, 13.1.4.

13 *Carpumque Novumque*: nine miles north of Carpi, Novi was the site of another castle of the Pio family; in 1498 Alberto granted Aldus substantial estates there.

15 repurposes Martial 3.60.5: *sunt tibi boleti, fungos ego sumo suillos*. The translation uses the modern Italian culinary terms for the mushrooms named here. Curiously, in Martial they respectively embody high- and low-quality cuisine.

23 Cf. the letter to Caterina: *secundum accentus . . . moderatio dictionum*.

5

An Elegiac Poem by Julius Caesar Scaliger (1484–1558) on Sickness and Healing

Bobby Xinyue

Introduction

Julius Caesar Scaliger (1484–1558) ranks as one of the best known classical scholars of the early modern period.[1] His fame among students of Greek and Latin literature derives mainly from his posthumously published *Poetices libri septem* (Lyon 1561), an ambitious work of poetic theory and literary criticism in the manner of Aristotle's *Poetics*, Horace's *Ars Poetica*, and Vida's *De arte poetica*.[2] Yet, to view Scaliger purely through the lens of the *Poetice* would do him a disservice. As well as being a practitioner of medicine and a scholar of natural philosophy and linguistics,[3] Scaliger was also a prolific poet. The sheer quantity of his verse compositions collected in the *Poemata in duas partes divisa* (1574) reflects Scaliger's immense productivity throughout his career. But it is the erudition on display that attests to Scaliger's wide-ranging humanistic interests and profound sensibility to classical literature.

There exists a biography of Scaliger written by his son, Joseph Justus Scaliger, a fine scholar and poet in his own right.[4] While this *vita* is a useful source in many respects, for it sheds light on some of the events and figures mentioned throughout the elder Scaliger's works, it has been shown that much of the biographical information concerning Scaliger's family ancestry, education and early career is at best unverifiable and at worst entirely fictitious. Regarding the first forty years or so of Scaliger's life, all we can be certain of is that he moved to France from his native Italy in *c.* 1525 and began practising medicine in Agen.[5] As we shall see, the image of Scaliger as a Veronese noble descended from the once-ruling house of the Della Scala (from which derived his name 'Scaligero'), who fled his ancestral home and endured family tragedies and prolonged hardships before enjoying a successful career in France, was purely the product of Scaliger's self-mythologization, which his son not only reproduced but even embellished in the *vita*.

Despite the difficulties presented by the sources, however, modern scholarship has made various attempts to reconstruct Scaliger's activities prior to his time in Agen.[6] A more credible picture of a man who grew up in Venice and studied in Padua has since emerged, though much remains unknown. The picture of Scaliger's life in France is much clearer. While practising medicine in Agen, Scaliger gradually established a reputation as a scholar, philosopher and scientist through a series of publications. He attacked Erasmus' view on Cicero with a pair of virulent speeches (1531, 1537);[7] wrote a highly influential treatise on Latin grammar (1540);[8] and produced commentaries on the works of Hippocrates (1539),[9] Theophrastus (1566)[10] and Aristotle (1619),[11] amongst others. At the end of his life, in 1557, Scaliger offered – in the course of fifteen books – a merciless review of Girolamo Cardano's scientific treatise, *De subtilitate*.[12]

Alongside these, Scaliger composed a diverse range of Latin poetry, nearly all of which was collected in the *Poemata*.[13] A significant number of compositions were concerned with poetry; and in this respect the *Poemata* and the *Poetice* cohere productively.[14] Conventional subjects such as poetic inspiration and the value of poetry open the collection; but there are also harangues against the tastelessness of contemporary society and despondent reflections on the vocation of poetry. Eulogies of contemporary Neo-Latin poets and scholars (such as Pietro Bembo, Girolamo Fracastoro and Giovanni Pico) are not in short supply;[15] nor are satires and iambic epigrams that lend insight into Scaliger's bitter relationship with his enemies (in particular Étienne Dolet).

A more chronological account of Scaliger's verse productions gives us a better sense of the development of his poetic interests. His first collection, *Nova epigrammata*, published in 1533, was a creative reimagining of the lost elegiac poetry that Aristotle was said to have written – 'an eye-catching and novel way of combining humanist and scholastic modes of writing'.[16] A year later, Scaliger produced a collection of elegies under the title *Lacrymae* (Paris 1534). In the next decade Scaliger wrote a significant amount of poetry, which appeared together in a collection called *Poematia* (Lyon 1546), dedicated to his patroness Costanza Rangona. Among these were the *Heroes* (first published in 1539) and *Heroinae*, composed in elegiac couplets, which celebrated illustrious men and women from classical antiquity to the early modern period; the *Thaumantia*, a collection of erotic elegiac poems; and, perhaps most notably, fifty-nine hendecasyllabic poems in the style of Catullus, to which Scaliger gave the title *Manes Catulliani*.[17] It was also during this period that Scaliger began work on the *Poetice*, which drew on the insights of Horace and quoted amply from Vergil.[18] The topics and genres of

Scaliger's poetic output at this time showed that he was especially interested in elegy *grosso modo*[19] and that he framed his compositions as belonging to and inheriting a poetic tradition that extended from Aristotle to his day.

The poem chosen for commentary is the second lament in the *Lacrymae* (= *Poemata* 1.529–30), entitled '*In Alpibus aeger Apollinem et Aesculapium alloquitur*' ('Sick in the Alps he addresses Apollo and Asclepius'). The collection – originally containing nine poems, later expanded to twelve in the *Poemata*, all in elegiacs – purports to be autobiographical and deeply personal. The first lament dramatizes Scaliger's exile from his native Italy; the second recounts his suffering and alleviation from a bout of fever; the third is dedicated to his lover, Angela Paulina, who committed suicide after she was misinformed that Scaliger had been killed at the Battle of Ravenna; and the final poem laments the death of Scaliger's two-year old daughter Margarita. A key question to be explored in the commentary is what we are to make of Scaliger's poetic autobiography, both in the immediate context of the '*In Alpibus aeger*' and in the broader context of Scaliger's self-fashioning.

A further point of interest is the poem's generic affiliations and literary dialogues. The '*In Alpibus aeger*' sits somewhere between a self-lament and a hymn; as such, the poem draws on a number of models from the classical literary canon. First and foremost, Scaliger engages closely with Catullus 68, a poem (or perhaps two separate, but thematically connected, poems) that deals with death, emotional distress and timely intervention. No less visible is the presence of Latin love elegy and Ovid's exilic corpus in Scaliger's poem. The vulnerable self-positioning of the elegiac subject in Propertius' poetry (cf. Prop. 1.17 about the poet's lament in a lonely place), along with Ovid's desperate laments about his exilic suffering and deteriorating condition, characterize the poetic persona of Scaliger. As a hymn to Apollo and Asclepius, Horatian lyric exercises a significant influence on the '*In Alpibus aeger*'. In particular, we are reminded of *Odes* 1.21, a paean of sorts; *Odes* 2.7, which dramatizes the poet's rescue by Mercury; and the triad of *Odes* 2.13, 2.17 and 3.4, which allude to Horace's near-fatal encounter with a falling tree and the divine protection he received from Faunus (cf. 2.17.27–9). Amid all the classical allusions (both specific and impressionistic), the language of Christian prayer also makes itself felt at the start of Scaliger's poem. The interplay between the classical and the Christian, healing and salvation, self-pitying and authorial mythologization, combine to enliven (and complicate) the picture of Scaliger as poet, physician and patient.

Notes

1. For an overview of Scaliger's life and works, see esp. Hall 1950; Patrizi 1989; Jensen 1990: 15–50.
2. Deitz / Vogt-Spira 1994–2011.
3. See the variety of contributions in Cubelier de Beynac / Magnien 1986.
4. *Epistola de vetustate et splendore gentis Scaligerae et Julii Caesari Scaligeri vita* (Leiden 1594). On Joseph Justus Scaliger, see Grafton 1983 and 1993.
5. There is no way of confirming Scaliger's claim that he entered France as the personal physician of Antonio della Rovere, the bishop of Agen (see Hall 1950: 90–1).
6. See Richards 1962; Billanovich 1968.
7. *Oratio pro Marco Tullio contra Desiderium Erasmum Roterodamum* (Paris 1531) and *Adversus Desiderii Erasmi Roterodami dialogum Ciceronianum oratio secunda* (Paris 1537). Combined, edited and translated by M. Magnien, *Jules-César Scaliger, Orationes Duae contra Erasmum* (Geneva 1999).
8. *De causis linguae Latinae* (Lyon 1540); see further Jensen 1990.
9. *Hippocratis liber de somniis cum J. C. Scaligeri commentariis* (Lyon 1539); see further De Smet 2008.
10. *Commentarii et animadversiones in sex libros de causis plantarum Theophrasti* (Lyon 1566); see further Blank 2010.
11. *Aristotelis historia de animalibus. Iulio Caesare Scaligero interprete, cum eiusdem commentariis* (Toulouse 1619); see further Perfetti 2000: 155–81.
12. *Exotericarum exercitationum liber XV. De subtilitate, ad Hieronymum Cardanum* (Paris 1557); see further Sakamoto 2016.
13. For an overview, see Costanzo 1961: 7–37.
14. Clements 1954.
15. On Scaliger's praise and 'canonization' of Neo-Latin poets, see Ludwig 1979; Reineke 1988; Rolfes 2001.
16. Haugen 2007: 844.
17. On the *Manes Catulliani*, see Pomeroy Harrington 1932.
18. The *Poetice* was originally conceived with the aim of educating Scaliger's eldest son, Silvio, on the matters of poetry; see Hall 1945.
19. In his *Poetice* Scaliger recognizes the flexibility of the elegiac couplet; see Deitz / Vogt-Spira 1994–2011: 3.202, with brief discussion by Houghton 2017: 99.

Bibliography

Billanovich, M. (1968), 'Benedetto Bordone e Giulio Cesare Scaligero', *Italia medievale e umanistica*, 11: 197–256.

Blank, A. (2010), 'Julius Caesar Scaliger on Plant Generation and the Question of Species Constancy', *Early Science and Medicine*, 15: 266–86.
Blank, A. (2018), 'Julius Caesar Scaliger', in: M. Sgarbi (ed.), *Encyclopedia of Renaissance Philosophy*, Cham (https://doi.org/10.1007/978-3-319-02848-4_879-1).
Clements, R. J. (1954), 'Literary Theory and Criticism in Scaliger's *Poemata*', *Studies in Philology*, 51: 337–60.
Costanzo, M. (1961), *Dallo Scaligero al Quadrio*, Milan.
Cubelier de Beynac, J. / Magnien, M., eds (1986), *Acta Scaligeriana: Actes du Colloque International organisé pour le cinquième centenaire de la naissance de Jules-César Scaliger (Agen, 14–16 septembre 1984)*, Agen.
Cummings, R. (2017), 'Epigrams', in: V. Moul (ed.), *A Guide to Neo-Latin Literature*, 83–97, Cambridge.
Deitz, L. / Vogt-Spira, G. (1994–2001), *Iulius Caesar Scaliger. Poetices libri septem: Sieben Bücher über die Dichtkunst*, 6 vols, Stuttgart.
De Smet, I. (2008), 'Of Doctors, Dreamers and Soothsayers: The Interlinking Worlds of Julius Caesar Scaliger and Augur Ferrier', *Bibliothèque d'Humanisme et Renaissance*, 70: 351–76.
Feeney, D. C. (1992), '"Shall I Compare Thee . . ."? Catullus 68B and the Limits of Analogy', in: A. J. Woodman / J. Powell (eds), *Actor and Audience in Latin Literature*, 33–44. Cambridge.
Grafton, A. (1983), *Joseph Scaliger: A Study in the History of Classical Scholarship I: Textual Criticism and Exegesis*, Oxford.
Grafton, A. (1993), *Joseph Scaliger: A Study in the History of Classical Scholarship II: Historical Chronology*, Oxford.
Hall, V. (1945), 'Preface to Scaliger's *Poetices libri septem*', *Modern Language Notes*, 60.7: 447–53.
Hall, V. (1950), *Life of J. C. Scaliger (1484–1558)*, Philadelphia.
Haugen, K. L. (2007), 'Aristotle my Beloved: Poetry, Diagnosis, and the Dreams of Julius Caesar Scaliger', *Renaissance Quarterly*, 60: 819–51.
Houghton, L. B. T. (2017), 'Elegy', in: V. Moul (ed.), *A Guide to Neo-Latin Literature*, 98–112, Cambridge.
Jensen, K. (1990), *Rhetorical Philosophy and Philosophical Grammar: Julius Caesar Scaliger's Theory of Language*, Munich.
Kristeller, P. O. (1952), 'Review of Hall, *Life of J. C. Scaliger* (1950)', *The American Historical Review*, 57: 394–6.
Lindheim, S. H. (2021), *Latin Elegy and the Space of Empire*, Oxford.
Ludwig, W. (1979), 'Julius Caesar Scaligers Kanon neulateinischer Dichter', *Antike und Abendland*, 25: 20–40.
Patrizi, G. (1989), 'Della Scala, Julius Caesar', *Dizionario Biografico degli Italiani*, 37.
Perfetti, S. (2000), *Aristotle's Zoology and Its Renaissance Commentators (1521–1601)*, Leuven.
Pomeroy Harrington, K. (1932), 'The *Manes Catulliani* of J. C. Scaliger', *Classical Journal*, 27: 596–610.

Reineke, I. (1988), *Julius Caesar Scaligers Kritik der neulateinischen Dichter: Text, Übersetzung und Kommentar des 4. Kapitels von Buch VI seiner Poetik*, Munich.

Richards, J. F. (1962), 'The *Elysium* of J. C. Bordonius', *Studies in the Renaissance*, 9: 195–217.

Rolfes, S. (2001), *Die lateinische Poetik des Marco Girolamo Vida und ihre Rezeption bei Julius Caesar Scaliger*, Munich / Leipzig.

Sakamoto, K. (2016), *Julius Caesar Scaliger, Renaissance Reformer of Aristotelianism: A Study of his Exotericae exercitationes*, Leiden.

Vandiver, E. (2000), 'Hot Springs, Cool Rivers, and Hidden Fires: Heracles in Catullus 68.51–66', *Classical Philology*, 95: 151–9.

Source of Latin text

Julius Caesar Scaliger, *Poemata in duas partes divisa*, Heidelberg 1574.

Latin text

In Alpibus aeger Apollinem et Aesculap[ium] alloquitur

Magne minorque dei, quanquam mihi magnus uterque,
    magne pater, solo sed patre nate minor,
magne pater, medicas si rite sacravimus aras,
    si colui praesens altera sacra puer,
5 aspice me, miserum, extorrem, rerum omnium egenum,
    quem tenet ignoto barbara terra sinu;
aspice me dulcis linquentem luminis haustus,
    cuius adhuc nullus pectore gustus inest,
8a [ah necdum mihi, decurso per mille labores,
8b   quinque nigros signant turbida lustra dies,]
quique bonis infans carui miser exul avitis,
10   quique tuli duri vulnera servitii,
nulla cui maesto ridens Aurora reluxit,
    nulla cui faciles condidit hora deos,
quem divus genitor fraudavit lumine diro
    funere, quem diro funere diva parens.
15 saltem non potuit serae ventura senectae
    praeterita exoriens spes relevare mala?
at me perpetuus crudeliter obsidet aestus,
    nec maior Sicula est ignibus Aetna meis.
accipe qua tristis expugnat Sirius umbras,
20   qua steriles rapidus Cancer hiulcat agros,
aut in desertis Libyes ubi letifer atros
    per populos siccis Auster anhelat equis,
et quaecunque gravi pariter quocunque sub orbe
    fervida languentem colligit hora sitim.
25 illa sitis, sitis illa leves mihi condiet haustus:
    sic miser in mediis ardeo mersus aquis.
ecce igitur misero facilis succurrit Apollo,
    et defert gelido gramine laetus opem.
vos ego fatales suci, vos gramen adoro:
30   vivificus vestro caule superbit honos,
unde mihi licuit fugientem ducere vitam
    funeraque extructis tollere fulta rogis.
vosne ab Hyperboreis spiravit Cynthius auris?

English translation

Sick in the Alps, [Scaliger] addresses Apollo and Asclepius

Great and lesser gods, though each of you is great to me,
great father [and] son, lesser but only to the father:
great father, if I duly honoured your healing altars,
if I was there to tend to your second set of rites as a boy,
look upon me, wretched, exiled, destitute of all possessions,   5
whom a barbarian land holds in her unfamiliar bosom;
look upon me, leaving behind the breaths of sweet life,
in whose insides there is as yet no taste of food or water,
[ah, having passed through a thousand toils, not yet
do twenty-five troubled years mark the dark days for me,]
who, a wretched exile since infancy, was separated from my fine ancestors,
who endured the wounds of harsh servitude,   10
on whose sorrow no smiling Dawn has shone a light,
for whom no hour has established favourable gods,
[whose] divine father has deprived him of life by a terrible death,
another terrible death also deprived him of his divine mother.
These misfortunes aside, could the rising hope of a late old age to come   15
not even lighten the sufferings of the past?
Yet a constant thirst cruelly possesses me,
and the Sicilian Aetna is no greater than my fire.
Learn, where Sirius storms the gloomy shades,
where scorching Cancer splits the barren fields,   20
or where in the Libyan dessert the deadly south wind
pants on its parched horses through the dark peoples,
and whatever blazing season likewise harsh under whatever oppressive region
brings up a debilitating thirst.
That thirst, that very thirst, will flavour my light breaths: 25
so wretchedly do I burn, plunged in the midst of waters.
But look! Kindly Apollo runs to the aid of the wretched one
and happily brings help with ice-cool grass.
You, fateful moisture, [and] you, grass, I revere you:
life-giving beauty is splendid in your stalk.   30
From which I could draw the life-breath [that was] fleeing [from me],
and remove the corpse already propped on heaped pyres.
Did Cynthius blow you in from the Hyperborean winds?

vosne sub Odrysio pastor habet nemore?
35 vosne ab Acidaliis misit Venus aurea campis?
aut Paphio facilis fonte rigavit Amor?
qui mihi conceptos in morem fulminis aestus
iussistisque atris ignibus ire faces?
non Venus aut tanto statuit puer ales honore.
40 ah quantum flammarum illa, vel ille trahunt.
unde igitur? Pholoes glacialia pectora nosco.
unde fuit toties mors mihi, vita venit.

Did the shepherd have you in his Odrysian grove?
Did golden Venus send you from her Acidalian fields 35
or kindly Amor soak you with the Paphian spring,
who ordered for me the heat that took hold like a thunderbolt
and the torches with their black fires to leave?
Not Venus nor the winged boy of such great honour made that decision.
Ah how great are the flames she and he bring in their wake! 40
So where from? I recognise the frozen heart of Pholoe:
from the place which was so often [a source of] death for me, life came.

Commentary

Title: *In Alpibus aeger . . .*: in the first edition of the text (1534) Scaliger gives a much longer title: *In Alpibus Ligurum cum aegrotaret procul a medicis, vehementi febre contractam sitim conqueritur. quam tandem sedatam dicit non herbis, sed amicae frigore. Apollinem et Aesculapium alloquitur* ('When [the poet] was sick in the Ligurian Alps far from physicians, he laments the thirst brought on by a violent fever. He tells of its eventual alleviation not by herbs, but by the coolness of his sweetheart. He addresses Apollo and Asclepius'). The more concise title that appears in the later edition, along with other emendations (see below 8a–b), is the work of the author's son, the compiler of the *Poemata*, Joseph Justus Scaliger.

1 *Magne minorque dei* refers to Apollo and Asclepius. The juxtaposition of *magne* and *minor* is unusual; the only classical parallel is Plautus, *Cistellaria* 522 (*di . . . omnes, magni minuti*). The invocation of divinities at the start of an elegy is not uncommon (cf. Prop. 2.28, 3.17; Ov. *Trist.* 1.2, 1.10). This opening underscores the poem's generic affiliation with both lament and hymn (especially paean, typically addressed to Apollo).

2 *pater . . . nate*: the father and the son in question are Apollo and Asclepius, but it is impossible to read this line without thinking of the language of Christian prayer, which regularly calls on God the Father and God the Son. This Christian allusion adds another dimension to the poem's generic hybridity. Apollo's paternity of Asclepius is uncontested in classical literature (cf. *Hom. Hymn.* 16.1; Pind. *Pyth.* 3.5; Diod. Sic. 5.74.6; Ov. *Met.* 2.620; Paus. 7.23.7).

3–4 Scaliger's self-presentation as a devotee of the two chief healing gods of classical antiquity serves to highlight his successful career as a doctor.

4 *praesens* may evoke the idea of divine epiphany and is especially fitting in a prayer; for its use in such contexts cf. Cic. *Nat. D.* 2.6.2: *praesentes saepe di vim suam declarant* ('the gods often manifest their power in bodily presence'); Verg. *Aen.* 9.404: *tu, dea, tu praesens, nostro succurre labori* ('you, goddess, you, be present, run to help our effort').

altera sacra: refers to poetry, which also falls under Apollo's patronage along with medicine.

puer: for predicative use of *puer* in a similar context (i.e. keenness on poetry since youth), cf. Ov. *Trist.* 4.10.19: *at mihi iam puero caelestia sacra placebant* ('but even as a boy the heavenly rites delighted me').

5-16 A highly fictionalized autobiographical account of the poet's sorrows. The principal events described, most of which appear to belong to an early period of Scaliger's life, find their way into Joseph Scaliger's biography of his father. However, none of these life-shaping events – exile, destitution, orphanhood, servitude – can be confirmed by any extant documents (Kristeller 1952; Blank 2018). Yet Scaliger's autobiographical fiction is worthy of critical attention precisely because of its lack of credibility and highly stylized poetic form. Ovid's relentless lament about the misery and hardship of his exile, which also lacks confirmatory evidence, but has come to define the poet's persona in the *Tristia* and *Epistulae ex Ponto*, looms large in Scaliger's multitude of complaints here. To a lesser extent, this passage may also have been informed by the kind of autobiographical details scattered across Propertius' elegies (cf. 1.21–22 on the death of his relatives). Rather than offering an accurate record of his misfortunes, the intertextual layering of Scaliger's pathetic self-portrait serves to reassert his 'credentials' as a poet of lament.

5 *aspice me* is used twice by Propertius at 1.15.3 and 2.34.55.

miserum, extorrem, rerum omnium egenum: evokes Aeneas' account of the misfortune that has befallen his men, cf. Verg. *Aen.* 1.597–8: *nos . . . terraeque marisque | omnibus exhaustos iam casibus, omnium egenos* ('us, now worn out by every kind of disaster on land and sea, and destitute of everything'); see also Livy 2.6.2 (Tarquinius): *extorrem, egentem ex tanto modo regno* ('banished, [and] lately destitute of great power').

6 *barbara terra* appears no fewer than three times in Ovid's *Tristia* (3.1.18, 3.3.46, 4.4.86). Both the sentiment and the language of 5–6 further evoke Ov. *Fast.* 4.82: *me miserum, Scythico quam procul illa solo est* ('wretched me, how far she [i.e. Sulmo] is from the Scythian land').

7 *dulcis linquentem luminis haustus*: for poetic usage of *lumen* meaning 'life', see e.g. *lumen ademptum* ('with life taken away', Catull. 68.93; also Ov. *Trist.* 4.4.45). The meaning of *haustus* as 'breath' derives from its original verbal form *haurio* ('to drink up, inhale'), cf. Verg. *Georg.* 4.220–1: *haustus | aetherios* ('draughts of air').

8 *gustus*: uncommon in poetry, but frequent in prose scientific texts (see esp. Plin. *HN* and Sen. *NQ*).

8a–b This couplet was excised from the 1574 edition of the *Poemata*. The removed text claims that Scaliger's life has been in turmoil for nearly twenty-five years (*necdum . . . | quinque . . . turbida lustra*), which sets up the catalogue of griefs that follows (9–14). It is unclear why Joseph Scaliger discarded these lines: it may be that the temporal specificity of this couplet was not compatible with Joseph Scaliger's wish to present the *Poemata* as the culminating *opus* of his father's verse compositions.

decurso: a middle use of the passive participle.

9 *infans ... exul* fleshes out *extorrem* in line 5. Joseph Scaliger's biography of his father records that Scaliger's family was forced to abandon their castle in La Rocca at Riva in 1484, when it came under attack from the Venetians; Scaliger was only a few days old at the time (cf. Joseph Scaliger 1594: 30–1; Hall 1950: 88).

avitis: a reference to Scaliger's claim that he descended from the ruling family of Verona, the Della Scala – a claim that was challenged even by the contemporaries of Joseph and has since been debunked in modern scholarship (see Billanovich 1968).

10 *duri ... servitii*: it is unclear what this refers to. According to his son, Scaliger endured poverty and spent an unhappy time at a Franciscan convent in Bologna (Joseph Scaliger 1594: 35–6).

11 The personification of Aurora (cf. *ridens*) is a common feature in the poetry of Vergil, Ovid and Statius; there is also a hint of Lucretius' allegorization of the gods, cf. *largo diffuso lumine ridet* ('smiles in widely diffused light', *DRN* 3.22).

12 *faciles ... deos*: another Ovidian expression, cf. *Trist.* 1.5.15: *di tibi sint faciles* ('may the gods favour you'); *Her.* 16.282; *Pont.* 4.4.30; note also *Tr.* 4.1.53: *sint, precor, hae saltem faciles mihi* ('I pray that they [i.e. the Muses] are at least kind to me').

13–14 Scaliger's father was apparently killed at the Battle of Ravenna in 1512 (along with Scaliger's elder brother), while his mother died soon after from grief; see Joseph Scaliger 1594: 33–5; also Arnoul Le Ferron (a friend of Scaliger's), *De rebus gestis Gallorum ...* (Paris 1549: 63b). The tragic consequence of the Battle of Ravenna also provides the dramatic backdrop for the next poem in the *Lacrymae* (= *Poemata* 1.530–2), a lament on the death of a certain Angela Paulina, who was said to be Scaliger's lover at the time. It is worth repeating that none of these events and figures can be verified by sources independent of Scaliger's circle.

15–16 The usage of the '*saltem* + negative' construction (cf. *OLD* s.v. *saltem* 2) within a rhetorical question conveys effectively Scaliger's desperation. Both Scaliger's sentiment and language recall the dark pessimism of Lucan 1.522–3 <u>nequa futuri</u> | <u>spes saltem trepidas mentes levet</u> ('not any hope even for the future relieved their frightened minds').

16 *exoriens* is most commonly used to describe the rising or appearance of celestial bodies (cf. *OLD* s.v. *exoriens* 2), thus anticipating the imagery of 19–20.

17 Scaliger describes the principal symptom of his illness. The treatment of fever is a major topic in the Hippocratic corpus (esp. *Epidemics* 1), Celsus (esp. *De Medicina* 2 and 3) and Galen. As a practising doctor and humanist, Scaliger must have been familiar with Latin translations of the works of Hippocrates and Galen, which flourished in Italy in the late fifteenth century.

18 Catullus compares his burning love for his girl to Mount Etna: *cum tantum arderem quantum Trinacria rupes* ('when I was burning as much as the Trinacrian rock', Catull. 68.53).

19–24 supplement the comparison between fever and volcanic fire in line 18 with proverbial expressions of heat from classical literature. A *tricolon crescens* of sorts can be observed in lines 19–22, during the course of which the images also subtly veer from the meteorological to the ethnographical.

19–20 On the association between Sirius ('Dog Star') and hot weather in Latin poetry, see esp. Tib. 1.7.21; Verg. *Aen.* 10.273; Luc. 10.211–12; Sil. 16.99; cf. also Ov. *Am.* 2.16.3–4 (where *stella canis* is used instead of *Sirius*) and *Ars Am.* 2.231 (*sitiensque Canicula*). The association of heat with Cancer ('Crab') derives from the fact that the sun is positioned in the zodiacal sign of Cancer at the summer solstice; in poetry, see e.g. Lucr. 5.616; Ov. *Met.* 2.83, *Fast.* 6.727; Luc. 10.259.

20 *hiulcat agros*: an unmistakable echo of Catull. 68.62: *cum gravis exustos aestus hiulcat agros* ('when heavy heat cracks open the burnt fields').

21-2 *desertis Libyes* (note the Greek genitive ending of *Libyes*) looks back to *Sicula ... Aetna* in line 18. The display of geographical and ethnographical knowledge is especially common in Latin elegy (see e.g. Prop. 1.6.1–4, 3.7, 3.22.1–18, 4.3.7–10, 33–40; Tib. 1.7.17–22; Ov. *Am.* 2.16.19–22; *Ars Am.* 1.223-6; note also Hor. *Carm.* 2.20, 3.4.29–36, 4.14.41–50). Roman imperial expansion directs the Augustan poets' perspective on the world (see Lindheim 2021); the assertion of classical erudition underpins Scaliger's couplet here.

siccis ... equis: recalls artistic depictions of the horses of the wind.

23 *quaecumque ... quocunque*: the pointed lack of specificity, underscored by the repetition of the indefinite pronoun, conveys the idea that the speaker is worn out by his illness.

24 *languentem*: the bodies of the *amator* and *puella* in Augustan elegy are particularly prone to enfeeblement (cf. Prop. 1.13.15, 2.34.59; Ov. *Am.* 2.10.35; *Ars Am.* 2.692; *Her.* 18.161; *Rem.* 511). On the corporeal vulnerabilities of the exiled Ovid, see *Tr.* 3.3.39; *Pont.* 1.4.3.

26 *aquis*: most probably refers to the Alpine climate. The paradox of suffering from thirst while surrounded by a watery environment recalls and further develops Ov. *Her.* 16.211–12: *nec proavo Stygia nostro captantur in unda | poma, nec in mediis quaeritur umor aquis* ('nor does my ancestor catch at fruits in the Stygian wave or seek water in the midst of waters'). The sensory contrast between *ardeo* and *aquis* further enlivens the imagery. In the *Poetice* Scaliger identifies the interplay between unlikely conjunctions as a central feature of epigrams; see Deitz and Vogt-Spira 1994–2011: 3.204, with further discussion by Cummings 2017: 86–7.

27–8 Scaliger employs the classical trope of divine epiphany to dramatize his unexpected salutary relief. *Succurrere* is commonly used in the context of both (appeals to) divine assistance (cf. Prop. 2.16.13; Tib. 1.3.27; Verg. *Aen.* 9.404) and medical intervention (note its frequent usage by Celsus in the *De Medicina*). In Ovid's account of the foundation of the cult of Asclepius in Rome following a plague, the Romans first pray to Apollo for assistance: *utque salutifera miseris succurrere rebus | sorte velit . . . orant* ('and they begged that [Apollo] would wish to succour them in their wretched state with his health-bringing fate', Ov. *Met.* 15.632–3). There is also a palpable hint of Catull. 68.57–62 in Scaliger's presentation of the *gelidum gramen* (28). Earlier, in line 20, Scaliger uses the Catullan expression *hiulcat agros* (cf. Catul. 68.62) to describe the intensity of his fever. In poem 68, where Catullus was suffering from his burning passion for his beloved (cf. *torruerit*, 68.52; *arderem*, 68.53), the poet compares the timely assistance of Allius to a cool stream that refreshes the parched traveller (*qualis . . . | rivus muscoso prosilit e lapide | . . . | dulce viatori lasso in sudore levamen, | cum gravis exustos aestus hiulcat agros*, 'just as a stream leaps out from a mossy stone, a sweet refreshment for the traveller in his tired sweat when heavy heat cracks open the burnt fields', 68.57–62). The idea that a 'saviour' (Apollo/Allius) brought 'cooling' aid to the 'burning' poet underpins both this passage and Catullus' simile. On the use of similes in Catull. 68, see Feeney (1992) and Vandiver (2000).

29 The anaphora of *vos* is a typical expression of hymnic praise, but the entire sentence is strongly reminiscent of Catull. 64.24: *vos ego saepe meo vos carmine compellabo* ('You shall I often address, you in my poetry'). *Sucus* can also mean the juice of ambrosia or nectar, especially in the context of the divine (cf. Hor. *Carm.* 3.3.35; Verg. *Aen.* 12.419; Ov. *Met.* 2.120). Scaliger's choice of this word further blurs the line between natural cure and divine intervention, reality and imagination.

30 *vivificus*: not attested in extant classical texts, but used with some frequency by Christian authors from Zeno of Verona onward. The transition from *adoro* (29), which also has strong Christian associations in post-classical

texts, to *vivificus* widens the rhetorical scope of this couplet to encompass Christian prayer.

31–2 are particularly melodramatic and rich in literary references. *fugientem ducere vitam* evokes a number of pathetic figures from canonical poetic texts: (i) Vergil's Dido (*me si fata meis paterentur ducere vitam auspiciis*, 'if the fates allowed me to lead my life according to my own fortune', Verg. *Aen.* 4.430); (ii) the grieving mother clutching a corpse in Lucan's *Bellum Civile* (*membra ... fugiente rigentia vita*, 'limbs stiffening with life fleeing', Luc. 2.25); and (iii) possibly a hint of the dying Orpheus in Vergil's *Georgics* (*anima fugiente vocabat*, 'he called as the soul escaped', Verg. *Georg.* 4.526). The funerary image in line 32 recalls Ovid's lament on the death of Tibullus: *ille tui vates operis, tua fama, Tibullus | ardet in extructo, corpus inane, rogo* ('that poet of your own work, your own glory, Tibullus burns, an empty corpse, on the mounted pyre', Ov. *Am.* 3.9.5–6).

funera: poetic plural for 'corpse', cf. Prop. 4.11.3.

33–8 present another 'tricolon' (see 19–22) and another virtuosic display of classical erudition. The anaphoric *vos* (33, 34, 35) refers back to the life-saving *gramen* (28–9), which the poet has already established as the work of Apollo (27). Thus, the present passage, in which Scaliger ruminates on the origin of the *gramen*, is essentially redundant. However, in the process of exploring alternative origins, Scaliger shows off his knowledge of pagan gods and their tutelary or healing roles. The four divine figures mentioned – Apollo, Orpheus, Venus and Cupid (Amor) – are variously associated with providing poets with inspiration, protection or alleviation, especially (but not exclusively) in the genre of elegy. Their introduction into the poem, therefore, not only reinforces Scaliger's elegiac self-fashioning, but also subtly integrates this poetic lament into the literary tradition of Roman elegy. Moreover, Scaliger's ostentatious search for divine candidates finds a precedent in Horace's *Odes* 1.2, a lament of sorts. In that poem, Horace surveys a number of gods who might come to Rome's rescue (Hor. *Carm.* 1.2.25–40), before settling on Mercury–Caesar as the ultimate saviour of the Romans (1.2.41–52).

33 *Cynthius*: a common epithet of Apollo as the god of poetry. Cynthian Apollo tells Vergil / Tityrus to adhere to Callimachean poetic principles (cf. Verg. *Ecl.* 6.3–5) and inspires elegists with his art (cf. Prop. 2.34.80).

34 The *pastor* in question is Orpheus, whose Thracian origin is referenced with the phrase *Odrysio ... nemore* (cf. *Odrysius dux*, Val. Fl. 5.99; *Odrysius vates*, Stat. *Sil.* 5.1.203). Orpheus is the master poet–singer of classical antiquity; his role as a healer derives partly from the idea that the power of his song can soothe troubled souls and partly from his association with magic

(cf. Plin. *HN*. 30.7). For the linking of Apollo and Orpheus as healers, note especially Eur. *Alc*. 965-72: κρεῖσσον οὐδὲν Ἀνάγκας | ηὗρον οὐδέ τι φάρμακον | Θρήσσαις ἐν σανίσιν, τὰς | Ὀρφεία κατέγραψεν | γῆρυς, οὐδ' ὅσα Φοῖβος Ἀ- | σκληπιάδαις ἔδωκε | φάρμακα πολυπόνοις | ἀντιτεμὼν βροτοῖσιν ('I have found nothing that is stronger than Destiny, neither the medicine contained in the Thracian tablets that the voice of Orpheus has inscribed, nor the remedies that Apollo has given to the songs of Asclepius, to heal the manifold suffering of mortals').

35 *Acidaliis*: 'Acidalia' is a classical epithet of Venus, cf. *matris Acidaliae* (Verg. *Aen*. 1.720).

Venus aurea: cf. Ov. *Her*. 16.35, 291; *Met*. 1.277; Verg. *Aen*. 10.16.

36 *facilis . . . Amor*: cf. Prop. 1.9.23; also Tib. 1.3.57: *quod facilis tenero sum semper Amori* ('as I am always compliant with tender Love').

37-8 *iussistis* (38) makes clear that *qui* (37) refers to both Venus and Amor. *atris ignibus* (38), extremely rare in prose, is commonly used in poetry; cf. Verg. *Aen*. 4.384; Ov. *Fast*. 2.561; Luc. 3.98; Stat. *Theb*. 6.81. The quick sequence of *aestus* (37), *ignibus* (38) and *faces* (38) reminds readers of the intensity of Scaliger's fever (cf. *aestus*, 17; *ignibus*, 18).

39-40 Having flirted with the imagery of elegiac poetry in the previous two couplets (cf. *Venus aurea*, 35; *facilis . . . Amor*, 36), Scaliger now engages explicitly with trope of the fire of love (cf. e.g. Ov. *Met*. 7.9-18 [Medea]). The idea here is that it is inconceivable that Venus and Cupid, who usually inflame the elegist's passion, could have quelled Scaliger's feverish heat. Another layer of humour derives from the interplay between the metaphorical fires of love and fever, pitting the overdramatic psychological suffering of the *amator* against the physical agony brought on by an illness. *tanto . . . honore*: ablative of quality.

41 *Pholoes*: genitive of the Greek proper noun Pholoe, the name of Scaliger's lover (cf. *amicae* in the poem's original longer title). A certain Pholoe appears three times in Horace's *Odes* (*Carm*. 1.33.5-9, 2.5.17, 3.15.7); on the first two occasions she is a reluctant lover (cf. *asperam . . . Pholoen*, 1.33.6; *Pholoe fugax*, 2.5.17) – a quality that Scaliger's Pholoe appears to share, as *glacialia pectora* puns on emotional and real frost.

42 While there are not any direct allusions, the poem's final line evokes the trope whereby that which wounds also heals, as in the story of Telephus and the spear of Achilles (cf. Apollod. *Epit*. 3.17-20), which Ovid is particularly fond of (cf. *Met*. 12.112; *Trist*. 1.1.99-100, 2.19-20, 5.2.15-16).

6

Two Poems by Piero Vettori (1499–1585)

Agnese D'Angelo[1]

Introduction

Piero Vettori (1499–1585) was the most important Italian scholar of the sixteenth century, mainly known for his editions of classical authors and his miscellaneous work, the *Variarum lectionum libri*.[2] Unlike other scholars of his age, he never published his poetry, and one might think that he never indulged in such activity. Yet, some unpublished poems by Vettori are preserved in a manuscript held at the Bayerische Staatsbibliothek in Munich. Clm 750 is a miscellaneous manuscript, assembled in 1729 by one of Vettori's descendants, Francesco Vettori.[3] From fol. 129 onwards it contains a section entitled 'Versi latini e volgari di Piero Vettori'. The dozen Latin poems show significant differences in metre, themes and material aspects (handwriting, watermarks etc.), and they were probably not meant to be published as a collection. They might have been put together by Vettori's son, Iacopo, and later bound into the manuscript with other original materials by Francesco Vettori in the eighteenth century.[4] The two poems presented here were selected because of some shared features: they are both addressed to a friend, their theme is poetry, and they are in hendecasyllables. Essentially, they represent two different examples (more traditional for the first poem, with innovative elements in the second) of Catullan poetry in the sixteenth century.[5]

The first poem is addressed by Vettori to Pietro Carnesecchi (1508–67) as a token of gratitude for the gift of the latest literary work of their common friend, Marcantonio Flaminio (1498–1550).[6] Since Carnesecchi and Flaminio met in Naples in 1540, this date represents an obvious *terminus post quem* for this poem. The tone of the poem does not suggest that Flaminio was dead; therefore, it must have been written before 1550. It might be possible to take the dating of the poem further back: in lines 10–11 Vettori states that he appreciates the book of Flaminio because it often mentions Carnesecchi, and three poems are addressed to him by Flaminio in the anthology *Carmina quinque illustrium poetarum*, published in 1548.[7] In conclusion, Vettori probably wrote this poem between 1548 and 1550.

If much is known about the relationship between Carnesecchi and Flaminio, it is more difficult to reconstruct their friendship with Vettori.[8] It is not by chance that very little evidence remains of Vettori's fellowship with these scholars: both Flaminio and Carnesecchi were close to Reform movements, and the latter was sentenced to death and burnt for heresy by the Inquisition. Not everything concerning Flaminio was erased: Flaminio addressed a poem to Vettori, to congratulate him on his edition of Aristotle's *Rhetoric*,[9] and Vettori praised Flaminio as *optimus nostri temporis poeta* in his *Variarum lectionum libri XXV* (IX 9, p. 132). Yet, when in 1586 Francesco Vettori, Piero's nephew, published his correspondence,[10] he omitted a letter addressed to Cardinal Pole, in which the humanist mourned the death of Flaminio.[11] In all likelihood, an even worse *damnatio memoriae* might have occurred for any letter that mentioned the heretic Carnesecchi. The two were old friends, but, to my knowledge, no direct correspondence between them survives, whereas some letters from Flaminio to Vettori are preserved.[12] Therefore, this short poem represents an interesting witness to the relationship between the three humanists.

The poem embodies the characteristics of Catullan poetry in the Renaissance. Echoes and poetic devices from Catullus can be identified in every line, to the point that it can sound like a Catullan cento. It is not only the metre and the quotations that mark this poem as deeply Catullan: the very relationship between Vettori, Carnesecchi and Flaminio mirrors that of Catullus and his close friends. As Julia H. Gaisser pointed out: 'it was the Catullan manner, and the persona it represented, that made Catullus the natural model for the personal poetry of the Renaissance. The poets looked into his poems as into a mirror and saw the young Catullus, with his loves, his enemies, and his circle of fellow poets.... Thus, they wrote love poems in imitation of Catullus, but also poems about poetry and friendship.'[13] This was particularly true of Flaminio, who used Catullus as a standard for praise or blame,[14] and contemporary sources testify that Carnesecchi, too, wrote poetry.[15] In this short poem, then, Vettori recreated the world of Catullus and, at the same time, reproduced the dynamic of the scholarly circles of the Humanism that looked up to the Veronese poet as a literary model.

The second poem deploys more innovative features. Some elements are still strictly Catullan: the metre (hendecasyllables), the dedication to a friend (in this case anonymous), the reflections on poetry and some overt references. Yet, the poem on the whole reproduces qualities that can be traced back to the *recusatio-excusatio* of Augustan poets.[16] The first 11 lines contain a *praeteritio*:[17] Vettori states that, if only the Muses had granted him the poetic ability, he would gladly praise his friend, and then proceeds to list all his qualities. This device (claiming the impossibility to talk about something, and then doing it) is widely attested, for example, in Catullus and Horace.[18] The second and longer section of the poem contains the *recusatio-excusatio*. Vettori must face the grim reality: he is not a skilled poet, and the Muses do not love him. In doing so, he echoes programmatic poems from Horace, Propertius and Ovid. However, there is an interesting difference: while the classical poets used this *topos* in order to justify their choice of writing non-epic literature (be it odes, satires, elegies) Vettori does not indicate a poetic genre more suited to him.[19] On the contrary, he focuses only on his vain effort to succeed as a poet. Having no information on the addressee of this poem, it is not possible to determine how serious this declaration of modesty was. It is worth remembering, however, that Vettori (unlike the Augustan poets) obtained the support of the Medici through his activity as a teacher: he was no professional poet, and he seems to be well aware of it.

Finally, it should be noted that the two poems feature elements (both in vocabulary and content) that link back to Cicero's works. This is not surprising: among Latin authors, Cicero was undoubtedly the dearest to Vettori, who devoted most of his life to the study of the great orator's *opera*.[20]

Notes

1 I would like to express my gratitude to all those who took part in the workshop held in London on 28 June 2022 and to the editors of this volume for their suggestions, and especially to Professor Stephen Harrison for having shared with me his forthcoming work on vertical juxtaposition in Catullus.
2 For an account of Vettori's life, see Rüdiger 1896, Niccolai 1912, Mouren 2014 and Piras 2020.
3 On Vettori's library and Francesco's reorganization of it, see Mouren 2010.
4 I believe the first to gather these poems was Iacopo Vettori, and not Francesco, because the title of this section (*Versi latini e volgari di Piero Vettori*) is written in his handwriting. Only Iacopo's Greek handwriting has been studied (Mouren 2000: 438–9), but for his Latin hand see the *nota possessionis* in Munich, BSB, Res/A.gr.c. 147 and P.o.it. 18.
5 See Ludwig 1989; Gaisser 1993: 193–254; Parenti 2009.
6 For useful biographical notes, see Rotondò 1977 and Pastore 1997. Rüdiger 1896: 62 n. 2 defines this poem as 'Dankhendecasyllaben'.
7 The poems addressed to Carnesecchi are now edited in Flaminio 1993 (V 17, p. 157; V 31, p. 170; VI 35, p. 213). For Flaminio's poems see also Parenti 2020: 751ff.
8 Maddison 1965: *passim*.
9 Flaminio 1993: 161.
10 Vettori 1586.

11 Cesarini Martinelli 1983: 713. The letter had already been published, together with the answer by Cardinal Pole, in 1561; see Brutus 1561: 239–47.
12 See 'Appendice III' in Giannotti 1932. Carnesecchi, however, is mentioned in some letters addressed to Vettori in Bandini 1758–60. For more information about Vettori's relationship with the Reform movement, see Caponetto 1979, where unedited letters addressed to Vettori by Flaminio are mentioned, and Lo Re 2006.
13 Gaisser 1993: 193–4.
14 *Non sunt Flaminio malo poeta | digna carmina, sed tuo Catullo*; see Gaisser 1993: 195 and 379 n. 6.
15 Galluzzi 1822: 67.
16 See Wimmel 1960: *passim*; Hopkinson 1988: 98–101; Cameron 1995: 454–83.
17 On the difference between *recusatio-excusatio* (concerning the poetry) and *praeteritio* (concerning the theme) see Serrao 1995. *Praeteritio* is a typical apologetic technique according to Bundy 1972: 46–7; see also Cameron 1995: 455: 'Of course, in many cases, as with that other linked device the *praeteritio*, the act of refusal is itself the compliment.'
18 Perrotta 1972: 194.
19 Cameron 1995: 455: 'The *recusatio* is an apology by an author of erotic, sympotic or bucolic poetry for not writing in a higher style, in effect a variation on the affected modesty topos.'
20 Consider, for instance, the editions of Cicero's *Letters to Friends* discussed by Mouren 2009.

Bibliography

Bandini, A. M. (1758–60), *Clarorum Italorum et Germanorum epistolae ad Petrum Victorium senatorem Florentinum*, 2 vols, Florence.
Bargaeus, P. A. (1989–90), *Carmina: Carminum Appendix*, ed. Paola Gianfilippi de' Parenti, Tesi di laurea, Università degli studi di Padova.
Brutus, J. M., ed. (1561), *Epistolae clarorum virorum*, Lyon.
Bundy, E. L. (1972), 'The "Quarrel between Kallimachos and Apollonios" Part I: The Epilogue of Kallimachos's "Hymn to Apollo"', *California Studies in Classical Antiquity*, 5: 39–94.
Cameron, A. (1995), *Callimachus and His Critics*, Princeton.
Caponetto, S. (1979), *Aonio Paleario (1503–1570) e la riforma protestante in Toscana*, Torino.
Cardini, R. / Coppini, D., eds (2009), *Il rinnovamento umanistico della poesia. L'epigramma e l'elegia*, Florence.
Cesarini Martinelli, L. (1983), 'Pier Vettori e gli umanisti tedeschi', in: *Firenze e la Toscana dei Medici nell'Europa del Cinquecento: Atti del Convegno internazionale di studi (9–14 giugno 1980). Vol. II: Musica e spettacolo. Scienze dell'uomo e della natura*, 707–26, Florence.

Fitzgerald, W. (1996), *Catullan Provocations: Lyric Poetry and the Drama of Position*, Berkeley / Los Angeles / Oxford.
Flaminio, M. (1993), *Carmina: Testo e note a cura di Massimo Scorsone*, Turin.
Gaisser, J. H. (1993), *Catullus and His Renaissance Readers*, Oxford.
Galluzzi, R. (1822), *Storia del Granducato di Toscana di Riguccio Galluzzi istoriografo regio. Vol. III*, Florence.
Giannotti, D. (1932), *Lettere a P. V., pubblicate sopra gli originali del British Museum da R. Ridolfi e C. Roth, con un saggio illustrativo a cura di R. Ridolfi*, Florence.
Hardison, O. B. (1962), *The Enduring Monument: A Study of the Idea of Praise in Renaissance Literary Theory and Practice*, Chapel Hill.
Harrison, S. (forthcoming), 'Vertical juxtaposition in Catullus 64', *Paideia*.
Hopkinson, N. (1988), *A Hellenistic Anthology*, Cambridge.
Lo Re, S. (2006), 'Piero Vettori e la «natione todesca» a Siena: Irenismo e Inquisizione al tempo di Francesco de' Medici', *Bollettino della Società di Studi Valdesi*, CXXIII, n. 199: 51–92.
Ludwig, W. (1989), *Litterae Neolatinae: Schriften zur neulateinischen Literatur*, Munich.
Maddison, C. (1965), *Marcantonio Flaminio: Poet, Humanist and Reformer*, London.
McKeown, J. C. (1989), *Ovid: Amores. Volume II. A Commentary on Book One*, Leeds.
McKeown, J. C. (1998), *Ovid: Amores. Volume III. A Commentary on Book Two*, Leeds.
Mouren, R. (2000), 'L'identification d'écritures grecques dans un fonds humaniste: l'exemple de la bibliothèque de Piero Vettori', in: *I manoscritti greci tra riflessione e dibattito, atti del V° colloquio internazionale di paleografia greca (Cremona, 4–10 ottobre 1998)*, 433–41, Florence.
Mouren, R. (2009), 'Une longue polémique autour de Cicéron: Paolo Manuzio et Piero Vettori', in: Sordet 2009: 80–91.
Mouren, R. (2010), 'Quatre siècles d'histoire de la bibliothèque Vettori: entre vénération et valorisation', in: Wagner / Reed 2010: 241–67.
Mouren, R. (2014), *Biographie et éloges funèbres de Piero Vettori*, Paris.
Niccolai, F. (1912), *Pier Vettori*, Florence.
Parenti, G. (2009), 'La tradizione catulliana nella poesia latina del Cinquecento', in: Cardini / Coppini 2009: 63–100.
Parenti, G. (2020), *Poeti latini del Cinquecento. Vol. II*, Pisa.
Pastore, A. (1997), 'Flaminio, Marcantonio', *Dizionario Biografico degli Italiani* 48 (https://www.treccani.it/enciclopedia/marco-antonio-flaminio).
Perrotta, G. (1972), *Cesare, Catullo, Orazio e altri saggi*, Rome.
Piras, G. (2020), 'Vettori, Piero', *Enciclopedia Italiana* (https://www.treccani.it/enciclopedia/pietro-vettori_%28Enciclopedia-Italiana%29/).
Pontanus, I. I. (1978), *Hendecasyllaborum libri*, ed. L. Monti Sabia Naples
Rotondò, A. (1977), 'Carnesecchi, Pietro', *Dizionario Biografico degli Italiani*, 20. (https://www.treccani.it/enciclopedia/pietro-carnesecchi_%28Dizionario-Biografico%29/).

Rüdiger, W. (1896), *Petrus Victorius aus Florenz: Studien zu einem Lebensbilde*, Halle.

Serrao, G. (1995), 'All'origine della *recusatio-excusatio*: Teocrito e Callimaco', *Eikasmos*, 6: 141–52.

Sordet, Y., ed. (2009), *Passeurs de textes: Imprimeurs et libraires à l'âge de l'humanisme*, Turnhout.

Thomson, D. (1997), *Catullus: Edited with a Textual and Interpretative Commentary*, Toronto / Buffalo / London.

Vettori, P. (1586), *Petri Victorii epistolarum libri X, orationes XIIII, et liber de laudibus Ioannae Austriacae*, Florence.

Wagner, B. / Reed, M., eds (2010), *Early Modern Books as Material Objects*, Munich.

Wiltshire, S. F. (1977), 'Catullus Venustus', *CW*, 70: 319–26.

Wimmel, W. (1960), *Kallimachos in Rom: Die Nachfolge seines apologetischen Dichtens in der Augusteerzeit*, Wiesbaden.

Source of Latin text

A digital facsimile of ms. Clm 750 is available at the following link: https://www.digitale-sammlungen.de/en/view/bsb00125547?page=,1. The two poems can be found at fol. 143–4 [II] and 151 [I]. I believe that the handwriting of the main text is that of Iacopo, Vettori's son, while the corrections and adjustments were written by Vettori himself. Therefore, I have adopted these changes in the main text, as they represent the final version of the poems by their author. The footnotes give the readings that I have excluded and that can be considered authorial variants.

Latin text

[I] *Ad Petrum Carneseccam*

Iucundissime amice Carnesecca,
multis Flaminii tui libellum
de causis, lepidum ac perelegantem,
qui constat numeris Catullianis,
5 amavi, et merito in dies diesque
semper plus amo, nec capit meum cor
ulla unquam satias quiesve habendi
illum ipsum in manibus, teram ut fricemque
nolens aureolum sacrum libellum:
10 in quis[2] non minimum, tuum quod illic
nomen invenio frequens, amatum
meo a me ingenuo, pioque amore
supra cetera cuncta, quae unquam[3] amavi.
Sed quis tam lepidum bonum sodalem
15 non totis amet intimis medullis?
Ergo tu, salibus tuis venustus,[4]
non solum facis undique ipse ameris
verum ut qui ex animo te amant amarunt
magis nomine eo magisque amentur.

---

[2] First hand *queis*.
[3] First hand *olim*.
[4] First hand *venustis*.

English translation

[I] *To Pietro Carnesecchi*

Most genial friend Carnesecchi, for many different reasons I have loved the witty and most refined book composed in Catullan verse by your Flaminius. And, deservedly, I love it more day after day, and my heart never gets sated or tired of keeping it in my hands, to the point that I am unwillingly consuming and wearing down this precious and venerable book. One of these reasons, and not a small one, is that I often find your name in it, a name that I love with my pure and devoted love more than anything else I have ever loved. But who would not love with all his heart a friend so witty and fine? Therefore, charming and witty as you are, not only do you make yourself lovable in every way, but also you make those who love and loved you from the bottom of their heart be loved more and more on that account.

[II]

Si me diligerent novem Sorores
et ferrent[5] oculis, amice magne,
ut tu[6] commemoras (vides in uno
hoc qui non satis), omnibus relictis
5   rebus, ingenium tuum, decusque
mores ingenuos, salisque plenos,
virtutem eximiam, bonos parentes,
genus nobile, clara facta priscae
domus, ac merito probatae in omni
10 bonis tempore, niterer vocare
ad coelum numero gravi ac severo.
Atque haec materies foret profecto
illis viribus apta, quas foverent[7]
summo cum studio atque amore Musae.
15 Nunc, cum uix faciem pudicam earum
unquam (est quod grave) viderim misellus,
frustra ipsas rogo. Respuunt amantem
ignotum, utque aliquem procum impudentem,
pellunt: nec subitum, novumque vultum
20 fas sibi accipere in suum sacellum
putant. Inde igitur fugatus, ausim
nil magnum: mihi quod satis molestum
haud posse, ut cuperem exitum parare[8]
huic desiderio pio atque honesto,[9]
25 haesit quod mi animo diu ac vehementer.[10]
Tu vero (facilis tua ac benigna[11]
quae est natura[12]) volens mihi libensque
ignosces, minime illa dona danti
quae tibi dare cum ardeam, negantur
30 ab his, quae id tribuunt bonum atque donant.

---

[5] First hand *ferrentque in.*
[6] First hand *passim ut.*
[7] First hand *fovissent.* – The ending of this word was deleted, and only the first five letters are readable, but *fovissent* seems the most plausible variant.
[8] First hand *ad finem vocare.*
[9] First hand *hoc desiderium pium atque honestum.*
[10] First hand *vementer.*
[11] First hand *est comisque.*
[12] First hand *quae natura.*

[II]

If the nine sisters loved me and held me dear, my great friend, the way you say they do (and in this only do you lack judgment), I would lay aside all other occupations, and your talent and beauty, your noble character, full of wit, your distinguished virtue, your righteous parents, your noble birth, the illustrious deeds of your ancient house, deservedly respected by honest men in every age, all this I would strive to proclaim to the sky, in a grave and solemn metre. But this subject would surely be suitable for the forces of those that the Muses fostered with the greatest fervency and love. Now, since I have barely ever seen (miserable me!) their chaste appearance (which is hurtful), I call for them in vain. They turn down the unknown lover and reject him like some shameless suitor; and they do not consider it lawful to accept in their shrine a new, recently arrived face. So, chased away from there, I dare nothing great; and this ineptitude is quite painful for me, since I would like to fulfil this pure and honest desire, that has long and forcefully been fixed in my heart. But, since you are lenient and gracious by nature, you will gladly forgive me if I do not at all give you those gifts, although I burn to give you them, but they are refused by those who grant and bestow this good.

Commentary

[I] *Ad Petrum Carneseccam*

1 The very incipit of the poem reveals its model: *iucundissime* echoes Catullus 14.2 (*iucundissime Calve, munere isto*). It is not only the terminology that relies on Catullus 14, but also the theme: in both poems a book is given as a present to the author. While Catullus reproaches Calvus for his ironic gift (a collection of bad poems), Vettori sincerely admires Flaminio's poetry: it is possible to notice here, then, the first case of reversal of the model, a widespread feature in these two poems by Vettori. In one of the poems addressed to Carnesecchi Flaminio too echoed this line (5.17.14: *iucundissime Carnesece, abibo*).

2–3 *libellum* | ... *lepidum* recalls Catullus 1.1 (*cui dono lepidum novum libellum*), but Vettori separates the words over two lines and reverses their order, while preserving their original metrical positions. The abundant phrasing of l. 3 (*lepidum ac perelegantem*) might echo Catullus 6.2 (*ni sint illepidae atque inelegantes*). It is worth noting that here, again, the model is reversed from a negative to a positive sense. *Perelegans* is rare and only used in prose; Vettori probably remembered it from Cicero (e.g. *Pro Plancio* 58).

4 Hendecasyllables 'were so strongly associated with Catullus that they immediately identified their user as a Catullan' (Gaisser 1993: 195). *Numeris Catullianis* is used, in the same metrical position, by Bargeo (*carminum appendix* 1.20.26) and Pontano (*Hendecasyllaborum libri* 2.37.6).

5 Cf. Catullus 38.3: *in dies et horas*.

8 The line manifestly reproduces the ending of Catullus 23.22 (*quod tu si manibus teras fricesque*), but, once again, the model is completely reversed: in Catullus 23 the expression refers to Furius' faeces!

9 Another echo of Catullus 14 (14.12: *di magni, horribilem et sacrum libellum!*), combined with the *aureolus libellus* of Cicero, *Lucullus* 135. Once more, the quotation from Catullus expresses the opposite of Catullus' line.

11–19 For the polyptoton of *amo* cf. Catullus 8.5: *amata nobis, quantum amabitur nulla*. Both here and in lines 16–18 Vettori reproduces a stylistic feature, vertical juxtaposition, that is characteristic of Catullus' poems (see Harrison, forthcoming). Vettori in these lines employs vertical anaphora plus polyptoton (*amatum* | ... *amore* | ... *amavi* | ... *ameris* | ... *amarunt* | ... *amentur*; type

A in Harrison, forthcoming); we may compare other vertical juxtapositions in Catullus, e.g. Catullus 3.3-4 (final anaphora), 5.7-9 (final anaphora and rhyme), 9.10-11 (final polyptoton), and two cases of final anaphora and polyptoton (8.11-12 and 23.5-6).

12 For *ingenuus amor* cf. Horace, *Odes* 1.27.16. The other adjective, *pius*, is more frequently found with *amor*: e.g. Vergil, *Aen.* 5.296; Ovid, *Met.* 10.451.

15 Cf. Catullus 58.13: *omnibus medullis*; Ovid, *Met.* 9.484: *totis . . . medullis*.

16 'For Catullus . . . *venustas* is an expression of a way of life and, more importantly, of an aesthetic ideal for his poetry itself' (Wiltshire 1977: 319; cf. Fitzgerald 1996: 35, on *venustus*; 96, on *venustas*). *Venustus* is a keyword not only in Catullus, but also in the Neo-Latin poets that imitate him: Flaminio himself uses it twice for Carnesecchi (5.17.8 and 21).

17 Cf. Catullus 45.20: *mutuis animis amant amantur*. On vertical juxtaposition at line-end see note on ll. 11-19.

19 Cf. Catullus 29.11: *eone nomine, imperator unice*.

[II]

1 Cf. Martial 5.6.18 (*si novi dominum novem Sororum*), another poem in hendecasyllables. The idea that only those to whom the Muses grant their favour can succeed as poets is already in Hesiod, *Theog.* 81-4 ('Whomever among Zeus-nourished kings the daughters of great Zeus honor and behold when he is born, they pour sweet dew upon his tongue, and his words flow soothingly from his mouth'; trans. Most). The theme will be developed by Callimachus (e.g. *Aetia* 1, fr. 1 Pf., ll. 1-2: 'Often the Telchines mutter against me, against my poetry, | who, ignorant of the Muse, were not born as her friend' and ll. 37-8: '. . . for whomsoever the Muses did not look at askance as a child they will not reject as a friend when he is old'; trans. Harder), and, from its Hellenistic version, it will be incorporated into Augustan poetry (e.g. Horace, *Odes* 1.26.1: *Musis amicus*).

2 *In oculis ferre* means 'to cherish someone, to hold someone dear'. It is first attested in Terence (*Eun.* 401), but it is mainly found in Cicero's works (e.g. *Har. resp.* 48; *Tusc.* 2.63). Cicero is also the only author who, like Vettori here, uses the expression without the preposition *in* (*Ad familiares* 16.27.2; see *TLL* s.v. *oculus*, p. 447 col. 1).

5-10 In this short catalogue of virtues Vettori summarizes centuries of theory on personal praise. The first three lines (5-7) contain the so-called *notatio* that lists the 'goods of character' of the dedicatee, that is, his moral qualities. This was, at least according to Cicero, the only true form of praise (*De oratore* 2.342): *genus, forma, vires, opes, divitiae cetera quae fortuna det, aut extrinsecus aut corpori, non habent in se veram laudem, quae deberi virtuti uni putatur* ('Family, good looks, bodily strength, resources, riches and the rest of the external or personal gifts of fortune do not in themselves contain any true ground for praise, which is held to be due to virtue alone'; trans. Sutton). Yet Cicero goes on to concede that also the 'goods of nature and fortune' should be included in the praise, as they allow true virtue to reveal itself: *sed tamen, quod ipsa virtus in earum rerum usu et moderatione maxime cernitur, tractanda in laudationibus etiam haec sunt naturae et fortunae bona* ('but nevertheless, as it is in the employment and wise management of these that virtue itself is very largely discerned, a panegyric must also treat of these goods of nature and of fortune'; trans. Sutton). Compare the listing of Lollius' virtues by Horace (*Odes* 4.9.35-44). The following lines (7-10) employ the topics of *effictio*, the listing of the 'goods of nature and fortune', which include praise of nation, family and birth (see Hardison 1962: *passim*; for a discussion of *effictio* and *notatio* see 30ff.). It might be worth noting that, while the *notatio* usually included the narration of the deeds of the praised person, Vettori celebrates exclusively the *clara facta priscae | domus* (ll. 8-9).

10-11 Vettori combines different sources. Like Catullus with Flavius in 6.17 (*ad caelum lepido vocare versu*), the humanist wishes to honour his friend, but Catullus' *lepidus versus* becomes a *numerus gravis ac severus*. This expression echoes the famous *recusatio* of Ovid, *Am.* 1.1.1-2 (*arma gravi numero violentaque bella parabam | edere*) and the *incipit* of Martial's epigram 1.35 (1.35.1-3: *versus scribere me parum severos | nec quos praelegat in schola magister, | Corneli, quereris*), two poems that contain a refusal of serious poetry.

12-14 In these few lines Vettori accumulates many keywords from *recusatio* poems of the Augustan age. The first is *materia/materies*: although it is found predominantly in prose, the word occurs frequently in Ovid, who uses it twice in the programmatic first elegy of the *Amores* (1.1.2: *materia conveniente modis*; 1.1.19: *nec mihi materia est numeris levioribus apta*; cf. McKeown 1989: 13). In referring to the poet's lack of ability (mainly to justify the refusal of epic poetry), *vires* is used by Horace (*Satires* 2.1.12-13: *cupidum, pater optime, vires | deficiunt*), Propertius (2.10.5-6: *quod si deficiant vires audacia certe | laus erit* and 2.10.11-12: *iam, carmine, sumite vires, | Pierides, magni nunc erit oris opus!*), Ovid (*Epistulae ex Ponto* 3.4.79: *ut desint vires, tamen est laudanda voluntas*). *Aptus* has the technical meaning of 'as befits the proprieties of the genre' (McKeown 1998: 375), and in this sense it is a characteristic word of *recusatio* poems: see Ovid (*Am.* 1.1.19; 2.1.4: *non estis teneris apta theatra modis*; 2.17.21-22: *carminis hoc ipsum genus inpar; sed tamen apte | iungitur herous cum breviore modo*) and Propertius (3.9.7: *omnia non pariter rerum sunt omnibus apta*).

17-18 For the idea of the direct and privileged relationship between the Muses and the poets, see note on ll. 1-2. In these lines another traditional image is added: that of the Muses allowing into their presence only those who they cherish. In Latin literature the first to employ it was Ennius (*Annales* 208 Sk.: *neque Musarum scopulos*), ironically reversed by Catullus in poem 105, where the Muses defend the Pimpleian mountain from Mentula and his literary pretensions (see Thomson 1997: 541-2). Another relevant parallel is Propertius 3.1, with the poet asking Callimachus and Philetas to allow him to join them in their sacred grove (3.1.1-2: *Callimachi Manes et Coi sacra Philitae, | in vestrum, quaeso, me sinite ire nemus*). But, unlike the classical poets, Vettori is rejected by the Muses. This allows the humanist to introduce a new image. *Procum impudentem* (l. 18) depends on Cicero's *Brutus* (330): *nos autem, Brute, quoniam post Hortensi clarissimi oratoris mortem orbae eloquentiae quasi tutores relicti sumus, domi teneamus eam saeptam liberali custodia et hos ignotos atque* **impudentes procos** *repudiemus tueamurque ut adultam virginem caste et ab amatorum impetu quantum possumus prohibeamus* ('As for us, Brutus, since with the death of Hortensius we are left to be the guardians of orphaned eloquence, let us keep her within our own walls, protected by a custody worthy of her liberal lineage. Let us repel the pretensions of these upstart and impudent suitors, and guard her purity, like that of a virgin grown to womanhood, and, so far as we can, shield her from the advances of rash admirers'; trans. Hendrickson). With this simile, eloquence is compared to a young girl, orphaned after Hortensius' death, and Cicero must be her guardian and repel the advances of unworthy wooers. In Vettori's poem, too, the Muses, like young girls, flee from an unworthy lover; this unworthy suitor, however, is the humanist himself. Vettori, in depicting himself as an incompetent poet, reverses these traditional images in a new and effective picture.

23 *Cupidus* is used by Horace to express the opposition between the desire to write epic poetry and the ability to realize it in *Sat.* 2.1 (2.1.12-13: *cupidum, ... vires | deficient*).

28-30 Poetical ability as a gift of the Muses appears already in Homer (*Od.* 8.64), Hesiod (*Theog.* 30-2) and Archilochus (fr. 1.2). For Latin poets see, e.g.,

Horace (*Epist.* 2.1.243: *ad libros et ad haec Musarum dona vocares*) and Propertius (3.3.33–4: *diverseque novem sortitae iura Puellae | exercent teneras in sua dona manus*). For the impossibility of writing good poems without the Muses' approval, in addition to what is noted above on ll. 1–2 and 12–14, see also Horace, *Odes* 1.6.10 (*Musa potens vetat*).

7

Jean Dorat (1508–1588): The Latin Lyrics of a Greek Professor

Stephen J. Harrison

Introduction

Jean Dorat or Daurat (Johannes Auratus, 1508–88) was born as Joan Dinemand near Limoges to a family of minor nobility.¹ After study at the Collège de Limoges he came to Paris, where he was tutor to the pages of François I and (from 1547) principal of the Collège de Coqueret, associated with the University of Paris. There he was teacher and mentor to a group of young poets that included Jean-Antoine de Baïf, Pierre de Ronsard, Rémy Belleau, Pontus de Tyard and Joachim du Bellay; with Dorat and the later addition of the dramatist Étienne Jodelle, they numbered seven and named themselves La Pléiade, in emulation of the similar group of seven Greek poets of Hellenistic Alexandria.² Most of them produced works of verse in French that were versions or adaptations of classical texts, by which they hoped to rival the achievements of Petrarch and his successors in Italy. Dorat became *poeta et interpres* ('poet and translator/interpreter') to Henri II and professor of Greek (1556–67) at the Collège Royal (the future Collège de France), where he was a colleague of the great scholars Denis Lambin and Adrien Turnèbe, and lectured on a wide range of Greek poets from Homer to the Hellenistic period.³

His main scholarly publication was an edition of Aeschylus' *Prometheus Bound* (Dorat 1548), a reprint for his students of the Aldine *editio princeps* of 1518 with his own corrections and conjectures. This made significant contributions to the text and was the first edition of any play of Aeschylus published in France.⁴ Modern scholars have drawn attention to his further conjectures and interpretations published in the work of his contemporaries and students, covering all three great Greek tragedians;⁵ and recent research has also revealed more about his influential teaching, which presented allegorical and moral interpretations of Greek texts, especially Homer.⁶ In later life, apart from many occasional poems, he published a propagandistic prose work justifying the St Bartholomew's Day Massacre of Protestants (Dorat 1576); in his last years, his pupils put together an extensive collection of his poetry in both Greek and Latin (Dorat 1586).⁷

This contribution presents three items from his extensive output, all lyric; the first and second are selected parts of longer poems. The first is an ode that celebrates a spring near Paris in imitation of Horace's poem to the *fons Bandusiae* (*Odes* 3.13); the second is an ode that adapts the opening of Pindar's *Olympian 2* for the celebration of Dorat's most distinguished student, Pierre de Ronsard, using the Greek poem's original metre; and the third is another Horatian ode (in Alcaics) to a major military and political figure of the time – François, Duc de Guise – which uses elements from Horace's political odes.

Notes

1 For his life and career see Demerson 1983, Demay 1996 and de Buzon and Girot 2002.
2 On the Greek Pleiad (named after the constellation of seven 'sister' stars) and its uncertain membership, see Fantuzzi and Hunter 2004: 434–5. On the French group see Chamard 1939–63.
3 See Pfeiffer 1976: 102–7.
4 See Mund-Dopchie 1979, Gruys 1981: 22–30 and the work of Matteo Taufer (Taufer 2006a, 2006b, 2011). Dorat's future colleague Turnèbe was to produce an edition of the whole of Aeschylus in 1552.
5 See Avezzù 2021 (Euripides); Taufer 2008 (Sophocles).
6 See Pfeiffer 1976: 102–6, Ford 1995 and 2000, and Bizer 2011: 59–80.
7 For a modern verse translation of selected poems of Dorat into English see Slavitt 2000.

Bibliography

Avezzù, G. (2021), 'Dalla scuola di Jean Dorat: annotazioni rinascimentali inedite all'«Elettra» di Euripide', *Eikasmos*, 32: 315–30.
Bizer, M. (2011), *Homer and the Politics of Authority in Renaissance France*, New York / Oxford.
Blänsdorf, J. (1993), 'Aspekte eines poetischen Themas in der neulateinischen Dichtung Italiens und Frankreichs', in: J. Blänsdorf / D. Janik / E. Schäfer (eds), *Bandusia: Quelle und Brunnen in der lateinischen, italienischen, französischen und deutschen Dichtung der Renaissance*, 1–72, Berlin / Boston.
Carroll, S. (2009), *Martyrs and Murderers: The Guise Family and the Making of Europe*, New York / Oxford.
Charmard, H. (1939–63), *Histoire de la Pléiade*, 4 vols, Paris.
de Buzon, C. / Girot, J. E., eds (2002), *Jean Dorat: Poète humaniste de la renaissance*, Geneva.

Demay, H. (1996), *Jean Dorat (1508-1588): 'L'Homère du Limousin', âme de la Pléiade, et poète des rois*, Paris.
Demerson, G. (1979a), *Jean Dorat: Les Odes latines*, Clermont-Ferrand.
Demerson, G. (1979b), 'L'ode pindarique latine en France au xvième siècle', in: P. Tuynman / G. G. Kuiper / E. Keßler (eds), *Acta Conventus Neo-Latini Amstelodamensis*, 285-305, Munich.
Demerson, G. (1983), *Dorat en son temps, culture classique et présence au monde*, Clermont-Ferrand.
Demerson-Barthelot, G. (1974), 'L'attitude religieuse de Dorat', *Humanistica Lovaniensia*, 23: 145-87.
Desguine, A. (1936), 'Arcueil et les écrivains du xvie siècle', *Le Vieil Arcueil*, 26: 225-30.
Desguine, A. (1948), *Au sujet de l'aqueduc romain de Lutèce dit d'Arcueil-Cachan*, Paris.
Dorat, J. (1548), *Aeschylus: Promētheus desmōtēs. Prometheus Vinctus*, Paris.
Dorat, J. (1576), *Ad belli ciuilis auctores et eorum socios*, Paris.
Dorat, J. (1586), *Poematia*, Paris.
Fantuzzi, M. / Hunter, R. (2004), *Tradition and Innovation in Hellenistic Poetry*, Cambridge.
Ford, P. (1995), 'Jean Dorat and the Reception of Homer in Renaissance France', *International Journal of the Classical Tradition*, 2: 265-74.
Ford, P. (2000), *Jean Dorat: Mythologicum, ou, Interprétation allégorique de l'Odyssée, X-XII et de L'hymne à Aphrodite*, Geneva.
Gherardi, P., ed. (1572), *In foedus et victoriam contra Turcas iuxta sinum Corinthiacum Non. Octob. 1571 partam poemata uaria*, Venice.
Girot, J. E. (2002), *Pindare avant Ronsard*, Geneva.
Gruys, J. A. (1981), *The Early Printed Editions (1518-1664) of Aeschylus*, Nieuwkoop.
Guillon, R. (1548), *De generibus carminum Graecorum*, Paris.
Lampridio, B. / Amalteo, G. B. (1550), *Carmina*, Venice.
Lauvergnat-Gagnière, C. (1988), *Lucien de Samosate et le lucianisme en France au XVIe siècle: athéisme et polémique*, Geneva.
Mayer, C.-A. (1984), *Lucien de Samosate et la Renaissance française*, Geneva.
Mund-Dopchie, M. (1976), 'Le premier travail français sur Eschyle, le *Prométhée enchaîné* de Jean Dorat', *Les lettres romanes*, 30: 262-74.
Pfeiffer, R. (1976), *History of Classical Scholarship from 1300 to 1850*, Oxford.
Schmitz, T. (1993), *Pindar in der französischen Renaissance: Studien zu seiner Rezeption in Philologie, Dichtungstheorie und Dichtung*, Göttingen.
Simonin, M. (1990), *Pierre de Ronsard*, Paris.
Slavitt, D. R. (2002), *The Latin Odes of Jean Dorat*, Washington.
Taufer, M. (2006a), *Jean Dorat, editore e interprete di Eschilo*, Amsterdam.
Taufer, M. (2006b), 'L'Eschilo di Jean Dorat', *Lexis*, 24: 361-79.
Taufer, M. (2006c), '«Marginalia» eschilei di Jean Dorat: otto emendamenti all'«Orestea»', in: G. Avezzù / P. Scattolin (eds), *I classici greci e i loro commentatori*, 181-99, Rovereto.

Taufer, M. (2008), 'Congetture di Jean Dorat al «Filottete»', in: G. Avezzù (ed.), *Didaskaliai II: Nuovi studi sulla tradizione e l'interpretazione del dramma attico*, 187–218, Verona.

Taufer, M. (2011), 'Il «Prometheus Vinctus» di Jean Dorat: qualche stravaganza congetturale', *Ítaca*, 27: 103–9.

Source of Latin text

The edition of Demerson 1979a, with occasional modification of punctuation and orthography, and her numeration of these poems have been used.[1]

---

[1] I print one conjecture of my own, *si* for *seu* in Ode 4.29 (see commentary there).

Latin text

Text 1: Ode 3 – to the Spring of Arcueil

This poem derives from a walk taken in summer 1549 by Dorat and his students (including Ronsard, who wrote a French poem 'Les Bacchanales' about the same occasion)[2] to Arceuil, then outside Paris, but now in a southern suburb of the city some 5 km from the centre.[3] There they picnicked beside a clear spring, connected with the remains of a Roman aqueduct, which had earlier supplied Paris.[4] The full ode contains eighteen stanzas (72 lines), of which the first seven are presented here. The poem begins with a line that recalls the opening line of Horace, *Odes* 3.13, drawing a parallel with the Horatian spring of Bandusia, and contains a number of allusions to that famous ode.[5] Its asclepiadic metre is Horatian and close to (though not identical with) that of *Odes* 3.13.[6]

Metre: First Asclepiad

O Fons Arculii sydere purior,
Aestum marmoreo frigore qui domas,
Quamvis arua furens Erigones canis
    Lentis excoquat ignibus,
5 Seu tu nomen habes arcubus a tuis,
Quorum reliquiae semirutae patent
Moles, quae geminis nunc quoque cornibus
    Incumbunt geminae tibi:
Magni forsan opus regis apostatae,
10 Qui, missus Latii finibus aduena,
Sedes hic posuit, iugera Gallici
    Princeps multa tenens soli.

---

[2] Conveniently quoted by Blänsdorf 1993: 59–63. Other poetic students of Dorat also wrote about the aqueduct and its surroundings: see Desguine 1936.
[3] Demerson 1979a: 273.
[4] See Desguine 1948 for a full account.
[5] See Blänsdorf 1993: 59–63.
[6] 3.13 is written in the Third Asclepiad; Dorat's poem uses the related Second Asclepiad, found e.g. in Horace, *Odes* 1.6.

English translation

O spring of Arcueil, clearer than a star,
You who tame the heat with your marble chill,
Though the raging Dog of Erigone
Roasts the fields with its slow fires,

   Whether you take your name from your arches,   5
Whose remains lie open to view as crumbling masses,
Which still as a pair lean over you
With their pair of horns:

   Perhaps the work of the great apostate ruler,
Who, sent as an incomer from the bounds of Latium,   10
Set his dwelling here, an emperor possessing
Many acres of Gallic soil,

Seu fors grata tibi causa uetustior
　　　Huius nominis est, atque libentius
15　Audis Herculis fons, et ouans tui
　　　　　Crescis laudibus Herculis.

　　　Nam fama est et in haec clauigerum loca
　　　Aduenisse patrem, sive tricorporis
　　　Cum monstri domitor gente ab Iberica
20　　　Victorem retulit pedem,

　　　Seu tunc Hesperidum cum decus auferens
　　　Sylvis ac pretium, ditibus aurei
　　　Mali ponderibus tardus, Atlanticis
　　　　　Vix undis caput extulit.

25　Hinc Grais etiam Gallicus Hercules
　　　Notus, cuius erat forma catenula,
　　　Aures quae traheret pensilis aurea
　　　　　Vulgi, orator et eloquens.

Or whether a fortunate chance is an older cause
Of this name of yours, and you are happier
To be called the spring of Hercules, and glorying 15
You grow with the praise of your own Hercules.

For the story goes that the club-bearing father
Came even to this location, whether when as tamer
Of the triple-bodied monster he made his victorious return
From the people of Iberia, 20

Or on that occasion when, bearing away his glory and reward
From the forest of the Hesperides, slowed by the rich weights
Of the golden fruit, he was barely able to project his head
From the waves of the Atlantic.

Thus was the Gallic Hercules known also to the Greeks, 25
Whose emblem was a miniature chain,
Which, hanging down in gold, could direct the ears of the crowd,
And who was an eloquent speaker.

Commentary

1–8 The poet's initial address to the spring recalls in phrasing and metre the opening line of Horace, *Odes* 3.13: *o fons Bandusiae splendidior uitro*; the theme of the water's cooling effect in the heat of the Dog-Star (2–4) is also drawn from that poem (3.13.9–12: *te flagrantis atrox hora Caniculae | nescit tangere, tu frigus amabile | fessis vomere tauris | praebes et pecori vago*).

2 *marmoreo* suggests that the spring flowed through one of the marble conduits linked to the aqueduct.[7]

3–4 *Erigones canis* recalls Columella 10.1.400: *canis Erigones* (the Athenian princess Erigone was the mythical owner of the dog Maera catasterised in the Dog-Star – for her story see Hyginus, *Fabulae* 130); *furens* puns on raging heat (cf. Horace, *Odes* 3.29.18) and rabid dog, while *lentis excoquat ignibus* recalls Horace, *Odes* 1.13.8: *quam lentis penitus macerer ignibus*.

5–8 The initial *seu tu* of line 5 looks back to Horace's address to the wine-jar in *Odes* 3.21.2: *seu tu*; the etymological speculation of *seu … seu* (here first suggesting the derivation Arceuil/*arcus*) recalls the poetic antiquarianism of Propertius (4.2.9–12) and Ovid (*Fasti* 2.479–80), but is also in the donnish manner of Dorat himself.[8] Lines 5–8 describe the remains of the Roman aqueduct at Arceuil;[9] for *tu nomen habes* cf. Martial 4.31.5: *sed tu nomen habes*, for *semirutae … moles* cf. Mantuan, *De calamitatibus temporum* 1.709: *semirutae moles*. The 'twin horns' over the spring seem to describe the shape of a now incomplete arch of the ruined aqueduct.

9–16 The learned poet first suggests that the aqueduct might have been the work of the future Roman emperor Julian the Apostate (331–63, emperor 361–3) during his governorship of Gaul in 355–60, when he was at least once quartered in Paris (Ammianus 20.4.1); Dorat may have read some of Julian's works.[10] For 9 *magni … opus regis* cf. *Elegiae in Maecenatem* 2.150: *et magnum magni Caesaris illud opus*, for 10 *finibus aduena* cf. *Dirae* 80: *nostris in finibus advena*, for 11 *sedes … posuit* cf. Silius 12.361: *sedes posuere* and for 11–12 *iugera Gallici … multa … soli* cf. Tibullus 1.1.2: *culti iugera multa soli*. The second suggestion of Arceuil's derivation of its name from Hercules (13–16)

---

[7] For plans and images of these see Desguine 1948.
[8] See Demerson 1983: 206.
[9] Described a generation later (1585–6) in the *Diarium* of the Dutch antiquarian Aernout van Buchel, citing Dorat's poem: see http://www.romanaqueducts.info/aquasite/parijsdiarium.html for his text, and Desguine 1948: 37 for his sketches.
[10] As suggested by Demerson-Barthelot 1974: 155. The aqueduct is likely to date from before Julian: see Desguine 1948: 15–17.

points to another distinguished and even earlier visitor, and it might reflect the self-presentation of the French Valois kings as Hercules, common to François I, Henri II and Charles IX.[11] For 14–15 *libentius audis* (where *audis* = Greek *klueis*, 'are spoken of as') cf. Horace, *Satires* 2.6.20: *seu Iane libentius audis*, and for 16 *crescis laudibus* cf. Horace, *Odes* 3.30.7–8: *usque ego postera | crescam laude recens*. Note the vertical juxtaposition of rhyming noun and epithet at line-end in both 11–12 and 15–16, an Horatian ornamental word-order.[12]

17–28 These three stanzas combine two of Hercules' traditional labours in the course of which he might have passed through France on his return journey to Greece (that of overcoming the triple-bodied Geryon in Spain and that of gaining the apples of the Hesperides in the far West) with the somewhat whimsical and older 'Celtic' version of the hero (see below); the last too is local and relevant for a French readership. 17 *fama est* is a Vergilian formula for referring to a previous source (*Aen.* 3.578), very fitting here with this triple allusion. 18 *sive* (followed by *seu* at 21) presents another pair of antiquarian variants, while 17 *claviger* is an Ovidian epithet for Hercules (*Met.* 15.284), and 18 *pater* is used of him by Propertius (4.9.71). 18–19 *tricorporis ... monstri* recalls Silius 13.201: *monstrum Geryones immane tricorporis irae*. The two labours of Hercules as described here look back to major classical Latin texts: 19–20 echo Vergil's summary of the Geryon episode at *Aen.*8.202–3: *tergemini nece Geryonae spoliisque superbus | Alcides aderat ... victor* (the personification of 20 *victorem ... pedem* also recalls Ovid, *Fasti* 4.858: *victorem terris impositura pedem*), while the account of the apples of the Hesperides in 21–4 draws on Lucan's version at 9.360–6: *syluis* and *aurei/mali* pick up 9.360 *aurea silva*, while *ditibus* recalls 9.361 *divitiisque* and *auferens* and *pretium* pick up 9.365 *abstulit ... pretium* (note how the assonating and metrically equivalent *auferens* and *aurei* are vertically juxtaposed at line-end). Dorat adds the amusing picture of Hercules walking through the sea with only his head above the waves, weighed down by the apples of gold: 24 *undis caput extulit* recalls Vergil, *Georg.* 4.352: *caput extulit unda* (of a water-nymph). 25–28 look specifically and in detail to the Greek writer (*Grais ... notus*) Lucian's comic depiction (at *Herakles* 3) of Herakles Ogmios, the Celtic Hercules, who attracts men to follow him by his entrancing eloquence (cf. *orator et eloquens*): 'That old Heracles of theirs drags after him

---

[11] See Blänsdorf 1993: 61. The late François I was depicted as the Gallic Hercules (with an allusion to Lucian, see on 17–28) on a celebratory arch in Henri II's entry into Paris in June 1549, a very recent event that Dorat may be recalling (see https://essentiels.bnf.fr/fr/image/1d8315e7-7c1d-48cf-b7c0-a80fb8c3ae66-francois-ier-hercule-gaulois).

[12] Cf. e.g. *Odes* 1.2.13–15: *vidimus flavum Tiberim retortis | litore Etrusco violenter undis | ire*, 1.6.17–19: *nos convivia, nos proelia virginum | sectis in iuvenes unguibus acrium | cantamus*.

a great crowd of men who are all tethered by the ears! His leashes are delicate chains fashioned of gold and amber, resembling the prettiest of necklaces...' (ὁ γὰρ δὴ γέρων Ἡρακλῆς ἐκεῖνος ἀνθρώπων πάμπολύ τι πλῆθος [cf. *uulgi*] ἕλκει [cf. *traheret*] ἐκ τῶν ὤτων [cf. *aures*] ἅπαντας δεδεμένους. δεσμὰ δέ εἰσιν οἱ σειραὶ [cf. *catenula*] λεπταὶ χρυσοῦ [cf. *aurea*] καὶ ἠλέκτρου εἰργασμέναι ὅρμοις ἐοικυῖαι τοῖς καλλίστοις). Lucian was a favourite Greek author of the French Renaissance,[13] and the Gallic Hercules was highlighted by Dorat's former pupil Du Bellay in the conclusion of *La Défense et Illustration de la langue française*, the Pléiade manifesto of 1549, as a justification for the group's proclamation of a new classicism for French literature. The non-classical diminutive *catenula* (26) is found at Maffeo Vegio, *disticha* 1. 84; for *aures* ... *uulgi* (27–8) cf. Horace, *Odes* 2.13.32: *bibit aure uulgus*, and note how the assonating *aures* and *aurea* are neatly balanced at the start and end of the same line.

---

[13] See e.g. Mayer 1984 and Lauvergnat-Gagnière 1988.

Text 2: Ode 4 – to Pierre de Ronsard

This technically brilliant poem of around 1550 is addressed to Dorat's former pupil and fellow Pléiade member Pierre de Ronsard (1524–85), the leading poet of the French Renaissance. It responds explicitly (8–15) to Ronsard's French odes imitating the Greek lyric poet Pindar in his first collection *Quatre livres des Odes* (1550). Dorat's Latin poem is much more closely related to Pindar than Ronsard's work, suiting his expertise as a scholar of Greek poetry;[14] it also surely reacts to the appearance in the same year of the Italian Benedetto Lampridio's *tour de force* Latin renderings of Pindar, using the complex original Greek lyric metres.[15] Dorat's ode begins with a close translation of the opening of *Olympian* 2, and his poem (142 lines in full) closely replicates that poem's metre and triadic structure, with identical strophe and antistrophe followed by an epode; Dorat has four triadic systems where the original has five. Only the first triad of Dorat's poem is presented here.

In accordance with the understanding of Pindaric metre of his own time (preserved for us in Guillon's 1548 analysis),[16] Dorat's lines are sometimes shorter than those printed in modern texts of Pindar,[17] and as a result he allows (e.g. in lines 12–14) the splitting of words across two metrical units that are in fact a single unit. This splitting is familiar from the Sapphic lyrics of Horace (*Odes* 1.2.19–20), Catullus (e.g. 11.11–12) and Sappho herself (e.g. 31.7–8 V.), but is not practised by Pindaric lyric. The *Odes* of Horace, a natural resource for Latin lyric, are an important intermediary for the language of the poem.

Metre: paeonic (identical with Pindar, *Olympian* 2)

---

[14] See Schmitz 1993: 16. For the fashionability of Pindaric versions in French poetry of this period see Demerson 1979b, Schmitz 1993: 16–26 and Girot 2002. Ronsard's Pindarising in the 1550 collection was largely limited to using triadic structures in the praise of great men.
[15] Lampridio 1550. Cf. Schmitz 1993: 24–5.
[16] Guillon 1548: 10–38 has a complete metrical analysis of the Olympians.
[17] For an analysis of Dorat's metrical scheme cf. Demerson 1979: 280; for a modern analysis of the metrical scheme of *Olympian* 2 cf. Willcock 1995: 140–2.

Latin text

Lyrae potentes Camoenae,	Strophe
Agite, quis deum herosve	
Homo quis fidibus inseri	
Poscit? Satis Pisa iam	
5 Iovisque memoratus	
Olympus, sacrum et	
Herculis patris opus:	
At nunc patriae principem	
Chelys, apud Celticos	
10 Decus grande populos,	
Decet nos suo	
Sibi Pindari can-	
tu personare, numeros-	
que Gallicos Latiis	

15 Remunerari haud inultos.	Antistrophe
Itaque par pari reddens,	
Nova plectra resequar nouis:	
Clauumque clauo uelut	
Retundam ego reperta	
20 Meis Italis	
Patria indigenaque,	
Ronsarde, tua: o flos virum, et	
Decus olivi, aut illius	
Virilis, quo oblinitur	
25 Et artus terit	
Amyclaea pubes,	
Aut illius, quod hilares	
Fere Camoenae obolent.	

Nam si quis artem sinuosaque	Epode
30 Corporis uolumina uolet	
(Quibus corpus apte	
Vel in equum, vel de equo	
Volans micat in audacibus	
Pugnis), stupebit dicatum gravibus umbris	
35 Musarum, agilibus quoque	
Saltibus Martis expedisse membra.	

English translation

Muses who rule over the lyre,
Come, which god or hero,
Which man demands to be introduced
Into your strings? Already Pisa and the Olympus
Of Zeus are sufficiently commemorated,   5
And the holy work
Of father Hercules:
But now it is the prince
Of the native lyre, the mighty ornament
Among the Celtic peoples   10
That we should make
Resound to himself
In the song of his own Pindar,
And by my Latin metres

Repay his French ones with full requital.   15
And so, rendering like for like,
I will follow his new measures with new ones:
And like a nail with a nail
Hammer out your native
And indigenous creations,   20
Ronsard, by my Italian ones:
O flower of men, and
Ornament of the olive oil,
Both of that manly kind
With which is smeared and rubs its limbs   25
The youth of Sparta,
And of that kind with which
The joyful Muses are generally scented.

For if someone will wish for the skill
Of the flexible turnings of the body   30
(By which the body can fittingly
Fly to horse or from horse,
Flashing out in the boldness of battle),
He will be stunned that one who is dedicated
To the sober shade of the Muses has also   35
Freed his limbs in the agile leapings of Mars.

Commentary

1–7 A close rendering in the same metre of Pindar, *Olympian* 2.1–4: ἀναξιφόρμιγγες ὕμνοι, | τίνα θεόν, τίν' ἥρωα, τίνα δ' ἄνδρα κελαδήσομεν; | ἤτοι Πίσα μὲν Διός· Ὀλυμπιάδα δ' ἔστασεν Ἡρακλέης | ἀκρόθινα πολέμου·, 'Hymns that rule the lyre, what god, what hero, and what man shall we celebrate? Indeed, Pisa belongs to Zeus, while Heracles established the Olympic festival as the firstfruits of war'. Dorat uses Horace's imitation of the same opening at *Odes* 1.12.1–3: *quem virum aut heroa lyra vel acri | tibia sumis celebrare, Clio? | quem deum?* For 1 *lyrae potentes Camoenae* cf. *Odes* 1.6.10: *lyrae Musa potens*; for 7 *Herculis patris* see on 3.18 above, for 8 *patriae principem* cf. Manilius 1.7: *patriae princepsque paterque*.

8–14 The poem turns to addressing Ronsard, fittingly echoing Horace's self-description as the national lyric poet at *Odes* 4.3.23: *Romanae fidicen lyrae* in *patriae principem | Chelys*; 10 *Decus grande* recalls Horace's description of Maecenas at *Odes* 2.17.4: *grande decus* (note the jingling *decus* and *decet* in line-initial vertical juxtaposition)[18] while the juxtaposition of *Gallicos Latiis* elegantly suggests how Dorat's Latin poem is a response to Ronsard's French versions of Pindar (see above).

15–28 The address to Ronsard continues. 15 *haud inultos* ('with full requital'; the litotes recalls comic language – Plautus, *Men.* 521, Terence, *HT* 918) is ironic, suggesting that Dorat's poem is reciprocal 'revenge' for Ronsard's collection. Note the triple paired polyptotons 16 *par pari* (colloquial, 4 x in Plautus), 17 *nova . . . novis* (neatly set at either end of the line) and 18 *clavum . . . clavo* (homely and proverbial, cf. Cicero, *Tusc.* 4.75); for 17 *nova plectra* of a new style of poetry, pointing to Ronsard's then innovative Pindarism, cf. Statius, *Silvae* 1.2.2, while 19–20 *reperta* and *Italis* in a context of poetic cultural exchange recall Lucretius 1.136–7: *nec me animi fallit Graiorum obscura reperta | difficile inlustrare Latinis versibus esse*; for the laudatory terms 22 *flos virum* and 23 *decus olivi* cf. Verg. *Aen.* 8.500: *flos veterum virtusque virum* and Catullus 63.64: *decus olei* (of the young and handsome Attis). Dorat represents the young Ronsard as both a Pindaric-style athlete and a poet, reflecting the latter's initial military training at the royal school for squires, followed by his turning to poetry after a debilitating illness.[19] This dichotomy is reflected in the twin ancient uses of olive oil for anointing both ancient athletes (here represented as in Propertius 3.14 by the hardy Spartans; for *Amyclaeus* = Spartan cf. Vergil, *Georg.* 3.345, for *pubes* cf. e.g. Vergil, *Aen.* 2.477: *Scyria pubes*) and party-goers, suitable for festive goddesses such as the Muses

---

[18] An Horatian stylistic ornament – cf. e.g. *Odes* 1.20.2–3, 1.21.14–15, 1.38.5–6.
[19] For Ronsard's life see Simonin 1990.

(compare the fragrantly oiled hair of the personified Elegy at Ovid, *Am.* 3.1.6); for 27 *hilares* cf. Martial 7.8.1: *hilares ... Musae*. Here and in line 1 Dorat uses the Italian name of the Muses (*Camenae* in classical Latin) because of his stress on writing in Latin. Note the parallel prefixes of the two balancing verbs *oblinitur* and *obolent*.

29–36 At 29 *si* is my conjecture for the illogical *seu* of Dorat 1586 (the expected second *seu* presenting an alternative does not materialise and 'whether' makes no sense here).[20] 29–30 *artem sinuosaque ... volumina* is hendiadys, equivalent to *artem sinuosorum uoluminum* (for the phrase cf. Vergil, *Aen.* 11.753: *sinuosa volumina*, of a writhing snake). For 33–4 *audacibus | pugnis* cf. Vergil, *Aen.* 9.625: *audacibus ... coeptis* (in battle). 34 *dicatum* suggests the classical poet's semi-divine status as *vates*, 'poet/priest/prophet' (cf. e.g. Horace, *Odes* 3.1.29–32); the phrase *gravibus umbris* is found at Seneca, *HO* 710. The shade as the location for poetic activity recalls the world of Vergil's *Eclogues* (1.1, 10.75) and the poet's leisured lifestyle in the 'cool grove', *gelidum nemus*, pictured at Horace, *Odes* 1.1.30; it contrasts with the sun-exposure of military existence (cf. Horace, *Odes* 3.2.5). 36 *saltibus Martis*: for leaping in the warfare of classical epic cf. Vergil, *Aen.* 12.287, 326, 681. 36 *expedisse membra*: for this phrase in a battle context cf. Caesar, *Gall.* 4.24.4: *omnibus membris expeditis*. The epode looks back to Ronsard's earlier military training here, pointing to its unusual combination with his current literary skill; the two fields of endeavour are consistently contrasted in Augustan poetry (e.g. Tibullus 1.1.3–6; Horace, *Odes* 1.1.23–5; Propertius 3.4 and 3.5).

---

[20] Demerson 1979a retains *seu*, but translates it as *si*. *Seu* is an easy (phonetic?) error for *si*; in line 30 Demerson 1979a convincingly prints *uolet* for the *uelit* of Dorat 1586, the future tense paralleling that of 34 *stupebit* and providing a fuller alliteration with *uolumina*; so this may have been a negligently printed passage in general in the first edition.

Text 3: Ode 11 – to the Duc de Guise

This poem celebrates the return to France from Italy in late 1557 of François, Duc de Guise (1519–63). Guise, the cousin, adviser and chief general of Henri II (and maternal uncle of Mary, Queen of Scots),[21] had been recalled from campaigning in Italy and was about to besiege Calais. He would rapidly capture that city in January 1558, a major propaganda victory for the French since Calais was the last part of France then occupied by England, which was at that time allied with the Emperor Charles V against the French.

Dorat's ode uses Horace's Alcaic stanza and echoes some of Horace's odes in the same metre concerned with the victories of Augustus and his family in war, against Cleopatra (1.37) and against the peoples of eastern Europe (4.4). It was rapidly published in Dorat's *Odae Triumphales* (1558) as part of a cycle of Horatian-style odes on the successful Calais campaign.[22]

Similar Horatianising lyric poems celebrating military victories were common in sixteenth-century Neo-Latin; for example the Alcaic odes written by George Buchanan on the same topic of the capture of Calais (1558) and on the relief of Metz (1553)[23] or those composed to celebrate the Battle of Lepanto in 1571.[24] Dorat's poem is set in late 1557, but its publication in the collection of 1558 means that his readers would be well aware that Guise's return was followed by a triumphant conclusion.

Metre: Alcaics

---

[21] For his colourful career see Carroll 2009: 59–170.
[22] For this collection and its context see Demerson 1979a: 300–7.
[23] *Miscellanea* 1 and 8.
[24] The large collection of poems on the battle in Gherardi 1572 contains a number of Alcaic odes (380–408).

Latin text

    Solvant Camoenae triste silentium,
    Solvant, et acri Guisiaden lyra
        Cantent, remoto iam Britanno
            Moenibus a patriis tumultu.
5 Nuper secundus dum terere Annibal
    Fastus superbos tenderet Alpium,
        Ausi feroces tum Britanni
            Gallica sunt penetrare rura
    Orbata tanto praeside, tot virum
10 Cum caesa foede milia, pro nefas,
        Tot vincta ductorum pudendis
            Bracchia nobilium catenis.
    Iam gloriari quidlibet insolens
    Iactabat Anglus, celsa Lutetiae
15   Se templa fundo diruturum
           Sacrilegis spoliata dextris.
    Sed Guisiani fama ferociam
    Gentis superbae contudit ocius:
        Vix ductor auditur redire
20   Guisius, et fugitant Britanni,
    Vt forte viso cum cane Thessalo
    Immanis ausi conscius aufugit
        Agna lupus laxis remissa
            Faucibus horribilique dente.
25 Nec mirum, agebat non stimulus ducem
    In bella simplex: mixtus erat dolor
        Acer pudori, capta signa
            Gallica, se revocatum ab ausis,
    Vt Poenus olim, Scipio cum ureret
30 Arces Elissae, iam Capitolio,
        Cuncto timente iam Senatu,
            Signa domum revocare iussus.

Jean Dorat (1508-1588)

English translation

Let the Muses unseal their sad silence,
Unseal it, and sing of the son of Guise with shrill lyre,
Now that the British turbulence
Has been removed from our country's walls.
   When lately that second Hannibal strained 5
To wear down the lofty pride of the Alps,
Then the ferocious Britons dared to penetrate
The fields of France, then robbed
   Of so great a commander, when so many thousands
Of men were foully slaughtered, o wickedness, 10
So many arms of noble leaders
Bound in shameful chains.
   Insolent enough to make any kind of boast,
The English were already vaunting
That they would destroy the lofty shrines of Paris 15
From their foundations, once despoiled by their sacrilegious right hands.
   But the fame of him of Guise crushed the ferocity
Of this proud people all too rapidly:
Barely was the news heard of the leader's return
Than the Britons took to flight. 20
   Like perhaps when, at the sight of a Thessalian hound,
A wolf, conscious of its monstrous enterprise, flees away,
Dropping a lamb from its loosened jaws
And terrifying teeth.
   And no wonder, for no single goad drove the leader 25
To war: fierce pain was mixed with shame,
The capture of French standards,
his recall from his bold deeds,
   Like the Carthaginian of old, when Scipio was burning
The citadels of Elissa, and when the Capitol and the whole Senate 30
Was already in a state of fear, was ordered
To recall his standards home.

Commentary

1–8 The idea of the Muses ending a mournful silence in celebration echoes Horace, *Odes* 2.10.17–18: *quondam cithara tacentem | suscitat Musam*. 1 *triste silentium* is a phrase from Livy (1.29.3), while *solvant... silentium* is a nicely alliterative variant of the more common *silentium rumpere* (Horace, *Epodes* 5.85 etc.). Note how verb and object elegantly enclose the opening line and how the verb is repeated at the start of lines 1–2 (cf. similarly Horace. *Odes* 1.3.1–2). 2 *acri... lyra* recalls Horace, *Odes* 1.12.1: *lyra... acri* (an ode of praise for Augustus), while the Greek-termination patronymic *Guisiaden* echoes *Odes* 1.15.21 *Laertiaden* and is the first of three elegantly varied Guise-terms naming the honorand (cf. 17 *Guisiani*, 20 *Guisius*). 3 *remoto... Britanno* looks back to *Odes* 4.4.47–8: *remotis | ... Britannis* (in a different sense but in a war ode), while 4 *moenibus a patriis* recalls Vergil, *Aeneid* 11.882: *moenibus in patriis*. For 5 *nuper* of recent war news cf. Horace, *Odes* 4.14.8: *Vindelici didicere nuper*; Guise's role (5) as a second Hannibal crossing the Alps (the other way) recalls Lucan's similar description of Caesar at 1.303–5.

5–6 The bold metaphor *terere... fastus*, suggesting blunting the sharp edges of the mountains, is combined with the personifying *fastus superbos* (cf. e.g. Propertius 3.25.15: *fastus... superbos*); note the careful vertical juxtaposition of the parallel alliterative expressions *terere Annibal | ... tenderet Alpium*.[25]

7 for the *ferocia* of the Britons cf. Tacitus, *Agr.* 11.5: *plus tamen ferociae Britanni praeferunt*.

8 *Gallica... rura* is a phrase of Lucan (1.394, 2.429), who also uses *penetrare* of invading foreign territory (8.216: *Medorum penetrare domos*).

9–12 refer to the disastrous recent French loss of the battle of Saint-Quentin of August 1557, in which the French commander Anne de Montmorency and many others were captured fighting against the forces of Charles V in Picardy;[26] the Horatian echo in 11–12 implicitly compares it with Rome's catastrophic defeat at the Battle of Carrhae (53 BCE).

9 Cf. Ovid, *Met.*14.88: *orbataque praeside pinus* and *Ibis* 144: *tanto praeside* (of Augustus).

9–10 Cf. Lucretius 5.999: *virum... milia*, Vergil, *Aen.*10.498: *caesa manus iuvenum foede*, Seneca, *Ag.* 35: *pro nefas*.

---

[25] Cf. similarly Horace, *Odes* 1.14.16–17: *nuper sollicitum | ... nunc desiderium* (again at line-end).
[26] See Carroll 2009: 79 (7,000 French prisoners).

11-12 Cf. Horace, *Odes* 3.5.21-2 *civium* | *retorta tergo bracchia libero*; *ductorum* ... *nobilium*, though plural, points to Guise's captured rival, the Duc de Montmorency. Note once again the careful vertical juxtaposition of three parallel pairs of related and rhyming words *vincta ductorum pudendis* | *bracchia nobilium catenis*.

13-20 narrate the triumph of the English, followed by their supposed immediate flight on the news of Guise's coming return.

13 recalls the rash confidence of Cleopatra at the Battle of Actium (Horace, *Odes* 1.37.10-11: *quidlibet inpotens* | *sperare*); the promise to burn Paris to the ground (14-15) also matches Cleopatra's supposed hopes to do the same to Rome in the same ode (1.37.6-8: *dum Capitolio* | *regina dementis ruinas* | *funus et imperio parabat*); the 'lofty temples' of Paris, suggesting the cathedral of Notre-Dame and the Sainte-Chapelle, are a neat modernisation of Horace's elevated Capitoline shrine (cf. also Vergil, *Aen.* 8.653: *Capitolia celsa*).

15-16 Note the chiastic ordering of initially alliterating words (*diruturum* | *sacrilegis spoliata dextris*); cf. Ovid, *Met.* 14.539: *sacrilega ... dextra*.

17 For the alliterative pairing cf. Tacitus, *Agr.* 27.1: *fama ferox*.

18 for *gentis superbae* cf. Vergil, *Aen.* 1.523: *gentis frenare superbas*, for *contudit* cf. Horace, *Odes* 3.6.10: *contudit impetus*.

19-20 evoke the return of the great warrior Achilles to the battle in the *Iliad* after an extended absence, instantly striking terror into the enemy (Homer, *Iliad* 20.45): note the related movements of return and flight (*redire* | ... *fugitant*). Dorat outdoes Homer by stating that the mere news of Guise's return was enough to send the English into flight, an encomiastic exaggeration.

21-28 The poem concludes with fulsome praise of Guise, beginning with an Homeric-style simile (21-4) comparing the retreating English to a wolf who sees a hound and drops its prey; this comparison draws on those at Vergil, *Aen.* 9.565-6 (wolf takes lamb, 565 *agnum*), 11.812 (wolf kills herdsman or bullock and then flees, *conscius audacis facti*) as well as taking its location from Horace, *Odes* 1.37.17-20 (Augustus pursuing Cleopatra is like a hawk chasing a dove or hare in Thessaly); for *faucibus horribilique dente* cf. Horace, *Odes* 2.19.24: *unguibus horribilique mala*.

25-8 describe Guise's motives: pain at his country's previous humiliation at Saint-Quentin and at the shameful capture of its standards[27] (again a feature shared with Rome at Carrhae: cf. Horace, *Odes* 3.5.18-19: *signa ... Punicis* |

---

[27] Some 57: see Carroll 2009: 79.

adfixa delubris, Ovid, *Tr.* 2.1.228: *Parthus eques timida captaque signa manu*), and regret at his recall from his campaign in Italy. Such mixed motives are a regular feature of heroic psychology in the battles of Vergil's *Aeneid*: cf. 10.398: *mixtus dolor et pudor armat in hostis*, 10.871, 11.807, 12.665.

29–32 The recall of Guise to France from Italy is said to match the recall of Hannibal (*Poenus*) from the same Italy in 203 BCE to defend his threatened homeland at the end of the Second Punic War (Livy 30.20.1). Livy (28.42.13) reports fears in the Senate at Rome that Hannibal might attack the city as a last desperate effort before leaving Italy; these are the fears referred to in lines 30–31. Livy also mentioned later fears amongst the Carthaginians that Scipio might besiege Carthage and set it on fire (30.7.4, 9), something that line 29 seems to claim he really did; in fact the war was ended by a treaty without an attack on the city (Livy 30.16.8–15, 30.43.1–10).

30 *Arces Elissae* = Carthage (cf. Vergil, *Aen*.1.298: *Karthaginis arces* and the same poet's use of Elissa, the secondary name of Carthage's founder's Dido: *Aen*. 4.335, 4.610, 5.3).

30–31 The pairing of Capitol and Senate points to the fact that the Senate often met in the Capitol at this date (cf. e.g. Livy 28.38.14). The poem ends as it began (5) with an allusion to the great Carthaginian general and Guise's emulation of his deeds; Guise outdoes Hannibal here as the latter was unable to prevent his country's defeat on his return, but Guise was to win a great victory, as readers in 1558 would have been well aware.

8

Janus Dousa (1545–1604): The Satires of a Dutch Scholar

David Andrew Porter

Introduction

Janus Dousa (Jan van der Does, 1545–1604) was born in Noordwijk in South Holland. He became lord of Noordwijk at the age of five after the death of both his parents, and when he was older, the lordship of Kattendijke passed to him from his uncle. He was educated at Lier, Delft, Louvain, Douai and Paris, and notably studied Greek under Jean Dorat at the Collège Royal. Active during the Dutch Revolt against the Spanish and the notorious Duke of Alba, he was appointed commander of Leiden, his home since 1571, and was an envoy to Queen Elizabeth of England in 1572.[1] Soon after William the Silent founded Leiden University, Dousa was named as curator of the library, where he remained for the next twenty-nine years. Throughout his life he established scholarly connections throughout Europe, and he was particularly proud of bringing the philologist and philosopher Justus Lipsius to Leiden.[2]

Janus Dousa finished eight satires in total.[3] The first two were published in 1569; and three more appeared in a new volume of poetry printed in 1575, which was soon followed by an expanded second edition in 1576. Finally, all eight surviving satires were published posthumously in 1609.[4] A few other humanists connected with Janus Dousa wrote Latin verse satires. Lambertus Hortensius (1500/1–74), for example, dedicated his first (of two) books of satires to Dirck van Zuylen van der Haer, who was also Janus Dousa's father-in-law. Whatever Dousa's appreciation of Hortensius' satires, he at least went as far as addressing to him a complimentary epigram.[5] And Dousa refers favourably to Hortensius' historical scholarship on more than one occasion.[6] But of all the Latin satires of the early modern period – many of which are little more than polemic or scholastic exercises in epideictic rhetoric – Dousa's compositions rank among the best. His first satire is presented here in full and concerns itself with an accusation of academic plagiarism. The selections from his third satire address his role in Spanish intervention in the

Low Countries. Dousa also produced editions of and commentaries on Horace, Catullus, Plautus and other Roman authors; his interest in classical poetry, history and scholarship is reflected in his poetry.

Notes

1 Vermaseren 1955: 50. On his life see Heesakkers 1976; Heesakkers / Reinders 1993.
2 See Heesakkers 1987.
3 Dousa 1609: 333–404.
4 On this publication, see Heesakkers 1975.
5 Dousa 1603: fol. 29v.
6 Maas 2011: 65.

Bibliography

Arnade, P. J. (2008), *Beggars, Iconoclasts, and Civic Patriots: The Political Culture of the Dutch Revolt*, Ithaca (NY).
van Crombruggen, Henri (1955), *Janus Lernutius 1545–1619: een biografische studie*, Brussels.
Devos, F. (2006), 'François Thorius (Thooris) et son fils Raphaël médecins, poètes et mathématiciens de la Renaissance' (https://meteren.pagesperso-orange.fr/FicheN16.htm).
van Dorsten, J. A. (1962), *Poets, Patrons, and Professors: Sir Philip Sidney, Daniel Rogers, and the Leiden Humanists*, Leiden / Oxford.
Dousa, Janus (1569), *Epigrammatum lib. II; Satyrae II; Elegorum lib. I; Silvarum lib. II*, Antwerp.
Dousa, Janus (1579), *Novorum poematum*, 2nd edn, Leiden.
Dousa, Janus (1603), *Echo, sive Lusus imaginis jocosae, quibus titulus Halcedonia*, The Hague.
Dousa, Janus (1609), *Poemata pleraque selecta*, Leiden.
Filelfo, F. (1502), *Satyrarum hecatostichon decades decem*, Venice.
Geurts, P. M. M. (1977), *De Utrechtse kanunnik Philippus Morus, Neolatijns dichter*, Nieuwkoop.
Graevius, Johannes, Geogius (1680), *Catullus, Tibullus et Propertius ex recensione Johannis Georgii Graevii*, Utrecht.
Heesakkers, C. L. (1975), 'Petrus Scriverius as the Publisher of the Poemata of Janus Dousa', *Quaerendo*, 5.2: 105–25.
Heesakkers, C. L. (1976), *Praecidanea Dousana: Materials for a Biography of Janus Dousa Pater (1545–1604): His Youth*, Amsterdam.
Heesakkers, C. L. (1985), 'Le procurateur Obertus Giphanius (5 novembre 1566 – 4 janvier 1567)', in: R. Feenstra / C. M. Ridderikhoff (eds), *Études*

néerlandaises de droit et d'histoire présentées à l'Université d'Orléans pour le 750e anniversaire des enseignements juridiques: 133–53, Orléans.

Heesakkers, C. L. (1987), 'Twins of the Muses: Justus Lipsius and Janus Dousa Pater', in: A. Gerlo (ed.), *Juste Lipse (1547–1606): Colloque international tenu en mars 1987*, 53–68, Brussels.

Heesakkers, C. L. / Reinders, W. M. S. (1993), *Genoeglijk bovenal zijn mij de muzen: de Leidse Neolatijnse dichter Janus Dousa (1545–1604)*, Dimensie.

Heesakkers, C. L. (1998), '"To Attract the Attention of that Snobbish Queen", Dousa's Latin Ode to Elizabeth (1573) in its Historical Context', in: E. M. Knottenbelt / M. Rudnik-Smalbraak (eds), *A Fusion of Horizons: In Dialogue with Dominic Baker-Smith*, 131–6, Amsterdam.

Heesakkers, C. L. (2006), 'Twee Leidse boezemvrienden van Justus Lipsius: Janus Dousa en Jan van Hout', *De Gulden Passer*, 84: 1–26.

Heesakkers, C. L. (2009), 'Propaganda poética en la Guerra de Flandes. Dos odas y una sátira latinas de Janus Dousa', *Revista de Estudios Latinos*, 9: 149–90.

Hortensius, Lambertus (1552), *Satyrae VIII. ad nobilem uirum D. Theodoricum Zulenum, D. à Zevender*, Utrecht.

Maas, C. (2011), '"Hadrianus Junius" Batavia and the Formation of a Historiographical Canon in Holland', in: D. van Miert (ed.), *The Kaleidoscopic Scholarship of Hadrianus Junius (1511–1575): Northern Humanism at the Dawn of the Dutch Golden Age*, 38–68, Leiden.

Simons, R. (2009a), 'Janus Dousa: Satira 1 – Text, Übersetzung, Kommentar', *Neulateinisches Jahrbuch*, 11: 155–77.

Simons, R. (2009b), '"Ein humanistischer Plagiatstreit" und seine Inszenierung. Zu Gestalt und Funktion der ersten beiden Satiren des Janus Dousa', in: E. Lefèvre / E. Schäfer (eds), *Ianus Dousa: Neulateinischer Dichter und Klassischer Philologe*, 69–92, Tübingen.

Spohnholz, J. (2017), *The Convent of Wesel: The Event that Never was and the Invention of Tradition*, Cambridge.

Susius, Jacobus (1590), *Carmina tam sacra quam prophana, ex bibliotheca Iac. Susii D.F.P.N.*, Leiden.

Venturini, G., ed. (1972), *Gaspare Tribraco: Satirarum liber dedicato al duca Borso d'Este*, Ferrara.

Vermaseren, B. A. (1955), 'De werkzaamheid van Janus Dousa Sr. (1604) als geschiedschrijver van Holland', *Bijdragen en Mededelingen van het Historisch Genootschap*, 69: 49–109.

Wauters, A. (1885), 'Grobbendonck (Gaspar Schets, Seigneur de)', *Biographie Nationale de Belgique* (Brussels), VIII: 314–24.

Source of Latin text

For Satire 1, Simons' 2009 edition has been used, with minor differences in punctuation and orthography, and checked against the 1569 and 1609 editions. Satire 3 is based on the 1609 edition, collated against the 1576 text.

Simons' critical edition, German translation and commentary are helpful. Many classical parallels are mentioned that are not repeated here.

Text 1: Satire 1 – To Franciscus Thorius Bellio

This programmatic satire is addressed to the humanist François de Thoor (1525 – before 1601), a scholar who was also connected with the Pléiade circle in France (Devos 2006). Dousa's impetus for writing this poem was an act of academic theft. In 1566 Lucas Fruterius, a scholar and friend of Dousa, passed away. Obertus Giphanius (Hubert van Giffen, 1534–1604), personally entrusted with the philological notes of Fruterius, was later suspected, by Dousa and others, of passing some of the deceased scholar's brilliant remarks off as his own. Another satire by Dousa, addressed to Janus Lernutius, makes the claims of plagiarism even more explicit.[1] Dousa expresses his anger at Giphanius' appropriation of his colleague Fruterius' work, as well as alluding to accusations that Giphanius plagiarised Denis Lambin's edition of Lucretius.[2] This satire first circulated amongst a circle of readers familiar with the background of the events and some evidence of this survives. This evidence includes a letter from New Year's Eve, 1579, in which Justus Lipsius sent some of these satires of Dousa to Lernutius (van Crombruggen 1955: 33). Publication then expanded Dousa's circle of readers to the more general public.

Metre: dactylic hexameter

---

[1] The full second satire was printed with a Dutch translation in Heesakkers / Reinders 1993: 22–7.
[2] For more details of this controversy see Heesakkers 1976: 116–22; Heesakkers 1985: 133–53; Heesakkers / Reinders 1993: 21–8; Simons 2009b: 70–6.

Latin text

Satyra I. Ad Franciscum Thorium Bellionem.

    Semper ego Harpocrates tantum? nunquamne licebit
    Nunc hunc, nunc alium depingere rite colore
    Quemque suo, et tumidi cristas contundere Galli?
    Impune ergo mihi leges minitetur, et urnam
5 Hic, atque ille? Impune fidem iurataque fallens
    Numina, deposito laqueum mandabit amori?
    Non tantum Scheto debet Bithynicus aeris,
    Quantum ludibrii mihi Fannius, alter ab illo,
    Quem toties vexat ridentis pagina Flacci.
10 Sed tamen expediet nomen puto. Cur ego semper
    Creditor esse velim? Scribit mala carmina Codrus:
    Num minus ergo sibi plausum movet, hostibus iram?
    Et iam tentat idem quivis, gaudetque, Thori, in se:
    Quod modo dum faciat, nec amico, nec sibi parcit.
15 Quid vetat et nosmet Lucili exempla secutos
    Fastidire minas, quorum sibi conscia mens est?
    Hoc iubet et pietas, et amici Manibus olim
    Pacta fides, umbraeque dolor (quis nescit?) inultae.
    Adde, oti quod nunc satis est solennis, et ipsa
20 Materia ingenium faciat mihi, restibilis ceu
    Hydra, nec Herculeis unquam cessura lacertis.
    Temporibus quid enim nostris corruptius? Aut quid
    Turpe magis? Leno uxoris Petronius audit.
    Vendit Pantolabus fumos, periuria Flaccus.
25 Est, qui tutoris se nomine ventilet et rem
    Atterat haeredum longo sufflamine litis:
    Digni omnes venia, me iudice, quod scelere uno
    Contenti vivunt. Nam cur inducere mentem
    Possim aliter, quoties devoti stigmata Fanni
30 Mi subeunt? Quae si quis singula nosse laboret,
    Idem percurrat scelerum genus omne necesse est.
    Ocyus expediam certe, quot scorta Philoenus,
    quot Lalage moechos habeat, quot nocte dieque
    Et calices, et pota viros exsorbeat Aegle.

English translation

Satire 1. To François de Thoor of Bailleul

Will I always be merely a Harpocrates? Will I never be allowed
to sketch out now this person, now that one, each according to his
own colour, and smash the comb of the puffed-up Gallus?
Will this man and that one, threaten the laws and [judge's] urn
against me with impunity? With impunity betraying the faith and gods   5
he has sworn to, will he hand over the noose to a discarded lover?
     Bithynicus does not owe as much money to Schets
as Fannius is indebted in mockery to me, the second comer after him,
whom the page of laughing Flaccus so often troubles.
But I think he will eventually clear his name. Why should I always   10
be willing to be a creditor? Codrus writes wicked verses:
does he really thereby provoke less applause for himself and anger from his
    enemies?
And already everyone tries the same thing, Thorius, and is self-satisfied:
but as long as he can do it, he shows no consideration for neither friend nor
    himself.
So, what prevents us, we who are aware of Lucilius' examples,   15
from following them and disregarding the threats?
     Duty even demands this, and the confidence made with the Manes
of a friend, and the pain (who doesn't know it) of the unavenged shadow.
Say, that is now enough of common leisure, and may the
matter itself be an inspiration to me, as the Hydra   20
is regenerated, and never yields the arms of Hercules.
What indeed is more corrupt than our times? Or what
is more shameful? Petronius is said to be his wife's pimp.
Pantolabus sells vapours, Flaccus sells false oaths.
There is another, who blusters in the name of a guardian, and   25
the heirs' resources are worn away by the long drag of a lawsuit:
I judge all these worthy of forgiveness, because they live content
with a single offence. For how could I make up my mind
otherwise, as often as the marks of the devoted Fannius
intrude upon my thoughts? If anyone troubled to familiarize himself with
    each one,   30
he would need to mull over every type of sin.
I would certainly relate more promptly: how many whores Philoenus has,
how many strumpets Lalage has, how many nights and days
and cups and men the drunk Aegle has sucked down.

35 Promptius enumerem Blaesi mendacia, quotque
    Testamenta resignarint Labienus, et Hermes.
    Nam quota pars Geldri vitia haec sunt pectoris? Hic et
    Livor edax, hic insidiae cum mille nocendi
    Artibus, et sedem fixisse videtur Enyo.
40   Horrendam mitto rabiem fastumque referre.
    Nec libet antiquam plagii renovare querelam:
    Quod te felicem quondam, Lambine, cerebri
    Et vidi et pleno memini posuisse theatro,
    Parrisiis, tunc cum miserandus et hostibus ipsis
45 Fannius introrsum detracta pelle pateret.
    Indignum scelus, et nullo satis igne piandum:
    Sed tamen heu levius, quam quod sibi vulturis idem
    Et placet haeredis sub nomine, Frutericisque
    Vendere se plumis male suppositicius audet.
50 Haec ego cum video, non possum ferre Sodales,
    Non possum! Nam tot quis in uno crimina cernens
    Carminibus parcat, nisi sit plagiarius idem
    Atque aliquis Fidentini de gente superstes?
         Magna inter similis concordia, participesque
55 Criminis eiusdem: nec enim bene seditioso
    Displiceat Gracchus: ut nec Catilina Cethego,
    Nec furi Verres. 'Cur non tibi gratuler hanc rem,
    Cur tibi non plaudam Fanni?' Callistratus inquit.
    Credo, quod in partem venturus et ipse rapinae est.
60 Sic placet ergo tibi, Fanni: quem spe libeat si
    Hac fraudare semel, a te desciscet ad hostes
    Continuo, poenaeque, tuae se pascet amore.
    Gryllus cum dominum tolerare diutius, et se
    Non posset, 'quid', ait, 'melius, quam transfuga partis
65 Adversae domino fiam? nisi verbere malo
    Semper, et a titulis non degenerare parentum.'
    Sic nunc ille miser, sese dum credit herile
    Excussisse iugum, nulli non servit, ut ipsi
    Esse putem dominos ferme totidem, quot amicos.
70   Omnes nostrimet nos poenitet: atque hominem vix
    Invenias, cui sors placeat sua. Navibus aptus
    Castra sequi mercator, et esse triarius optat.
    Quid miles? Ride, mercaturae dare nomen.
    Uxori queritur sese nupsisse beatae

I could enumerate even faster the lies of Blaesus, and how many 35
wills that Labienus and Hermes have unsealed.
For how small a portion of these vices is in the heart of Gelder? And here is
gnawing envy, here are treacheries with a thousand means
of causing harm, and here Enyo seems to have set her seat.
    I decline to recall the horrible madness and pride. 40
Nor am I willing to renew the old complaint about plagiarism:
which you, Lambinus, once fortunate in temperament,
I both saw and remembered you had presented to a packed theatre,
at that time when Fannius, after his skin had been stripped, opened
    inwardly
invoking the compassion of the Parisians, and even his enemies. 45
Shameful sin, no fire sufficient for atonement.
But, nevertheless, alas, more trifling than that which at the same time
pleases himself under the guise of vulture and heir, and
spurious, wrongly dares to advertise himself with the feathers of Fruterius.
When I see this, I cannot endure it, friends, 50
I cannot! For who can discern so many crimes in one individual
and spare him in poems, if he were not also a plagiarist
and one descending from the race of Fidentinius?
    There is great concord among those who are alike and share
crimes in common: for the seditious will not much 55
dislike Gracchus, and Catiline will not dislike Cethegus,
nor Verres the thief. 'Why would I not congratulate you in this matter,
why would I not applaud you', says Callistratus.
I think this is because he himself will come into a portion of the robbery.
So, then it pleases you, Fannius, if it should suit you, 60
to deceive him in this prospect, he will desert you for the enemy
without further ado, and with passion feast himself on your punishment.
When Gryllus could no longer bear his lord
and himself, he said 'what is better than defecting
to my lord's enemies? Unless I prefer a relentless 65
beating, and to fall short of the titles of my parents.'
So, now that wretched man, as long he himself
has cast off the master's yoke, thinks he does not serve anyone, so that
he has, I suppose, almost as many masters as friends.
    All of us are dissatisfied with our lot: and you could hardly 70
find a man who is pleased with his fate. The merchant suited for ships
strikes for military camps, and desires to join the reserves.
What about the soldier? Laugh, that he lends his name to trade.
The old man complains that he has married a rich

75 Priscus, et 'o utinam vitae me Parca priori
   Restituat'. Contra, 'peius quid caelibe lecto?',
   Flaccus ait. Molles vivant sine compare Galli.
   Ipse ego si fati contentum munere, si me
   Laetum sorte mea, et quod res est, praedico, 'Non es
80 Quod simulas!', mox Aulus ait, 'qui testibus uti,
   Iane, reformidas, et aperto vivere voto
   Conscius ipse tibi.' Quid ad haec ego? Nempe quod horae
   Non unius homo. Vocor in certamen et ipse
   Votorum: non ut patrui legar unicus orbi
85 In tabulis haeres, turba plorante nepotum
   Nec formosa mihi contingat ut uxor, et infans
   Nascatur patri similis: sed quod magis ad rem
   Pertinet, ut tandem plagiis vaga ponere finem
   Curet turba suis, alieno dives in aere:
90 Quos inter primum nisi iure meretur honorem
   Fannius, interream. Quare est mihi saepe vocandus
   Ad partes, nec non blando sermone monendus,
   Ut privas ostentet opes, et scrinia vitet
   Tangere, quae niveis vehit anxia Gloria pennis
95 Fruterica signata manu. Quid post ea? Multos
   Ut versus faciat, desit ne scilicet unquam,
   Quod mecum ridere satis tu Bellio possis.

woman, and 'oh, if only Fate would restore my 75
old life back to me.' On the contrary, 'what is worse than a bachelor's bed',
says Flaccus. Let the effete Galli live without a companion.
If I myself am content with the gift of fate, if I am
happy with my own lot and circumstance, I proclaim, 'You are not
what you pretend to be!', soon Aulus says, 'Ianus, 80
you shrink back from bringing witnesses forward, and self-consciously
living with unconcealed desire.' What do I say to this? But truly that man
does not exist for a single hour. I say I am also caught up in that same struggle
of desires: not that I should be listed as the heir of the will
of the childless uncle, while a mob of descendants wail 85
nor that a beautiful wife should come to me and a child
born resembling his father: but what pertains more to this
matter, that finally the roaming crowd, rich in debt,
should care to put an end to their thievery:
I would be undone if Fannius does not justly deserve the first place of honour 90
among these. Therefore, I must often summon him to play
his parts and admonish him with flattering speech,
to show his own possessions, and refrain from touching
the book-boxes, sealed by the hand of Fruterius,
which anxious Fame carries with him on snow-white feathers. And what next? That 95
he make many verses, so that there never be something lacking
about which you, Bellio, can sufficiently laugh with me.

Commentary

1 Juvenal's first satire begins (1.1): *Semper ego auditor tantum? numquamne reponam*. Dousa sets the tone for his Juvenalian satire by echoing his predecessor's opening line, while *auditor* is replaced by the erudite reference to Harpocrates, the god of silence and secrets, adapted from the Egyptian goddess Horus by the Greeks. Like Juvenal before him, Dousa professes the satirical imperative to castigate vice.

2 *depingere*: cf. Persius 6.79: *depinge, ubi sistam*, though modern editions often prefer *depunge*: a reminder of the value of checking classical references in early modern texts against contemporary editions.

3 Cf. Horace, *Odes* 4.3.8: *quod regum tumidas contuderit minas*; Juvenal 13.233: *cristam promittere galli*. Simons (2009a: 165) notes that *gallus* was printed in lower case in the first 1569 edition, but the word was later capitalized for the 1609 text. This allows Juvenal's 'crested cock' to mean a puffed-up *Gallus*, a eunuch priest of Cybele, a slight on the masculinity of Giphanius, the target of this satire. Cf. Persius 5.186: *grandes Galli*.

4 Cf. Horace, *Epistles* 2.2.105: *impune legentibus*; *Sermones* 2.1.47: *leges minitatur et urnam*. *urna*: a vessel for casting voting-tablets.

5 Cf. Horace, *Sermones* 1.4.126: *hic atque ille*, in the same metrical position. Ovid, *Heroides* 2.23–4: *iurata reducunt | numina*.

6 Cf. Juvenal, 10.53: *mandaret laqueum*. The meaning is something like, 'go hang yourself'.

7 Gaspar Schets (Gaspar Schetus Corvinus, 1513–80), Lord of Grobbendonk: a statesman with literary interests (Wauters 1885). Later, during the Dutch Revolt, he was active on the Spanish side, unlike Dousa, who fought against the invading Spaniards. *Bithynicus* is a name from Martial 6.50.5; if it refers to one of Dousa's contemporaries. the allusion is now obscure.

8 *Fannius*: the pseudonym of Obertus Giphanius, with antecedents in Horace. Cf., in connection with books, *Sermones* 1.4.21–23: *beatus Fannius ultro | delatis capsis et imagine, cum mea nemo | scripta legat*. It also puns on the pronunciation of his surname. Giphanius is the primary target of this satire. Dousa follows the example of the Roman satirists in not using the real name of his target, though the reference would have hardly escaped his intimate readers. Cf. Vergil, *Eclogues* 5.49: *alter ab illo*.

Janus Dousa (1545–1604) 175

9 *ridentis . . . Flacci*: refers to the Roman poet Horace, whose satire was characterized by provoking laughter, whether directed at vices, at others or towards oneself. Horatian satire is usually considered milder than Juvenal's (and Dousa's) mode of satire.

10 *ego semper* in Juvenal often introduces a question, cf. line 1.

11 *mala carmina*: cf. Horace, *Sermones* 2.5.74. The name *Codrus* is usually applied to a bad poet: cf. Vergil, *Eclogues* 5.11, 7.22; Juvenal 1.2, 3.203, 3.208.

12 Anger (here: *ira*) or indignation (*indignatio*) are common motives for Juvenalian satire.

13 *in se*: One metrical allowance for formal verse satire was that a poetic line could end in a monosyllabic word or even two monosyllabic words (especially when introducing a clause continuing into the following line), something usually avoided in epic and other genres. Janus Dousa is generous in his employment of this metrical freedom in his Latin satires. In this ninety-seven-line satire five lines end in monosyllables, ten in double monosyllables. Most Neo-Latin verse satirists did not utilize the metrical freedoms of ancient satire, and this is almost never commented on in Renaissance poetic manuals or commentaries on Roman satire.

Thori: the dedicatee of a Latin poem is usually addressed somewhere in its text, here quite late.

15 Cf. Horace, *Sermones* 1.4.6: *hinc omnis pendet Lucilius*, 1.10.56: *quid vetat et nosmet Lucili scripta legentis*. Lucilius was the original creator of Roman satire. Though only fragments of his work survive, early modern satirists often regarded him as their predecessor.

16 *conscia mens*: A common expression in Neo-Latin verse satire: cf. Tribraco, *Satirae* 3.88; Filelfo, *Satyrae* 5.5.49.

17 *Manibus*: The metre helps clarify *Mānēs*, not *manus*.

19 Cf. Horace, *Sermones* 2.7.111–12: *adde, quod idem | non horam tecum esse potes*.

20 *restibilis*: an unpoetic word (Simons 2009a: 168). Classical satire admitted more prosaic diction than other genres of classical poetry.

21 Hercules' second labour was to kill the Lernean Hydra; a task impeded by the Hydra's tendency to regenerate two new heads for every old one cut off.

23 *audit*: the meaning here is 'is said to be'.

24 *Pantolabus*: a pseudonym borrowed from Horace, *Sermones* 1.8.11 and 2.1.22. Duplicitous heirs are ubiquitous in satire.

26 Cf. Juvenal 16.50: *nec res atteritur longo sufflamine litis*.

27 The man who imagines he would be happier in another life was a commonplace in classical poetry: cf. Horace, *Sermones* 1.1.2; Juvenal 14.179.

29 Dousa uses *stigmata* again in connection with the poems of Giphanius in the final verses of his second satire (2.2.71–3; cf. Simons 2009a: 169).

32 *Ocyus*: a common medieval and Neo-Latin spelling of classical Latin *ocius*, which endured into the early nineteenth century.

33 *Lalage*: from Horace, *Odes* 1.22.

34 *Aegle*: another name from Martial 1.72.3. This epigram was directed against a plagiarist named Fidentinus; so the borrowing is apt for this satire.

35 *Blaesi*: *blaesus* means 'lisping'; so the name is appropriate for a liar. The name is from Martial's epigrams (8.38.14), that great repository of pseudonyms.

36 *Labienus*: from Martial 12.16, where he is depicted in unflattering sexualized terms.

37 *Geldri*: Giphanius was from Gelderland.

39 *Enyo*: the goddess of war. Between 1502 and 1543 Gelderland was the location of a series of wars between the dukes of Burgundy and Guelders (another name for Gelderland).

41–5 Here the satire alludes to the allegation that Giphanius had plagiarized Dionysius Lambinus' (Denis Lambin, 1520–72) 1563 edition of Lucretius.

45 Cf. Horace, *Sermones* 2.1.64: *detrahere et pellem*.

46 Cf. Juvenal 13.54: *grande nefas et morte piandum*.

48 *Frutericisque*: usually writers of dactylic hexameters do not end their lines with words of more than three syllables. But the example of ancient satire was more permissive of polysyllabic line-endings, as expressed here and in lines 54 and 55. Lucas Fruterius (Lucas Fruytier, 1541–66) was another Neo-Latin poet and friend of Janus Dousa.

50 *Sodales*: friends among the Republic of Letters. Cf. Juvenal 3.60: *non possum ferre, Quirites*.

54-7 Cf. Juv. 2.24-7. Tiberius Gracchus was an ancient Roman political leader known for his agrarian reforms. Catiline was the political enemy of Cicero; Gaius Cornelius Cethegus was his fellow conspirator. Gaius Verres was a Roman magistrate, famous for his misrule of Sicily and was also prosecuted by Cicero.

58 *Callistratus*: another name from Martial 12.42.1, there referring to an effeminate homosexual, here referring to the philologist Gulielmus Canterus: one of the very few scholars who sided with Giphanius in these controversies.

63 Plutarch's dialogue *Gryllus* suggests that animals are rational and that men are pigs.

67-9 Cf. Persius 5.73-5.

82 Cf. Persius 2.7: *et aperto vivere voto*.

88 Cf. Juvenal 13.240-1: *nam quis | peccandi finem posuit sibi?*

92 *partes*: Translated as 'parts', but the plural of *pars* often simply means 'character', 'part' or 'role' in a singular sense.

94 The goddess Gloria is also personified in Horace, *Sermones* 1.6.23.

Text 2: Satire 3 – To Willem van Zuylen van Nijevelt (lines 1–41, 168–177, 272–292, 315–324)

While Janus Dousa's early satires were concerned with the injustices of academic life, the beginnings of the Dutch Revolt against the Spanish, also referred to as the Eighty Years' War, led to the creation of three more satires by Dousa appearing in 1575. These were soon republished in an expanded edition of his poetry in 1576, which was more widely circulated and soon received the compliments of Justus Lipsius.[3] These satires shifted from philological to political themes, as they directly address the takeover of the government by the Duke of Alba and more generally the Spanish intervention in the Low Countries.[4] Aside from Dousa's satires, there were two similar war satires published by Dousa's friend, the Dutch nobleman Jacobus Susius (Jakob Suys, 1520–92), in 1590, although these were likely written during the Duke of Alba's governorship of the Netherlands (1567–73).[5] Susius addressed the first of these satires to Janus Dousa, but his style is very different: Susius expresses more bitterness and anger than Dousa, especially when describing the sack of his home in Mechelen on 2 October 1572.[6] Dousa maintains a more Horatian diplomatic tone in his satire, though he does not refrain from describing the injustices of foreign invasion and depravities he witnesses.

This poem is dedicated to Dousa's friend, the Utrecht nobleman Willem van Zuylen van Nijevelt (c. 1538–1608).[7] The selections chosen are intended to convey both a sense of the style of this satire and illustrate some of Dousa's historical, religious and diplomatic preoccupations.

Metre: dactylic hexameter

---

[3] Heesakkers 2006: 2.
[4] A critical edition of two Latin odes and another satire on this occasion are provided in Heesakkers 2009.
[5] Susius 1590: 5–13.
[6] Cf. Susius 1.27–30: *Bella sepulta forent, auratis aurea pennis | Lucida PAX fana atque domos urbesque bearet. | Bello iura silent. Ius bello, Vis teritur vi. | Tunc vitium viget atque furor, Lernamque malorum | Cernere, et horrendi barathri est basta ora recludi.* The reference to the hydra Lerna refers to a bronze statue in Antwerp, which was designed by Jacques Jonghelinck, was built from the cannons that the Spanish had captured at Jemmingen and depicted the Duke of Alba as Hercules crushing the hydra Lerna (on this statue see Arnade 2008: 200–2).
[7] Perhaps also a relative of Dousa's wife Elisabeth van Zuylen van de Haar?

Latin text

Satyra III. Ad Gulielmum Niueldium.

O rem ridiculam valde, nimiumque, iocosam,
Cui damus hanc? Gulielme tibi! Tu namque putare
Esse meas aliquid tricas apinasque solebas.
Iam tum cum patria simul a tellure profectos,
5 Iactatosque diu, non terris dico, sed alto,
Exceptos tandem hospitio Gravesanda Britanno
Remige Londinum porro transmisit, et inde
Kinstonum, illius visuros Principis ora,
Principis Augustae: cui ut est nil, sic nihil unquam
10 Aut fuit, aut alia posthac aetate futurum est,
Doctrina, eloquio, forma, et pietate secundum.
Quare quicquid id est tibi habe: quantum quidem abunde
Totis paene decem risum tibi suggerat annis.
Quod tamen ante tibi quam narrare incipiam, unum
15 A te etiam Gulielme velim prius ipse doceri.
Nota tibi credo patria est tua, sex licet inde
Extorris fueris annos: sed et Amsteliorum
Usurpasti oculis fortasse ac naribus urbem;
Hic, ubi nil Arabum spirant de messe Plataeae.
20 Utram plus sapere, aut virtutibus esse priorem
Harum igitur censes? Age dic quaeso! ad me etenim quod
Attinet, ex illis, si quis Deus: Elige, dicat,
Elige utram malis, quid responsurus ei sim
Non video, nisi quis Traiectum dicat, eo quod
25 Maxima pars illic Bullata incedit, et unctum
Rasa caput, glabrior mentum undique, quam puto volsus
Ludius, atque ideo tonsoribus annua praestans.
De genere hoc, lucri quos pascere suevit odor, non
Ex lotio, verum quod oleto spurcius ipso
30 Est etiam, humanis ex ossibus aera ruentes,
Functorumque cadaveribus, bustisque piandis,
Quos, uti commentum placet ipsis, nocte dieque
Nunc frictos, nunc elixos, tostos modo, et assos
Februa flamma coquens ambureret, ambustosque

English translation

Satire 3. To Willem van Zuylen van Nijevelt

O to whom do I give this absurdly funny and
excessively droll thing? To you, Willem! For you used to
reckon my trifles and nonsense were something.
Even then, when they departed together from their ancestral land
and were for a long time thereafter scattered about, I say not on land, but on
  the high sea,   5
after finally receiving hospitality at Gravesend, was sent further on with
  British
rowers to London, and from there
to Kingston, to gaze upon the visage of the Sovereign,
the August Sovereign: for whom there is none, nor was there
ever any, nor will there be any in any future age thereafter,   10
equal to her in learning, eloquence, beauty and piety.
Therefore, keep to yourself whatever thing this is: so long as it still
may at least amply supply you with laughter after nearly ten whole years.
However, before I begin to tell you about it: there is first still one thing
I would like to be taught by you, Willem.   15
I believe that your fatherland is well-known to you, although you have been
exiled from there for six years, but also perhaps
you have experienced the city of Amsterdam through your eyes and
  nostrils;
here, where no Arabs breathe the harvest of Plataea.
So, which of these two things do you think takes precedence: 20
being wiser or more virtuous? Come on, please tell me! As far as
I'm concerned, if some god should say 'choose one of those',
'choose whichever you prefer', I cannot see how
I should respond to him. Unless one should say 'Utrecht', because
the greatest number of people walk along there with degrees and tonsured: 25
the head anointed, the chin all together smoother than, I think,
a depilated actor, and so thereby supplying the barbers their yearly stipends.
Regarding this class, the smell of lucre used to nourish them, not
from urine (the truth is even fouler in its filth itself
than that) but rather rushing at the money from human bones,   30
and the corpses of the departed, and honoured tombs,
which, in order that the scheme be pleasing to them, are by night and day
now fried, now boiled, now baked and roasted,
a purgative cooking blaze should burn, and ice

35   Mersaret gelida, sacrae absque piamine Bullae,
     Ac Missis foret, et setosi aspergine sceptri,
     Quae linquenda sibi, ac tota de mente fuganda
     Omnia, cum caenis Saliaribus, et vice grata
     Craterum, Venerumque, vident examine, Missam
40   Si missam facere, ac Christo dare nomina vellent,
     Cum sacrisque suis Latium eiurare Baälem.

168 Ut taceam caecos aditus per mille cuniclos,
     Aenea tot tormenta, pilas, ignitaque, tela,
170 Et certos scloporum ictus, plumbumque volucre:
     Nitrati immensam vim pulveris, atque alia huius
     Multa modi, quae si non singula, at omnia iuncta
     Constantes etiam valeant percellere mentes.
     Adde Diplomata nunc (hoc est oleum adde camino)
175 Regia, terrificas legas, edicta libellos.
     Tentando assidue queis credula corda popelli
177 Paulatim labefactare, et convellere certant.

272 I nunc, dispositis et per loca certa veredis
     Arragonas, gelidaeque, nives transscende Pyrenes.
     Ipso uti Madridi convento Rege, Triumphos,
275 Et maria, et montes, cuncta aurea denique tecum
     Inde domum referens, Alba ridente revorti
     Pollicitis possis satur, et spe dives opima:
     Aut meritis confide tuis, bellator, et omni
     Maiorem te crede metu, frustraque Philippi
280 Signatis tabulis et fretus imagine cerea,
     Heu Parmae Ducis illecebris potiora Solonis
     Omnia, et Auriaci monitus postpone salubres.
     Scilicet ut custos Verga veniente creatus
     Carceris, aut Gandavae arci praefectus ab Alba.
285 In matutinam tandem educaris arenam,
     Pompeium Hispanis, Tragicis tamen absque cothurnis
     Et larva saltaturus: mox truncus iniqua
     Parte tui, sudibusque caput praefixus acernis,
     Spectaclum patriis praebens miserabile Belgis,
290 Naenia Bruxellae fias urbi, interea dum,
     Credo, dispendi faciat ne temporis hilum,
292 In tabula placide a Caio depingitur Alba.

should douse the charred remains, without the expiation 35
of the holy papal Bull and Masses and sprinkling of the bristly sceptre,
which must be forsaken by them, and everything must be routed from the
      mind
completely, with Salian feasts, and the pleasing exchange
of wine-bowls and sex, they see in the balance, the Mass,
if they would wish to perform the mass, and give names to Christ, 40
and would wish with their saints to abjure the Roman Baal.

That I pass over blind attacks through thousands of tunnels, 168
so many bronze cannons, balls and flaming weapons, bullets,
and the sure shot of guns and flying lead: 170
the immense power of gunpowder, and other things
of this kind, which, if not individually, are all together
capable of overpowering even implacable courage.
Add now diplomats (this is adding oil to the furnace),
royal edicts, terrifying laws, pamphlets. 175
All for attacking the credulous hearts of the rabble,
which they vie little by little to whittle away and batter down. 177

Go now, on relay horses through the settled places, 272
and transcend the icy snow-capped Aragonese Pyrenees.
When meeting the King himself at Madrid, bringing triumphs
and seas and mountains and finally all the gold home 275
with you from there. With laughing Alba you were able to turn back
sated with promises and laden with ample hope:
or rather trust, soldier, your merits, and believe
yourself better than every fear, and in vain rely on Philip II's
sealed tablets and his wax image, 280
alas, the enticements of the Duke of Parma are worth more than
everything of Solon. Also, neglect the healthy counsels of Orange.
Of course, as de Vargas arrived, you were made by Alba the warden
of the prison or commander of the castle at Sas van Gent.
Finally, you were brought up to the morning show at the sands, 285
Pompey to the Spaniards, yet about to dance without the tragic
boots and mask: soon deprived of your unworthy
part, and your head fastened on maple stakes,
providing a miserable spectacle to native Belgians,
Naenia, you come to the city of Brussels, meanwhile, while 290
I believe that it does not make up for a whit of lost time,
Alba is painted placidly on boards by Caius. 292

315 Confiteor: sed Democritos nos esse putabis,
    Non Heraclitos: quod si Gulielme nec istis
    Contentus fueris, o tum bis terque quaterque
    Te miserum, fatique mali, quem protinus a me
    Mille die, totidem noctu sine fine iocosa
320 Per caput, et salient latus omne poemata circum.
    O te tum miserum. Sed utut Gulielme futurum est,
    Promissum ante oculos hoc semper habere memento,
    Non te, non quenquam immeritum laesurus opinor
    Bilem hosti, tibi risum uni, sociisque movebo.

I confess: yet you will think me a follower of Democritus, 315
not Heraclitus: but if you, Willem, are not happy with either of
those options, oh, then you are twice, thrice and four times
an unfortunate with an evil fate, as forthwith from me
for a thousand days, and as many nights, without ceasing the jesting,
poems will dance through my head and around on every side. 320
Oh, you are so wretched. But, Willem however it may be:
remember to always keep this promise before your eyes,
I suppose neither you nor anyone will lash at the undeserving
bile of the enemy, I will provoke laughter from you, both alone and with
    friends.

Commentary

1 *O rem ridiculam* recalls the opening of Catullus 56, an erotic poem. As is the case in the opening of this satire, part of the playfulness of Catullus' poem stems from the ambiguity of as to what *res* refers. The scholar J. C. Scaliger, who greatly influenced Dousa, commented on the opening lines of Catullus' poem, *O rem ridiculam, Cato, et iocosam | dignamque auribus et tuo cachinno*, '*ut satyricus*', linking the poem with the satire genre (Graevius 1680: 81). Dousa later wrote another parody of this poem in *Praecidanea pro Q. Valerio Catullo* (Dousa 1581: 68–9).

2–10 These lines recall Catullus 1, with the dedication of his poetry to Cornelius Nepos.

4 Cf. Lucan 7.56–7: *nec non et reges populique queruntur Eoi | bella trahi patriaque procul tellure teneri*, which also refers to those prevented from returning to their homeland.

9–11 Dousa describes his journey to England and meeting with Queen Elizabeth near the end of the year 1572. Both Dousa and Van Zuylen van Nijevelt were part of an informal mission to attempt to persuade the queen to aid the Dutch resistance to the Spanish (see Heesakkers 2009: 153–5; van Dorsten 1962: 122–3; on two of Dousa's Latin odes written on this occasion, see Heesakkers 1998).

13 *risum* suggests Horatian satire. Van Zuylen van Nijevelt was himself for a period, beginning in 1568, an exile in Emmerich, in the Duchy of Cleves, where he worked as a Reformist and pro-Orange bookbinder (Spohnholz 2017: 74).

19 *Plataeae*: Plataea is an island off the coast of Libya, mentioned by Herodotus, *Histories* 4.151; cf. Propertius 2.29a.17: *afflabunt tibi non Arabum de gramine odores*.

20 Cf. Horace, *Epistles* 1.18.17: *plus quam se sapere et virtutibus esse priorem*.

21–2 *ad me ... quod | attinet*: prosaic.

23 Cf. Terence, *Hecyra* 465: *et tamen utrum malis scio*.

24 Van Zuylen van Nijevelt was from Utrecht. Another personage from Utrecht mentioned in the poem is Philippus Morus, a canon and Neo-Latin poet with whom Dousa had previously exchanged poems, who is chided for his advocacy of the duke of Alba (1.129–31, not included here; cf. Geurts 1977: 83–6).

25 Cf. Juvenal 14.5: *heres bullata*. In late medieval Latin, *doctor* or *magister bullatus* referred to someone granted a degree by decree and thus had a low academic standing. Compare John Skelton's poem: 'Doctors that learned be | Nor bachelors of that faculty | That hath taken degree | In the universitie | Shall not be objected for me. | But Doctor Bullatus | Parum litteratus, ...'

26 Cf. Plautus, *Aulularia* 402: *glabriorem reddes mihi quam volsus ludiust*.

24-7 Dousa complains that Utrecht is full of ignorant monks.

28-29 Cf. Suetonius, *Vespasian* 23: *atqui ex lotio est*. When Titus complained to his father, the emperor Vespasian, about a tax on the disposal of urine, Vespasian showed him a gold coin and asked if it smelled offensive. Titus replied in the negative, so Vespasian observed that money does not smell foul even if its origins are filthy. *Pecunia non olet* became proverbial.

29-31 According to the satire, the Roman Emperor may have made a profit from urine, but these monks profit from the relics made of even fouler human remains.

33-6 Though the bodies of heretics and witches were burned, both protestants and Catholics regarded cremation with abhorrence and at odds with the Christian belief in the final resurrection of the body.

36 *setosi ... sceptri* refers to the *aspergillum* used in the Catholic Mass for sprinkling of water: often it was a brush with long hairs.

38 *Saliaribus*: *Salii*, the leaping priests of Mars, dressed as ancient warriors when performing rituals. The *Saliaris cena* was an annual feast, but the term came to refer to an expensive meal.

Cf. Horace, *Odes* 1.4.1: *vice grata*.

168-77: This passage describes the martial, legal and propaganda onslaughts by the Spanish.

169 *tela*: classical Latin for spears or missile weapons more generally, but in this context it refers to modern 'bullets'.

174 Cf. Horace, *Sermones* 2.4.321: *hoc est oleum adde camino*.

272-80 Fernando Álvarez de Toledo, the third Duke of Alba, often referred to 'Alba' or 'Alva', was sent by King Philip II to Brussels on 22 August 1567. He was notorious for his repression of the Flemish nobility, whom he suspected of Calvinism and disloyalty, and the subsequent destruction of Mechelen and other cities. His actions shocked moderate Catholics and protestants alike. Dousa comments on his return to Spain in 1573.

280 Cf. Ausonius, *Parentalia* 20: *signatis quam tu condideras tabulis*.

281 *Parmae Ducis*: Ottavio Farnese, the Duke of Parma, who was married to Margaret of Parma, the Governor of the Netherlands, before the appointment of the Duke of Alba. Ottavio's son Alexander was made a general of the Spanish army in 1578 and later himself became the Governor-General of the Netherlands.

Solonis: Solon, the great Athenian lawmaker.

282 *Auriaci*: Willem van Oranje or William the Silent.

283 *Verga*: Juan de Vargas, the Duke of Alba's henchman.

284 *Gandavae*: Sas van Gent, site of a fortress, seized by the Spanish in 1583.

285 *matutinam . . . arenam*; cf. Mart. 14.125.1.

286 *Pompeium*: The Roman statesman Pompey served in the Sertorian War in Spain.

286–7 Athenian tragic actors wore masks and thick boots.

290 *Naenia*: goddess of funerals.

292 *Caio*: Willem Adriaensz Key (1516–68) painted the Duke of Alba. Dousa likely knew the story that, when Key was painting the Duke, he overheard a plot that lead to the execution of Lamoral, Count of Egmont and Philip de Montmorency, Count of Hoorn, the famous first leaders of the Dutch Revolt. After hearing of their deaths, Key himself allegedly died of grief.

315–16 Democritus and Heraclitus were known respectively as the laughing and crying philosophers. The choices here are that one can be happy or sad.

320 Horace, *Sermones* 2.6.34: *centum per caput, et circa saliunt latus*.

9

Editing Cicero (and Translating Aratus) in Sixteenth-Century Europe: Jan Kochanowski (1579) and Hugo Grotius (1600)

Daniele Pellacani

Introduction

In his younger years[1] Cicero produced the first Latin translation of Aratus' *Phaenomena*, a Greek didactic poem of the Hellenistic period that consists of an astronomical section (vv. 1–732) followed by a catalogue of weather-signs (vv. 733–1154). The *editio princeps* of Cicero's *Aratea*, edited by Victor Pisanus and published by Antonio da Strata (Venice 1488) reproduced a manuscript owned by Giorgio Valla, which is likely to be identified with Montpellier, École de Medicine, H 452, fol. 70r–82v: it therefore only contains Cicero's verses preserved in the direct tradition.[2] Périon, in his 1540 edition, was the first who also published fragments from the indirect tradition, supplementing the missing lines with parallels from Vergil and especially from the translations of Aratus' poem made by Germanicus (first cent. CE) and Avienius (fourth cent. CE). Further fragments of the indirect tradition were added in Morel's edition (Paris 1559; 1569[2]), which served as basis for the *Aratea* published by Patricius in his collection of Cicero's fragments (Venice 1561; 1565[2]): but Patricius made extensive revisions to Cicero's poem,[3] thanks to the collaboration of Paolo Manuzio and Jan Kochanowski (*Cochanovius meus*), his compatriot and fellow student at the University of Padua.[4]

Jan Kochanowski (Sycyna 1530 – Lublin 1584), destined to become the father of Polish poetry,[5] was a Latin poet as well as a classical scholar, as testified by his edition of Cicero's *Aratea* (Cracow 1579) in which he chose to supplement the missing hexameters with a personal Latin translation of Aratus' *Phaenomena*.[6] For this work, not lacking in brilliant conjectures, Kochanowski used the *Aratea* editions of Morel and Lambin (Paris 1566; 1573) as well as Turnèbe's *Adversaria* (Paris 1564).[7] On the whole, the perspective is more poetic than philological, as testified by the choices not to differentiate graphically his own verses from those of Cicero and to rewrite entire hexameters by Cicero in order to make them more consistent with the Greek model.[8] Kochanowski's interest in Aratus and the Latin *Aratea* matured during his Paduan years (1552-8) through his friendship with the scholar and future bishop Andrzej Patrycy Nidecki, but received new stimulus during a short trip to France (late 1558–spring 1559), in which Kochanowski, thanks to his friend Carolus Utenhove, got to know two poets who attempted poetic translations of Aratus' *Phaenomena* in those years: Rémy Bellau, who produced a French version in Alexandrine lines (published posthumously in 1578, but already partly collected in the 'Seconde Journée' of *La bergerie*, 1565) and Nicholas Allen, who translated it into Latin hexameters (Paris 1561).[9] Possibly it was this experience that persuaded Kochanowski not only to supplement Cicero's *Aratea* with a Latin translation of his own, but also to produce a Polish translation of Aratus' poem, a project on which he started working already on his return from France, but which would be published only in 1585, after his death.[10] This peculiar interaction between Greek poetry, Cicero's poetic fragments and original Polish poetry would characterise, even more significantly, Kochanowski's most memorable work, *The Laments* (*Treny*: 1580[1]; 1583[2]), which includes, like stones in a mosaic, translations of Cicero's poetic fragments that are themselves translations of Homer and the Greek tragedians: this intertextual perspective is already stated in the work's epigraph, the quotation of Cicero's translation of Hom. *Od.* 18.136–7 (= Cic. fr. 31 Bl.): *tales sunt hominum mentes, quali pater ipse | Iuppiter auctiferas lustravit lumine terras*.[11]

The same choice to integrate the lost verses of Cicero's *Aratea* with a Latin translation of his own was made again – apparently independently of Kochanowski – by a young Hugo Grotius (Hugo de Groot: Delft, 1583 – Rostock 1645). In 1600 Grotius – probably at the instigation of his teacher J. J. Scaliger, who had just edited Manilius' *Astronomica*[12] – published the *Syntagma Arateorum*, in which he printed the Greek text of Aratus' *Phaenomena* along with the Latin translations of Cicero, Germanicus and Avienius, followed by exegetical notes.

Universally known for his activities as a diplomat and jurist,[13] the Dutch humanist devoted himself, from his youth, to classical studies as well as poetry, to the point that Lucian Müller did not hesitate to define him as the most noteworthy of all Dutch Latin poets.[14] From a philological point of view, the most striking feature of the *Syntagma Arateorum* is undoubtedly the text of Germanicus, supplemented in numerous *loci* thanks to the use of ms. Leiden, Voss. Lat. Q 79, a Carolingian illuminated manuscript that represents the most authoritative witness of the ζ branch of Germanicus' tradition, unknown to previous editors (who only knew manuscripts belonging to the μ branch).[15]

With regard to the text of Cicero's *Aratea*, Grotius consulted ms. Leiden Voss. Lat. F 121 (fol. 1v–2v)[16] as well as the editions of Périon, Morel, Lambin and the *Adversaria* of Turnebus, which are never cited, with the consequence that the conjectures of these scholars were for centuries considered ingenious intuitions of the young Grotius.[17] A similar attitude can also be recognised from an analysis of his translation of Aratus, where Grotius shows himself to be indebted in some cases to the solutions devised by Allen,[18] who is never mentioned.

From a literary perspective, his Latin translation of Aratus is particularly significant because it anticipates later developments of Grotius' poetic production: during his imprisonment in Loevestein Castle (1618–21), he would conceive a cultural project aimed at 'transferring the facets of Greek poetry that he considered most important to Latin, Western culture',[19] a project that would materialise in the following years with the Latin translations of Stobaeus' *Anthologion*, the epigrams of the *Anthologia Graeca* and the tragedies of Sophocles and Euripides.[20]

Notes

1 For the problematic chronology of Cicero's *Aratea* see Pellacani 2015: 8–15.
2 Cic. *Arat.* fr. 34.1–471; the other verses of the direct tradition (472–80) are only transmitted by ms. London, British Library, Harley 647 (IX[1]) and its descendants: see Pellacani 2024a.
3 See Buescu 1941: 146. The poetic fragments represent Nidecki's most significant addition to the edition of Cicero's fragments published by Carlo Sigonio (1559; 1560), one of his Paduan teachers: see Grouchala 1991: 450–1; Axer 1996: 170–1.
4 See for example Grouchala 1991: 452–3.
5 On Kochanowski cf. the essays collected in Bilinski 1985; on his poetic production see in particular Weintraub 1952; Pelc 1986.
6 Kochanowski 1579: *M.T. Ciceronis Aratus, Ad Graecum exemplar expensus et locis mancis restitutus* ..., Cracoviae 1579 (repr. Cracoviae 1612).
7 For an analysis of Kochanowski's textual criticism see Bilinski 1984: 224–31 and especially Grouchala 1989: 117–28; for previous *Aratea* editions referred by Kochanowski see Grouchala 1989: 160.
8 On the poetic, rather than philological, value of Kochanowski's edition, see in particular Axer 1996: 173–5, but also Grouchala 1989: 129–43, who analyses some verses of Cicero rewritten by Kochanowski in order to emend errors of interpretation.
9 *Ad Illustrem et inclytum principem Eduardum semarum ... Nicolai Aleni Essentani Angli, Arati Phaenomena*, Parisiis 1561; a reference to Allen's translation can perhaps be recognised in the epigram placed by

Kochanowski in the preface of his edition, where, recalling the Latin translators of Aratus, he also names a *doctor Britannus*: see Bilinski 1984: 216. For Kochanowski's possible connections with Bellau and Allen, see Grouchala 1989: 68–71.

10 *Phaenomena Albo Wyraz Znakow Polnocnych*, published in the edition of Kochanowski's works edited by Jan Januszewski (Cracow 1585); in this Polish version only the astronomical section of the poem is translated. For the chronology of the two translations see Grouchala 1989: 78–92, who believes that the Latin translation was written in Czarnolas, where Kochanowski lived from 1574, after his retirement from public life (see also Axer 1996: 172). Grouchala 1991: 455 points out that in the preface to his second edition of Cicero's fragments (1565) Nidecki encouraged Kochanowski to undertake a Polish translation of Aratus' poem.

11 Axer 1996: 176: 'nel ciclo che gli avrebbe dato l'immortalità nella poesia polacca, scritto a meno di due anni di distanza [sc. from his *Aratea* edition] Kochanowski continuò a trattare le traduzioni ciceroniane dal greco come sfida e come ispirazione'; see also Cytowska 1979; Axer 1979; 1984: 164–5.

12 Cf. Bruhel 1961: 46 n. 102.

13 On Grotius' biography see Kahn 1983; Nellen 2014; for his education at Leiden University see also van Dam 1996.

14 Müller 1867: 78. For an overview of Grotius' poetic production see Eyffinger 1982; 1982b; 1984; Nellen / Rabbie 1991.

15 For the manuscript tradition of Germanicus see Pellacani 2024b. Thanks to the intercession of Janus Dousa, Grotius obtained a state subsidy to purchase the manuscript from the heirs of Jacob van Suys; the picture of the constellations preserved in this codex served as model for the engravings by Jacob de Gheyn that form the iconographic apparatus of the *Syntagma Arateorum*: cf. van Dam 1996. For the Greek text of Aratus, Grotius collated ms. Heidelberg, Palat. Gr. 40: see Buhle 1793: xxiv.

16 Buescu 1941: 65.

17 Buescu 1941: 109, 117–18, 148–9.

18 For this translation, published in 1561, see n. 9.

19 Eyffinger 1984: 92.

20 On this 'second phase' of Grotius' poetic production see Eyffinger 1982: 68–72; 1984: 92–5.

Bibliography

Axer, J. (1979), 'Smok i słowiczki. Wokół wersów 1–14 «Trenu I» Jana Kochanowskiego', *Pamiętnik Literacki*, 70: 187–91.

Axer, J. (1984), 'Aratus – miejsce poematu w twórczości Kochanowskiego', in: T. Michałowska (ed.), *Jan Kochanowski i epoka renesansu: W 450 rocznicę urodzin poety 1530–1980*, 159–67, Warsaw.

Axer, J. (1996), 'La fortuna dei frammenti poetici di Cicerone nella Polonia del Cinquecento', *Ciceroniana*, 9: 169-76.
Bilinski, B. (1984), 'Gli *Aratea* ciceroniani: edizione e traduzione di Jan Kochanowski poeta rinascimentale polacco', *Ciceroniana*, 5: 213-35.
Bilinski, B., ed. (1985), *Jan Cochanowski: Giovanni Cocanovio, poeta rinascimentale polacco (1530-1584)*, Wrocław et al.
Buescu, V. (1941), *Cicéron: Les Aratea*, Bucharest (repr. Hildesheim 1966).
Buhle, J. T. (1793), *Arati Solensis Phaenomena et Diosemea*..., Leipzig.
Bruhel, C. M. (1961), 'Josef Justus Scaliger: Ein Beitrag zur geistesgeschichtlichen Bedeutung der Altertumswissenschaft', *Zeitschrift für Religions- und Geistesgeschichte*, 13.1: 45-65.
Cytowska, M. (1979), 'Nad «Trenami» Jana Kochanowskiego: Od motta do genezy poematu', *Pamiętnik Literacki*, 70: 181-6.
Eyffinger, A. (1982a), *Inventory of the Poetry of Hugo Grotius*, Assen.
Eyffinger, A. (1982b), 'Outlines of Hugo Grotius' Poetry', *Grotiana*, 3: 57-75.
Eyffinger, A. (1984), 'Hugo Grotius, Poet and Man of Letters', in: Grotius Committee (ed.), *The World of Hugo Grotius (1583-1645)*, 83-95, Amsterdam / Maarssen.
Grouchala, J. (1989), *«Aratus» Jana Kochanowskiego - warsztat filologiczny poety*, Warsaw / Kraków.
Grouchala, J. (1991), 'Andrzej Patrycy Nidecki i Jan Kochanowski - wydawcy Cycerona', *Filomata*, 406: 446-58.
Kahn, E. (1983), *The Life and Works of Hugo Grotius (1583-1645)*, Pretoria.
Kidd, D. (1997), *Aratus: Phaenomena*. Edited with Introduction, Translation and Commentary, Cambridge.
Müller, L. (1867), *Hugo Grotius als Latijnsch dichter beschouwd*, Haarlem.
Nellen, H. J. M. (2014), *Hugo Grotius: A Lifelong Struggle for Peace in Church and State (1583-1645)*, Leiden.
Nellen, H. / Rabbie, E. (1991), 'Grotius' Fame as a Poet', in: A. Dalzell / C. Fantazzi / R. J. Schoeck (eds), *Acta conventus Neo-Latini Torontonensis*, 539-48, New York.
Pelc, J. (1986), *Jan Kochanowski: poète de la Renaissance (1530-1584)*, Paris.
Pellacani, D. (2015), *Cicerone. Aratea e Prognostica. Introduzione, traduzione e note*, Pisa.
Pellacani, D. (2019), 'Tradurre un'*ekphrasis*: gli *Aratea* di Cicerone', *Res Publica Litterarum*, 42: 124-51.
Pellacani, D. (2024a), 'Cicero. *Aratea*', in: J. Stover (ed.), *The Oxford Guide to the Transmission of the Latin Classics*, Oxford.
Pellacani, D. (2024b), 'Germanicus', in: J. Stover (ed.), *The Oxford Guide to the Transmission of the Latin Classics*, Oxford.
van Dam, H.-J. (1996), 'Hugo de Groot: Filoloog en dichter in Leiden', in: H. J. M. Nellen and J. Trapman (eds), *De Hollandse jaren van Hugo de Groot (1583-1621)*, 67-86, Hilversum.
Weintraub, W. (1952), 'Kochanowski's Renaissance Manifesto', *The Slavonic and East European Review*, 30.75: 412-24.

Kochanowski: Latin text

[Source of Latin text: Kochanowski 1579]

In order to analyse how Kochanowski integrated his own translation into his edition of Cicero's *Aratea*, the beginning of Aratus' astronomical section will be scrutinised (for its text see Appendix). After the proemial hymn to Zeus, Aratus begins his catalogue of the constellations, taking as starting point the celestial axis and the north pole, around which the two Bears wheel (19–48). Of this section, only six fragments of Cicero's translation have been preserved,[1] corresponding to about 15 hexameters. In the text of Kochanowski here they are not italicized to distinguish them clearly from the verses translated by Kochanowski (in italics).

22 Caetera labuntur celeri caelestia motu,
    Cum caeloque simul noctesque diesque feruntur.
    Axis stat semper, neque partem inclinat in ullam:
25 *Sed medius magnae pervadens viscera terrae,*
    Pracipitem coeli radiantis sustinet orbem.
    Extremusque adeo duplici de cardine vertex,
    Dicitur esse polus: *latet alter mersus in undis:*
    E regione alter Boream super arduus extat.
30   Hunc arcti circum geminae voluuntur: easdem
    Plaustra etiam dicunt, et imago est proxima plaustris,
    Lumina si obtineant sua temonesque rotaeque,
    Quodsi forte ursas magis appellare libebit:
    Ora micant obversa feris: capite altera tergo
35 *Imminet alterius: cursus recupinus utrique.*
    Si qua fides famae, Cressa tellure profectas
    Iuppiter in coelo, victus pietate, locavit:
    Dictaeo quod ab iis foret enutritus in antro,
    Saevum Curetes cum delusere parentem.
40 Ex iis altera apud Graios Cynosura vocatur,
    Altera dicitur esse Helice: *latera huius, et ardens*
    Cauda illustratur stellarum lumine claro,
    Quas nostri septem soliti vocitare Triones.
    Hanc Graii observant, pelagi per caerula nautes,

---

[1] Cic. *Arat.* fr. 3–8 Soub.; Kochanowski obviously omits fr. 4b *hic* [*est qui*] *terra tegitur*, first identified by Soubiran (Paris 1972).

English translation

The other celestial bodies slide in rapid motion,   22
and day and night are dragged along with the sky.
The axis always stands still and does not tilt even slightly,
but crossing in the middle the great earth's bowel   25
holds the fast sphere of the shining sky.
The axis' extreme points
are called poles: one is hidden, submerged by waves,
the other rises high in the hemisphere above Boreas.
    Around him the two *Arctoi* turn: they are also called   30
Waggons, and their appearance is similar to a waggon
if the yoke-beams and wheels had stars of their own;
but perhaps it is more correct to call them Bears: the beasts' snouts
shine one in front of the other, with her head one looms
over the other's back: both move with their paws facing up.   35
If legend can be believed, Jupiter, as a sign of respect,
placed them in the sky, originating from the land of Crete,
for he was fed by them in the cave of Dicte
when the Curetes deceived his cruel father.
One of these is called Cynosura by the Greeks,   40
the other is named Elice: its flanks and shining
tail are illuminated by the clear light of the stars,
which our people are used to call the seven oxen.
The Greeks look at her when they sail the blue sea;

45   *Germanae numero stellarum, dispositúque*
     Par Cynosura, polum sublimis lustrat eundem.
     Hac fidunt duce nocturna Phoenices in alto.
     Sed prior illa magis stellis distincta refulget,
     et late prima confestim a nocte videtur:
50   Haec vero parva est, sed nautis usus in hac est.
     Nam cursu interiore brevi convertitur orbe:
     Atque haec Sidonias nunquam est frustrata carinas.
         Has inter, veluti rapido cum gurgite flumen,
     Torvus draco serpit subter, superáque revolvens
55   Sese: conficiénsque sinus e corpore flexos,
     Oceano tingi metuentes implicat Arctos.

Cynosura, equal to her sister in number of stars and position,   45
travels, high, the same heaven.
On her the Phoenicians rely as a night guide on the high sea.
But the other shines brighter thanks to her stars
and is much the first to be recognised at nightfall;
Cynosura, on the other hand, is small, but it is useful for sailors: 50
in fact, with a faster path, it revolves in a smaller circle
and never mislead the ships of Sidon.
   Between the Bears, in the likeness of a river with raging currents,
the grim Serpent streaks, writhing on high
and down below: and forming sinuous coils with his body   55
envelops the Bears that fear plunging in the Ocean.

Commentary

22–9 *The Axis and the Poles* (= Arat. 19–26)

This section includes two Ciceronian fragments that, like the following ones, are taken from the long self-quotation that Cicero inserts in *De natura deorum* 2, within the speech of the Stoic Balbus. *Arat.* fr. 3 Soub. (21–2 = *Nat. D.* 2.104) describes the continuous movement of the constellations around the celestial axis; fr. 4 (27–8 = *Nat. D.* 2.105) defines the two poles as the extreme points of the axis, a concept reinforced through the iconic *ordo verborum*. In emphasising the axis' fixity, Kochanowski reverses the order of the model (24: *Axis stat semper* = ἄξων αἰὲν ἄρηρεν; *neque partem inclinat in ullam* = οὐδ' ὀλίγον μετανίσσεται), a solution perhaps influenced by Germ. 19: *axis stat motus*[2] *semper vestigia servat*. A similar choice can be recognised in the description of the two poles, whose antithesis is emphasised by the chiastic structure (28–9: *latet alter mersus in undis | e regione alter Boream super arduus extat*): the reference to the ocean – which Arat. 25–6 pleonastically refers to the north pole (ὁ δ' ἀντίος ἐκ βορέαο | ὑψόθεν ὠκεανοῖο) – is anticipated to explain the invisibility of the south pole (*latet alter mersus in undis*: cf. Arat. 25: οὐκ ἐπίοπτος), a solution influenced by Germ. 22–3, where the south pole is defined as *pars mersa sub undas | Oceani*. The tendency towards emphasis is achieved through adjectivisation and the use of the attributive present participle, an ecphrastic feature often used in Cicero's *Aratea*:[3] the axis *medius magnae pervadens viscera terrae* (cf. Stat. *Theb.* 9.451: *cavae ... viscera terrae*; *Silv.* 3.1.113: *invitae ... viscera terrae*) | *praecipitem coeli radiantis sustinet orbem* (same line-ending in Cic. *Arat.* fr. 34.73, but cf. the description of Atlas at Verg. *Aen.* 8.137: *aetherios umero qui sustinet orbis*), a translation that expands Arat. 22–3: ἔχει δ' ἀτάλαντον ἁπάντη | μεσσηγὺς γαῖαν περὶ δ' οὐρανὸς αὐτὸν ἀγινεῖ (perhaps assuming the *varia lectio* οὐρανόν, accepted by modern editors).

30–56 *The Bears* (= Arat. 26–48)

Arat. 26–7 Δύω ... | Ἄρκτοι, emphasised by the strong hyperbaton, is translated by replacing the numeral with the poetic *geminus*, thus forming a phrase attested in Prop. 2.22.25; Ov. *Met.* 3.45; Manil. 3.382, 5.19. Here Kochanowski adapts the Greek name to Latin morphology (*Arcti*), a form

---

[2] This is the incomprehensible text found in the editions prior to Grotius 1600, who printed *axis at immotus* on the basis of the Leiden manuscript.
[3] See Pellacani 2019: 134 *et passim*.

rare in poetry, but attested in Hygin. *Astr.* 3.1.95. The wordplay of Arat. 27: Ἄρκτοι ἅμα τροχόωσι, τὸ δὴ καλέονται Ἅμαξαι, which introduces the alternative name for these constellations, is replaced by the polyptoton framing v. 31, clearly modelled on Germ. 26-7: *plaustraque quae facies stellarum proxima verae,* | *tres temone rotisque micant sublime quaternae* (note also the replacement of the Germanican chiasmus with the epic coordination *temonesque rotaeque*). For the reference to the third appellation (*Vrsae*), Kochanowski merges Germ. 24 *Romani cognominis Vrsae* with Germ. 27-8 *si melius dixisse feras, obversa refulgent* | *ora feris*, as confirmed both by the conditional phrase and by the words *ora micant obversa feris* (with *variatio* in the *ordo verborum* and in the verb indicating brightness).

As the *aition* of these two constellations, Arat. 30-5 reports the catasterism of the bears that fed the infant Zeus while he was hidden in Crete to escape the violence of his father Cronos. In translating this section, Kochanowski combines several models: the ablative *Cressa tellure*, which translates Κρήτηθεν, is taken from Germ. 32 *Cresia . . . tellus*; the description of the catasterism combines the first half of Ov. *Met.* 13.843 with Lucr. 5.1188: *in caeloque deum sedis et templa locarunt* (but cf. also Cic. *Arat.* fr. 34.145-6: *Eridanum . . . in parte locatum* | *caeli*); and an explicit reference to Jupiter's *pietas* is made in Avien. *Arat.* 111: *custoditae referens pia dona salutis*. Like Germanicus and Avienius, Kochanowski omits the geographical reference to Mount Ida, while the iconic hyperbaton *Dictaeo . . . in antro* recalls Verg. *Georg.* 4.152, where it is stated that the bees, attracted by the cymbals of the Curetes, *Dictaeo caeli regem pavere sub antro*; for the rare verb *enutritum* cf. Ov. *Met.* 4.289: *Naiades Idaeis enutrivere* (sc. Hermaphroditus) *sub antris*, perhaps mediated by Verinus, *Flam.* 2.42.59: *Castaliis quamvis sis enutritus in antris*.

In lines 40-4 Kochanowski inserts two Ciceronian fragments that are quoted, in this order, in *Nat. D.* 2.105; while fr. 6 translates Arat. 36-7, fr. 5 represents an independent expansion by Cicero, who, through a 'translator's note', provides the Latin name for Ursa Maior.[4] In *Nat. D.* 2.105 the two fragments are linked by a prose insertion – *cuius* (sc. *Helices*) *quidem clarissimas stellas totis noctis cernimus* –, which Kochanowski reworks in poetic form (41-2) by omitting the temporal determination and instead emphasising, also through alliteration, the brightness of the constellation, in accordance with a characteristic feature of Cicero's *Aratea*:[5] *et ardens* (the same line-ending at [Ov.] *Hal.* 113) again attests to the use of the attributive present participle; *lumine claro* (the same line-ending at Catull. 64.408; Avien.

---

[4] For the order of these two fragments see Pellacani 2015: 88.
[5] See Pellacani 2015: 20-1; 2019: 137-9.

Arat. 484) modifies the Ciceronian phrase *claro cum lumine* (*Arat.* fr. 34.277; 298; 323; 389; but cf. also 263 *claro collucens lumine Cancer* and the clausulae of *Arat.*107 *lumine claret*; 180 *lumine clarae*).

Arat. 37–44 reports the different modes of navigation of the Greeks, who follow Ursa Maior, easier to recognise but more distant from the north pole, and the Phoenicians, who instead orient themselves by following Ursa Minor; Cicero quotes twice only the lines relating to the Phoenicians (fr. 7 = *Nat. D.* 2.106 and, partially, *Ac.* 2.66). In v. 44 Kochanowski condenses *Arat.* 37–8: Ἑλίκῃ γε μὲν ἄνδρες Ἀχαιοὶ | εἰν ἁλὶ τεκμαίρονται ἵνα χρὴ νῆας ἀγινεῖν in the periphrasis *pelagi per caerula nautes* (for the expression *pelagi caerula*, not classical, cf. Petrus Damiani, *Carm.* 81.3: *pelagi mihi caerula sulcat* and, with identical metrical placement, Gambara, *Navig.* 2.273–4: *pelagique ad caerula proras | convertunt*); the noun *nautes* – which appears both in the 1579 and the 1612 editions – must be understood as an allograph of *nautae*, unless one assumes a misprint for *nantes*, which would constitute a further example of the attributive present participle. Lines 45–6 find no parallel in the Greek text: here too Kochanowski reworks the prose expression that Cicero, in *Nat. D.* 2.106, uses to connect the two poetic quotations: *parilibusque stellis similiter distinctis* (= *Germanae numero stellarum, dispositique | Par Cynosura*) *eundem caeli verticem lustrat parva Cynosura* (= *polum sublimis lustrat eundem*, with double *variatio* of the noun designating the pole and the adjective qualifying Cynosura). Line 52, which closes the section, translates *Arat.* 44: τῇ καὶ Σιδόνιοι ἰθύντατα ναυτίλλονται, reworking Germ. 47: *Sidoniamque ratem numquam spectata* [sc. *Cynosura*] *fefellit*: note the double synonymic *variatio* of *Sidoniam ratem* with *Sidonias . . . carinas* (cf. Avien. *Arat.* 136: *Sidoniis . . . carinis*, with identical metrical position) and of *fefellit* with the alliterative *est frustrata*.

Arat. 45–8 introduces the constellation of the Serpent, which meanders, river-like, between the two Bears. Kochanowski quotes the Ciceronian translation of *Arat.* 45–7 (fr. 8 = *Nat. D.* 2.106) and supplements it with his own translation of *Arat.* 48: Ἄρκτοι, κυαννέου πεφυλαγμέναι ὠκεανοῖο. He is clearly inspired by Verg. *Georg.* 1.246: *Arctos Oceani metuentes aequore tingi*, which in turn is part of a rewriting of *Arat.* 45–7 (Verg. *Georg.* 1.244–6: *maximus hic flexu sinuoso elabitur Anguis | circum perque duas in morem fluminis Arctos, | Arctos Oceani metuentes aequore tingi*):[6] in Kochanowski the

---

[6] For the influence of Vergil's *Georgics* see Axer 1996: 174: '[Kochanowski] colmò le lacune con alcuni versi propri, il cui ideale era rappresentato dal modello virgiliano delle *Georgiche*.'

different *ordo verborum* and the substitution of the nexus *aequore Oceani* with the simple *Oceano* enable insertion of the verb *implicat*, necessary because in Cic. *Arat.* fr. 8 the subject is the Serpent (and not the Bears, as in Arat. 47–8).

Grotius: Latin text

[Source of Latin text: Grotius 1600]

In his edition of Cicero's *Aratea*, Grotius – unlike Kochanowski – takes care to distinguish graphically his own translations from the Ciceronian hexameters: this graphic solution, perfectly consistent with the philological aims of his work, would be maintained in Cicero's *Opera omnia* edited by Orelli, Baiter and Halm (Zurich 1861), which reprints Grotius' edition, including his additions (vol. 4, pp. 1013–47). Once again, presented here is the beginning of the astronomical section of the poem.

  Caetera labuntur caeleri celestia motu,
20 Cum caeloque simul, noctesque diesque feruntur;
  Axis at immotus nunquam vestigia mutat,
  Sed tenet aequali libratas pondere terras;
  Quem circum magno se volvit turbine coelum:
  Extremusque adeo duplici de cardine vertex
25 Dicitur esse Polus, *quorum hic non cernitur, ille*
  Ad Boream, Oceani supera confinia tendit:
  Quem cingunt Vrsae celebres cognomine Plaustri,
  Quas nostri septem soliti vocitare Triones.
   Alterius caput, alterius flammantia terga
30 *Aspicit, inque vicem pronas rapit orbis in ipsos*
  Conversas humeros. Crete (si credere fas est)
  Ad caeli nitidas axes venere relicta:
  Iupiter hoc voluit, quem sub beneolentibus herbis
  Ludentem Dicti, grato posuere sub antro,
35 *Idaeum ad montem, totumque aluere per annum,*
  Saturnum fallunt dum Dictaei Corybantes.
  Ex his altera apud Graios Cynosura vocatur
  Altera dicitur esse Helice, *quae monstrat Achivis*
  In pelago navis quo sit vertenda, sed illa
40 *Se fidunt duce nocturna Phoenices in alto.*
  Sed prior illa magis stellis distincta refulget,
  Et late prima confestim a nocte videtur.
  Haec vero parva est, sed nautis usus in hac est:
  Nam cursu interiore brevi convertitur orbe,
45 Signaque Sidoniis monstrat certissima nautis.
  Has inter, veluti rapido cum gurgite flumen,
  Torvu' Draco serpit, subter, superaque revolvens
  Sese, conficiensque sinus e corpore flexos,
  Quos cani tangunt immunes gurgitis Arctoi.

English translation

The other celestial bodies slide in rapid motion,
and day and night are dragged along with the sky. 20
But the axis, motionless, never changes position,
but keeps the earth in balance, balancing its weight;
around it the sky revolves in a great vortex.
The axis' extreme points
are called poles: one of them is not visible, the other 25
rises above Ocean's horizon, on the side of Boreas.
   Around him the Bears wheel: they are known as the Waggons,
which our people usually call the seven oxen.
One's head gazes at the flaming hips
of the other, and the rotation moves them into a prone position, 30
on their backs. If you can believe it, they went up
into the sky's bright vault after leaving Crete:
Jupiter willed it, whom they deposited, when he was a child,
on the fragrant meadows of Dicte, inside a beautiful cave
near Mount Ida, and fed him for a whole year, 35
while the Corybantes of Dicte deceived Saturn.
One of these is called Cynosura by the Greeks,
the other is named Elice. It is she who among the waves shows
to the Achaeans where to direct their ship; but on the other
the Phoenicians rely as a night guide on the high sea. 40
But the first shines brighter thanks to her stars
and is much the first to be recognised at nightfall;
Cynosura, on the other hand, is small, but it is useful for sailors:
in fact, with a faster path, it revolves in a smaller circle
and shows infallible signs to the Sidonian sailors. 45
   Between the Bears, in the likeness of river with raging currents,
the grim Serpent streaks, writhing on high
and down below: and forming sinuous coils with his body,
which the Bears, free from contact with the grey sea, touch.

Commentary

19-26 *The Axis and the Poles* (= Arat. 19-26)

After quoting Cic. *Arat.* fr. 3, Grotius (21-3) completes the description of the celestial axis by reworking Germ. 19-21: *axis at immotus semper vestigia servat | libratasque tenet terras et cardine firmo | orbem agit*: the literal quotation of the first half verse is accompanied by the *variatio* of *semper vestigia servat* in *numquam vestigia mutat*, with double antonymic (and isoprosodic) substitution that leaves the sense, as well as the metre, unchanged (for the line-ending *vestigia mutat* cf. Germ. 439; 522); at line 22 Germanicus' phrase *libratas tenet terras* is completed by the ablatival phrase *aequali ... pondere*. This last is attested in poetry only in Marrasio, *Carm.* 30.16-8: *et lances geminas aequali pondere Librae | intravit* (sc. *sol*) as a variation of *aequato pondere* employed, likewise with reference to Libra / Claws in Germ. fr. 4.27 Bl.: *aequato libratae pondere Chelae* and Manil. 4.548: *aequato ... sub pondere Librae*. Consistent with the Greek text he adopted (περὶ δ' οὐρανὸς αὐτὸν ἀγινεῖ: see *Notae*, p. 2: 'Mihi non displicet Mathematicorum lectio: περὶ δ' οὐρανὸς αὐτὸν ἀγινεῖ – Leontius: καὶ ἄξων λέγεται ἐπεὶ περὶ αὐτοῦ ὁ οὐρανός ἄγεται'), Grotius states that it is the sky that rotates (*se volvit*) around the axis (*quem circum*); with *magno ... turbine* he adapts to the sky a phrase attested in Flavian epic, especially referring to winds (Val. Fl. 6.353; 8.366-7; Sil. 12.570).

The reference to the two poles (24-5 = Cic. *Arat.* fr. 4) is completed with a fairly faithful translation of Arat. 25-6: line 26 combines an incipit attested in Priscian's *Periegesis* (96, 543, 556) with the line-ending of Avien. *Orb.* 323; with *Oceani confinia* Grotius understands the reference to the Ocean as a poetic metonymy for the horizon, consistently with his exegesis of Arat. 26 (*Notae*, p. 2: '*Aratus ubique horizontem vocat oceanum, ut et Homerus*').

27-49 *The Bears* (= Arat. 26-48)

In introducing the Bears, Grotius – unlike Kochanowski and the ancient Latin translators – does not give the Greek name of these constellations, but only the Latin names *Vrsae* – *Plaustra* (the line-ending, which modifies Germ. 25: *Romani cognominis Vrsae*, is possibly influenced by Allen's translation: *cognomine plaustra vocarunt*). Reversing the order in which the fragments are quoted in *Nat. D.* 2.105, Grotius inserts here Cic. *Arat.* fr. 5 (*quas nostri septem soliti vocitare Triones*), assuming that the relative *quas* refers to both constellations. This solution would be adopted by all later editors (with the exception of Ewbank and Pellacani), but it contradicts the *testimonium*, where *quas* clearly refers to the stars of Ursa Maior (*Nat. D.*

2.105: *Helice, cuius quidem clarissimas stellas totis noctibus cernimus, 'quas... Triones'*: see Pellacani 2015: 88). The description of the reciprocal position of the two Bears (29-31) is again presented as a *variatio in imitando* of Germ. 29-31: *caput alterius super horrida terga | alterius lucet: pronas rapit orbis in ipsos | decliveis umeros*.

Lines 31-6 report the catasterism of the two Bears. The aside *si credere fas est* appears, in the same metrical position, in Sil. 3.425, but the line-ending *credere fas est* is already in Manil. 3.553; 4.896; v. 32 combines Verg. *Aen.* 6.790: *magnum caeli ventura sub axem* (Anchises announcing to Aeneas the future apotheosis of Iulus' line) and Stat. *Silv.* 1.2.212-3 (the hyperbolic description of Stella's joy, who, at the announcement of his wedding, *ire polo nitidosque errare per axes | visus*). The description of the cave on Dicte is clearly influenced by Allen's translation, where the Curetes *muscoso procul occoluere* [*sc. Iovem*] *sub antro | Dictamo fultum molli, et bene olentibus herbis*: note on the one hand the rendering of the epithet εὐῶδες[7] with the periphrasis *sub beneolentibus herbis* (at line-end as in Allen), on the other hand the expression *grato posuere sub antro*, which modifies Allen's translation through an echo of Hor. *Carm.* 1.5.3 (*grato, Pyrrha, sub antro*); the reference to *Corybantes*, instead of Curetes, is clearly influenced by Germ. 38: *Dictaei ... Corybantes*.

At lines 36-7 Grotius inserts *Arat*. fr. 5, in which Cicero mentions the names of the two Bears; the following comparison between Greek and Phoenician navigation (*Arat*. fr. 7) is introduced by the translation of Arat. 37-8: Ἑλίκῃ γε μὲν ἄνδρες Ἀχαιοί | εἰν ἁλὶ τεκμαίρονται ἵνα χρὴ νῆας ἀγινεῖν, where the Homeric εἰν ἁλί is rendered by a half-line that echoes Lucr. 4.432 *in pelago nautis*, thus reproducing the *variatio synonymica* of the model (Arat. 38: εἰν ἁλί = *in pelago*; 39: θάλασσαν = *in alto*). In quoting Cic. *Arat*. fr. 7 Grotius corrects the transmitted *hac* (referring to Cynosura) with *se*, thus opting for the reflexive construction of *fido*. After the quotation, the section is concluded with the translation of Arat. 44: τῇ καὶ Σιδόνιοι ἰθύντατα ναυτίλλονται, where the verb *monstro* forms a sort of ring composition (cf. 38) that rounds off the *excursus*; the phrase *certissima signa* is attested in Verg. *Georg*. 1.439, and then in Germ. 5; 255; 521 (but in reference to constellations).

The passage ends with the quotation of Cic. *Arat*. fr. 8, which introduces the Serpent, completed by Grotius' translation of Arat. 48; unlike

---

[7] Moving from the meaning of this epithet, Grotius (*Notae*, p. 2) corrects the transmitted Δίκτῳ (dative of a masculine or neuter toponym not attested elsewhere) with Λύκτῳ, a conjecture recently accepted by Kidd 1997: 186-7 (*contra* Martin 1998: 80-1: 'c'est peut-être trop facile, et on ne peut pas vraiment dire que Lyctos soit *près de l'Ida*').

Kochanowski, Grotius reproduces the syntax of the Greek model, with the Bears (designated by the Grecism *Arctoi*) as the subject of *tangunt*: he chose this verb because in the Greek text of Aratus he prints the *varia lectio* φύονται (which he understands in the sense of its compound ἔμφυω: 'to attach', 'to grasp'), and not the technical φέρονται accepted by modern editors. In translating κυανέου πεφυλαγμέναι ὠκεανοῖο with *cani ... gurgitis* he preserves, even with variation, the chromatic detail, recalling a phrase attested in Catull. 64.18 and later in *Ciris* 514; Stat. *Theb.* 11.43; Avien. *Arat.* 308: overall, the expression can be interpreted as a triple *variatio synonymica* of Germ. 63: *tumidis ignotae fluctibus Arctoe.*

Appendix: Aratus, *Phaenomena* 19–48[8]

Greek text

Οἱ μὲν ὁμῶς πολέες τε καὶ ἄλλυδις ἄλλοι ἐόντες
20 οὐρανῷ ἕλκονται πάντ' ἤματα συνεχὲς αἰεί·
αὐτὰρ ὅγ' οὐδ' ὀλίγον μετανίσσεται, ἀλλὰ μάλ' αὕτως
ἄξων αἰὲν ἄρηρεν, ἔχει δ' ἀτάλαντον ἁπάντη
μεσσηγὺς γαῖαν, περὶ δ' οὐρανὸς αὐτὸν ἀγινεῖ.
Καί μιν πειραίνουσι δύω πόλοι ἀμφοτέρωθεν·
25 ἀλλ' ὁ μὲν οὐκ ἐπίοπτος, ὁ δ' ἀντίος ἐκ βορέαο
ὑψόθεν ὠκεανοῖο. Δύω δέ μιν ἀμφὶς ἔχουσαι
Ἄρκτοι ἅμα τροχόωσι, τὸ δὴ καλέονται Ἅμαξαι.
Αἱ δ' ἤτοι κεφαλὰς μὲν ἐπ' ἰξύας αἰὲν ἔχουσιν
ἀλλήλων, αἰεὶ δὲ κατωμάδιαι φορέονται,
30 ἔμπαλιν εἰς ὤμους τετραμμέναι. Εἰ ἐτεὸν δή,
Κρήτηθεν κεῖναί γε Διὸς μεγάλου ἰότητι
οὐρανὸν εἰσανέβησαν, ὅ μιν τότε κουρίζοντα
Δίκτῳ ἐν εὐώδει, ὄρεος σχεδὸν Ἰδαίοιο,
ἄντρῳ ἐγκατέθεντο καὶ ἔτρεφον εἰς ἐνιαυτόν,
35 Δικταῖοι Κούρητες ὅτε Κρόνον ἐψεύδοντο.
Καὶ τὴν μὲν Κυνόσουραν ἐπίκλησιν καλέουσιν,
τὴν δ' ἑτέρην Ἑλίκην. Ἑλίκῃ γε μὲν ἄνδρες Ἀχαιοὶ
εἰν ἁλὶ τεκμαίρονται ἵνα χρὴ νῆας ἀγινεῖν·
τῇ δ' ἄρα Φοίνικες πίσυνοι περόωσι θάλασσαν.
40 ἀλλ' ἡ μὲν καθαρὴ καὶ ἐπιφράσσασθαι ἑτοίμη
πολλὴ φαινομένη Ἑλίκη πρώτης ἀπὸ νυκτός·
ἡ δ' ἑτέρη ὀλίγη μέν, ἀτὰρ ναύτῃσιν ἀρείων·
μειοτέρη γὰρ πᾶσα περιστρέφεται στροφάλιγγι·
τῇ καὶ Σιδόνιοι ἰθύντατα ναυτίλλονται.
45 Τὰς δὲ δι' ἀμφοτέρας οἵη ποταμοῖο ἀπορρὼξ
εἰλεῖται, μέγα θαῦμα, Δράκων, περί τ' ἀμφί τ' ἐαγὼς
μυρίος· αἱ δ' ἄρα οἱ σπείρης ἑκάτερθε φύονται
Ἄρκτοι, κυανέου πεφυλαγμέναι ὠκεανοῖο.

---

[8] According to Grouchala 1989: 46 it is impossible to determine the edition of Aratus used by Kochanowski for his translation. Since the second part of this chapter is devoted to Grotius' translation, I reproduce the Greek text of Aratus published by him in Grotius 1600.

English translation

The numerous stars, scattered in different directions,
sweep all alike across the sky every day continuously for ever. 20
The axis, however, does not move even slightly from its place,
but just stays for ever fixed, holds the earth
in the centre evenly balanced, and round it the sky rotates.
Two poles terminate it at the two ends;
but one is not visible, while the opposite one in the north 25
is high above the horizon. On either side of it two
Bears wheel in unison, and so they are called the Waggons.
    They keep their heads for ever pointing to each other's loins,
and for ever they move with shoulders leading, aligned
towards the shoulders, but in opposite directions. If the tale is true, 30
these Bears ascended to the sky from Crete by the will
of great Zeus, because, when he was a child, then
in fragrant Dicte near Mount Ida, they deposited him
in a cave and tended him for the year,
while the Curetes of Dicte kept Cronus deceived. 35
Now one of the Bears men call Cynosura by name,
the other Helice. Helice is the one by which Greek men
at sea judge the course to steer their ships,
while Phoenicians cross the sea relying on the other.
Now the one is clear and easy to identify, Helice, 40
being visible in all its grandeur as soon as night begins;
the other is slight, yet a better guide to sailors,
for it revolves entirely in a smaller circle:
so by it the Sidonians sail the straightest course.
    Between the two Bears, in the likeness of a river, 45
winds a great wonder, the Serpent, writhing around and about
at enormous length; the Bears touch either side of its coil,
keeping clear of the dark-blue ocean.[9]

---

[9] The English translation is that of Kidd 1997, with modifications.

10

John Barclay (1582–1621): The *Argenis* as a Statian Scholar's Novel

Ruth Parkes

Introduction

John Barclay was born in Lorraine in 1582 to a French mother and a Scottish father, the jurisprudence scholar William Barclay. He studied at the university of Pont-à-Mousson in Lorraine, where his father taught. Evidence of Barclay's wide classical learning is provided by the variety of Greek and Latin authors, including Homer, Euripides, Seneca, Ovid and Pliny, cited in his first publication, his 1601 commentary on Statius' *Thebaid*, which originated during his university education. Moving to England in 1605, he was connected to James I's court for a decade. He died in 1621 in Rome, where he had relocated in 1616.

The (all Latin) literary output of Barclay was a varied one: it included such pieces as his 1603 poem upon James I's coronation, *Regi Jacobo Primo, carmen gratulatorium*, his 1606 collection of poems, *Sylvae*, and an edition of his father's posthumous text *De Potestate Papae* (1609). This chapter treats John Barclay's posthumously published romance novel *Argenis* (1621). In this work, Barclay's prose is interspersed by thirty-seven verse sections (in various metres, but with dactylic hexameter predominating). Barclay's adoption of this prosimetric format follows on from his use of it in his earlier novel, the satirical *Euphormionis Lusinini Satyricon* (1605–7), which critics such as de Smet (1996) have placed in the Menippean tradition.

Whilst Barclay's *Argenis* no longer has the popularity attendant upon its original publication, the novel still garners critical interest, notably surrounding its impact upon later literature and in the area of contemporary political resonance.[1] Another concern is the work's literary form and tradition. Connors (2005) has shown that Petronius' prosimetric Latin novel *Satyrica* was a key model for the *Argenis*, as it had been for Barclay's earlier work, *Euphormionis Lusinini Satyricon*. Even though Barclay would have had even less text of the *Satyrica* than is now available for modern readers (prior to c. 1650 the *Cena Trimalchionis* was known only in fragmentary form), he would have had access to some portions. It is similarly important to set the work against the ancient Greek novel tradition, particularly Heliodorus' *Aethiopika* (Connors 2005; Zurcher 2007; Bearden 2013: 128–57). Barclay's use of non-prose intertexts has also attracted critical attention. Connors (2005) has looked at the novel's use of two Latin epics, Vergil's *Aeneid* and Ovid's *Metamorphoses*.[2] Given that the ancient novel had itself exploited epic, Barclay's entwining of these two traditions seems especially fitting. Traditional drama may have had an impact: for instance, in Barclay's use of a five-book structure.[3] Certainly, the work demonstrates an interest in spectacle, as evidenced by *Argenis* II.3.2–3 (the victory procession), III.23.2–6 (the masque) and III.5.6 (Radirobanes' viewing of a play and other entertainments).

Two sections of the *Argenis* have been selected for scrutiny. The first passage, from book 2, contains a verse celebration of a beautiful bracelet that the Sicilian king Meleander chooses as a present for the foreigner Poliarchus (the disguised King of Gaul), who had been in Sicily for more than a year and who had helped Meleander with the island's civil dissension (*Arg.* I.4.2; III.13.5). The beauty and value of the bracelet helps convey the value that Meleander places on Poliarchus' friendship: the king is trying to regain Poliarchus' favour and bring him back to Sicily (Meleander had previously believed the aspersions of the trouble-stirring Sicilian Lycogenes against Poliarchus and accused him of treason). The king decides to send the bracelet as if it were coming from his daughter Argenis, following the advice of Cleobulus (*Arg.* II.6.4): at this point, he is unaware of Argenis' amorous feelings towards Poliarchus (who had travelled to Sicily in order to seek out Argenis). By the time of the second extract, from book three, Lycogenes has been defeated, but the ambitious Sardinian king Radirobanes poses a threat to Sicily. As he had informed Meleander at *Argenis* III.5.2, he wishes to marry Argenis. In awareness of the presence of a rival, Archombrotus, Radirobanes resolves to use treachery as an aid, bribing those close to Argenis (*Arg.* III.5.5). Whilst he is contemplating the corruption of Argenis' nurse, Selenissa, he sees a play and takes heart from that part which depicts the wavering Eriphyle, a character from Greek myth, succumb to greed (*Arg.* III.5.6). Following Argenis' rejection of his advances (*Arg.* III.5.8), Radirobanes passes on a picture in a jewelled case to garner Selenissa's support (*Arg.* III.5.8).

The particular focus of this chapter lies in the value of looking at the *Argenis* from the angle of Barclay's scholarly experience of Statius' *Thebaid*, the late first-century CE epic on the war of the Seven against Thebes. Hence its material includes Barclay's comments on the *Thebaid* (1601), alongside his lemmata drawn from Bernartius' 1595 text, and two passages of Statius, taken from *Thebaid* 2.269–30 and 4.187–21 (using Hill's 1983 edition[4]). Barclay's work on Statius does not cover the full twelve books of the Latin epic, its incompletion being attributed by the preface to the intervention of Barclay's father. The need to halt progress on the project affected the final output: some 160 pages are devoted to commentary on the first four books, followed by thirty pages of notes on books five to eight (Berlincourt 2013: 76). It is clear from Barclay's observations that he was very familiar with the poem, including books nine to twelve, where circumstances had precluded exegesis. As befits his stated aim in the preface of illuminating the poet (Berlincourt 2013: 176), Barclay's notes have a pedagogical thrust, typically explicating the epic in various ways. His notes often give mythical background: for example, Barclay comments on his quotation of *Thebaid* 2.299 (*viderat hoc coniunx perituri vatis*, 'the wife of the doomed seer had seen this'): 'Eryphile Amphiarai coniunx, cui monili illo in donum dato persuasit Polynices ut coniugem ad suscipiendum in Thebanos bellum compelleret' ('Eryphile, wife of Amphiaraus, whom Polynices persuaded by that well-known necklace, given for a gift, to force her husband to enter upon war against the Thebans'). The notes also point to relevant material elsewhere in the poem (here Barclay goes on to cross-reference the appearance of the story in *Thebaid* 4). Exegesis is scant compared to modern scholarly commentaries, with frequent gaps. So, for example, there are only two comments dealing with *Thebaid* 4.187–213: the observation that *Thebaid* 4.187 refers to Amphiaraus and the clarification of *Thebaid* 4.190 (a reference to the fated overwhelming of Amphiaraus' foreknowledge of Apollo's warnings) *obrueratque deum* ('she [Atropos] had crushed the god') as *divinos monitus obruerat* ('she had crushed divine warnings'; see *Theb.* 3.451–551 for Amphiaraus' divination).

One value of approaching the *Argenis* through the lens of Barclay's scholarship is that it allows explication of parts of the novel. In his note on *Thebaid* 2.274 Barclay gives information about the wizard craftsmen known as the Telchines. Within the note he quotes Ovid, *Metamorphoses* 7.365–7 on the Telchines: *Ialysios Telchinas, | quorum oculos ipso vitiantes omnia visu | Iuppiter exosus fraternis subdidit undis* ('and the Telchines of Ialysus, whose eyes, marring all things by their very gaze, Jupiter hated and plunged under his brother's waves'). Immediately after this, Barclay presents his interpretation of *Metamorphoses* 7.367: *in silices nimirum commutavit* ('without doubt he changed them into rocks'). This exegesis sheds light on the meaning and origin of the description of the Telchines at *Argenis* II.6.6.21 as *nondum ... naufraga saxa* ('not yet shipwrecking rocks'). The use of mythical content apparently derived from the *Metamorphoses* reinforces the Ovidian spirit already conjured in this line by the presence of a metamorphosis and use of *nondum* to refer to an as yet unrealized future (for which see Solodow 1988: 63).[5]

A yet stronger benefit, however, lies in the illumination of Barclay's artistic techniques. Our knowledge of Barclay's deep understanding of the *Thebaid* invites us to bring this epic to the fore as an important intertext for the *Argenis*.[6] He draws on the *Thebaid*'s diction, material and even structure (he mimics Statius' references to Harmonia's necklace in *Thebaid* 2 and 4 through evoking these passages in two distinct parts of the novel). Through the intertextuality, we can see a more sophisticated and sensitive response to the *Thebaid* than is evident in the largely pedagogical notes of Barclay's commentary.

Statius treats Eriphyle's necklace in two separate sections. The first is at *Thebaid* 2.265–305, which provides a description and history of Harmonia's cursed necklace, which Amphiaraus' wife Eriphyle covets as she sees it worn by Polynices' bride, Argia. The second section shows Argia deciding to give up her necklace after weighing up the issue. She knows that, if Eriphyle is bribed, Amphiaraus will join the other chiefs and the expedition against Thebes can commence. The relevant parts of these two sections are cited in an appendix, together with a translation; the commentary on Barclay's text makes it clear where verbal and thematic parallels occur.

Notes

1 Note, for example, its engagement with contemporary debates (cf. Parkes 2022: 260). For literary reception, see e.g. Invernizzi 2017.
2 For Ovid, see also Parkes 2022: 264–6.
3 IJsewijn (1983), 13. Morrish Tunberg (2013: 76 n. 8) sees the influence of Plautus in the characterization of Radirobanes.
4 There are a few occasions where Hill's text does not accord with the text that Barclay would have found in Bernartius. So, for example, at *Theb.* 4.193 Hill's reading *scit et ipsa (nefas!)* differs from Bernartius' text, *scit et ipse nefas*, and at *Theb.* 4.204 Hill reads *(infandum!) . . . minanti* whereas Bernartius prints *(heu superi) . . . minaci*. However, this should not affect our appreciation of the intertextuality: whilst we should note that at *Thebaid* 4.199 Barclay would have read *deposuit nexus*, rather than *exuerat cultus*, Statius' application of *cultus* to the necklace at *Thebaid* 2.302 and 4.195 still allows use to see overlap in diction. Translations are my own.
5 Cf. Barclay's use of *nondum* at *Arg.* III.23.5 and II.12.3 at Ovidian-rich moments (Parkes 2022: 264 n. 28 and 264–5 n. 29).
6 This area has been somewhat neglected. Parkes (2022: 261 n. 5) contains a brief discussion of engagement with Statius' *Thebaid* (and also Statius' other epic, the *Achilleid: ibid.*, 269 n. 67; 275 n. 117).

Bibliography

Barclay, John (1601), *In P. Statii Papinii Thebaidis libros iiii. commentarii et in totidem sequentes notae, cum argumentis summam cuiusque libri seriem ac materiam explicantibus, authore Ioanne Barclaio, Guilmi I. Cti. Filio. Pontimussi, apud Melchiorem Bernardum*, Pont-à-Mousson.

Barclay, John (2004), *Argenis*. Edited and translated by Mark Riley and Dorothy Pritchard Huber, 2 vols, Assen.

Bearden, E. B. (2013), *The Emblematics of the Self: Ekphrasis and Identity in Renaissance Imitations of Greek Romances*, Toronto / Buffalo / London.

Berlincourt, V. (2013). *Commenter la Thébaïde (16e–19e s.): Caspar von Barth et la tradition exégétique de Stace*, Leiden / Boston (Mnemosyne Suppl. 354).

Connors, C. (2005), 'Metaphor and Politics in John Barclay's *Argenis*', in: S. J. Harrison / M. Paschalis / S. A. Frangoulidis (eds), *Metaphor and the Ancient Novel*, 245–74, Groningen (Ancient Narrative Supplementum 4).

de Smet, I. (1996), *Menippean Satire in the Republic of Letters 1581–1655*, Geneva (Travaux du Grand Siècle 2).

Hill, D. E. (1983, 1st edn), *P. Papini Stati Thebaidos libri XII. Recensuit et cum apparatu critico et exegetico instruxit*, Leiden (repr. 1996 with corrigenda).

IJsewijn, J. (1983), 'John Barclay and His Argenis: A Scottish Neo-Latin Novelist', *Humanistica Lovaniensia*, 32: 1–27.

Invernizzi, D. (2017), 'L'Argenis di *John Barclay* (1582–1621) e la sua influenza sul Romanzo Italiano Seicento', PhD diss., Università Cattolica del Sacro Cuore (online at: DocTA – Doctoral Theses Archive).

Morrish Tunberg, J. (2013), 'An Old Wife and the Tale that She Tells in Barclay's Argenis', in: S. Tilg / I. Walser (eds), *Der neulateinische Roman als Medium seiner Zeit / The Neo-Latin Novel in its Time*, 73–82, Tübingen (NeoLatina 21).

Parkes, R. (2022), 'Sicily, the Classical Tradition and Interpretative Possibilities in John Barclay's *Argenis*', *International Journal of the Classical Tradition*, 29: 260–80.

Solodow, J. B. (1988), *The World of Ovid's Metamorphoses*, Chapel Hill.

Zurcher, A. (2007), *Seventeenth-Century English Romance: Allegory, Ethics, and Politics*, New York.

Source of Latin text

The 2004 edition of the *Argenis* by Mark Riley and Dorothy Pritchard Huber has been used as the basis for the text given.

Latin text

Text 1: *Argenis* II.6.5-6

Metre of II.6.6: elegiac couplets

II.6.5 ... *Inter cetera erat armilla ex serico texto, quod totum varii generis lapilli sic implebant, per suos colores distributi ut aliquot ferarum aut fugam figurarent aut iram, quas hic telis venatores sequebantur, hic excipiebant venabulis. Pretium gemmis et operi ingens, quippe quod talentis quinquaginta indicabatur. Multi Siculorum hanc viderant, plures audierant celebratam non ignobilis poetae opera, quem suo fulgore ad hos versus rapuerat.*

II.6.6
Dicite, surgenti confinia litora Phoebo,
    Quam nitidus vestris hic deus exit aquis?
Cum tingit virides hilari fulgore smaragdos,
    Aut facit, o adamas, te sibi luce parem,
5 Pallentemve onychem, varium vel iaspida miscet,
    Vel cui purpureo nomen ab igne venit,
Caeruleasque notas et flammis implet et auro,
    Ceu variat puras comptior Iris aquas.
Hae tamen haud uno cunctae sub litore gemmae
10   Nascuntur. Nam cui gloria tanta solo?
His nitet immensus Ganges, his flavus Hydaspes;
    Est et Erythrai lucida concha sali.
Una omnes armilla tenet, par omnibus una,
    Omnis in haec Oriens lucida texta coit.
15 Di superi! Pretium nitidae formamque coronae!
    Quam volet amplecti tanta corona manum?
Ut natat in solidis lux alternata lapillis!
    Oraque venantum quam bene gemma facit!
Dives en hic cervus, quem ditia tela fatigant,
20   Et leo, quem pretio cerne tumere suo.
Lemnius an nondum Telchines naufraga saxa
    Artifici gemmas sic posuêre manu?
Digna quidem Iovis haec vibrare armilla lacerto,
    Cum quatit imbrifera luce coruscus humum.
25 Ipsa, licet dives, placata hoc munere Iuno,
    Poneret offensi iurgia saeva tori.
At te seu veri seu famae gloria tangit,
    O quisquis tanta bracchia dote coles,
Vince animo censum, ne haec optima saxa putentur,
30   Tuque genus Pyrrhae vilior esse lapis.

English translation

II.6.5 ... Among the rest was a bracelet of silken fabric which gems of varied kind so covered all over, shared out through their colours, that some depict the flight or anger of wild beasts which the hunters here were following with their spears and here were intercepting with their hunting-spears. The cost was great for the jewels and for the workmanship, since it was priced at fifty talents. Many of the Sicilians had seen this, more had heard it praised by the work of a not undistinguished poet, whom the work brought to these lines by its gleam.

II.6.6 Speak, you shores that are adjacent to the rising sun, how radiantly does this god emerge from your waters, when he colours your green emeralds with cheerful brilliance or, o diamond, makes you shine like himself, [5] or he mixes the pale onyx or variegated jasper, or the stone whose name comes from crimson fire, and he fills blue-green marks with both flames and gold, in the same way as the rather adorned Iris marks clear waters with contrasting colours. Yet these gems do not all exist on one shore. [10] For what ground has such great glory? The boundless Ganges glitters with these, the light yellow Hydaspes with those. There is also the bright pearl of the Erythraean sea. One bracelet contains all, one equal to all; the whole of the East comes together into this shining woven work. [15] Heavenly gods! What value and beauty of the radiant circlet! What hand will such a great circlet wish to surround? How vacillating light comes and goes on the solid stones! How well does the jewel make the faces of hunters. Look, this rich stag which precious arrows assail, [20] and a lion which – see! – swells by its own worth. Did Vulcan or the Telchines, not yet shipwrecking rocks, so place the jewels with skilled hand? Indeed, this bracelet is worthy for Jupiter to brandish on his arm when he shakes the ground, flashing with rain-bearing light. [25] Juno herself, though wealthy, would be appeased by this present and set aside the fierce abuse concerning her bed that had been offended against. But, o whoever shall adorn your arm with such great gift, whether the glory of truth or of fame affects you, overcome the wealth in your mind lest these stones are thought the best [30] and you, who belong to Pyrrha's race, are thought to be a cheaper stone.

Commentary

This section gives information about the bracelet and provides a poet's celebration of it. Interest in the radiance of precious stones and their play of light has a long-standing history: see, for example, Posidippus, *Lithika*, Pliny, *Natural History* 37.80–81, the description of jewels at Heliodorus, *Aethiopika* 2.30.3, and Herodias' commentary on jewellery at Act IV, Scene 2 of Grimald's *Archipropheta* (1546). Here the luminosity of the individual stones that make up the bracelet is suggested through an exploration of how sunlight reacts with various precious stones from India and the Red Sea in their uncut state. The bracelet's craftsmanship is brought out with reference to details of a hunting scene that has been engraved onto the precious stones. The elegant style of the verses (note, for instance, the chiastic enclosure of line 13 by *una*, 'one', juxtaposed with a form of *omnis*, 'all') may reflect rival artistic craftmanship.

As shown by the portrayal of Achilles' shield at Homer, *Iliad* 18.478–608, descriptions of works of art go back to the early beginnings of classical literature. This continued to be a feature of epic, as illustrated by the depictions of Harmonia's necklace by Statius and Nonnus (*Dion.* 5.135–89), but was not exclusive to that genre. Of particular note, in light of the *Argenis*' literary models, is the presence of ecphrasis in the ancient novel tradition, as, for example, at Achilles Tatius, *Leucippe and Clitophon* 2.11.2–3 (Calligone's necklace), Heliodorus, *Aithiopika* 3.4 (Charicleia's breast band adorned with serpents; cf. Barclay's ornamental fabric bracelet) and *Aethiopika* 5.14 (where the amethyst of Nausicles' ring has a pastoral picture carved upon it; cf. Barclay's engraved hunting scene).

Certain details send the reader back to Statius' depiction of the necklace of Harmonia. Statius had also stressed the splendour of the jewellery (Stat. *Theb.* 2.297: *donis Argia nitet*; 4.191: *fulgurat . . . auro*; 4.200: *nitidis ornatibus*), and Harmonia's necklace similarly contains emerald (Stat. *Theb.* 2.276; cf. *Arg.* 3) and *adamas* (*Theb.* 2.277: *adamanta*, used with the meaning 'adamant'; cf. *Arg.* 4: 'diamond'). Moreover, both Barclay's portrayal of the bracelet and the description of Harmonia's necklace in *Thebaid* 2 contain the use of 'Lemnian' to designate Vulcan (*Arg.* 21, as at Statius *Thebaid* 2.269), the reference to the Telchines in the context of crafting (*Arg.* 21; cf. *Theb.* 2.274) and an allusion to Jupiter's firebolt (*Arg.* 24; cf. *Theb.* 2.278–9 for the thunderbolt ashes within the necklace).

Those who recognize the Statian intertext can perceive potentially disturbing overtones in the poet's positive presentation of the bracelet. Suspense and uncertainty are added, as the reader wonders whether the bracelet will bring doom as Harmonia's cursed necklace did. This is especially the case once we come across Lycogenes' order that the bracelet be imbued with poison (*Arg.* II.7.1; a suspicious Eristhenes has informed Lycogenes that he thinks Meleander is trying to win Polynices' friendship by the gift). If we remember that Statius' ornament was drenched in poison (*Theb.* 2.285), we may even see that the intertextuality helps prepare such a plot twist.

II.6.5

cetera: We have previously been informed that these are things brought by a Syrian merchant.

ex serico texto . . . varii generis lapilli: The bracelet has various kinds of jewels (emerald, diamond, onyx, jasper, pyrite, blue stone) attached to silken fabric.

II.6.6

1 *Phoebo*: the sun (from Phoebus Apollo, the sun god).

6 *Vel cui purpureo nomen ab igne venit*: i.e. pyrite, which derives its etymology from the Greek word for 'fire'.

8 *Iris*: Iris is the Greek goddess of the rainbow. The reference is to a rainbow's reflection of its colours onto water.

11 *Hydaspes*: the Jhelum river, a tributary of the Indus.

12 *Erythrai . . . sali*: the Red Sea.

19–20 There is a play upon the richness (19: *dives, ditia*) and price (20: *pretio*; cf. 15: *pretium*) of the precious stones and the impressiveness of the animals and weapons.

21 The way in which the future metamorphosis of the Telchines into rocks is pictured may be relevant in light of Poliarchus' later shipwreck described at II.10.1 (when the ship that Poliarchus is on sinks, he escapes into a lifeboat, which goes on to become shipwrecked by rocks).

Lemnius: i.e. Vulcan: see Barclay (1601) on Statius *Thebaid* 2.269: *dictus ab insula Lemnos sibi sacra*, 'called from the island of Lemnos which was sacred to him'.

24 This refers to Jupiter hurling his signature weapon, the thunderbolt. With *imbrifera luce*, cf. Vergil, *Aen.* 8.429, where *tris imbris torti radios* ('three rays of coiled rain') contribute to the thunderbolt that the Cyclopes are forging.

26 A reference to Juno's famously angry reactions to the serial infidelities of her husband.

30 This conceit picks up the mythological story that the human race derived from the stones thrown over the shoulders of Pyrrha and her husband Deucalion (see e.g. Verg. *Ecl.* 6.41: *lapides Pyrrhae iactos*; Ovid, *Met.* 1.390–415; Barclay 1601 on Stat. *Theb.* 3.560, of Deucalion and Pyrrha: *qui coniectis a tergo saxis humanum genus repararunt*, 'who renewed the human race after stones had been thrown from behind'). The moral warning about the dangers of valuing precious stones too highly is a lesson that it would have been well for Selenissa to heed (see *Arg.* III. 5.7).

Latin text

Text 2: *Argenis* III.5.6-8

Metre of III.5.7: iambic trimeters, as befitting its putative derivation from a play and the referencing of the cursed history of the necklace in classical tragedy, as, for example, Sophocles' now fragmentary *The Epigoni*.

III.5.6 ... *Sed in auspicium traxit quod largitioni intentus non absimilem victoriam aspexit in theatro, in quod Argiam et Eriphylen poeta produxerat: hanc divino monili mercantem crudele suffragium; illam munere victam et coniugis fata prodentem. Inter cetera istos versus, quibus Eriphyle accepto proditionis pretio exultabat, sic laudavit ut confestim ad se praeciperet afferri et aliquoties tacito voto perlegeret.*

III.5.7
Absiste tandem, cura. Sat sterili vigil
Marcore cecidit vultus. O grates, Dei,
Favistis omnes. Teneon' armillam manu?
Meamque teneo? Vota, cecidistis bene.
5 Nunc tuta, nunc excelsa, nunc caelo fruor.
His se decora sueverat gemmis Venus
Ornare Marti. Tyrius has stupuit gener
Ardere collo coniugis. Quis hic decor?
Quis radiat ipso non minor Phoebo dies?
10 Quo pergis, amens? Di, fides, lares, amor,
In pretia deposcuntur. Heu nimio tibi
Armilla stabit. Poteris infelix tuum
Damnare bello coniugem? Bellum vetant
Sagae volucres, Delphicus pater vetat,
15 Et omne sacris exta quod praebet pecus.
Funesta merces! Vidua, si tantum potes
Sic esse felix. Melius – ah pietas! – malos
Omitte cultus. Trahitur en! dubia vice
Instabile pectus; sic ut incertam ratem
20 Non unus atro ventus involvit freto.
Sic nempe simplex! sorte nunc dubitas frui,
Quam fata praebent? Quid times vanas aves?
Ne bella fiant, reddere armillam voles?
Haec ipsa bellum faciat; haec regnum est mihi,

English translation

III.5.6 ... But he, while he was occupied with bribery, took for a portent that he saw a not dissimilar victory in the theatre, where a poet had presented Argia and Eriphyle: this one purchasing a cruel vote by a divine necklace, that one conquered by a gift and betraying the destiny of her husband. Among other things, he so praised those verses in which Eriphyle exulted after she had received the price for the betrayal that he immediately commanded them to be brought to him and would read them through a number of times in silent prayer.

III.5.7 Care, cease at last. My watchful face has fallen enough with unprofitable wasting. O gods, thanks, you have all shown favour. Do I now hold the necklace in my hand? Do I keep it as my own? Wishes, you have turned out well. [5] Now am I safe, now exalted, now I enjoy heaven. With these jewels Venus had been accustomed to decorate herself beautifully for Mars. The Theban son-in-law was stunned that these gleamed on the neck of his wife. What is this ornament? What light shines not less than the Sun himself? [10] Where are you heading, insane one? The gods, loyalty, household gods, love are demanded in recompense. Alas, for you the bracelet will stand at the price of too great a cost. Will you, you wretch, be able to doom your husband to war? Prophetic birds forbid war, the Delphian father forbids, [15] and the entrails that all the herd provides for rites. Deadly bribe! If you are able to be thus blessed so much, you will be a widow. Better – ah piety! – abandon the evil finery. Lo, my inconstant breast is pulled in wavering succession: [20] just as more than one wind has overwhelmed an unsteady ship in a dark sea. So without doubt you are being simple! Do you now hesitate to enjoy the fortune that fate offers? Why do you fear truthless birds? Will you want to return the necklace, so the war does not happen? Let this itself cause war. This is a kingdom to me [25] and better than Thebes. The unfortunate augur returns, hateful piety, and my mind does not trust itself. What do I do? O hard lot, when my wretched mind fears what it desires! Yet if you pass your life worthy of this divine gold, [30] if the sacred bracelet befits your looks, claim this as a great gift of the gods to you. If by chance you are of little importance to your husband, dare to do what you fear. But if he cherishes you and wishes you to match the chief goddesses in wealth, he himself would desire this for you bought by his own blood.

25 Meliusque Thebis. Augur infelix redit,
    Invisa pietas, mensque non credit sibi.
    Quid agimus? O sors dura, cum timet miser
    Quod optat animus! Digna caelesti tamen
    Si vivis auro, sacra si tuos decet
30 Armilla vultus; vindica hoc ingens tibi
    Munus deorum. Coniugi si fors tuo
    Es vilis, aude quod times. Sin te colit,
    Opibusque summas optat exaeques deas.
    Tibi ipse cupiat sanguine hoc emptum suo.

III.5.8 *Laetus Radirobanes huius exempli augurio, postquam finitis ludis in aulae interiora recessum est, Argenidi in conclavi ipso patris eadem narravit quae antea regi* . . .

III.5.8 After people had gone back into the inner part of the palace following the end of the plays, Radirobanes, who was cheerful because of the omen of this example, related to Argenis in the very chamber of her father the same things which he had before said to the king ...

Commentary

Radirobanes savours these lines because he sees Eriphyle as a model for Selenissa. The nurse will, indeed, follow in Eriphyle's footsteps by betraying trust for gain. In an ominous side to the mythical parallelism, this will similarly lead to her death, although she will commit suicide (*Arg.* IV.3.5) whereas Eriphyle is killed by her avenging son, Alcmaeon.

Barclay adapts the same mythical material as Statius, the story of the transference of the necklace from Argia to Eriphyle, but takes a different angle. Statius had shown the deliberations of Argia leading to her decision to lose the necklace in return for what she thought would benefit Polynices. The necklace was described as entering Eriphyle's house at *Thebaid* 4.211-12. Barclay creates a dramatic monologue for Eriphyle, who is in possession of the ornament, and gives her the internal debate over what to do with the jewellery. The presence of some shared diction encourages us to think of the Statian material. So Eriphyle's use of the word *cultus* (*Arg.* III.5.7.18, 'finery') may pick up its appearances at *Thebaid* 2.302 and 4.195 whilst Eriphyle's description of the ornament as *sacra* ('sacred') at *Argenis* III.5.7.29 may resonate with this adjective's use at *Thebaid* 2.298 and 4.198 (where there is ambiguity as to whether *sacer* is employed with its meaning of 'accursed'). Furthermore, in both instances, reference is made to the fact it is made of gold (*Arg.* III.5.7.29; cf. Statius' description of Harmonia's necklace as golden at *Theb.* 2.298, 4.191, 4.192, 4.205, 4.211). Compare also Eriphyle's characterization of herself as *excelsa* (*Arg.* III.5.7.5, 'exalted') with *Thebaid* 4.195, where Eriphyle longs to *excellere*, 'be preeminent', in the finery.

The self-exhortations of the two women have very different outcomes. Eriphyle's decision to doom her husband for profit stands in contrast to Argia's selfless resolution to help Polynices (she does not realize that he will die at Thebes). The intertext serves to emphasise the shocking nature of the treachery of Eriphyle – and hence that of Selenissa.

III.5.6

divino monili: since it was made by the god Vulcan; cf. *Arg.* III.5.7.28: *caelesti* ('divine').

crudele suffragium: 'vote' (*suffragium*) presumably refers to the tradition that Amphiaraus had agreed to Eriphyle having sway over disagreements between himself and Adrastus due to a previous dispute (Apollod. *Bibl.* 3.6.2; Diod. Sic. 4.65.5-6). It is 'cruel' as it will lead to Amphiaraus' death at Thebes.

III.5.7

3 *armillam*: translated as 'necklace' here and at line 23. The term *armilla* usually denotes a bracelet or armlet. However, at *Argenis* III.5.6 the ornament is described as *monile*, 'necklace' (following the classical Latin tradition of labelling Harmonia's item of jewellery as a *monile*). The description of the bracelet sent to Poliarchus may have influenced Barclay's application of the word.

4 *Vota*: At *Thebaid* 4.193-4, Statius shows Eriphyle wishing to exchange her husband for the gift.

6-7 It would seem that Venus used the ornament, which her husband Vulcan had made, to adorn herself during her adulterous relationship with Mars. In the *Thebaid* the necklace is made by Vulcan as a gift for Harmonia, the daughter of Mars and Venus.

7 *Tyrius . . . gener*: i.e. the Theban Polynices (*Tyrius* signifies 'Theban' since the founder of Thebes, Cadmus, came from Tyre). He was son-in-law to Adastus, king of Argos, through his marriage to Argia.

10 *Quo pergis, amens?*: echoing the chorus' address to Amphitryon at Seneca, *Hercules Furens* 1033.

13-15 In the *Thebaid* Amphiaraus is warned off war by divination such as extiscipy (*Theb.* 3.456-9) and augury (e.g. at *Theb.* 3.546-7, he sees his fatal descent through earth).

14 *Delphicus pater*: an honorific phrase designating Apollo, who had a cult at Delphi.

26 *pietas*: Eriphyle, described as 'impious' (*impia*) at *Thebaid* 2.303 and 12.123, rejects 'piety', which she had been struggling with (17), and decides to send her husband on the expedition, even though it will result in his death.

Appendix: Model Passages from Statius' *Thebaid*

Latin text

Statius, *Thebaid* 2.269–305

    Lemnius haec, ut prisca fides, Mavortia longum
270 furta dolens, capto postquam nil obstat amori
    poena nec ultrices castigavere catenae,
    Harmoniae dotale decus sub luce iugali
    struxerat. hoc, docti quamquam maiora, laborant
    Cyclopes, notique operum Telchines amica
275 certatim iuvere manu; sed plurimus ipsi
    sudor. ibi arcano florentes igne zmaragdos
    cingit et infaustas percussum adamanta figuras
    Gorgoneosque orbes Siculaque incude relictos
    fulminis extremi cineres viridumque draconum
280 lucentes a fronte iubas; hic flebile germen
    Hesperidum et dirum Phrixei velleris aurum;
    tum varias pestes raptumque interplicat atro
    Tisiphones de crine ducem, et quae pessima ceston
    vis probat; haec circum spumis lunaribus unguit
285 callidus atque hilari perfundit cuncta veneno.
    ...
    tunc donis Argia nitet vilesque sororis
    ornatus sacro praeculta supervenit auro.
    viderat hoc coniunx perituri vatis, et aras
300 ante omnes epulasque trucem secreta coquebat
    invidiam, saevis detur si quando potiri
    cultibus, heu nihil auguriis adiuta propinquis.
    quos optat gemitus, quantas cupit impia clades!
    digna quidem: sed quid miseri decepta mariti
305 arma, quid insontes nati meruere furores?

English translation

The Lemnian god, so ancient belief goes, had fabricated this as a dowry ornament for Harmonia on her wedding day: he had long grieved at Mars' secret affair, after punishment in no way hindered the love that had been captured nor did avenging chains correct it. The Cyclopes worked on this, though skilled in greater projects, and the Telchines, known for their creations, [275] competed to help with friendly hand. But the greatest exertion was Vulcan's. There he makes a circle of emeralds glowing with hidden fire, adamant struck with ill-starred shapes, eyes of the Gorgon, ashes left on the Sicilian anvil from the last thunderbolt, [280] and crests shining from the brow of green serpents; here is the lamentable fruit of the Hesperides and the dreadful gold of Phrixus' fleece. Then he interweaves various blights, the chief snake torn from Tisiphone's black hair and the most noxious power which attests Venus' girdle. He cleverly smears these with lunar spume [285] and drenches all with cheerful poison.... Then Argia shines with the gift and, outshining with the cursed gold, surpasses the mean ornaments of her sister. The wife of the doomed seer had seen this and [300] before all the altars and feats was secretly nurturing a fierce envy, if only it might be granted her to possess the cruel finery. Alas, she was in no way helped by auguries close at hand. What groans, what disasters does the impious woman wish for! She indeed deserves them: but what have the deceived arms of her wretched husband deserved, [305] what the innocent madness of her son?

Statius, *Thebaid* 4.187–213
```
      iamque et fatidici mens expugnata fatiscit
      auguris; ille quidem casus et dira uidebat
      signa, sed ipsa manu cunctanti iniecerat arma
190   Atropos obrueratque deum, nec coniugis absunt
      insidiae, vetitoque domus iam fulgurat auro.
      hoc aurum vati fata exitiale monebant
      Argolico; scit et ipsa (nefas!), sed perfida coniunx
      dona viro mutare velit, spoliisque potentis
195   inminet Argiae raptoque excellere cultu.
      illa libens (nam regum animos et pondera belli
      hac nutare videt, pariter si providus heros
      militet) ipsa sacros gremio Polynicis amati
      exuerat cultus haud maesta atque insuper addit:
200   'non haec apta mihi nitidis ornatibus' inquit
      'tempora, nec miserae placeant insignia formae
      te sine: sat dubium coetu solante timorem
      fallere et incultos aris adverrere crines.
      scilicet (infandum!), cum tu claudare minanti
205   casside ferratusque sones, ego divitis aurum
      Harmoniae dotale geram? dabit aptius isto
      fors decus, Argolicasque habitu praestabo maritas,
      cum regis coniunx, cum te mihi sospite templa
      votivis implenda choris; nunc induat illa
210   quae petit et bellante potest gaudere marito.'
      sic Eriphylaeos aurum fatale penates
      inrupit scelerumque ingentia semina movit,
      et grave Tisiphone risit gavisa futuris.
```

And now even the will of the prophetic seer, which had been stormed, flags. Indeed, he saw the fortunes and dire signs, [190] but Atropos herself with her hand had fitted arms to him as he hesitated and crushed the god. Nor is his wife's treachery lacking, and the house already glitters with forbidden gold. Prophecies warned that this gold would be deadly to the Argive seer. She herself also knew (oh horror!), but the faithless wife would like to exchange her husband for the gift [195] and is bent on the spoils of royal Argia and on being preeminent in the appropriated adornment. Willingly (for she sees that, if the prophetic hero fights in concert, the minds of the princes burdened with war sway in this direction), she herself without unhappiness had taken off from her bosom the accursed ornament of her beloved Polynices and added besides: [200] 'These are not fit times for me to wear glittering ornaments', she said, 'nor should I take pleasure in decorating my wretched beauty without you. It is enough to beguile my anxious fears with the solace of companions and cause my unkempt hair to sweep over the altars. Should I (unspeakable thought!) [205] wear the dowered gold of wealthy Harmonia when you are enclosed in a threatening helmet and clank in your armour? Fortune will give me an ornament more suitable than this, and I shall surpass the Argive wives in dress when I am wife of a king and must fill the temples with votive choirs upon your safe return. Now let her put it on [210] who requests it and can rejoice while her husband is at war.' So the fatal gold burst into the house of Eriphyle and set in motion the seeds of great crimes, and Tisiphone laughed harshly, rejoicing in what was to come.

11

Spare Muses: Epigrams by the Cambridge Don James Duport (1606–1679)

Thomas Matthew Vozar

Introduction

The Cambridge don James Duport is best known today for his instructions to undergraduates, among which is featured the advice: 'Use your self, (and what if every day) to write some short Epistle, or Essay, or Theame or sometimes verses. *Nulla dies sine linea* ['no day without a line'].' Duport, as a prolific composer of poetry in the classical languages throughout his life, lived by his own rule.

The son of a Jesus College don who contributed to the King James Bible, Duport matriculated at Trinity College in Michaelmas 1622 and was elected as a fellow in 1627 shortly after taking his first degree. In 1630 he received his MA and was ordained, and the following year he delivered a satirical speech on alchemy as the university's *praevaricator* or commencement orator. His first major work was a paraphrase of the Book of Job in Greek hexameters published by the university press in 1637, which helped him win the post of Regius Professor of Greek two years later. Duport's version of Job even appeared in the 1642 curriculum of the newly founded Harvard College, making it one of the first Greek textbooks in use in North America, and he would later compose similar paraphrases of other parts of the Old Testament.

In the 1640s, amidst the English Civil Wars, he delivered a series of lectures on Theophrastus, which were published several decades after his death. Despite his royalist politics he retained his Trinity fellowship throughout the Interregnum and was only forced to give up the Regius Professorship in 1654. After the Restoration in 1660 he was made a royal chaplain and, in 1664, Dean of Peterborough. In 1668 he became master of Magdalene College, and he served a term as Vice-Chancellor of the university in 1669–70.

Duport's major work of scholarship, *Homeri Gnomologia* (1660), offers an extensive commentary on maxims, *sententiae* and other quotable bits from the *Iliad* and the *Odyssey*. But his scholarly interests are equally on display throughout his poems, which were collected and published by the university printer in 1676 under the title *Musae Subsecivae* ('*Spare Muses*'). This volume of some 600 pages shows the influence of Martial especially, and it testifies to Duport's continuing admiration of Homer: the figure of Zoilus, the carping critic who earned the epithet 'Homeromastix' ('Homer-whipper'), is a recurring antagonist. The small selection included here, meant to represent something of the range of Duport's Latin verse, features epigrams on a Jesuit's expurgated edition of Martial, the Greek motto of a Cambridge pub, bathhouse etiquette according to Theophrastus, the royalist propaganda piece *Eikon Basilike*, Claudius Salmasius' defence of the executed Charles I, the Scottish translator of Vergil John Ogilby, comparable phrases in the *Iliad* and Deuteronomy, Julius Caesar Scaliger's criticism of Homer, professional actresses on the Restoration stage and a blind poet who may be identified as John Milton. Replete with puns, wordplay, splashes of Greek and learning not worn lightly, Duport's Latin epigrams reveal how this Cambridge scholar's donnish wit and passion for classical literature flourished throughout some of the most tumultuous decades in English history.

Metres: elegiac distichs, Alcaics, hendecasyllables, hexameters

Bibliography

Alho, T. (2022), 'A Prevaricator Speech from Caroline Cambridge: James Duport (1606–79), *Aurum potest produci per artem chymicam*', in: G. Manuwald / L. R. Nicholas (eds), *An Anthology of Neo-Latin Literature in British Universities*, 203–17, London.

Clarke, E. (2003/4), 'George Herbert and Cambridge Scholars', *George Herbert Journal*, 27.1–2: 43–52.

Cunich, P. / Hoyle, D. / Duffy, E. / Hyam, R. (1994), *A History of Magdalene College Cambridge 1428–1988*, Cambridge.

Duport, J. (1660), *Homeri Gnomologia*, Cambridge.

Duport, J. (1676), *Musae Subsecivae, seu Poetica Stromata*, Cambridge.

Duport, J. (1712), 'Praelectiones in Theophrasti Characteres', in: P. Needham (ed.), *Theophrasti Characteres Ethici*, 177–474, Cambridge.

Forster, H. (1982), 'The Rise and Fall of the Cambridge Muses (1603–1763)', *Transactions of the Cambridge Bibliographical Society*, 8.2: 141–72.

Heap, G. V. M. (1981), 'James Duport's Cambridge Lectures on Theophrastus', in: H. W. Stubbs (ed.), *Pegasus: Classical Essays from the University of Exeter*, 84–97, Exeter.

Knight, S. (2015), 'University', in: S. Knight / S. Tilg (eds), *Oxford Handbook of Neo-Latin*, 233–48, Oxford.

Money, D. (2015), 'Epigram and Occasional Poetry', in: S. Knight / S. Tilg (eds), *Oxford Handbook of Neo-Latin*, 73–86, Oxford.

Monk, J. H. (1826), 'Memoir of Dr. James Duport, Regius Professor of Greek, and Dean of Peterborough', in: *Museum Criticum; or, Cambridge Classical Researches*, vol. 2, 672–98, Cambridge.

O'Day, R. (2008), 'Duport, James (1606–1679)', *Oxford Dictionary of National Biography*.

Prancic, T. / Doelman, J. (2000/1), '"Ora pro me, sancte Herberte": James Duport and the Reputation of George Herbert', *George Herbert Journal*, 24.1–2: 35–55.

Preston, C. D. / Oswald, P. H. (2011), 'James Duport's Rules for His Tutorial Pupils: A Comparison of Two Surviving Manuscripts', *Transactions of the Cambridge Bibliographical Society*, 14.4: 317–62.

Trentman, J. A. (1978) 'The Authorship of *Directions for a Student in the Universitie*', *Transactions of the Cambridge Bibliographical Society*, 7: 176–201.

Trevelyan, G. M. (1943), 'Undergraduate Life under the Protectorate', *Cambridge Review*, 64: 328–30.

Vozar, T. M. (2022), 'Alcaics on Restoration Actresses by the Cambridge Classical Scholar James Duport', *Early Theatre*, 25.2: 83–8.

Vozar, T. M. (2023), 'A Cambridge University Greek Textbook at Harvard College in 1642', *New England Quarterly*, 96.1: 64–73.

Weise, S. (2022), 'Great Britain', in: F. Pontani / S. Weise (eds), *The Hellenizing Muse: A European Anthology of Poetry in Ancient Greek from the Renaissance to the Present*, 482–557, Berlin.

Source of Latin text

The Latin texts have been edited from Duport 1676, with minor changes to spelling and punctuation.

Latin text

In Raderi Martialem castratum

Raderus ad Lectorem.

Lascivis epigrammatis omissis,
castum do tibi, amice, Martialem;
qualem nempe legat Cato vel ipse,
vel Lucretia et audiente Bruto.

Lector ad Raderum.

5 Zoilus argutos ne possit rodere libros,
   vis inde obscenum, Radere, eradere carmen:
sic facis, ut Marco hoc Marcus non castior ullus,
   nec Cicero, aut Brutus, nec virtus ipsa Catonis,
nec Seneca aut pater, aut Lucanus, Marcus uterque,
10 Corduba Bilbilicos quin et legat ipsa lepores.

In signum delphini Cantabrig. oenopolio appensum, cum hoc symbolo, ἢ πίθι, ἢ ἄπιθι

Aspice delphinum, Bacchi praenobile signum,
   Bacchi, cui delphin tam bene notus erat.
In delphinas enim is nautas mutaverat olim;
   in pisces mutant nunc quoque vina viros.
5 Quid nisi pisces nempe natantes semper in udo
   sunt homines, qui sic nocte dieque bibunt?
Dumque hi Graecantur, sua Graece oracula fundit
   Pythius an dicam? an Delphicus? iste tripos:
ἢ πίθι, ἢ ἄπιθι, si non bibis, hinc et abibis:
10   Mutus amat piscis per sua signa loqui.

English translation

On Rader's castrated Martial

Rader to the reader:

The lascivious epigrams having been omitted,
I give you, friend, a chaste Martial,
such as even Cato himself would assuredly read,
or even Lucretia while Brutus listens in too.

The reader to Rader:

Lest Zoilus be able to gnaw away at the witty books,   5
you, Rader, want to eradicate the obscene poetry from them:
you make it so that no Marcus more chaste than this Marcus,
not Cicero or Brutus, nor Cato's virtue itself,
not Seneca or his father, or Lucan, both Marcuses,
even Cordoba herself could really read Bilbilican delights.   10

On the Sign of the Dolphin Hung over the Cambridge Tavern with this Motto: 'Either Drink, or Go Away'

Look at the dolphin, the celebrated sign of Bacchus,
    of Bacchus, to whom the dolphin was so well known.
For he had once turned sailors into dolphins;
    now likewise wine turns men into fish.
What else of course but fish, always swimming in the wet,   5
    are the men who drink thus, night and day?
And while they imitate the Greeks, so does that tripod – should I say
    Pythian? or Delphic? – pour out its oracles in Greek.
E pithi, e apithi: 'if you're not drinking, you'll also get out of here',
    so the mute fish loves to say through its signs.   10

In sordidum alieno oleo se in balneis ungentem. Ex Theophr. Charact.
Περὶ Βδελυρίας Ἐιπὼν, σαπρόν γε τὸ ἔλαιον ἐπρίω, τῷ παιδαρίῳ τῷ ἀλλοτρίῳ ἀλείφεσθαι.

Dum non vult oleum consumere sordidus ullum,
    parcit et ampullae, dum lavat ipse, suae:
accusat puerum, unguentum quasi vile parasset;
    et merito, sordes scilicet istud olet.
5 Tum miser alterius sumit de pyxide: nempe
    non oleum perdit, perdit at hic operam:
nam qui sic gratis alieno ex aere lavatur,
    saepe licet lotus, sordidus usque manet.

In librum Regii Martyris Caroli I vere aureum, cui titulus, Ἐικὼν Βασιλική

Siqua coli meruit divini regis imago,
    icone adorari sanctus et ipse sua;
quis non, rite colens tam sanctum in imagine regem,
    libri esset supplex iconolatra tui?
5 Hic pietas, doctrina, fides, patientia, certant:
    pulchrior in terris nulla tabella fuit.
Nulla vorax tinea, aut informis blatta, nec ullus
    consumet librum hunc iconoclasta dies.
Carole, tu martyr sanctissimus ipse, tuique
10   martyrii haec icon regia testis erit.
Zoilus interea Regem negat iconis huius
    autorem, et non es, Carole, pictor, ait.
Sic ubi sacrilegum temeraverat omnia vulgus,
    reddita nec regi regis imago fuit.
15 At quis lineolam hanc potuit, nisi noster Apelles,
    ducere? Quis facere hoc, rex nisi martyr, opus?

On a Dirty Cheapskate Washing Himself in the Baths with Someone Else's Oil. From Theophrastus, *Characters*, 'On Beastliness': 'Saying "You Bought Putrid Oil," Polishing off with Someone Else's'

As long as the dirty cheapskate didn't want to use up any oil,
    he was also sparing with his own flask as he washed himself.
He accused the boy as if he had bought cheap ointment,
    and deservedly: that filth of his own obviously reeks.
Then the miser takes from someone else's box: he certainly   5
    doesn't waste the oil, yet here he wastes his labour:
for he who's thus washed for free on someone else's change,
    though he may be often bathed, still remains a dirty cheapskate.

On the Truly Golden Book of the Royal Martyr Charles I Entitled the *Royal Icon*

If the divine king's image at all deserved to be revered
    and he himself to be adored as a saint in his own icon,
who, rightly revering so holy a king in the image,
    could not be a humble iconolater of your book?
Here piety, learning, faith, patience contend: 5
    there was no tablet more beautiful on earth.
No ravenous worm or ugly moth, nor any
    iconoclast shall consume this book in time.
Charles, you most holy martyr yourself, this royal icon
    will also be the testimony of your martyrdom.   10
Meanwhile Zoilus denies that the king is the author of this icon,
    and says 'you, Charles, are not the painter'.
Thus, where the profane mob had defiled all things,
    the king's icon was not rendered to the king.
Yet who could draw this delicate line, except our Apelles?   15
    Who could fashion this work, except the martyr king?

In viri illustrissimi, et πολυμαθεσάτου Claudii Salmasii librum, cui titulus, Defensio Regia

Doctorum Coryphaee, magne Claudi,
linguarum simul omnium artiumque,
Salmasi, iubar atque lumen ingens,
quot illustria saeculo dedisti
5 tu vastae monumenta lectionis,
rari et iudicii ingenique fetus!
Et primum Polyhistorem Solini
illustras critica face, atque Plini
ingentes aperis abinde gazas,
10 thesaurum et physices petis profundum.
Stupendae hoc opus eruditionis.
Cultum pumice tum tuo et politum
Augustae Historiae volumen: inde
usurae expositae, ipsa res, modusque,
15 pactum et fenebre rite constitutum.
Tum Patris quoque Pallium vetustum
Afri, en emaculatum et illud omni
sua sorde, plicis et evolutum.
Mitto caetera; quis tuae valebit
20 doctrinae monumenta tot referre,
cedro digna, perenniora et aera,
ipso et marmore permanentiora?
Quae cum singula posteri videbunt,
venturique avide legent nepotes;
25 At Defensio Regia eminebit,
palmam et praeripiet vel universis.
O vere scheda regia! hanc ob unam
omnes quotquot ubique in orbe reges,
aeternum tibi principesque debent.
30 Sacratae themidos politicesque
arcas excutis hic penuque totum.
Hic Regalia vindicasque iura,
majestatis et es ruentis Atlas:
Hic monstrum grave, multiceps, cruentum,
35 horrendum, novus Hercules trucidas,
et contundis Hydram rebellionis,
infernos iugulasque regicidas.
Hinc, vir maxime, principum patronus,

On the Book of the Most Illustrious and Most Learned Man, Claudius Salmasius, Entitled the *Royal Defence*

Great Claudius, chorus-leader of the learned,
at the same time of all languages and arts
the splendour and prodigious lamp, Salmasius,
how many times have you granted to the age
the illustrious monuments of your vast reading 5
and the offspring of your rare judgment and genius!
You first illuminate the *Polyhistor* of Solinus
with a critical torch, and from this
you break open the massive treasures of Pliny,
and seek after a deep storehouse of natural history. 10
This is a work of stupendous erudition.
Next, adorned and polished by your pumice,
the volume of the *Augustan History*: from there
the matter itself and manner of usury exposed
was set down and established after the usurious fashion. 15
Then likewise the ancient *Cloak* of the African
Father, behold it cleansed of all its
squalor and unravelled from its fold.
I pass over others: who shall prevail to relate
so many monuments of your learning, 20
worthy of cedar, and more lasting than bronze,
and more permanent than marble itself?
When those to come shall look upon each of these,
and future descendants shall read them,
yet the *Royal Defence* shall stand out 25
and snatch away the palm from all the rest.
O truly royal shield! On account of this one
all kings, however many and wherever in the world,
and princes are in your eternal debt.
Here the arks of sacred law and politics 30
you examine wholly into the innermost part.
Here too you assert the laws of kings,
and you are the Atlas of collapsing majesty:
Here a menacing monster, many-headed, bloody,
horrendous, you, a new Hercules, slaughter, 35
and you crush the Hydra of rebellion
and the infernal throats of regicides.
For this, most great man, are you called patron of princes,

hinc tu regius advocatus audis.
40 Macte hoc elogio ac honore: doctum,
Salmasi, te alias, et eloquentem;
hic te praeterea pium, probumque, et
malis temporibus bonum, probasti.

In sortilegium Ogilvii librarium

Sortilego libros pretio dum vendis, Ogilvi,
   grandibus inprimis Virgiliumque typis:
annon hae sortes vere sunt Virgilianae?
   Auri sacra fames; sors venit ista tibi.
5 Nescia mens hominum fati sortisque futurae;
   carmen hoc emtores sortilegosque notat.
Sunt bona, sunt quaedam mediocria, sunt mala plura;
   tales sunt sortes, bibliopola, tuae.

In illud Homericum, ἔπεα νιφάδεσσιν ἐοικότα χειμερίῃσιν, comparatum cum Deuter. 32.2

Mens an vox hominis praegnans fecundaque nubes,
   a qua verba, velut tot meteora, fluunt.
Candida verba et crebra nives sunt; grandia grando;
   ore Pericleo fulgura missa volant.
5 Fulmina vibrantur, validaeque tonitrua linguae,
   rostra tenent nati cum, Zebedae, tui.
Sermo super teneras distillans molliter herbas,
   et ros doctrinae ceu pluvialis aquae.

Gratiarum una a Junone Somno in matrimonium data. Hom Il. ξ Quod neque placet κριτικωτάτῳ Julio Scaligero Poet. l. 5. c. 3

Displicuit Critico, quod nupta est Gratia Somno;
   ac si dormites hic et Homere senex.
Gratia non dormire solet, nec denique debet:
   ergo, Somne, tibi non bene iuncta Charis.
5 Quin et Cimmerios procul aestu et sole recessus,
   Somne, tenes; feret hanc Gratia nuda plagam?
Incedunt Charites sine veste et tegmine; forsan
   frigidum et indociles sic tolerare Iovem.
Tu quae donasti nupta tam dispare Somnum,
10   defendas Charitem, pronuba Iuno, tuam.

for this are you called the royal advocate.
Be blessed with this inscription and honour: elsewhere you have 40
proven yourself learned, Salmasius, and eloquent;
here, moreover, you have proven yourself pious
and virtuous and good in evil times.

On Ogilby's Bibliomancy

While you're selling books that cost a fortune, Ogilby,
    and above all Vergil in grand type,
are these fortunes not in fact truly Vergilian?
    'Accursed hunger for gold': that fortune comes for you.
'The mind of humans, ignorant of fate or future fortune': 5
    this verse applies to buyers and fortune-tellers.
'There are good things, some middling, many bad':
    such are your own fortunes, bookseller.

On the Homeric Phrase 'Words like Winter Snowflakes' compared with Deuteronomy 32.2

The mind, or voice, of man is a pregnant and fertile cloud
    from which words, like so many meteors, pour.
Dazzling words are also thickly snows: sublime from sublime,
    lightning-flashes sent from the Periclean mouth fly out.
Thunderbolts shake, and the thunders of a mighty tongue, 5
    when your sons, Zebedee, hold the rostra.
Speech softly trickles down over the delicate grasses,
    and the dew of learning like rainwater.

One of the Graces was Given in Marriage by Juno to Sleep (Homer, *Iliad* 14) Which Does not Please the Ever so Critical Julius Scaliger (*Poetics*, Book 5, Chapter 3)

It displeased the critic that Grace was wedded to Sleep –
    as if even you're nodding off here, old man Homer.
Grace isn't used to sleeping, nor indeed should she be:
    therefore, Sleep, Charis is not aptly joined to you.
And in fact, Sleep, you rule over the Cimmerians, withdrawn far 5
    from heat and sun: will a naked Grace bear this blow?
The Charites go about without clothing or cover, and thus
    perhaps not taught how to endure frigid Jove.
You who presented Sleep with a wife so dissimilar,
    bridesmaid Juno, should defend your Charis. 10

Aeris ipsa dea es; sit et illic mitior aer,
ut cum sponso habitet sic nova nupta suo.
Nugae! an grata minus caecorum haec somnia vatum,
quod physica haud queat, aut ethica, causa dari?

In Roscias nostras, seu histriones feminas

Nec femininum nomen hypocrita,
nec histrio, si grammaticae fides,
   et Prisciano; nempe solos
      esse viros decet histriones.
5 Hos tantum habebant pristina saecula,
dum castitas salva, atque modestia,
   nec liquerat iam Astraea terras
      virgineamve rubedo frontem.
Virtutis at nunc cum color exulat,
10 et femininum depuduit genus,
   viris remistus sexus alter
      occupat en hodie theatrum.
Herodis, Heinsi, non aliter tui
scenam Megaera et Tisiphone decent,
15   micatque drama Christianum
      Eumenidum facibus profanis.
Pars facta ludi femina comici,
sese ipsa ludos iam facit: Anglico
   Ἐκκλησιαζούσας theatro
20   ergo et Aristophanes dedisti?
Quousque frontem at, Roscia, perfricas?
Tandem pudor sit, nequitiae et modus:
   relinque scenam, pone soccos,
      pone, tibi male congruentes.
25 Silere discas, et sapere audeas,
et erubescas te dare publico.
   Sin dramatis pars esse pergas,
      non nisi κωφὸν agas πρόσωπον.

You are the goddess of air herself; and let the air be milder there,
   so that the new bride dwells thus with the groom.
Trifles! Are these dreams of blind poets less welcome
   because a natural or moral cause can scarcely be given?

On our Roscias, or Female Actors

Player is not a name for women,
nor is actor, if there be credit in grammar
   and in Priscian; surely it is proper
      that only men be actors.
Former times had them   5
as long as chastity was safe, and modesty,
   nor had Astraea yet departed from the earth
      or blush from the virgin's face.
Yet now, when virtue's hue goes into exile
and the race of women goes shameless,   10
   behold the other sex, mingled with men,
      today occupies the theatre.
Just so do Megaera and Tisiphone adorn the stage
of your *Herod*, Heinsius, not differently from yours,
   and the drama trembles with the profane   15
      torches of Christian Furies.
Woman has been made part of a comic play,
now she makes a spectacle of herself: have you
   therefore, Aristophanes, also produced
      the *Assemblywomen* for the English theatre?   20
Yet for how long, Roscia, do you lay aside shame?
Let there at last be shame for sin, and moderation:
   leave the stage, put away the slippers,
      put them away, as they fit you poorly.
You should learn to be quiet, and dare to be prudent,   25
and blush to present yourself in public.
   But if you insist on being part of the drama,
      do not play a role unless it is a silent one.

In citharoedum caecum

Salve, o Demodoce, et tantum non alter Homere,
   cui cantum, sed non lumen, Apollo dedit.
Seu capias nummos, citharam seu pollice pulses,
   in digitis oculos fers manibusque tuos.
5 In fide confidis, didicisti caecus ad unguem
   percutere articulis fila sonora tuis.
Dum nihil ergo vides, nil ultra credere curas;
   articulos fidei das fidibusque pares.
Si tua caeca fides est, atque professio caeca,
10   Romanae fidicen iam potes esse lyrae.

On a Blind Citharode

Hail, O Demodocus, and all but another Homer,
    to whom Apollo granted song but not light.
Whether you take money or you strike the lyre with thumb,
    you bear your eyes in your fingers and hands.
You confide in faith, and you have learned blindly how to strum   5
    the sonorous strings with your fingers to the nail.
So, as you see nothing, you take care to believe nothing more,
    and you render articles of faith equal to the strings.
If your faith is blind, and profession blind,
    now you can be a bard of the Roman lyre.   10

Commentary

In Raderi Martialem Castratum / On Rader's Castrated Martial

The practice of excising morally problematic passages from classical texts has a long history, on which see esp. S. Harrison and C. Stray (eds), *Expurgating the Classics: Editing Out in Greek and Latin* (2012). The Raderus of Duport's title is the German Jesuit Matthäus Rader (1561–1634), who published an expurgated Martial for the use of schools in 1599. For a vernacular epigram on the same subject cf. John Donne, *Satires, Epigrams, and Verse Letters*, ed. W. Milgate (1967), 54: 'Why this man gelded *Martiall* I muse, | Except himselfe alone his tricks would use, | As *Katherine*, for the Courts sake, put downe Stewes'. Duport distinguishes Rader from the persona of the reader by the use of different metres: the former speaks in hendecasyllables, the latter in hexameters.

3–4 Cato, Brutus and Lucretia are traditional exemplars of moral uprightness. Cf. Mart. 11.16.9–10: *erubuit posuitque meum Lucretia librum, | sed coram Bruto; Brute, recede: leget* ('Lucretia blushed and put down my book, but that was in the presence of Brutus; withdraw, Brutus, she will read it').

5–6 Duport plays on the name Raderus with *rodere* ('gnaw at, criticize') and especially *radere* ('wipe away, erase'), an effect my translation attempts to reproduce by rendering the latter as 'eradicate'.

7–9 Duport develops this theme on the basis of the fact that Martial, Cicero, Brutus, Cato and Lucan (though not the two Senecas) all share the praenomen Marcus.

10 *Bilbilicos*· Martial came from Augusta Bilbilis in the Roman province of Hispania Tarraconensis.

In signum delphini Cantabrig. oenopolio appensum, cum hoc Symbolo, ἢ πίθι, ἢ ἄπιθι / On the Sign of the Dolphin Hung over the Cambridge Tavern with this Motto: 'Either Drink, or Go Away'

The Dolphin was a storied Cambridge tavern and inn. Joseph Hall, *The Discovery of a New World or A Description of the South Indies* (1611), 65 confirms the motto: 'ἢ πίθι, ἢ ἄπιθι, such an inscription is upon the Dolphin in Cambridge'. Charles Henry Cooper, *Memorials of Cambridge*, vol. 2 (1861), 267 records that 'Edward Colbourne of the Dolphin tavern' was among those who made a donation between 1675 and 1695 for the establishment of Trinity College's library, with a gift of £5.

3 For the story of Dionysus transforming sailors into dolphins see *Hom. Hymn.* 7.

7 *Graecantur*: the sense seems to be that the men 'imitate the Greeks' or 'act in the Greek manner' by drinking heavily.

8 *Pythius . . . Delphicus*: both terms refer to the oracle at Delphi, in the latter case with a pun on the word for dolphin (*delphinus*).

In sordidum alieno oleo se in balneis ungentem. Ex Theophr. Charact. Περὶ Βδελυρίας Ἐιπών, σαπρόν γε τὸ ἔλαιον ἐπρίω, τῷ παιδαρίῳ τῷ ἀλλοτρίῳ ἀλείφεσθαι. / On a Dirty Cheapskate Washing Himself in the Baths with Someone Else's Oil. From Theophrastus, *Characters*, 'On Beastliness': 'Saying "You Bought Putrid Oil," Polishing off with Someone Else's'

The quotation in the title can be found in Theophr. *Char.* 30.8, under the heading Περὶ αἰσχροκερδείας ('On covetousness'), in modern editions. Duport used some version of Isaac Casaubon's text, in which the passage in question appears in the earlier chapter Περὶ βδελυρίας ('On beastliness'); see e.g. Isaac Casaubon (ed.), *Theophrasti Notationes Morum* (1638), 37. The inclusion of the poem in Duport's 1640s lectures on Theophrastus suggests that it was composed around this time; see Duport 1712: 390. It is not clear how Duport construed the dative παιδαρίῳ in the titular quotation (which modern editors correct to the vocative παιδάριον), as the word goes unmentioned in his lecture, and Casaubon's Latin translation fails to render it. For the sake of fidelity Duport's reading is retained, and my translation follows Casaubon's in omitting the word entirely. Duport plays throughout on the sense of *sordidus* as literally 'dirty' as well as 'stingy'; the word is thus translated here as 'dirty cheapskate'.

In librum regii martyris Caroli I vere aureum, cui titulus, Ἐικὼν Βασιλική / On the Truly Golden Book of the Royal Martyr Charles I Entitled the *Royal Icon*

The *Eikon Basilike*, a massively popular piece of royalist propaganda, was published in February 1649, within days of the killing of its purported author, Charles I. Given its attention to detractors of the book, Duport's poem was most likely written not long after October 1649.

4 *iconolatra*: literally 'icon-worshipper', here rendered into English as 'iconolater' (cf. the more common 'idolater').

6 This line is closely adapted from Mart. 10.32.6. The term *tabella*, appropriately, could refer to either a writing tablet (and hence a piece of writing) or to a picture. The *Eikon Basilike* was accompanied by an influential frontispiece engraved by William Marshall.

8 *iconoclasta*: probably a reference to John Milton's *Eikonoklastes*, published in October 1649. The word here occupies the same metrical position as the similarly formed but semantically opposite *iconolatra* in line 4.

10 *martyrii* ... *testis*: a play on the etymology of martyr, which literally means 'witness' (from Greek μάρτυρ).

11 The Zoilus referred to must be the anonymous author of the *Eikon Alethine*, published in August 1649, which calls into doubt the attribution of the *Eikon Basilike* to the king (Milton was content to assume the attribution for polemical purposes).

15 Duport compares the illustrator William Marshall to Apelles, renowned as the greatest of Greek painters.

In viri illustrissimi, et πολυμαθεσάτου Claudii Salmasii librum, cui titulus, Defensio Regia / On the Book of the Most Illustrious and Most Learned Man, Claudius Salmasius, Entitled the *Royal Defence*

Claudius Salmasius (1588–1653), among the most renowned classical scholars of his age, studied under Isaac Casaubon and in 1631 assumed the position at Leiden University formerly held by Joseph Justus Scaliger (son of Julius Caesar Scaliger). His *Defensio Regia*, an apology for the recently executed Charles I and an attack on the regicidal parliamentarians, was first published in 1649; it is best known today for the response it provoked from John Milton, *Pro Populo Anglicano Defensio* (1651).

7–10 *Et primum Polyhistorem ... petis profundum*: Duport here refers to Salmasius' *Plinianae Exercitationes in Caii Iulii Solini Polyhistora* (1629), a commentary on the Plinian *Polyhistor* of Solinus.

13 Salmasius' 1620 edition of the *Historia Augusta*, which notably included Casaubon's notes on the text.

14 Salmasius' works on usury, *De Usuris* (1638) and *De Modo Usurarum* (1639).

16 Salmasius' 1622 edition of *De Pallio* ('*On the Cloak*') by Tertullian, the Church Father from Roman Africa.

21 *perenniora ... aera*: cf. Hor. *Carm.* 3.30.1: *exegi monumentum aere perennius* ('I have built a monument more lasting than bronze').

34–5 *monstrum ... horrendum*: cf. Verg. *Aen.* 3.658: *monstrum horrendum, informe, ingens, cui lumen ademptum* ('a monster dreadful, hideous, massive, deprived of sight'). Duport may well have been inspired by the application of this Vergilian line to the blind Milton in Peter du Moulin, *Regii Sanguinis Clamor* (The Hague: Adriaan Vlacq, 1652), sig. A8v.

40 *elogio*: if this is meant to connote an epitaph or funerary inscription, the poem would have to be dated after Salmasius' death in September 1653.

In sortilegium Ogilvii librarium / On Ogilby's Bibliomancy

John Ogilby (1600–76) first published his English translation of the *Aeneid* in 1649. As Duport seems to refer to Ogilby selling his own books, the poem can probably be dated after the appearance of the 1654 edition, copies of which were printed 'for the Author, and are to be had at his House in Kings-head Court in Shoe-lane'. The *sortes Vergilianae* ('Vergilian fortunes') refers to an ancient tradition of book-based fortune-telling using randomly selected passages from the *Aeneid*.

1 *Sortilego ... pretio*: the adjective *sortilegus* signifies 'foretelling, prophetic, soothsaying', hence the phrase can be literally translated 'at a prophetic price'. But as my translation ('cost a fortune') seeks to convey, Duport seems to be playing on the dual sense of the root *sors* as both prophetic and economic, much like English 'fortune' (or Latin *fortuna*).

4 This line reproduces Verg. *Aen.* 3.57.

5 This line reproduces Verg. *Aen.* 10.501.

7 This line reproduces Mart. 1.16; Duport quietly switches to playing the *sortes* with the text of Martial.

In illud Homericum, ἔπεα νιφάδεσσιν ἐοικότα χειμερίῃσιν, Comparatum cum Deuter. 32.2 / On the Homeric Phrase 'Words like Winter Snowflakes' Compared with Deuteronomy 32.2

The Homeric phrase is from *Il.* 3.222. Deuteronomy 32.2 reads, in the King James Version: 'My doctrine shall drop as the raine: my speech shall distill as the deaw, as the smal raine vpon the tender herbe, and as the showres vpon the grasse'. This poem first appeared, in a slightly shorter form, in Duport's commentary on the Homeric phrase in question in Duport 1660.

3 Cf. Verg. *Aen.* 11.611: *crebra nivis ritu* ('thick as snow', lit. 'thick in the manner of snow').

4 The version in *Homeri Gnomologia* reads *fulmina jacta cadunt*.

5–6 These lines are absent in the version in *Homeri Gnomologia*.

6 Zebedee was the father of the Apostles James and John.

Gratiarum una a Junone Somno in matrimonium data. Hom Il. ξ Quod neque placet κριτικωτάτῳ Julio Scaligero Poet. l. 5. C. 3 / One of the Graces was Given in Marriage by Juno to Sleep (Homer, *Iliad* **14) Which Does not Please the Ever so Critical Julius Scaliger (***Poetics***, Book 5, Chapter 3)**

This epigram responds to a criticism of Homer made by the Italian scholar Julius Caesar Scaliger (1484–1558), who found the allegory of Grace or Charis marrying Sleep to be distasteful on both physical and ethical grounds. Duport discusses Scaliger's criticism in Duport 1660: 83.

1 *Displicuit* echoes Scaliger's diction in *Poetices Libri Septem* (1581), 544: *Neque placet, Gratias Somno in matrimonium dari* ('It is not pleasing that the Graces are given in marriage to Sleep').

2 Cf. Hor. *Ars P.* 359: *bonus dormitat Homerus* ('good Homer nods off').

5 The Cimmerians were a legendary people said to live in permanent darkness at the entrance of the underworld.

6 Cf. Hor. *Carm.* 4.7.5–6: *Gratia cum Nymphis geminisque sororibus audet | ducere nuda choros* ('Grace, together with the nymphs and her twin sisters, dares to lead the dances naked').

13 *grata*: a pun on *Gratia* ('Grace').

In Roscias nostras, seu histriones feminas / On our Roscias, or Female Actors

In the late-sixteenth and early-seventeenth centuries professional actors in the London playhouses were exclusively male: in the plays of Shakespeare and his contemporaries women's roles were played by boys or young men. During this period women could only participate in dramatic performances that were relatively private, like court masques. Professional actresses were only introduced after the Restoration of Charles II in 1660. Duport's response to this new cultural phenomenon must therefore date to the 1660s or early 1670s. For further discussion of this poem see Vozar 2022.

3 Priscian (*fl.* 500 CE) was a Roman grammarian, author of the *Institutiones grammaticae*.

7 Astraea was the virgin goddess of justice, whose departure marked the end of the mythological Golden Age.

13 A reference to the Neo-Latin tragedy *Herodes Infanticida* (1632) by the Dutch scholar Daniel Heinsius, which attracted claims of indecorum for featuring the pagan Furies (Allecto, Megaera and Tisiphone) in a biblical story.

19–20 Aristophanes' *Assemblywomen* treats a takeover of the Athenian government by women. If this refers to a specific play on the London stage, a possible candidate would be Edward Howard's comedy *The Six Days Adventure, or, The New Utopia* (1671), a notorious flop.

21 Roscia is a feminine version of the name of Quintus Roscius, the famous Roman actor who was a contemporary of Cicero.

25 Cf. Hor. *Epist.* 1.2.40: *sapere aude* ('dare to be wise').

28 κωφὸν … πρόσωπον: Duport's code-switching to Greek here would seem calculated to belittle.

In citharoedum caecum / On a Blind Citharode

The term 'citharode' (*citharoedus*, from Greek κιθαρῳδός) in the title signifies someone who sings accompanied by the cithara, a type of lyre. This poem could be read simply as a kind of self-contained literary game playing on the theme of 'blind faith' (*caeca fides*), but if a date of composition later in Duport's life is supposed, it is quite possible that there is a more specific target in mind – the blind poet John Milton. If that is the case, this would represent one of the earliest reactions to *Paradise Lost*, which first appeared in 1667. Milton's blindness, which his opponents dubbed divine punishment, here becomes the subject of mockery, yet the tone is perhaps not so much of rabid denunciation as of gentle ribbing – calling to mind Duport's humorous oration on alchemy in his capacity as Cambridge's *praevaricator* (commencement orator) in 1631.

1–2 Demodocus is a blind bard in the *Odyssey*; Apollo is the god of poetry and of light. For the phrasing of line 2 cf. *Od.* 8.44–45 and 8.64.

3 This might refer to the money paid to Milton for responding to Salmasius with *Pro Populo Anglicano Defensio* (1651). The Council of State seems to have awarded him £100, but Salmasius in his posthumously published *Responsio* would claim that Milton received as much as £4,000; see G. Campbell, *A Milton Chronology* (1997), 119. Interestingly, the combination of blindness with money is also found in Milton's sonnet on his blindness, first published in his 1673 *Poems*.

4 Cf. Plautus, *Asin.* 202: *semper oculatae manus sunt nostrae, credunt quod vident* ('our hands are always equipped with eyes, they believe what they see').

6 *ad unguem*: a proverbial expression idiomatically meaning 'exactly, perfectly', though Duport also plays on the literal sense 'to the nail'.

8 Duport puns on *articuli* as 'fingers' (line 6) but also as 'articles' of religion, and *fides* as 'faith' but also as a 'string' on a musical instrument.

10 Duport appropriates Hor. *Carm.* 4.3: *Romanae fidicen lyrae* ('bard of the Roman lyre') apparently to mean 'supporter of the Roman Catholic faith', though it is important to note that this is treated as something potential (*potes*), not actual. The insinuation would have obviously rankled the radical Milton, if he is indeed the target. While it might seem absurd on its face to picture Milton as a possible Catholic convert, it is nevertheless the case that Milton's radicalism could be conflated with Catholic dissent in the Restoration; on this point see N. Stogdill, 'Restoration Polemic and the Making of the Papist Milton', in: M. C. Fenton and L. Schwartz (eds), *Their Maker's Image: New Essays on John Milton*, Selinsgrove 2011, 177–90.

12

Writing a Woman Scholar: Poems around Birgitte Thott (1610–1662)

Trine Arlund Hass*

Introduction

In 1658 the Danish noblewoman Birgitte Thott (1610–62) published a Danish translation of philosophical works by Seneca, a remarkable scholarly accomplishment breaking new ground for translations of classical texts in Denmark. The prefatory material to the translation includes a series of so-called *carmina adoptiva* by established members of the learned republic of letters, particularly of Sorø Academy in Denmark, but also one by the famous Dutch scholar Anna Maria van Schurman. This section focuses on the volume's Latin *carmina adoptiva* and how they present and construct Thott as a female scholar.

Thott is among the most famous learned Danish women of the early modern period.[1] After her father's death in 1617, her learned mother, Sophie Below, ensured that her daughters had a thorough education. For Thott, as for so many others, widowhood, following an almost ten-year-long childless marriage to Otte Gøye (1632–42), allowed her to pursue further studies; languages especially interested her. Her home, Turebygaard on Zealand, functioned as a salon, but was plundered by Swedish troops in 1658, after which she never returned to live there. She moved in at Sorø Academy and, with the help of her friend – the master of the household, Jørgen Rosenkrantz – and the King's permission, she received an annuity from Sorø Academy from 1660. Sorø School in mid-Zealand was founded by Frederik II in 1586 as a boarding school for children of the nobility and bourgeoisie in a former Cistercian monastery established in 1162. In 1623, Christian IV expanded the school with an equestrian academy, which held status as a university from 1645 to 1665.[2]

Besides Seneca, Thott translated Cebes' *Tabula* and Epictetus' *Enchiridion* from Latin editions into Danish, wrote on genealogy and drafted a treatise *On the route to a happy life* (*Om vejen til et lyksaligt liv*). She furthermore conveyed international cultural debates to a Danish readership, including women, by translating works by, among others, Hall, Vives and Fuller, and had a vast network of learned men and women, including royalty, fellows of the University of Copenhagen and Sorø Academy and members of the clergy as well as international scholars.

Thott's translation entitled *Lucius Annaeus Seneca's writings in Danish* (*Lucii Annæi Senecæ Skriffter Fordanskitt*, 1658) is considered the second masterpiece of the Sorø Academy press.[3] It is a prestige volume of almost 1,000 pages in folio; it contains a detailed engraved titlepage and an engraved portrait of Thott; and the text is set in a great variety of fonts, most lavishly displayed in the section containing the *carmina adoptiva*.[4] Thott gives translations of *De beneficiis*, all of the *Dialogi* (except *De otio*), *De clementia* and all 124 of the *Epistulae morales*.[5] The texts are followed by excerpts from Justus Lipsius' explanations and reflections on the works, likewise in Danish translation by Thott, and some notes authored by her.[6]

The section of the *carmina adoptiva* is called a *tabula gratulatoria* by Marianne Alenius;[7] it is a mix of poetry and lyric prose in Latin and vernaculars.[8] Making up a substantial part of the prefatory paratexts of the translation, it is preceded by the approbation in Danish by Heinrich Ernst, a dedication by Birgitte Thott to 'the decent woman and all of the female gender who love virtue and insight' (*Det Loflige Fruen-Timmer Oc Alle dennem ibland Qvinde-Kiønnet, som elske Dyd oc Forstand*)[9] and Thott's address to the reader. After the *tabula* follows a Danish translation of Justus Lipsius' biography of Seneca.

In the order of the *tabula*, the authors represented are:[10]

a) Anna Maria van Schurman (1607–78), Dutch scholar, a central figure in the European network of learned women – Latin poem, text 1.
b) Vitus Bering (1617–75), famed poet of Latin verses, briefly professor of history at Sorø (1650–51), royal historiographer from 1650 – Latin poem, text 2, accompanying engraved portrait of Thott.
c) Jørgen Rosenkrantz (1607–75), master of the household (*Hofmester*) at Sorø Academy,[11] nobleman – Danish lyric prose.
d) Marcus Giöe Falcksen (1635–98), nobleman, Thott's brother-in-law – Latin poem, text 3.
e) Heinrich Ernst (1603–65), professor of law and moral philosophy at Sorø Academy – German poem.
f) Thomas Bartholin (1616–80), professor of anatomy, former student of philology, friend – Latin poem, text 4.
g) Hans Lauremberg (1590–1658), professor of mathematics, Classicist – Latin poem, text 5.
h) Johannes Faber († 1659), professor of eloquence at Sorø – Latin lyric prose.
i) Rasmus Hansen Brochmand (1626–64), professor of history at Sorø Academy – Latin poem, text 6.

j) Erik Eriksen Pontoppidan (1616–78), *poeta laureatus*, chaplain at Antvorskov Castle, later bishop of Trondheim – Latin poem, text 7.
k) Jesper Lauridsen Smith (1624–85), headmaster (*rektor*) of Sorø Academy 1656–60 – Latin poem, text 8.
l) Hans Clausen Rosing (1625–99), pastor in Tureby, friend of Thott, later bishop of Christiania – a Danish and a Latin poem, text 9.
m) Peder Schumacher (1635–99), student, later leading politician, ennobled as Count Griffenfeld and convicted of treason – Latin poem, text 10.

Constructing an academic network around Thott's intellectual practice, the *tabula* legitimizes and celebrates Thott as a scholarly authority and demonstrates an inextricable link between her person and the work, personal morality and scholarly competence. Her scholarly quality – Thott's remarkable grasp of Seneca's philosophy as well as her ability to elegantly transfer it into Danish – is the general focus, but most authors embed praise of her into a gendered discourse, while it is agreed that the volume will benefit readers of both genders.

The first poem by the established female scholar van Schurman confirms Thott to be part of an international trend and network, which Thott, with her dedication, invites readers to join. Van Schurman encourages national pride and celebration, in which the remaining poems can hardly be said to fall short. Pontoppidan's poem, by far the longest, embeds Thott into a historic tradition of learned women as well as a contemporary local tradition, first Northern, then Danish.

Across the poems, we see how qualities, areas and duties traditionally applying to women are infused with metaphorical meanings or in other ways used and challenged, in order to highlight the rarity of female scholarly accomplishments in general and at this level. Aspects of motherhood and childbirth are among the most frequent (van Schurman, Bering, Falcksen, Bartholin). Thott is also in many cases compared and connected to the Muses (van Schurman, Bering, Falcksen, Lauremberg, Pontoppidan) and to goddesses, especially Minerva, goddess of wisdom (Bering, Pontoppidan, Schumacher), and Diana or Phoebe, the moon and the female counterpart of Apollo, the sun and leader of the Muses, and the semantic sphere of the moon – light, shining, brightness (Bering, Falcksen, Pontoppidan, Smith).[12]

National (self-)assertion may have been further motivated by contemporary political circumstances. When the volume was published, Denmark was involved in the Second Northern War (1655–60). The relationship with Sweden had been unstable ever since the dissolution of the Kalmar Union in 1523. Danish King Frederick III declared war on Sweden in

1657 when the Swedish King Charles X Gustav was fighting in Poland. Nonetheless, he successfully countered the Danes, who agreed to a humiliating peace in early spring 1658, The Treaty of Roskilde. Already in the summer of that same year, however, Charles Gustav initiated new aggressions, including a siege of Copenhagen and the occupation of Zealand, which had direct consequences for Thott. This conflict was resolved by the Treaty of Copenhagen of 1660 after Charles Gustav's death, but new conflicts followed in the following centuries. Falcksen, Lauremberg, Pontoppidan and especially Smith set Thott's translation of Seneca, and its ability to further inner peace or moral strength, against the pressing hardship of the war. There may be an indirect, anti-Swedish dimension to calling Thott the Northern or Danish Minerva, while celebrating her practically as Stoic virtues embodied, since Queen Christina of Sweden, who abdicated in 1654 and publicly converted to Catholicism in 1655, was known for both these features too.[13]

Thott's status as a noblewoman (frequently mentioned in the poems), well-connected and a genuinely remarkable scholar means the *tabula* is not only beneficial to her. Yet being a woman means her situation is somewhat comparable to that of Schumacher, author of the last poem, who, of the contributors to the *tabula*, has least to offer in terms of authority. He and Falcksen are the youngest contributors, but Falcksen is a nobleman and his connection to Thott is clear; Schumacher is a commoner on his way up in society; he knew Brochmand's family well, which might have been how he got his poem included – it is quite a scoop. His poem shows off his education and grasp of Latin, announcing his skills and showing him able and willing to work in service of higher-ranking members of society, typically what young men in his situation would hope occasional poetry could help them accomplish. While established male scholars also printed celebratory adoptive texts in their works (see Text 1 in this volume), Thott as a learned woman, although well-connected, noble and twenty-five years Schumacher's senior, probably can be understood to rely almost as much as he did on the validation and support of established authorities in her professional pursuits. They both succeeded extraordinarily in transgressing the conditions in which they were born – Schumacher was ennobled and became the closest advisor to the king, but that Thott practically secured herself a university position is arguably even more remarkable.

Metre: All poems included are in elegiac couplets.

Notes

* I am grateful to Stephen Harrison especially as well as Marianne Pade, Karen Skovgaard-Petersen, Peter Zeeberg and the other contributors to this volume for constructive input on various aspects of my chapter. This was produced while I was a Junior Research Fellow at Linacre College and a visiting member of the Corpus Christi College Classics Centre at the University of Oxford funded by the Carlsberg Foundation.

1 On Thott, see Alenius 1983 and Alenius 2004; on early modern learned women, see e.g. Stevenson 2005 and Stevenson 2022; on learned women in Classics, see Wyles / Hall 2016.
2 On the history of the institution, see Mackesprang 1924-31.
3 Printed by Georg (Jørgen) Hantzch. See Dal 1982b: 40 and esp. Dal 1982a: 41-6 for a detailed description of the work in terms of measurements, material, fonts etc.
4 For a detailed technical description of the volume, see Dal 1982a: 41-4.
5 On Thott's selection of texts, the edition of the Latin text and her familiarity with translations in other languages, see Alenius 1983: 33-5.
6 Lipsius' Christian readings of Seneca were widely popular at the time. On this, the popularity of Seneca's prose texts in the seventeenth century and on the philosophical works vs. the tragedies, see Alenius 1983: 31-3.
7 Alenius 1983: 21.
8 Cf. Deneire 2014b and van Dam 2014 for mechanisms in this type of poetry.
9 Thott 1658: a2r.
10 Biographies of the contributors linked to Danish academia can be found in *Dansk Biografisk Leksikon*. On van Schurman, see e.g. de Baar et al. 1996; on her network de Baar 2004; for her works see Larsen / Maiullo 2021.
11 Olrik 1927-30: 5.
12 Wunder 1998 uses the dichotomy of the masculine sun and the feminine moon as a way to understand early modern German women. The female moon metaphors are abundant in the material; for masculine equivalents, see Pontoppidan, l. 51-4.
13 Åkerman 1991: 74-5.

Bibliography

Åkerman, S. (1991), *Queen Christina of Sweden and her Circle*, Leiden.
Alenius, M. (1983), 'Seneca-oversætteren Birgitte Thott: Et fagligt portræt', *Danske studier*, 78, 5-47.
Alenius, M. (2004), 'Birgitte Thott', trans. G. Kynoch, in: M. Stecher-Hansen et al. (eds), *Danish Writers from the Reformation to Decadence*, 443-51, Detroit / New York (*Dictionary of Literary Biography* 300).
Andersen, J. O. (1896), *Holger Rosenkrantz den lærde*, Copenhagen.
Brahe, T. (1573), 'In Vraniam Elegia Autoris', in: T. Brahe, *De nova stella*, Copenhagen.
Dal, E. (1982a), 'Birgitte Thotts Seneca, Sorø 1658', in: O. Hovmand et al. (eds), *Levende biblioteker*, 41-50, Copenhagen.

Dal, E. (1982b), *Dansk Provinsbogtryk gennem 500 år*, Odense.
Dansk Biografisk Leksikon på lex.dk. (https://biografiskleksikon.lex.dk).
De Baar, M. et al., eds (1996), *Choosing the Better Part: Anna Maria van Schurman (1607–1678)*, Dordrecht.
De Baar, M. (2004), '"God has Chosen You to be a Crown of Glory for all Women!" The International Network of Learned Women Surrounding Anna Maria van Schurman', in: S. van Dijk et al. (eds), *'I Have Heard about You!' Foreign Women's Writing Crossing the Dutch Border*, 108–35, Verloren.
Deneire, T., ed. (2014a), *Dynamics of Neo-Latin and the Vernacular*, Leiden.
Deneire, T. (2014b), 'Neo-Latin and Vernacular Poetics of Self-Fashioning in: Dutch Occasional Poetry (1635–1640)', in: Deneire 2014a: 33–58.
Dixon, S. (2007), *Cornelia: Mother of the Gracchi*, London.
Gruterus, J., ed. (1612), *Delitiae Poetarum Germanorum*, 6 vols, Frankfurt.
Hemelrijk, E. A. (1999), *Matrona docta: Educated Women in the Roman Élite from Cornelia to Julia Domna*, London.
Henry, M. M. (1995), *Prisoner of History: Aspasia of Miletus and Her Biographical Tradition*, Oxford.
Heywood, J., trans. (1560), *The Seconde Tragedie of Seneca Entituled Thyestes*, London (digitized facsimile of original in the Henry E. Huntington Library and Art Gallery, STC [2nd edn] 22226, Greg, I, 29(a); https://www.proquest.com/books/seconde-tragedie-seneca-entituled-thyestes/docview/2248516606/se-2?accountid=13042).
Ilsøe, H. (2011), 'Arild Huitfeldt', in: *Dansk Biografisk Leksikon på lex.dk* (https://biografiskleksikon.lex.dk/Arild_Huitfeldt).
Labalme, P. H. (1980), *Beyond their Sex: Learned Women of the European Past*, New York.
Larsen, A. R. / Maiullo, S., eds and trans. (2021), *Anna Maria van Schurman: Letters and Poems to and from Her Mentor and Other Members of Her Circle*, New York / Toronto (The Other Voice in Early Modern Europe: The Toronto Series 81).
Le Moyne, P. (1647/52), *The Gallerie of Heroick Women*, trans. H. Seile, London.
Mackeprang, M. et al. (1924–31), *Sorø: Klostret, Skolen, Akademiet gennem Tiderne*, 2 vols, Copenhagen.
Meunier, M. (1932), *Femmes pythagoriciennes: Fragments et lettres de Théano, Périctioné, Phintys, Melissa et Myria*, Paris.
Olrik, H. G. (1927–30), *Oversigt over Forstandere og Lærere ved den kgl. Skole i Sorø 1586–1737*, Sorø.
Pedersen, C. (1510), *Vocabularium ad usum dacorum*, Paris (www.renæssanceprog.dk).
Rostgaard, F., ed. (1693), *Deliciæ quorundam poetarum danorum*, 2 vols, Leiden.
Rørdam, H. (1879), 'Den kgl. Historieskriver Vitus Bering, en biografisk og litterærhistorisk Skildring', *Historisk Tidsskrift*, 5: 1–115.
Skovgaard-Petersen, K. (2002), *Historiography at the Court of Christian IV (1588–1648): Studies in the Latin Histories of Denmark by Johannes Pontanus and Johannes Meursius*, Copenhagen (*Renæssancestudier* 11).

Skoie, M. (2002), *Reading Sulpicia: Commentaries 1475-1900*, Oxford.
Stevenson, J. (2005), *Women Latin Poets: Language, Gender, and Authority from Antiquity to the Eighteenth Century*, Oxford.
Stevenson, J. (2022), *Women and Latin in the Early Modern Period*, Leiden (Brill Research Perspectives in: Latinity and Classical Reception in the Early Modern Period).
Thesleff, H. (1961), *An Introduction to Pythagorean Writings of the Hellenistic Period*, Åbo.
Treggiari, S. (2007), *Terentia, Tullia and Publilia: The Women of Cicero's Family*, London.
Tursen, J. (1561), *Vocabularius rerum*, Copenhagen (www.renæssancesprog.dk).
van Dam, H. J. (2014), 'Liminary Poetry in: Latin and Dutch: The Case of Pieter Bor's *Nederlantsche Oorloghen*', in: Deneire 2014a: 59-85.
Watts, E. J. (2017), *Hypatia: The Life and Legend of an Ancient Philosopher*, Oxford.
Weston, E. J. (2000), 'Catalogus Doctarvm Virginvm et Fæminarum', in: D. Cheney / B. Hosington (eds), *Parthenias* vol. 3, 282-303, Toronto.
Wider, K. (1986), 'Women Philosophers in the Ancient Greek World: Donning the Mantle', *Hypatia*, 1.1: 21-62.
Wyles, R. / Hall, E., eds (2016), *Women Classical Scholars: Unsealing the Fountain from the Renaissance to Jacqueline de Romilly*, Oxford (Classical Presences).
Wunder, H. (1998), *He Is the Sun, She Is the Moon: Women in: Early Modern Germany*, Cambridge, MA / London.
Zeeberg, P., ed. and trans. (1994), *Tycho Brahes Urania Titani: et digt om Sophie Brahe*, Copenhagen.
Zeeberg, P., ed. (2022), *Tycho Brahes bog om den nye stjerne*, Copenhagen.

Source of Latin text

The Royal Danish Library, Copenhagen, has three copies of Thott's Seneca, of which I have followed the digitized ex 2 (48-188 2°) – open access: https://soeg.kb.dk/permalink/45KBDK_KGL/143rgf3/alma99122577361605763.
The leaf with Albert Haelwegh's portrait and Vitus Bering's poem has, however, been consulted in ex 1 (Hielmst. 190 2°) as it is missing in ex 2 (48-188 2°). The third exemplar, donated to the library in 1917 as part of Vilhelm Bruun's collection (no shelf mark in the available catalogues), has not been consulted. In Pontoppidan's poem l. 38 *Sidronensis* has been corrected to *Stridonensis*.

Birgitte Thott (1610–1662) 263

Figure 12.1 Portrait of Birgitte Thott, copper etching by Albert Haelwegh after a painting by Abraham Wuchters. Bering's poem accompanying the portrait is included in *Deliciae quorundam Poëtarum Danorum collectae* (1693), with a note about its provenance. In The Royal Danish Library's ex 1 of Thott's volume, the portrait, in larger format than the book proper, is inserted bound in with the text at the end of the second quire (b) and folded up to fit. The portrait thereby sits immediately after van Schurman's poem (b4r), physically juxtaposing the two learned women. While Bering's poem declares Thott to be Minerva without her attributes, Alenius (1983: 8) suggests that the Minerva depicted on the volume's frontispiece has Thott's features.

Credit: 'Royal Danish Library, Shelfmark: 'Billedsamlingen. Danske portrætter. Thott, Birgitte (1610–1662) 2°.' URL:<http://www5.kb.dk/images/billed/2010/okt/billeder/object477323/en?id=%2Fimages%2Fbilled%2F2010%2Fokt%2Fbilleder%2Fobject477323>

Latin text

1. Anna Maria van Schurman

En Senecæ magnam nunc Fœmina nobilis umbram
    Et cineres tanti est ausa ciere Viri.
Huic dedit illa novam Arctoo sub sidere vitam,
    Atque novo edoctum iam facit ore loqui.
5 Corduba cede locum Annæi te gloria liquit,
    Dania quam merito vindicat una sibi
Cimbrica Musarum Decimæ gens necte corollas,
    Nympharumque chorus præmia Digna ferat;
Quid ni Parnassi sit Digna cacumine summo
10   Quæ parit huic vitam sed sine morte novam?

2. Vitus Bering

Pingitur abiecta procul ægide Pallas et hasta,
    Atque per Arctoas stat rediviva plagas.
Hoc vultu nostris affulget Tottia terris,
    Ingeniique decus præripit omne viris.
5 Tottia secreti quæ nunc penetralia Pindi
    Atque animi invadit nobilioris opes;
Id supplex Natura vides; edisserit artes
    Foemina, quodque viri discimus, illa docet,
Doctis foeta libris clarisque puerpera scriptis,
10   Et nova Palladio pignore facta parens.
Hactenus et Charites numeramus et ordine Musas
    Græcia quas vel quas Itala iactat humus,
Nomina quid libuit tot fingere vana Dearum?
    Non opus est, Lector, fingere; vera vides.

English translation

1. Anna Maria van Schurman

Look, a noble woman is now venturing to rouse up Seneca's great ghost
and the ashes of so great a man.
She has given him a new life under the Northern star
and taught him to speak a new language.
Cordoba, yield your place, Annaeus' glory has left you, 5
Denmark has justly won it for herself;
bind wreaths, Cimbrians, for the tenth Muse,
let the choir of nymphs bring worthy prizes;
of what is she worthy if not the highest summit of Mount Parnassus,
she who gives him life but a new one without death? 10

2. Vitus Bering

Pallas is depicted, having cast far aside her shield and spear,
she now stands revived in the Northern regions.
With her face Thott shines in our lands,
and she snatches every honour for her insight from men.
Thott now enters the innermost areas of Pindus 5
and the treasures of the nobler spirit.
This, Nature, you see, all overwhelmed:
a woman unfolds the arts, whatever we men learn, she teaches,
fertile with learned books, bearing brilliant writings,
and made a new parent by Palladian pledge. 10
Up until now we have listed both the Graces and Muses in due order,
those scattered in Greek or Italian lands,
Why was it our pleasure to fashion vain names for those goddesses?
Reader, there is no need to fashion anything, what you see, is genuine.

Commentary Text 1

1–2 possibly draw on Statius, *Silvae* 2.7.116–17: *... magna sacer at superbus umbra | noscis Tartaron*, where the dead Lucan, Seneca's nephew, is addressed by the poet, imagining how he might see the dead of Pharsalus in Elysium as well as Nero in Tartarus. Although Thott's translation does not include Seneca's tragedies, the passage brings their many ghosts to mind. The imagery seems to be popular – it is used for instance also by Jasper Heywood in the introduction to his translation of *Thyestes* of 1560, relating that Seneca's ghost appeared to him in a dream, *Full graue ... His eyes like Christ all shiende* (preface, l. 35–7), looking for someone to renew his name *and make me speake in straunger speech* (83), and by Tobias Sculerus in a poem about Gruter's Seneca, describing how Gruter calls Seneca back from the shadows (Gruterus 1612: VI 62).

3–4 Gendered wordplay on motherhood – giving birth (see also l. 10) and teaching young children to speak. Seneca's new Scandinavian homeland is plotted by reference to the Northern star (l. 3, for this see also Pontoppidan, l. 39). For l. 4 cf. Mart. 7.46.2: *Maeonioque cupis doctius ore loqui*.

5–6 Van Schurman presents the effect of Thott's scholarly effort in terms of a *translatio studii*: Seneca's homeland is no longer Cordoba but Denmark.

7 Van Schurman invests her own authority as a famed female scholar in naming Thott the tenth Muse, a most popular trope for learned women, but since it is used of van Schurman too, she is passing it on, inscribing Thott into a tradition.[2] Van Schurman invites Thott's homeland to celebrate her.

necte corollas: a popular expression in Neo-Latin, originating from a mix of Horace (*coronam nectere*) and Catullus (*corolla*), while Juvenal 6.51 has *necte coronam*.

10 *Quæ parit ...*: gendered metaphor.

---

[2] Stevenson 2022: 52. Ernst in his *approbation* likewise proclaims Thott as the tenth Muse: *Io triumphe! Dania peperit decimam Musam* (Thott 1658: a1v).

Commentary Text 2

Bering's poem accompanies the portrait of Thott (see Figure 12.1). At this time, he was the most popular Danish poet for verses paired with portraits in this style (Rørdam 1879: 18). The poem is no. 19 in *Deliciæ quorundam poetarum danorum* (Rostgaard 1693, II: 39–40).

1–2 The presentation of Thott as Minerva resembles Schumacher, l. 7–10. *Rediviva* as here, in the sense 'that lived again', is rare in classical Latin, but more frequent in Christian and Neo-Latin literature.

3 *vultu ... affulget*, pertaining to the semantic sphere of moon and moonshine, is used metaphorically in several of the poems. For the wording cf. Martial 5.6.9–11: *nosti tempora tu Iovis sereni, | cum fulgent placido suoque vultu | quo nil supplicibus solet negare.*

5 *Pindi*: Pindus, a mountain in Thessaly, seat of the Muses.

9–10 Gendered wordplay on pregnancy and childbirth.

10 *Palladio pignore*: intellectual issue by Pallas Athene.

11–12 rely on the most popular tropes used for learned women in this period, calling them or comparing them to Graces and Muses (Stevenson 2022: 52).

13 *Nomina ... vana*: cf. Lucan 1.313: *Marcellusque loquax et nomina vana Catones.*

Latin text

3. Marcus Giöe Falcksen

Languebat virtus, lento ceu pressa sopore,
    Non ætas pretium, non tulit æquus honos.
Ingenio illa tuo cunctis iam clara resurgit;
    Quisquis adest, lingua vir mulierque favet.
5 Ferrea sint Marti nec miti sidere natis
    Secula; tu musis aurea Juno refers.

4. Thomas Bartholin

Traximus ex nostro pridem præconia sexu,
    Nunc ex fœminea laus venit arte Viris.
Ingratus sævo Senecam Nero sustulit astu,
    En vitam reddit Docta BRIGITTA Seni.
5 Splendor fœminei sexus, Tibi fama procatur,
    Quamque studes aliis reddere tota tua est.

5. Hans Lauremberg

Vis animi effervens alienoque excita motu
    Permutat sexus munia sæpe sui.
Duxit Amazonidum lunatis agmina peltis
    Armatos contra Penthesilea viros;
5 Alcides famulas inter, muliebria pensa
    Versavit nata monstra domare manu.
TOTTIA sexum animis generosaque indole vincens
    Aonia palmam præripit arte Viris.
Sume colum posthinc Studiis inimica Juventus,
10   Fœmineo Musas linque librosque gregi.

English translation

3. Marcus Giöe Falcksen

Virtue was languid, as if oppressed by idle sleep,
the age did not bring prizes, nor did fair honour.
Thanks to your insight, virtue now re-emerges, bright for all;
all sorts of people approach it, men and women keep still.
Leave the iron age to Mars and those not born under a mild star; 5
you as Juno restore the golden age to the Muses.

4. Thomas Bartholin

For long, we have enjoyed recognition on account of our gender;
now praise comes from men as the result of female skill.
Ungrateful Nero destroyed Seneca with savage cunning;
but look, the learned Birgitte has given the old man his life back.
Lustre of the female gender, fame is courted by you; 5
The fame you strive to pass on to others, is entirely yours.

5. Hans Lauremberg

An ardent force of spirit summoned by strange commotion
often causes reversal of men's and women's duties.
Penthesilea led an army of Amazons with shields in half-moon shapes
against armed men;
although his hands were made for taming monsters, Alcaeus's grandson
    dwelled 5
among handmaids and plied women's skeins.
Thott, triumphing over her gender with her spirit and noble character,
snatches the first place in Aonian art from the men.
Take up the distaff, lads, hostile to studies from now on,
leave the Muses and books to the crowd of women. 10

Commentary Text 3

1–4 Falcksen dwells on the potential moral effect of the translation, implying that the unfolding Second Northern War is a sign of moral decay.

1 is metrically completely identical to Lucretius 6.1157, except for the caesura in the last two feet; *languebat* flags the model (6.1156–7: *atque animi prorsum tum vires totius, omne | languebat corpus leti iam limine in ipso*). Lucretius speaks of the effect of the plague on body as well as soul, while Falcksen focuses on the effect on the mind exclusively. In Lucretius (1.62–79) Epicurus stands up to superstition; Falcksen presents a more general positive effect of the Seneca translation on morals.

2 might echo Horace, *Epistles* 1.18.18 (*pretium aetas altera sordet*) while also referring to the declining ages of the world as in Ovid, *Metamorphoses* 1.89 and 1.115.

3 *clara resurgit*: recalls moon imagery.

4 Cf. Tibullus 2.2.2: *quisques ades, lingua vir mulierque fave.*

5–6 confirms that the present iron age of war may be relieved by a new golden age of letters brought about by Thott's translation. Since Juno is the goddess of childbirth, Thott is rather a birth assistant or midwife in l. 6 than giving birth (as often elsewhere), thereby approaching the metaphor Socrates famously applied to his philosophical praxis (Plato, *Theaetetus* 148e).

Commentary Text 4

1-4 Bartholin possibly alludes to van Schurman, using the same deictic particle *en* and the metaphor of Thott giving Seneca new life (l. 4) setting her against Nero, who ordered Seneca's suicide (l. 3). For *Ingratus . . . Nero* (l. 3), cf. Statius, *Silvae* 2.7.58.

5 According to contemporary Danish Latin dictionaries, *proco* = 'to court' and *procor* = 'to court' or 'to ask unshyly' (Pedersen 1510, *s.v. proco*; Tursen 1560, *s.v. procor*), which allows for a love relationship metaphor in the last couplet in which traditional gender roles are reversed: Thott is the suitor.

6 *tota tua est* probably originates from Martial (2.2.6, same metrical position), but is quite frequent in Neo-Latin poetry. In classical poetry, the phrase also appears in the poetry of Sulpicia, one of the few poems with a woman as author ([Tibullus] 3.10.14). While Caspar Barth in 1624 suggested that the poems, transmitted in book 3 of the Tibullan corpus, were written by Sulpicia, this notion only gained ground in the nineteenth century (Skoie 2002: 9, 127).

Commentary Text 5

1–2 Introducing parallel examples from classical mythology, Lauremberg builds the argument that extreme circumstances (such as the Second Nordic War) often cause men and women to swap duties.

3–4 quote Vergil's *Aeneid* 1.466–7 almost verbatim: *ducit Amazonidum lunatis agmina peltis | Penthesilea furens*.

5–6 allude to Hercules' one year of servitude, during which he was, according to some versions of the myth, serving Omphale and forced not only to do women's duties but also to wear female dress. For Hercules working with wool on that occasion, cf. Propertius 3.11.20: *tam dura traheret mollia pensa manu*; for *monstra manu . . . premens* in connection with Hercules cf. Vergil, *Aeneid* 8.289: *monstra manu geminosque premens eliserit anguis*.

7–8 Thott becomes the third argument. For the idea that learned women transgress their gender, see Labalme 1980: 4–5 and Pontoppidan, l. 65–8.

8 *Aonia*: 'Aonian / of Aonia', that is, 'of the Muses' (referring to the Aonian mountains in Boeotia, which include Mount Helicon, seat of the Muses).

Latin text

6. Rasmus Hansen Brochmand

TOTTIA feminei vere unica gloria sexus,
    Quæ superat multos nobilitate viros,
Doctrina et paucis doctorum cedere certat,
    Nullum non sexum nobilitare studet,
5 Se dignis virtutibus, et, quas exprimit ipsa,
    Summis, quas docuit mens sapiens SENECÆ;
Dum Scriptorem hunc Hispanum civem facit apte
    Danum, ut dignoscas scribere sic SENECAM.
TOT Dominæ similem vix unam hæc nostra tulerunt,
10   Forte dabant olim saecula Prisca pares.
Tullia talis erat docto dilecta Parenti;
    Talis erat Gracchos quæ tulit illa duos.

English translation

6. Rasmus Hansen Brochmand

Thott, a glory truly unique for the female gender,
who surpasses many men in nobility, in learning
and struggles to hold her own only against a few scholars,
strives to ennoble each gender
with worthy virtues – those she herself translates,   5
of the highest kind, as well as those Seneca's wise mind taught –,
all the while making that Spanish writer a proper Danish citizen,
in a manner that lets you recognize Seneca's way of writing.
Our many ages have hardly brought forth a single woman similar to Thott.
Maybe long ago, past times produced women equal to her.   10
Tullia was of this sort, beloved by her learned parent;
of such sort was she who bore the two Gracchi.

Commentary Text 6

Thott is aligned with Seneca as both a moral example and philosophical authority. The complexity of her relationship with Seneca is explored in gendered metaphors, comparing her to a daughter as well as mother of learned ancient Romans.

9 *tot* is a pun on Thott's name (l. 1), creating a sense of symmetry between this line and Tullia in l. 11. *Tot ... saecula* is furthermore the Christian ages, set against the pagan, *saecula Prisca*, in l. 10.

11 Tullia, Cicero's and Terentia's daughter, born between 79 and 76 BCE, died in 45 BCE. Her father's devotion to her is well-known, but according to Hemelrijk (1999) he showed little interest in her education.[3]

12 Cornelia, *c.* 190–115 BCE, the second daughter of Publius Cornelius Scipio Africanus, mother of Gaius and Tiberius Sempronius Gracchus, praised for her elegant Latin and considered an exemplary mother and wife also after antiquity (Dixon 2007).

---

[3] See e.g. Treggiari 2007 and for Tullia as well as Cornelia Hemelrijk 1999. On Cicero's interest in Tullia's education, see Hemelrijk 1999: 76.

Latin text

7. Erik Eriksen Pontoppidan

Mirabunda stupes merito iam Corduba, linguam
   ANNÆUM docuit DANA MINERVA suam.
Qui fandi monstrante viam genetrice Magistra
   Investis didicit Bætica verba loqui,
5 Et tandem vegetus, quæ non peritura, Latino
   Concinnata stylo Vir monumenta dedit,
Iam scite Arctois pandit sua dogmata verbis,
   Bætigena illustri nomine Danus erit.

Corcyræa decus Phæacæ gentis Agallis
10   Grammatica clarum nomen ab arte tulit,
At claret NOSTRAS, cui non suffecerit una
   Ars, supra sexum docta THALIA magis.
Ampla Tanagrææ tollatur ad astra Corinnæ
   Laus Phœbo dignis conciliata metris,
15 Mireturqve suæ Lesbis præconia famæ
   Sappho Pierii pars celebrata chori,
Cyrrhæis etiam Soror associata Camenis
   Prædives laudum DANICA MUSA cluit.
Fulvia diversas callebat Olympia linguas
20   Scilicet Ausoniæ Suada diserta plagæ;
Sed longe plures novit SÆDLANDICA PEITHO,
   Cui varia ad placitum prompta loquela fluit.
Arcanis Sophiæ studiis Milesia semper
   Aspasia, ut saperet, tota dicata fuit,
25 Pythagoræa sibi bene commentata Theano
   Promeritum magni fænus honoris habet:
Quicquid Aristocles, quicquid Sophus ille Stagiræ
   Utile proponat, NOSTRA SIBYLLA tenet,
Clarior et seris tradit sua nomina seclis
30   Cum Seneca docto Cimbrica scripta dare.
Stelligeras scrutata domos præclara Theonis
   Filia de stellis nobile scripsit opus:
Non contenta solo superas ascendit in oras,
   Ut vaga sollerti sydera mente notet,

English translation

7. Erik Eriksen Pontoppidan

A marvellous thing, no wonder you are stunned, Cordoba:
the Danish Minerva has taught Annæus her language.
He who, with his mother as a teacher showing him the way,
learned to say Spanish words in his boyhood
and who eventually, as a mature man, produced lasting 5
monuments, adapted to Latin style,
now spreads his teaching elegantly in Northern words;
born in Spain, he will be a Dane of great fame.

Corcyrean Agallis, the pride of the Phaeacian people,
won fame for her name in the art of grammar, 10
but the Thalia of our region, for whom one art was not enough,
shines brighter, is learned beyond her gender.
Let the praise of Corinna from Tanagra,
won by measures worthy of Phoebus, raise her to the great stars,
And let Sappho from Lesbos, 15
celebrated as a member of the Pierian chorus,
marvel at the praise of her fame;
our lady is associated with the muses of Cirrha too, as their sister,
so rich in praise that she has been called the Danish Muse.

Fulvia Olympia was well versed in different languages,
certainly an eloquent Suada of the Ausonian region, 20
but the Peitho of Zealand has mastered far more;
for her a variety of speech flows forth readily at will.
Aspasia of Miletus was always fully dedicated to secret studies of wisdom,
to pursue knowledge.
Theano, who devised Pythagorean matters for herself, 25
holds a well-deserved income of highest esteem
Our Sibyl grasps anything beneficial presented by Aristocles
and anything beneficial presented by the wise man of Stagira,
and she is more famous and transmits her name even to future ages
together with Seneca, who has been taught to render his works in the
    Cimbrian language. 30
Scrutinizer of the star-bearing houses, Theon's
daughter, how bright she was, wrote a fine work on stars:
not content with the ground, she strove towards the regions above,
to observe the wandering stars with her expert mind;

35 Et superat patuli stellata palatia cæli
    CIMBRICA, adesse Deo dum cupit, URANIE.
Es rimata sacri Marcella oracula libri,
    Ut Stridonensis plauderet inde Pater:
ARCTOA expendit vigili CONSTANTIA mente
40   Cum fructu veri cælica scita Dei,
Et contra exorsos prave sacra bella Sophistas
    Divina, ut vincat, tela vibrare potest.

BIRGITTÆ gens Scota suæ conamina grato,
    Ceu fas est, animo religiosa probet,
45 BIRGITTÆ manifesta suæ præsagia vatis
    Commemoret dignis Suecia tota modis,
BIRGITTÆ miranda suæ non dona tacebit
    Dania, sed meriti præco perennis erit.

Tres inter Danos generoso sanguine cretos
50   Doctrina ante alios eminuere viri:
Theiologum primas OLIGER, prælustris Apollo
    Et Patriæ Phœnix, conspicuumque iubar;
Astrigeri TYCHO summus scrutator Olympi,
    Alter Atlas, cœli Jupiter ille sui!
55 Assertor veri, princeps HVITFELDIUS Histor
    Non dubia memorans Regia gesta fide.

Sic tria fœminei celebrantur lumina sexus
    Danigeras inter Nobilitate satas:
Astrorum sollers speculatrix æmula fratris
60   BRAHÆA Aoniis hic operata sacris;
Pæonio celebris studio BELOVIA, multæ
    Et lingvæ et variæ gnara virago rei;
Omnigenæ vivum doctrinæ exemplar, honoræ
    Virtutis speculum Thespiadumque decus,
65 Mascula fœminei splendescens gloria cœtus
    THOTTIA, præsignis stella corusca domus,
Quæ Vir divina censeri mente meretur,
    Quæ potis est magnos anticipare viros.

the Cimbrian Urania also rises above the wide-spread sky's starry palace, 35
wishing to be near God.
You, Marcella, examined the holy book of prophecies and
so extensively that the Stridonian Father applauded it;
the Northern Firmness with her alert mind weighs celestial maxims
with the fruit of the true God 40
and is capable of brandishing divine spears at the sophists
who have wickedly arisen in sacred wars in order to gain victory.

Let the Scottish people commend the religious endeavours
of their Birgitta with grateful minds, as is right;
let all of Sweden commemorate 45
the manifest premonitions of their prophet Birgitta in worthy manner;
Denmark will not tacitly pass over their Birgitta's
marvellous gifts, but forever herald her merits.

Among Danes of noble blood three men
stand out from everyone else due to their learning: 50
the foremost theologian Holger, an illustrious Apollo,
a Phoenix of the Fatherland and a radiant beacon;
Tycho, the finest scrutinizer of starry Olympus,
a second Atlas, he is Jupiter of his own heaven!
The asserter of truth, Hvidtfeldt, the foremost historian, 55
recording regal deeds with unquestionable accuracy.

Likewise, three lights of the female gender are celebrated,
Danish-born, sprung from the nobility:
the expert observer of stars, emulator of her brother,
Brahe, devoted to the rites of the Muses here; 60
Below, famed for her Paeonian ventures,
a virago skilled both in many languages and a diversity of topics;
the living example of learning of all kinds, honour's and
virtue's mirror, the Jewel of the Muses,
the masculine shining glory of the feminine throng, 65
Thott, the flashing star of a pre-eminent house,
who due to her divine mind deserves to be evaluated as a man,
who is able to surpass great men.

Commentary Text 7

1–8: introduction
As in van Schurman's poem, Pontoppidan presents a type of *translatio studii*, addressing Seneca's native city Cordoba, which must be astounded that Seneca speaks a foreign language now. Seneca's quality is first linked exclusively to his Latin, alluding to Horace, *Carm.* 3.30.1 by calling it a monument to Latin style.[4] Thott is presented as Minerva in the text proper (l. 2) as well as in the inscription,[5] which furthermore, like van Schurman, l. 3, uses the Northern star to designate the location (reappearing as a metaphor for Thott in l. 39), but she assumes new forms through the poem.

4 *Bætica*: 'of Baetica', southern Spain, today Andalusia and part of Granada – Seneca's native region.

9–42: learned historical women
The general ordering principle of Pontoppidan's poem is comparisons. First Thott is set against women of history and the classical tradition, then grouped with namesakes and lastly with learned Danish men and women. Those selected seem to be popular examples in an early modern context – included e.g. in Elizabeth Weston's catalogue of learned women (published *c.* 1607; see Weston 2000).

9 *Agallis*: *fl.* second century BCE, female grammarian from Corcyra, worked on Homer. Phaeacia was identified with Corcyra.

11–12 *claret* ... *magis*: moon imagery, reinforced by the following couplet where Corinna is raised to the stars due to poetry worthy of Phoebus (cf. l. 29–36).

13 *Corinnæ*: Corinna, lyric poet from Tanagra in Boeotia, *fl. c.* 500 BCE.

18 Cf. also van Schurman, l. 7.

19 *Olympia*: Olympia Fulvia Morata (1526–55) was a famous Italian Classicist. A large collection of her Greek letters and Latin dialogues was published in Basel in 1558; Thott owned a later copy (Alenius 1983: 44). Tycho Brahe (l. 53–4) also compared his sister Sophie Brahe (l. 59–60) to Olympia Fulvia Morata (Zeeberg 1994: 170–6).

---

[4] Thott uses the Horatian image in her address to the reader, Thott 1658: b1v.
[5] *Arctoæ Palladi*, Thott 1658: c3v.

20-1 *Suada* ... *Peitho*: personified and deified persuasion in Latin and Greek respectively.

24 *Aspasia*: Pericles' partner, whose political insight Pericles admired, allegedly taught rhetoric and disputed with Socrates; a subject of jokes in comedies (Henry 1995).

25 *Theano*: wife of Pythagoras or Brotinus; fragments of her writings survive.[6]

27 *Aristocles*: supposedly the original name of Plato (cf. Apuleius, *De Platone* 1).

Stagiræ: Stagira, Aristotle's birthplace.

29-36 *Clarior* resumes the terminology of the moon imagery, which in the following blends in with the treatment of astrological science, most elegantly in l. 32, where Hypatia is *præclara* due to her work on the movement of stars.

31-2 Hypatia, *c.* 350-415 BCE, Alexandrian astronomer, philosopher, mathematician, literary critic; continued the astronomical work of her father, Theon, head of the Neoplatonic School at Athens. Some sources say that she was married to Isidorus the philosopher, but this is debated. The *Suda* records three writings by her, commentaries on Diophantus of Alexandria's *Arithmetica*, on Apollonius of Pergassus' *Conics* and on Ptolemy(?)'s *Astronomical Canon*; none of these survive.[7]

35-6 Urania, the muse of astronomy.

35 *palatia cæli*: quotes Ovid, *Metamorphoses* 1.176.

37-8 Marcella, *c.* 335-410/11 CE, founder of a religious community in Rome, friend of Jerome (= *Stridonensis*, born in Stridon, Dalmatia), active in the so-called Origenist Crises.

39-42 is recalling the initial presentation of Thott as Minerva, but here explicitly Christian.

39 *Arctoa ... constantia*: a word play on the North Pole or Northern Star, which does not move (for *arctous* in this meaning cf. Tycho Brahe, *Urania*

---

[6] Wider 1986: 30-4; Thesleff 1965; Meunier 1932. Weston 2000: 286 has her as Brotus' wife. On her marriage see Wider 1986: 29-30.
[7] On Hypatia and her reception in general, see Watts 2017. On her works, see also Wider 1986: 55. Wider 1986: 52 disputes her marriage to Isidorus; according to Watts 2017: 151 she chose to remain a virgin and never to marry, and, due to her position as head of her own school, she had to make this publicly known.

Titani, l. 276: *Et surdam et cæcam me facit Arctus Amor*, 'my love is constant, makes me deaf as well as blind'), and the Stoic virtue of *apatheia/constantia*; for Stoic *constantia* as a female virtue cf. e.g. Le Moyne's *Gallerie des femmes fortes* (1647, English translation 1652), esp. on Seneca's wife Paulina, pp. 66–83, likewise connected with Queen Christina of Sweden (Åkerman 1991: 75).

40 *Cum fructu veri . . . Dei*: see Augustine, *Sermo* 42.3: *sitis fructus mei, ut vobiscum sim, et omnes simus fructus Dei.*

43–8: famous Birgittae

Focus is now directed towards Northern Europe. The remaining three sections have a tricolon structure. In the first and last Thott is the third element. The last expands to a *tricolon auctum*, Thott's treatment becoming the conclusion of the poem.

43–4 Bridget/Bride/Bríd of Kildare, died in Kildare, but was from Scotland, *c.* 451–525 CE.

45–6 St Bridget of Sweden, *c.* 1303–73.

49–56: famous learned Danish noblemen

51–4 applies masculine terms of the radiant celestial bodies and deities equivalent to the frequent use of moon imagery of Thott and other learned women.

51–2 Holger Rosenkrantz, 1574–1642, nobleman, theologian, member of the Danish Council of State, friend of Tycho Brahe, father of Sorø's master of the household Jørgen Rosenkrantz, famed especially for his role as educator at his estate Rosenholm (Andersen 1896).

53–4 Tycho Brahe, 1546–1601, astronomer, poet, most famous for discovering a new star (supernova) on 11 November 1572, on which he published *De nova stella* (1573; see Zeeberg 1994; Zeeberg 2022).

55–6 Arild Huitfeldt, 1546–1609, first secretary of the Danish Chancellery 1573–80, member of the Danish Council of the Realm from 1586, published *Danmarks Riges Krønike*, a history of Denmark in ten volumes (1595–1604).[8]

---

[8] Discussed in Skovgaard-Petersen 2002. See Ilsøe 2011 for his biography.

57-62: famous learned Danish noblewomen; 63-8: conclusion

57 *lumina*: links the famous women to the semantic sphere of the moon or Diana, thereby underlining the symmetry of this and the preceding passage about learned Danish men, where Rosenkrantz and Brahe were called Apollo and Jupiter.

59-60 Sophie Ottesdatter Brahe, 1556/9-1643, worked on astrology, astronomy, chemistry, horticulture and genealogy; her brother respected her work.[9]

61-2 Marie Below, 1586-1651, Thott's aunt on her mother's side, accomplished in Latin and several other languages; *Pæonio* alludes to her vast production of poetry, but neither this nor her autobiography are preserved. Only a letter she wrote in Latin at the age of twelve to Holger Rosenkrantz survives as proof of her language skills. For the idea that learned women transgress their gender, see Labalme 1980: 4-5 and Lauremberg, l. 7-8.

63-8 Thott is in the end raised to the stars like Corinna (l. 11-2), taking the imagery of her being the Northern Star (l. 39) in a more conventional direction – she is a frontrunner, well-deservedly famous and a pride of her noble family. Throughout the poem Pontoppidan has argued that she measures up to the learned women of history, in the ancient world as well as in her own time and region. Building up to the conclusion with the symmetrical description of learned Danish men and women, beginning in l. 49, Pontoppidan presents a gender-balanced learned 'society' of noble Danes, in which Thott has not only deserved a place but must be considered a leading figure.

---

[9] Zeeberg 1994: 170-6 reproduces a description of Sophie and her faculties written by her brother in 1594.

Latin text

8. Jesper Lauridsen Smith

Sic Boream Phœbe fato meliore serenat,
    Et nova languentes poscit in arma manus.
Hactenus infames sicas vultusque minaces
    Sensimus, et torvi vota cruenta viri;
5 Non Latium, priscique magis sapuere Quirites,
    Cum fratres ageret vis inimica duos.
Nunc alius manet arma labor, sublimior ensem
    Lex rotat, et fasces littera sola beat;
TOTTIA nunc alias alio sub Marte secures
10   Exhibet, et fractos armat in arma viros,
Indomitos cohibet, Seneca præeunte, lacertos,
    Et solo mentes temperat ore feras.
Pande tuos, Borea, vultus, nam TOTTIA vitam
    Dum format, Boreas undique vivus erit.

9. Hans Clausen Rosing

Annæi summum quis Linguæ et Mentis acumen
    Exponet? Latia quis sine voce leget?
Tam facilem Danis Senecam nunc TOTTIA reddit,
    Ut Dani hunc Latia vel sine voce legant.
5 Annæus variis est linguis redditus ante;
    At lingua Annæi sæpe coacta fuit.
Felici Senecam sed TOTTIA transtulit ausu:
    Neutrius Linguæ sermo coactus erat.

English translation

8. Jesper Lauridsen Smith

Thus Phoebe clears up the North with a better fate
and calls the weary to arms of a new sort.
Up until this point we have felt a grim man's
infamous daggers, threatening faces and bloody pledges;
Latium or the old Quirites there were no wiser   5
back when hostile force drove two brothers.
Now different labour awaits arms, a higher law brandishes the sword,
and learning alone blesses the fasces;
Thott now, under another kind of Mars, displays another kind of axes
and equips broken men against warfare,   10
restrains untamed power, with Seneca in front,
and, using her voice alone, moderates raging minds.
Lay your face open, Boreas, for as long as Thott shapes life,
Boreas will be alive everywhere.

9. Hans Clausen Rosing

Who will present the supreme sharpness of Annaeus' language and mind?
Who will read him without the Latin tongue?
Thott now renders Seneca so accessible
that the Danes can read him even if they do not know Latin.
Annaeus has been rendered in various languages before,   5
but Annaeus' tongue was often forced.
Yet Thott has translated Seneca in a successful venture:
In neither tongue was the language forced.

Commentary Text 8

2 *poscit in arma manus*: cf. Ovid, *Heroides* 8.74: *vertit in arma manus*.

4 Smith builds his poem around the immediate political context – *torvi . . . viri* must refer to King Charles X Gustav of Sweden, Denmark's primary adversary in the Second Northern War.

5–6 It is common to compare situations of civil war with the falling out of the brothers Romulus and Remus (cf. e.g. Horace, *Epodes* 7.19).

5 *sapuere*: a standard perfect form in Neo-Latin (cf. e.g. Tursen 1561, *s.v. sapio*).

7–13 Introducing Thott and her translation, Smith follows the logic that the pen is stronger than the sword – she offers alternative *secures* (l. 9), the term implying especially the axes in the fasces of the lictors, so political markers, even an alternative to weapons entirely. Making available Seneca's philosophy and good morals, Thott holds the key to purging the region (l. 1) through moral education, using words alone (l. 12).

The focus on *Boreas*, the North (l. 1, 13, 14), rather than Denmark specifically, suggests Thott's work will affect the entire region of the conflict. It might be worth noting that Margrete I (1353–1412), who established the Kalmar Union in 1397, was initially buried in the church of Sorø Academy, then a Cistercian monastery; and while her body was soon stolen and moved to Roskilde Cathedral, the connection to Sorø may encourage comparison of Thott to her, a new uniting female force.

Commentary Text 9

1 *Mentis acumen*: common phrase in Neo-Latin occasional poetry.

2 *Latia ... sine voce*: cf. Silius Italicus 9.78–9: *quo ... si posceret usus, | noscere Gaetulis Latias interprete voces*

6 / 8 *lingua ... coacta / sermo coactus*: cf. Ovid, Ars Amatoria 3.293–4: *quid, cum legitima fraudatur littera voce, | Blaesaque fit iusso lingua coacta sono?*

Latin text

10. Peder Schumacher

Depositum cœli, cuius se DANIA Matrem
    Horret et hanc tantam se genuisse stupet,
TOTTIA, tam vastas muliebri pectore dotes
    Quis putet arctari? Credimus esse DEAM!
5 Quæ Latium Romamque sonat, vernacula Gallis
    Fatur, et attonitos detinet ore Deos!
Quæ quot verba facit linguis, tot gentibus orta
    Creditur, et quævis dejerat esse suam!
Fallor? an e cœlo nuper delapsa Minerva est
10   Humano vultu dissimulata Deam?
Nescio; certe illa est, et, si tantum Ægida ferret,
    iurarem, hanc ipsum parturiisse Jovem.

English translation

10. Peder Schumacher

A deposit from heaven, Denmark is amazed to be her mother
and astonished to have produced a woman so great,
Thott, such vast talents, who would have thought they could be
contained in a female breast? I think she is a goddess!
She sounds like Latium and Rome, converses with Gauls 5
as a native speaker and occupies startled gods with her talk!
She, who speaks as many languages as there are peoples,
appears to be a native speaker in each, and each of them vows she is theirs!
Am I wrong? Didn't Minerva just fall from the sky
concealing her divinity behind a human face? 10
I don't know – it must be her, and had she only carried her shield,
I would have sworn that Jupiter himself had borne her.

Commentary Text 10

1 Alenius (1983: 21) suggests two Vergilian parallels, *Aeneid* 7.620 and 11.595, the latter also used by Tycho Brahe (*In Uraniam elegia* 1573, l. 33–4 and 113; on Brahe see Zeeberg 2022), but *depositum cœli* is frequent in Neo-Latin poetry and the idea that Thott is on temporary loan from the heavens rather resembles Vergil, *Georgics* 1.504–5: *iam pridem nobis caeli te regia, Caesar, | invidet atque hominum queritur curare triumphos.*

10 *Humano vultu*: may echo Ovid, *Metamorphoses* 5.563: *virginei vultus et vox humana remansit.*

dissimulata Deam: cf. Ovid, *Fasti* 6.507–8: *dissimulata deam Latias Saturnia Bacchas | instimulat fictis insidiosa sonis.*

13

The Plinian Dolphin: Johann Matthias Gesner (1691–1761), *Carmina*

Gesine Manuwald

Introduction

The German classicist Johann Matthias Gesner, Latinized as *Jo. Matthias Gesnerus* (9 April 1691 – 3 August 1761), was one of the essential pioneers of the so-called 'new humanism', developing progressive forms of teaching classical languages and literature. Being an inspiring teacher, he produced scholarly editions of works by ancient authors, and he started to compile a Latin dictionary based on principles partly mirrored in today's *Thesaurus Linguae Latinae*. Gesner had a formative influence on the establishment of the newly founded Georg-August-Universität in Göttingen (Niedersachsen, Germany) and its library. In addition to all this activity, he wrote occasional poetry from his youth, some of which was published.[1]

Gesner (born in Roth near Nürnberg) came from a not particularly wealthy family; since his talent was spotted early, he received a thorough education, initially with the help of his stepfather and then supported by scholarships and initiatives of individuals. Already as a student at the university of Jena (in eastern Germany), he published occasional poetry as well as his first philological work *Philopatris dialogus Lucianeus*, demonstrating that the piece *Philopatris* attributed to the Greek writer Lucian could not have been written by him. In this period Gesner's mentor was the theologian Johann Franz Buddeus, who furthered his academic activities and then recommended the young man for the post of deputy headmaster at a grammar school in Weimar in 1715. In Weimar Gesner also assumed responsibility for the Duke's collection of coins and his library, the future Herzogin-Anna-Amalia-Bibliothek. That Gesner was able to obtain this position at the palace of Duke Wilhelm Ernst was due to the intervention of Buddeus and then Friedrich Gotthilf von Marschall called Greiff, later a friend of his. After the Duke's death in 1728 Marschall was removed from his office; then Gesner was relieved of his duties as librarian. He therefore left Weimar for Ansbach, to be a teacher at his former school; soon afterwards (1729) he was appointed headmaster of the Thomasschule in Leipzig, where he reformed the school rules and the curriculum. The composer Johann Sebastian Bach, a teacher of music at that school, is said to have been delighted at Gesner's arrival.

As the professors at the university of Leipzig did not allow Gesner to teach at the university, he left Leipzig when the Georg-August-Universität in Göttingen was founded on the initiative of King George II (named after him).[2] Gesner was one of the first professors to arrive in 1734: he was appointed professor of poetry and eloquence and also became director of the library; he subsequently created the *Seminarium Philologicum*, founded the Göttingen branch of the *Deutsche Gesellschaft* and was a member of the *Akademie der Wissenschaften zu Göttingen* since its foundation in 1751 (serving first as secretary and later as president).

At Gesner's death (in Göttingen) his oeuvre included several editions of ancient authors (e.g. Livy [1735], Quintilian [1738], Pliny the Younger [1739], Horace [1752], Claudian [1759]) as well as pedagogical works. Today it is thought that Gesner's editions of ancient texts were rather traditional and not as progressive as, for instance, the work of his contemporary Richard Bentley (1662–1742) in the United Kingdom, although Gesner correctly argued against the view proposed by another Cambridge Classicist, Jeremiah Markland, that the speeches Cicero delivered after his return from exile were not authentic (see Gesner's *Cicero restitutus*, 1753, 1754). At the same time it is widely acknowledged that Gesner's views on the organization of classical studies at university (especially for the training of future teachers) and his work on lexicography were influential. Generally, Gesner was more interested in historical context and interpretation and less in questions of transmission and textual criticism, and he also felt that the former was relevant for teaching. He outlined his ideas in *Institutiones rei scholasticae* (1715), where he describes what schools should achieve and what universities should teach.[3] For instance, he introduced the distinction between 'statary' and 'cursory' reading (i.e. spending a lot of time on the details of short passages versus reading longer stretches for content) and argued for the latter; he also published anthologies for this purpose (e.g. selections from Cicero [1717], from Pliny the Elder [1723], and from Greek Prose [1731]). He proposed that students training to be teachers should already get experience of school teaching during their studies.

After many years of work and various preliminary works Gesner published the *Novus linguae et eruditionis Romanae Thesaurus* in four volumes in 1749. This dictionary limited itself to ancient sources (excluding medieval and Neo-Latin ones), explained Latin words in Latin, not by translations into the vernacular, and organized individual entries chronologically according to the semantic development of each word. While the combination of factual and linguistic details in entries in the same dictionary was not continued, the principles for arranging the information on the meaning of words had an influence on the structure of the present-day *Thesaurus Linguae Latinae*.[4]

Gesner started writing occasional poetry when he was still young in order to earn money. The numerous poems written during his later career were linked to various occasions; for instance, there are poems in praise of King George or the city of Göttingen.[5] Gesner's occasional poetry includes a series of New Year poems, printed as book 2 entitled *Strenae s. Kalendae Ianuariae*, covering the years 1715 to 1729, in Gesner's *Carminum libri tres* (1743) and later editions. One of these poems (for 1 January 1727), dedicated to Gesner's friend Marschall, is particularly noteworthy since it is the result of a combination of scholarly erudition, enjoyment of poetry and an expression of feelings of friendship for the addressee. The poem was first published in Gesner's edition of the letters of Pliny the Younger (1739), since it responds to one of Pliny's letters (*Ep.* 9.33).[6] It was deemed to be of so much interest that it was included in a selection of Latin poems by recent German poets assembled by John Tobias Rönick in 1749.

In this letter to his friend Caninius Rufus, Pliny the Younger narrates an anecdote about a dolphin, noting that it would be good material for poetic treatment. Gesner takes up this suggestion and produces a poem on the subject; while he says that he had composed it twelve years earlier as a New Year poem,[7] he prints it underneath the text of Pliny's letter among his commentary notes.[8] A short summary of the story can also be found in the *Natural History* of Pliny the Elder (Plin. *HN* 9.26), a passage included in a section on dolphins in Gesner's edition of selections from this work.[9]

Metre: hexameter

Notes

1 On Gesner's biography, academic activity and writings see esp. Eckstein 1879; Schindel 1964; 1989; 2001a; 2001b: 11–17; Friedrich 1991; Jaumann 2004; Vielberg 2013: 1–26.

2 King George II had apparently planned the foundation of a university in Göttingen since summer 1729, along with one of his ministers, Gerlach Adolph von Münchhausen. Plans became more concrete from 1732, and on 14 October 1734 the first lecture took place, followed by the official inauguration on 17 September 1737.

3 For a modern edition with German translation and commentary see Vielberg 2013.

4 On the 'pre-history' of the *Thesaurus Linguae Latinae*, including Gesner's contribution, see Wick 2012.

5 On Gesner's occasional poetry, especially about the city of Göttingen and the university there, see Haye 2004.

6 On this letter (with references to earlier scholarship) see Beck 2016.
7 See the introduction to the poem in the Pliny edition: *Vtrum fecerit Caninius non dixerim: me certe excitauit Secundus, vt hoc sumerem ante XII annos argumentum carminis, quo honorem haberem veteri meo & literarum omnium in Vinariensi aula Patrono, cui mitem senectutem & beatum in rure suo, in quod recessit, otium, ex animi sententia precor. Licetne illud huc attexere? Et ponamus, monumentum non tam qualiscunque ingenii, quod ad tales ludos paullatim vt par est obdurescit, quam aeternae in virum immortaliter de nobis meritum pietatis. Hoc monumentum tibi, Plini Secunde, qui similes MARSCHALLI mei, & tui ipsius viros viuus complectebare, colebas mortuos, ad omnes posteros servandum commendamus. Est autem illud carmen, cuius aliquot similia olim nobis nata sunt. Et erunt forte amici quidam, quibus hunc libellum donabimus, ita blandi, vti rogent ea colligi, quibus deinde obtemperatum, in praefatione gloriari modeste possimus: Satisne probaui me poëtam? an melius, quam ipso carmine?*
8 In Gesner's Pliny edition the poem is connected to letter 9.33 (in line with the modern numbering of the letters), while in the editions of Gesner's poems there is a note after the title referring to letter 9.30 ('Vid. PLIN. *Epist. VIIII, 30.*').
9 Plin. *HN* 9.26: *alius intra hos annos Africo litore Hipponis Diarruti simili modo ex hominum manu vescens praebensque se tractandum et adludens nantibus inpositosque portans unguento peructus a Flaviano proconsule Africae et sopitus, ut apparuit, odoris novitate fluctuatusque similis exanimi caruit hominum conversatione ut iniuria fugatus per aliquot menses, mox reversus in eodem miraculo fuit. iniuriae potestatem in hospitales ad visendum venientium Hipponenses in necem eius conpulerunt.* – Printed in: *Chrestomathia Pliniana oder Auserlesene Stellen aus C. Plinii Secundi Historia naturali, nach den besten Ausgaben Harduini und Ioh. Frid. Gronovii recensiret, hin und wieder verbessert, und weitläuftfig erkläret. Auch mit einem Register versehen von Ioh. Matthia Gesnern*, Jena 1723 (p. 400).

Bibliography

Beck, J.-W. (2016), 'incidi in materiam.... Plinius und der Delphin (epist. 9,33)', *GFA*, 19: 61–87.
Eckstein, F. A. (1879), 'Gesner, Johann Matthias', *Allgemeine Deutsche Biographie (ADB). Band 9*, 97–103, Leipzig.
Friedrich, R. (1991), *Johann Matthias Gesner: Sein Leben und sein Werk*, Roth (Rother Miniaturen 2).
Haye, T. (2004), 'Göttingens Ruhm in: der Dichtung des Johann Matthias Gesner (1691–1761)', in: K. Grubmüller (ed.), *1050 Jahre Göttingen: Streiflichter auf die Göttinger Stadtgeschichte*, 48–77, Göttingen 2004.
Jaumann, H. (^{2}2009), 'Gesner, *Geßner*, Johann Matthias', *Killy Literaturlexikon*, Band 4, 202–4, Berlin.

Schindel, U. (1964), 'Gesner, Johann Matthias', *Neue Deutsche Biographie (NDB)*, 6, 348–9, Berlin.
Schindel, U. (1989), 'Johann Matthias Gesner, Professor der Poesie und Beredsamkeit 1734–1761', in: C. J. Classen (ed.), *Die Klassische Altertumswissenschaft an der Georg-August-Universität Göttingen: Eine Ringvorlesung zu ihrer Geschichte*, 9–26, Göttingen (Göttinger Universitätsschriften, Serie A: Schriften, Bd. 14).
Schindel, U. (2001a), 'Johann Matthias Gesner 1691–1761, Klassische Philologie, Ordentliches Mitglied seit 1751, Direktor seit 1753', in: K. Arndt / G. Gottschalk / R. Smend / Redaktion: R. Slenczka (eds), *Göttinger Gelehrte, Die Akademie der Wissenschaften zu Göttingen in: Bildnissen und Würdigungen 1751–2001*, 1.14–15, Göttingen.
Schindel, U. (2001b), 'Die Anfänge der Klassischen Philologie in: Göttingen', in: R. Lauer (ed.), *Philologie in: Göttingen: Sprach- und Literaturwissenschaft an der Georgia Augusta im 18. und beginnenden 19. Jahrhundert*, 9–24, Göttingen (Göttinger Universitätsschriften, Serie A: Schriften, Bd. 18).
Vielberg, M., ed. and trans. (2013), *Johann Matthias Gesner: Institutiones rei scholasticae – Leitfaden für das Unterrichtswesen*, Wiesbaden (Gratia 48).
Wick, C. (2012), 'Vorgeschichte eines Jahrhundertwerkes', *Akademie Aktuell* 1/2012: 34–9 (https://thesaurus.badw.de/fileadmin/user_upload/Files/TLL/12_wick.pdf).

Source of Latin text

C. Plinii Caecilii Secundi Epistolarum libri decem Gratiarum Actio Panegyricus cum adnotationibus perpetuis Io. Matthiae Gesneri, qui etiam vitam Plinii et indices auctiores emendationesque dedit cum privil. pot. pol. reg. et el. Sax., Lipsiae (Sumtibus Caspari Fritschii) M DCC XXXIX (pp. 418–21).

The poem is also included (with no textual variants, just minor differences in punctuation and orthographical conventions) in:

Io. Matthiae Gesneri. Eloq. et. Poes. in Acad. Georgia Aug. P. P. O. Acad. a Biblioth. Seminar. Philol. et Scholar. Maior. Inpsect. [sic] *Soc. Reg. Pruss. Sodalis Carminum libri III*, Wrocław 1743 (pp. 41–5).

Io. Matthiae Gesneri, Eloq. et. Poes. in Acad. Georgia Aug. P. P. O. Acad. a Biblioth. Seminar. Philol. et Scholar. Maior. Inspect. Soc. Reg. Pruss. Sodalis Opuscula minora. Tomus VIII. Carminum libros III. continens, Wrocław 1745 (pp. 41–5).

Recentium poetarum Germanorum carmina Latina selectiora, ex recensione M. Ioannis Tobiae Roenickii, Helmstedt 1749 (pp. 125–9).

Latin text

DELPHINVS PLINIANVS
ILLVSTRISSIMO HEROI
FRID. GOTTHILF
MARSCHALLO
GRYPHO,
IN STRENAE VICEM OBLATVS
VINARIAE
KAL. IANVAR. A. CIƆIƆCCXXVII
A
I. M. G.

Hoc unum, MARSCHALLE, tuis tibi deerat in hortis,
Fons salientis aquae, nymphis sedesque iocusque.
Hoc etiam tua cura tibi, an fortuna? parauit.
Qua puros capiunt passo specularia soles
5 *In lunam falcata sinu, qua maximus aestus,*
Exoritur iam dulce sitisque aestusque leuamen:
Lympha salit labro recidens excepta capaci.
An patiere, alto qui munera pectore spernis,
Piscis vt his in aquis nostro tibi munere ludat?
10 *Accipe, quem prisci commendat gratia saecli,*
Quique instar saecli vel solus, Plinius ille,
Traiani decus, atque sui laus unica Comi,
Quem primum laudet, cui non ignotus vterque,
Si tibi sit similis prisco reuocandus ab aeuo.
15 *Nec metus, vt labri Delphinum angustia magnum*
Terreat: ille per arentes te laetus arenas,
Ille per & montes, & per stabula alta ferarum,
Ingentem pietate virum pius ipse sequatur.

    Monstrorum genitrix terra Afra, Diarrhytos Hippo
20 *Qua colitur missis Roma de matre colonis,*
Humani ah! nimium vidit miracula piscis.
Imminet vrbs stagno. hoc vicino e gurgite ponti,
(Euripus qualis fluctus vomit atque resorbet)
Hauritque infusas vrgentibus aestibus vndas,
25 *Eructatque suum pelago residente liquorem.*
    Nauigat hic omnis populus, varioque natatu

English translation

The Plinian Dolphin
to the most illustrious champion
Frid[rich] Gotthilf
Marschall
[called] Greiff,
offered instead of a New Year present
of wine
on 1 January in the year 1727
by
I. M. G.

This one thing, MARSCHALL, was missing in your gardens,
a spring of cascading water, a home and an amusement for nymphs.
This your care (or a fortunate turn of things?) has provided for you as well.
Where the reflective surface catches clear sunshine, in a broad
curve formed into the shape of a moon like a sickle, where the heat is
    greatest,   5
there arises now a sweet alleviation of thirst and heat:
water rises up, springing back, having been caught in a capacious tub.
Will you allow, you who despise gifts with your lofty heart,
a fish to play in these waters for you by our gift?
Accept him, whom the esteem of a previous century commends,   10
and who is like a century even on his own, that Pliny,
the ornament of Trajan and the sole glory of his own Comum,
who is to be praised first by anyone to whom both [Pliny and Trajan] are
    not unknown,
if he, being similar to you, is to be recalled from a previous age.
No fear that the narrowness of the tub might frighten a big Dolphin: 15
it shall follow you happily through dry sand
and through mountains and through deep lairs of animals,
you a man outstanding in piety, pious itself.

The mother of monsters, the African land, Hippo Diarrhytus,
which is inhabited by colonists sent from Rome, the mother city,   20
ah, saw the miracle of a fish, that was, ah!, too human.
The city projects over a lagoon. From the nearby abyss of the sea
(just as the Euripus throws up and absorbs floods again)
it draws in the wave mixed with pressing heat
and spews out again its liquid as the sea settles down.   25
    The entire people here goes by sea and by various kinds of swimming

  Neptuni pecus exagitat. dubitaueris, alti
  Imperiumne Iouis, sceptra an fraterna sequantur?
  Non canibus matres hic irascuntur equisue,
30 Non trochus exercet, non puluerulenta palaestra,
  Non cursus, pueros: mare summa & sola voluptas.
  Exsuperat tam quisque alios, quanto altius aequor
  Ingressus, litusque simul nantesque reliquit.
   Huius amore puer reliquis audentior vnus
35 Accensus palmae, quae meta suprema laborum
  Illum erat ante diem, proferre interritus audet.
  Ipsamque ingreditur Neptuni feruidus aulam
  Nec tamen haec bilem mouisse audacia regi
  Creditur. en cara in primis de gente satelles
40 Occurrit puero Delphinus, & accipit vltro
  Aduenientem: & iam videas praeire sequentem,
  Pergentemque sequi, gyros iam ducere circum,
  Iamque subire pedes, equitandaque subdere terga,
  Ponere iam trepidum nouitate, iterumque subire,
45 Inque altum ferre, & vestigia flectere retro,
  Ludentumque gregi laeto sic reddere tandem.
   Fama exit, non est tota vulgatior vrbe
  Fabula, confertumque videt lux altera litus,
  Spectatum veniunt matres, veniuntque puellae:
50 Est, quae Delphinum obtendat, lectura tot inter
  Egregios iuuenes praestanti corpore amicum.
  Confestim redit ad certamina nota iuuentus.
  Delphini puer at vector discedere turba
  Cunctatur, fidei incertus, cautusque pericli,
55 Et pauidae parens genitrici. piscis ad horam
  Praesto est, & puerum cursu designat: at ille
  Cum reliquis celeri repetit sua litora planta.
   Delphinus sequitur rapido non ille volatu,
  Quo, quando vrgetur per Gallica * retia mugil, [note: Plin. H. N. 9, 8 f. 9.]
60 Verum inuitanti similis nutuque vocanti.
  Exilit hinc, & mergitur hinc, varioque natatu
  Spumeus implicitat crebros atque expedit orbes.
  Qualis vbi tenerae Melitaea gente catellus
  Alludit dominae, refugitque, venitque, caditque,
65 Et reuolutus humi subito emicat, atque lacessit

torments the herd of Neptune. Would you doubt whether
they obey the empire of high Jupiter or the brother's sceptre?
Here mothers do not get angry at dogs or horses,
nor does the trundling-hoop provide exercise for boys, nor the dusty
   athletic ground,   30
nor running: the sea is the supreme and sole joy.
Each one excels others by how much more deeply they have entered the sea
and leave the shore and the swimmers together behind.
   Kindled by desire for that victory, one boy, more audacious than the others,
dared to carry forward the point that was the final limit of the exertions   35
before that day, undaunted.
And he eagerly enters the very court of Neptune,
yet it is not believed that this audacity moved the bile of the king.
Look, from the most beloved herd, as a companion,
a Dolphin comes towards the boy and welcomes his approach   40
of its own accord: and you could see it now leading him as he followed
and following him as he went ahead, now drawing circles,
now coming under his feet and offering its back for riding,
now setting him down trembling at the novelty, now taking him up again
and carrying him onto the deep sea and again turning its path backwards,   45
thus finally returning him to the happy group of players.
   Talk about this gets out, no story is better known in the entire city,
and the next day sees a crowded shore,
in order to watch, mothers come, and girls come:
there is one who will use the Dolphin as an excuse, about to choose, among
   so many   50
excellent youths, a boyfriend of outstanding bodily shape.
Without delay the young people return to their familiar contests.
But the boy, the rider on the Dolphin, hesitates to go away from the crowd,
uncertain of his confidence and cautious in view of the risk,
and obeying his fearful mother. The fish is there on time   55
and marks out the boy by its course: but he,
with the others, revisits the shore with swift foot.
   The Dolphin follows, but not with that rapid flight
applied by the mullet when pressed by Gallic nets,
but similar to someone inviting and calling with a nod.   60
It springs forth here and dives in there, and, foaming from its various
   swimming moves,
it interweaves and disentangles frequent circles.
Just as where a puppy of the Melitaean breed
plays for a tender mistress, withdraws and comes and lies down,
and, being rolled up on the ground, suddenly darts up and makes an attack   65

Dentibus innocuis vestem, latratibus aures.
Vel qualis, iuuenes quando facilesque puellae
Lusibus ingenuis campo viridante calescunt,
Malo blanda petit iuuenem Galatea, fugitque
70 Illa quidem celeri pede, sed deprendier optat:
Itque reditque viam, ac vltro se amplexibus offert,
Quos vario cupit anfractu fugisse videri:
Talis Delphinus puerum pertentat amatum.
    Verum hic laetitiae medius, mediusque timoris
75 Blanditias sentit, sed respondere veretur.
Viderat ille cani quondam colludere hyaenam,
Sed lusus inter medios in deuia raptum.
    Omnia vincit amor; timor hic concessit amori.
Accedit venienti, alludit voce manuque,
80 Simonem appellans, & squamea tergora mulcens.
Adnatat, insilit in tergum, ferturque referturque,
Agnosci credit se, credit amari, amat ipse:
Insidias neuter metuit, fiducia crescit
Alterius tantum, quanto est mansuetior alter.
85   Nec non & reliqui dextra pueri atque sinistra
Vectorem comitantur, iter clamore frequentant:
Heus age dextrorsum frenis inflecte caballum,
Heus nunc siste gradum, nunc nunc calcaribus vrge.
    Verum & Delphino suus est comes alter; it vna
90 Spectator ludi non pars, comitatur euntem,
Deducit reducem, sed nil patiturue facitue
Ingenium praeter piscis, moresque ferinos.
    Alter at in litus pueris voluentibus exit,
Et iacet in siccis & cauda ludit arenis,
95 Inque suas pinna feruente reuoluitur vndas.
    Praua superstitio, millenum caussa malorum,
Hos etiam ludos, grata haec spectacula turbat.
Hoc in pisce Deos sibi placaturus Auitus
Naribus affundit croceos nardique liquores.
100 Ilicet acris odor novitate infestat & angit
Delphinum: refugit trepidans, & mergitur alto,
Nec nisi post aliquot languens emergere soles,
Offenso similis diffidentique, videtur.
    Mansisses! aeuo dignum pecus, inque profundis

Johann Matthias Gesner (1691–1761)

against her dress with innocent teeth, against her ears with barking.
Or just as, when young men and willing girls
grow hot with noble play on a verdant field,
charming Galatea challenges a young man with an apple and flees
with swift foot, but wishes to be caught: 70
and she walks and returns along the way, and she offers herself of her own
   accord to embraces,
which she desires to be seen to be fleeing with her various turning:
in such a way the Dolphin tests the boy it loves.
   But he, in between joy and fear,
senses the caressing, but he is afraid to respond. 75
He had once seen a hyena play with a dog,
but snatched away to remote places in the middle of the play.
   Love is victorious over everything; here fear gave way to love.
He approaches it as it came, he sports with voice and hand,
calling it Simo and stroking its scaly back. 80
He swims closer, jumps on the back and is carried back and forth,
he believes that he is understood, he believes that he is loved, he loves
   himself:
neither fears ambush, confidence grows
in one of them as much as the other becomes gentler.
   And, indeed, others too, on the right and the left side of the boy, 85
accompany the rider, throng the route with shouts:
Ho, turn the horse to the right by the reins,
ho, now stop its step, now urge it on with spurs.
   But for the Dolphin too there is another one as its comrade; it goes along
as a spectator, not part of the game, accompanies it as it moves, 90
escorts it when returning, but it does not bear or do anything
beyond the nature of a fish and the habits of wild animals.
   But the other slips away to the shore among the boys rolling along,
and it lies on dry sand and plays with its tail
and rolls back into its home of the waves with an eagerly moving fin. 95
   A perverted superstition, the reason for thousands of evils,
disturbs even these games, these welcome spectacles.
In the case of this fish, to placate the gods for himself, Avitus
scatters on its nostrils liquid saffron and nard-oil.
Instantly a sharp smell by its novelty annoys and chokes 100
the Dolphin: it withdraws trembling and dives into the deep sea,
and only after several days is it seen to be emerging weary,
similar to someone offended and diffident.
   Would you had stayed! A sea animal worthy of eternity, and would you
   had

105 Narrasses, animos hominum quam stulta teneret
 Relligio. sua sed miserum clementia perdit.
 Nam redit ad solitum, populo plaudente, theatrum,
 Paullatimque prior lasciuia redditur. orbem
 Rumores miro crebri de pisce pererrant.
110 Spectatum ingenti concurritur vndique turba.
 Nunquam tot chlamydas, trabeas tot viderat Hippo,
 Roma paludatos tot nunquam miserat illuc,
 Multum, GRYPHE, tui absimiles, & munerum auaros.
   Iam loca, quae tribuant ciues, iam lautia desunt.
115 Ira in inhumanos merito concepta Quirites
 Expetit in miserum, nec quidquam tale merentem.
 Ne sit, quod spectare velit damnosa Quirini
 Gens, in Delphini coniuratur caput insons,
 Tempore & obtruncant capto miseranda gementem.
120   Heu pietas! heu sancta fides! heu flebile fatum!
 Haec erat ergo tibi pro tanto debita amore
 Merces? sicne, viri, miseros tractatis amantes?
 Ergo Barbariae tibi, tellus improba, nomen
 Iure datum post haec merito, aeternumque manebit.
125 Te, Delphine, mori totum vetuere Camenae:
 Tam pisces inter memorabile nomen habebis,
 Quantum homines inter MARSCHALLI fama decusque
 Eminet, occultoque frequens celebrabitur aeuo.

narrated in the deep what a stupid superstition held the minds of human
   beings. 105
But its mildness destroys the poor [beast].
For it returns to the familiar theatre, with the people applauding,
and gradually its previous frolicsomeness returns. Widespread
rumours about the wonderful fish run through the world.
To watch, people come together in a huge crowd from everywhere. 110
Never had Hippo seen so many [Greek] cloaks, so many [Roman] robes,
never had Rome sent so many people in military garments there,
much different from you, GREIFF, and greedy for spectacles.
   Already places that the citizens can bestow, already provisions for guests
   are deficient.
Anger, justly conceived against savage Quirites [i.e. Roman citizens], 115
falls upon the poor one, not deserving anything of this kind.
So that what the pernicious nation of Quirinus would like to see does not
   occur,
a conspiracy is launched against the innocent head of the Dolphin,
and, having caught the appropriate moment, they slaughter it while it utters
   pitiable sighs.
   Alas, piety, alas, holy trust, alas, deplorable fate! 120
Was this then the reward owed to you in response
to such great love? In such a way, men, are you treating miserable lovers?
Thus, the name of 'Barbarian' given to you, wicked country,
rightly, will stay with you after this deservedly and for ever.
That you, Dolphin, should die completely the Camenae have forbidden: 125
among the fish you will have such a memorable name,
as among human beings the fame and glory of MARSCHALL
stands out and will be celebrated frequently over the unperceived course of
   time.

Commentary

Title: The poem's addressee is Friedrich Gotthilf von Marschall called Greiff (1675–1740), an influential civil servant and local politician, who served as first minister (1711–15) and chancellor (1725–28); he supported Gesner during his time in Weimar. 'Greiff' was the original family name of this family of the German nobility; from the beginning of the sixteenth century the title of a hereditary office ('Marschall', 'marshal') became part of the name, with the family name added as a second element.

1–128 The fact that a water feature was erected on the estate of his supporter and friend Friedrich Gotthilf von Marschall called Greiff serves as the starting point for Gesner to present him with a poem on fish as a New Year's gift. At the same time he honours Pliny as the author of the original letter. In the poem Gesner narrates the sequence of events in chronological order (vv. 19–119), as Pliny relates them in the letter: the town of Hippo enables an idyllic life by the sea coast; a boy dares to swim further out into the sea than others; between him and a dolphin a kind of friendship develops; the unusual interaction between the two turns into an sensation attracting lots of people, which destroys the idyllic way of life in the town. Eventually, the dolphin, regarded as the origin of these developments, is killed. The interlude presenting a magistrate guided by false religious beliefs has been taken over too. Gesner not only turns Pliny's narrative into a hexameter poem, but also elaborates some scenes and enriches the text with erudite information and allusions, including reminiscences of the works of a variety of prominent classical Latin authors.

The narrative of the dolphin story is framed by introductory verses directed at the addressee of the poem (vv. 1–18) and an epilogue featuring a lament at the ingratitude shown towards the dolphin and its *pietas* and *amor* towards human beings. The reference to *pietas* (v. 120) takes up a concept from the introduction, where it is said that Marschall is a man of great *pietas* (v. 18), who will be followed everywhere by the dolphin, who is equally characterized as *pius*. As a promising outlook at the end it is stated that the Muses will not let the glory of either the dolphin or Marschall disappear.

With this poem Gesner contributes to this lasting fame. In his version he makes the qualities of the dolphin more explicit and presents them in a positive light: the dolphin is presented as 'too human' (v. 21: *Humani ah! nimium ... piscis*); its *clementia* leads to the disaster (v. 106), and it is not rewarded for its love (vv. 121–2). Here Gesner may play with the ambiguity of a potential parallelism between the dolphin treated unjustly and Marschall, equally standing out by *pietas*. Marschall is addressed directly within the narrative (v. 113), when, in a disruption of the narrative coherence, he is set off from those who come to Hippo from Rome and expect to be entertained by the local population (vv. 111-13). In Pliny's version magistrates come and put pressure on the finances of the place; in Gesner's version, although the town also suffers from the large number of visitors, the anger of the locals against the dolphin is explained as an outlet for the anger towards 'savage Quirites [i.e. Roman citizens]' (v. 115: *inhumanos ... Quirites*) and their demands, and the killing of the innocent dolphin is presented as a kind of act of revenge against 'the pernicious nation of Quirinus' (vv. 117-18: *damnosa Quirini | Gens*).

Gesner will have expected the addressee to understand both the learned additions to Pliny's letter and the allusive comments, relating to himself, and also to enjoy the poetic description of the new water feature. Overall, when writing an occasional poem, the scholar Gesner did more than just create verses.

1-7 Marschall owned an estate in Oßmannstedt (northeast of Weimar), which was later developed into the Wielandgut, which still exists. There Marschall had apparently recently set up a water feature.

2 *Fons salientis aquae*: cf. Plin. *Ep.* 2.17.25: *haec utilitas haec amoenitas deficitur aqua salienti, sed puteos ac potius fontes habet; sunt enim in summo*; Hor. *Sat.* 2.6.2: *hortus ubi et tecto vicinus iugis aquae fons*.

4 *specularia*: literally window panes made from *lapis specularis*, a particular type of mineral that can be easily cut to size and is nearly as clear as glass. The phrasing alludes to an epigram by Martial (Mart. 8.14.1-4: *pallida ne Cilicum timeant pomaria brumam | mordeat et tenerum fortior aura nemus, | hibernis obiecta Notis specularia puros | admittunt soles et sine faece diem.*).

8 *alto ... pectore*: The phrasing is reminiscent of an expression in Vergil (Verg. *Aen.* 6.599-600: *sub alto | pectore*), but context and meaning are different.

9 Appropriately in line with the occasion of the new water feature and the nature of the gift, Gesner describes it as a 'fish': this 'fish' is a poem presenting another version of Pliny's story of the dolphin.

12 *Traiani decus*: Pliny the Younger (*c.* 61-113 CE) held several offices under emperor Trajan (r. 98-117 CE), including the role of provincial governor. While administering the province of Bithynia and Pontus, he exchanged letters with Trajan (Plin. *Epist.* 10). In 100 CE Pliny delivered a speech in the Senate including praise of Trajan, the basis for the extant *Panegyricus*.

Comi: Comum (modern Como), a city at the southern end of Lake Como in northern Italy and Pliny's birthplace.

17 *stabula alta ferarum*: cf. Verg. Aen. 6.179: *itur in antiquam silvam, stabula alta ferarum*.

19 *Diarrhytos Hippo*: Hippo Diarrhytus is the Latin name of the modern town Bizerte in Tunisia.

22 *e gurgite ponti*: cf. Lucr. 5.387: *ex alto gurgite ponti*.

23 *Euripus*: a narrow strait with strong tidal currents between the Greek island of Euboea and Boeotia in mainland Greece.

27 *Neptuni pecus*: i.e. the sea animals, described by a reference to the Roman sea god Neptune.

28 *Imperium ... Iouis, sceptra ... fraterna*: alludes to the power balance between the supreme god Jupiter and his brother Neptune.

29–31 *Non ..., | Non ..., non ..., | Non ...*: for such an emphatic anaphoric repetition cf. e.g. Catull. 64.63–65.

31 *sola voluptas*: cf. Verg. Aen. 3.660–1: *lanigerae comitantur oves; ea sola voluptas | solamenque mali*; 8.581–2: *dum te, care puer, mea sola et sera voluptas, | complexu teneo*.

51 *praestanti corpore*: a frequent Vergilian phrase, cf. Verg. *Georg.* 4.538: *quattuor eximios praestanti corpore tauros*; Aen. 1.71: *sunt mihi bis septem praestanti corpore nymphae*; 7.783: *ipse inter primos praestanti corpore Turnus*; 8.207: *quattuor a stabulis praestanti corpore tauros*.

59 Gesner's note on this line refers to a passage in the *Natural History* of Pliny the Elder, where he notes the swiftness of these fish, by which they can avoid the nets of fishermen, but may still be caught by dolphins (Plin. *HN* 9.31: *apparet acies, quae protinus disponitur in loco, ubi coniectus est pugnae. opponunt sese ab alto trepidosque in vada urgent: tum piscatores circumdant retia furcisque sublevant. mugilum nihilo minus velocitas transilit: at illos excipiunt delphini et occidisse ad praesens contenti cibos in victoriam differunt.*).

62 For the wording cf. Plin. *Ep.* 9.33.5: *delphinus exsilit, mergitur, variosque orbes implicitat expeditque*.

63–73 *Qualis ... | ... | Talis*: a series of similes illustrates the dolphin's behaviour towards the boy, indicating the love it feels, shown in play and not expressed openly, and presenting the relationship like that between a pet and a human or even two humans.

63 *Melitaea*: refers to the Dalmatian island of Melita (modern Mljet). The Elder Pliny discusses the medicinal benefits of Melitaean puppies (Plin. *HN* 30.43).

69 *malo... petit... Galatea*: that Galatea challenges a man with an apple and runs away while wishing to be seen is a motif taken from a song of one of the shepherds in Vergil's *Eclogues* (Verg. *Ecl.* 3.64–5: *malo me Galatea petit, lasciva puella, | et fugit ad salices, et se cupit ante videri.*).

78 *Omnia vincit amor*: a quotation from Vergil's *Eclogues* (Verg. *Ecl.* 10.69: *omnia vincit amor: et nos cedamus amori*), highlighting the erotic dimension of the relationship.

80 *Simonem*: According to Pliny the Elder Simo is a typical name used for dolphins because of the snub-nosed snout (*rostrum simum*) (Plin. *HN* 9.23: *lingua est iis contra naturam aquatilium mobilis, brevis atque lata, haut differens suillae. pro voce gemitus humano similis, dorsum repandum, rostrum simum. qua de causa nomen simonis omnes miro modo agnoscunt maluntque ita appellari.*). Gesner's annotated anthology of passages from Pliny the Elder (see Introduction) includes a comment (p. 404, n. 10) on the plausibility of the reasons for this name as reported by Pliny the Elder.

98 The proconsular legate Octavius Avitus (Plin. *Ep.* 9.33.9) is otherwise unknown. In Pliny the Elder this action is attributed to the proconsul Flavianus (Plin. *HN* 9.26).

111–12 characterizes groups of people by references to Greek (*chlamydas*) and Roman peacetime (*trabeas*) as well as Roman official military clothing (*paludatos*).

113 *Gryphe*: a Latinized version of 'Greiff' ('griffin'), an element of the addressee's name.

115 *Quirites*: the traditional formal designation of Roman citizens as civilians (taken up by *Quirini | Gens*). – In line with the description of the arrival of foreigners in the preceding lines (111–12), this wording suggests that the local population gets angry at the arriving Romans and aims to remove the dolphin, so that there is no longer a reason for visiting. The emphasis on 'Romans' and their characterization is added in Gesner's version.

117–18 *Quirini | Gens*: denotes the Romans, named after Quirinus, a name applied to the founder Romulus after his deification (for the phrasing see Sil. 16.76: *quis cedat toga et armiferi gens sacra Quirini*).

119 The anthology of poems published by Roenick (1749) has a note after this line, referring to Pliny's letter as an inspiration ('PLIN. Ep. l. IX. 33.'). That

the note is placed at this point may indicate that the final lines commenting on the story are Gesner's addition without a direct equivalent in Pliny's version. This section emphasizes the anthropomorphic presentation of the dolphin.

119 *Tempore . . . capto*: cf. Verg. *Aen.* 11.783–4: *telum ex insidiis cum tandem tempore capto | concitat.*

120 *Heu pietas! heu sancta fides!*: cf. Verg. *Aen.* 6.878: *heu pietas, heu prisca fides.*

125 *mori totum vetuere*: cf. Hor. *Carm.* 3.30.6: *non omnis moriar*; 4.8.28: *dignum laude virum Musa vetat mori.*

Camenae: Roman goddesses, also identified with the Greek Muses since Livius Andronicus (cf. Hor. *Carm.* 2.16.37–40: *mihi parva rura et | spiritum Graiae tenuem Camenae | parca non mendax dedit et malignum | spernere volgus*).

126 *memorabile nomen habebis*: cf. Ov. *Met.* 10.607–8: *seu vincar, habebis | Hippomene victo magnum et memorabile nomen.*

127–8 The wording is reminiscent of Horace's *Odes* (Hor. *Carm.* 1.12.45–8: *crescit occulto velut arbor aevo | fama Marcelli; micat inter omnis | Iulium sidus, velut inter ignis | luna minores.*).

14

Giovanni Pascoli (1855–1912): *Reditus Augusti*, an Horatian Mime

Francesco Citti*

Introduction

Giovanni Pascoli is a leading figure in late nineteenth-century Italian literature. Born in San Mauro di Romagna in 1855 into a rural petit-bourgeois family, he graduated in Greek in Bologna in 1882. During his university studies he joined the insurrectional socialists and spent several months in prison (1879); he remained faithful to his humanitarian ideals even afterwards. A poet and teacher, he taught Latin and Greek in high schools and went on to university posts, ending as professor at Bologna.

The fourth of ten children, his existence was marked by a series of family bereavements: the murder of his father in 1867, the death of his mother and five siblings. This explains the obsession – which pervades his poetry – with the family 'nest', which Pascoli tried to rebuild in Massa, where his sisters Ida and Maria joined him, and later in Castelvecchio di Barga, where he stayed until his death (1912).

His fame is mainly linked to his Italian poems, published in a series of collections during his lifetime, especially *Primi poemetti* (1904), *Poemi conviviali* (1904), *Odi e inni* (1906), *Nuovi poemetti* (1909), *Poemi italici* (1911) and posthumously *Poemi del Risorgimento*, *Poesie varie* and *Traduzioni e riduzioni* (1913). The latter contains some interesting attempts to reproduce Greek and Latin metres.

Alongside this vernacular production are some thirty Latin *Carmina* and sixty *Poematia et Epigrammata*,[1] thanks to which Pascoli was awarded thirteen gold medals at the prestigious international *Certamen Hoeufftianum*. He was the author of essays on politics, poetry and literature, both Italian and classical (especially Horace and Vergil, treated in the anthologies *Lyra* [1895[1], 1911[4]] – in which he comments among other texts on Catullus' short poems and Horace's lyric poetry – and *Epos* [1897[1], 1911[2]]), covering Latin epic from the beginnings to Claudian and including a commentary on the entire *Aeneid*.[2]

Pascoli profoundly renewed the Italian poetic tradition, reconnecting with European decadentism and symbolism. His prose work *Il fanciullino* attributes to the poet a child-like vision, according to a Platonic tradition (*Phaed.* 77e), revisited in the light of contemporary psychological theories; he thus establishes a magical-animistic relationship with reality, whose deep soul he discovers. The Child (a metaphor for the poetic function) 'is the Adam who gives the name to all that he sees and hears. He discovers the most ingenious similarities and relations among things'.[3]

For Pascoli, everything has its own language: hence the experimentation with a plurilingualism that contemplates onomatopoeia for the voices of nature (in *Myricae*, and not only), Grecisms for the Greek subject of the *Poemi Conviviali*, archaising Italian for the *Canzoni di Re Enzio* and Latin for the *Carmina*. Here, besides Vergil, Horace is a fundamental point of reference, both a source of inspiration and an *alter ego* of the poet who, already in an early prose work, defines him as *meus interpres*. The Horace of *mediocritas* is in harmony with the love of small things, proper to the Child ('He is not a poet who does not set himself in a vision that his eyes can measure. And big things, rich things, sublime things are not poetic if they are not felt and said by one who stands in wonder before them, precisely because he is small, is poor, is humble'[4]). In the name of *mediocritas*, Horace, seen as a *vates*, invites men 'to desert . . . the turbid city life for the quiet of the fields', to retreat to the *angulus*, the *ager Sabinus*, which Pascoli recreates on his Castelvecchio estate. As many as eight poems out of thirty are Horatian in theme or have Horace as their protagonist: *Veianius, Phidyle, Cena in Caudiano Nervae, Sosii fratres bibliopolae, Moretum, Ultima linea* and *Fanum Vacunae* as well as *Reditus Augusti*.

The *Reditus Augusti*, written in 1896, and awarded the gold medal at the *Certamen Hoeufftianum* in 1897,[5] is a metaliterary poem that reinterprets Horace's *Ode* 3.14. This ode was written in 24 BCE, to celebrate Augustus' return from Spain after a long convalescence: in the first part (ll. 1–12) Horace – in the guise of a *vates* or public orator – addresses the crowd (1: *o plebs*) to promote the public celebration in the streets of Rome; in the central strophe (ll. 13–16) he highlights how the peace restored by Augustus makes this day truly festive. In the second part (ll. 17–28) he orders his slave (17: *i . . . puer*) to make preparations for a private symposium. Doubts as to the unity of the ode and its real occasion have been raised by interpreters, already in Pascoli's time: not only does Horace in the two parts address different interlocutors, but he switches from the grandiose tone of the procession to the quotidian, if not comic, tone of the finale (23: *ianitorem*). For some the ode stages a *supplicatio*, when the prince is still far from Rome; for others it describes the prince's actual *adventus*.

Pascoli provides his interpretation of Horace's ode in *Lyra Romana* (1895: 285): 'Of this ode, variously judged amended and tortured, I know nothing more beautiful and more vivid and more joyful. However, the gladness at the end seems to end with a sigh. The poet is in the midst of the crowd waiting for Caesar, back from Spain. In the meantime, Livia, his wife, and Octavia, his sister, appear to meet their husband and brother. With them comes a procession of matrons: the mothers of the returning warriors and their wives. It is a moment of great movement in the crowd, as everyone pushes to see the illustrious matrons. Mischievous and equivocal words resound here and there, of those who feel bumped and beaten. The poet rebukes the people around him, also joking, and happily orders the banquet.'

For Pascoli the ode does not pose problems of unity, but is made up of several juxtaposed scenes, like a mime: moreover, in *Lyra Romana*, interpreting the ode, Pascoli anticipates some expressions that in his *Reditus* characterise the crowd. Explaining *male nominatis* (l. 11), Pascoli writes: 'I imagine someone saying: *Quid iste fert tumultus?* ... I also imagine that another man, or rather a woman says ... *Ista quidem, vis est.* ... The idea of this chattering is taken from Theocritus' *Adoniazousai*, where the crowd (ὄχλος) is mentioned very often.' For Pascoli, therefore, Horace was inspired by the *Adoniazousai*: thus he, in the *Reditus*, feels authorised to make even more explicit the references to Theocritus, who, in his mime, stages the chattering of two friends, Gorgo and Prassinoa, attending Adonis' feast.

In the last part of *Ode* 3.14, with the invitation to Neaera and Horace's meditation on his past youth, Pascoli senses a melancholic tone that produces an autobiographical mirroring in *Reditus*. When he wrote the poem, in 1896, Pascoli was forty-one years old, as Horace was in 24 BCE. 1896 was an emotionally painful year, due to the failure of his engagement: Pascoli mirrored himself in the frustration of a bachelor and melancholic Horace.

In the first part of the ode, then, Pascoli could perceive the voice of the Child: like Horace, who in the midst of a crowd becomes the spokesman of a collective feeling of celebration, the Child, too, according to Pascoli 'finds himself in a crowd and he sees flags go by and trumpets play. He casts out his word, and all the other people, as soon as he utters it, know it is the very same word they would have uttered. ... The poet is the one who expresses the word everyone had on his lips and no one would utter' (LaValva 1999: 43). In Pascoli's version Horace does not suffer emotional failure, but is recognised, precisely by Neaera, as a *poeta-vates*.

Metre: hexameter

Notes

* I thank the editors of this volume, particularly Stephen Harrison for his suggestions, and for kindly revising and greatly improving my English text.
1 To this corpus (established by Pistelli 1915, Gandiglio 1930 and Valgimigli 1970) should be added the texts collected by Traina / Paradisi 2008 and the poem *Leucothoe* published by Fera 2012.
2 For Pascoli's engagement with the poetry of Sappho and Catullus see Piantanida 2021: 23–52.
3 *Il fanciullino* 3 transl. LaValva 1999: 13–15.
4 *Il fanciullino* 9 transl. LaValva 1999: 37.
5 Text and Italian translation, with brief notes, in Valgimigli 1970: 148–55 and 608–9 and in Goffis 1978, vol. 2: 145–52; detailed commentary in Traina 1995; see also Goffis 1969: 185–91.

Bibliography

Barberi Squarotti, G. (1968), *Simboli e strutture della poesia del Pascoli*, Florence.
Fera, V. (2012), *Iohannis Pascoli e pago S. Mauri Leucothoe*, 1st edn, Messina.
Ferratini, P. (1990), *I fiori sulle rovine: Pascoli e l'arte del commento*, Bologna.
Ferratini, P. (1998), 'Pascoli prosatore e commentatore', in: *Orazio: Enciclopedia oraziana*, vol. 3, 395–7, Rome.
Fraenkel, E. (1957), *Horace*, Oxford.
Gandiglio, A. (1930), *Ioannis Pascoli Carmina*, Bologna.
Goffis, C. F. (1969), *Pascoli antico e nuovo*, Brescia.
Goffis, C. F. (1978), *Giovanni Pascoli: Opere*, vol. 2, Milan.
LaValva, R. (1999), *The Eternal Child: The Poetry and Poetics of Giovanni Pascoli*, Chapel Hill.
Pascoli, G. (1895), *Lyra Romana*, Livorno.
Pascoli, G. (1897), *Reditus Augusti, carmen praemio aureo ornatum in: Certamine Poetico Hoeufftiano*, Amsterdam.
Pascoli, G. (1911²), *Epos*, Livorno.
Pascoli, G. (1913), *Traduzioni e riduzioni*, raccolte e riordinate da Maria, Bologna.
Piantanida, C. (2021), *Sappho and Catullus in Twentieth-Century Italian and North-American Poetry*, London / New York.
Pistelli, E. (1915), *Ioannis Pascoli Carmina*, collegit Maria soror, edidit H. Pistelli, Bologna.
Tartari Chersoni, M. (1998), 'Pascoli poeta', in: *Orazio: Enciclopedia oraziana*, vol. 3, 390–5, Rome.
Traina, A. (1987), 'Pascoli, Giovanni', in: *Enciclopedia virgiliana*, vol. 3, 998–1005, Rome.

Traina, A. (1995²), *G. Pascoli: Reditus Augusti*, Bologna.
Traina, A. (2006³), *Il latino del Pascoli: Saggio sul bilinguismo poetico*, Bologna.
Traina, A. (2008³), *Giovanni Pascoli: Storie di Roma*, Milan.
Traina, A. / Paradisi, P. (2008²), *Appendix Pascoliana*, Bologna.
Valgimigli, M. (1970⁵), *Ioannis Pascoli Carmina. Giovanni Pascoli: Poesie latine*, Milan.
Woodman, A. J. (2022), *Horace: Odes Book III*, Cambridge.

Source of Latin text

The Latin text is based on the *editio princeps* (Amsterdam 1897), with minimal changes in punctuation.[1]

---

[1] I have also followed it by adopting quotation marks to introduce the lines of Horace and other characters (without distinguishing between monologue and dialogue, as some editors do): similarly, in manuscripts only the long dash is used. Preparatory manuscripts are preserved at Castelvecchio and available online; the autograph on which the *editio princeps* is based is now at Haarlem.

Latin text

REDITUS AUGUSTI

Cf. Theocr. XV passim, Hor. C. III. xiv.[2]

'Ὦ θεοὶ ὅσσος ὄχλος. Qui quandoque extrahar? Heia,
hoc age! Formicae numeroque modoque carentes.
Quo, puer, hinc diversus? Ἄνερ φίλε, μή με πατήσῃς.'
Haec modo compressis agitat labris, modo clara
5 Quintus Horatius exclamat per compita voce:
nempe Syracosias et amatum garrit Adonin,
interdum puerum castigat sollicitus, dum
festinos compescit, inertibus improbus instat:
adque forum molitur iter per plena popello
10 omnia, per plateas pedibusque rotisque sonantes.
'O me felicem' luctans aiebat in arcto
'staturae, nihilo si nostris ipse libellis
maior eram, libet ut tibi de me scribere, Caesar
(iamnunc in sextariolo mea carmina iusso
15 perlegere et triplex poteris laudare volumen!):
iam perrepsissem. Trudit nos turba, sues ut.
At nihil est, labor aut quod non perfecerit usus,
duraque temptando ceperunt Pergama Grai.
Huc concede, puer, latus et tege. Ni datur ultra,
20 huc prodisse sat est. Sistamus, μή τι πλαναθῇς.'
Tum circumventus vario clamore, velut si
nil prius audisset prorepens tale per urbem,
obstipuit; tamquam tacita cum nocte viator
nil praeter sonitumque pedum vocemque canentis
25 audiit ipse sui: postquam dormire sub alno
instituit, seu dura viae grave glarea corpus
excipit (aestivum tepido stat sidere caelum);
tum fractos crepitus acredula vibrat ad aures,
et tenui locusta quatit vertigine sistrum
30 et culices auras subtili murmure pungunt:
nec cessant ranae rixis resonare paludem
nec longe latrare canes nec rumpere bufo
turgidus ignoto liquidas a caespite bullas.

---

[2] The two main sources of the poem are indicated in the epigraph by the author.

English translation

THE RETURN OF AUGUSTUS

'Oh, my gods! What a crowd! How and when will I get away from them? Hey!
Come on! They are like ants, they have no number or limit.
Which way are you going away from here? *Please, sir, don't tread on me.*'
This is what Quintus Horatius now mumbles with closed lips,
now exclaims aloud among the crossroads: 5
he chatters of course verses from the *Syracusan Women* or *Adoniazousai*,
meanwhile chastises the slave impatiently, while he
restrains those who are hurried and rudely pushes those who are slow to move:
he forces his way towards the forum through places all full of people,
through the streets resounding with footsteps and wheels. 10
'I am so lucky', he says, struggling in the crush,
'to have my stature: if I were no bigger than my small books,
as you enjoy writing about me, Caesar,
(you may read soon my verses, as you wished,
in the measure of a pint-pot, and praise the three volumes), 15
I would have crept through by now. The crowd pushes us like a drove of pigs.
But there is nothing that effort or practice will not overcome:
by dint of trying the Greeks took the difficult Troy.
Come here, boy, and cover my flank. If we can go no further,
let's be content with getting here. Let us stop, *so you don't get lost.*' 20
Then, surrounded by a variety of clamour, he was astonished,
as if he had not heard anything like it before, crawling
through the city: as when, in the silence of the night, the traveller
hears nothing but the trampling of his footsteps and
his own singing voice; after he has taken to sleeping under 25
an alder, or the hard gravel of the road
has taken the weight of his body (the summer sky stands there with its warm stars),
then the tree frog vibrates its trembling croak in his ears,
and the grasshopper shakes its rattle with gentle spinning,
and the mosquitoes sting the air with subtle buzzing. 30
Nor do the quarrelling frogs cease to make the swamp resonate,
nor dogs to bark in the distance, or the bloated toad
to burst its liquid bubbles from an unseen clod.

Hic media clamans in turba Graeculus: 'O plebs,
35 non aliter Iove natus' ait, 'cui pulchra Iuventas
se iussu patris in celso sociavit Olympo
(umbra locis maestis volitat levis: ipse superne
inter securos celebrat convivia divos);
maximus Hispana, cives, redit ultor ab ora,
40 Geryonae redit armento taurisque potitus;
tergeminumque nefas anima spoliaverat...' 'Ohe
desine, iam satis est.' 'Immo cum pace loquatur,
Aule propola, tua. Melli est audire disertos.'
'Palliolum, credo, copam iuvat.' 'Hoc habet!' 'Hercle,
45 ante lacum furnumve rear nos esse: silete
atque tacete: aegro quidam de Caesare narrat
nescioquid.' 'Vapide (iam verbo principis utor)
se princeps habet. En subito morbus furit. Omnes
exanimi medicis instare deosque precari...'
50 'Morte quidem, cives, laurus venale τι χρῆμα.
nunc urbem repetit, petiit qui praemia laudis,
laudis avens tantum nec tantum prodigus aevi...'
'Graeculus insanit.' 'Quae nunc nova turba?' 'Quid istinc
truditis?' 'Adveniunt matronae'. 'Conspice cunctas
55 vittatas'. 'Mulierne est an dea?' 'Livia.' 'Gaudet
nimirum natum mox complexura tribunum.'
'At soror Augusti me detinet. Ut pia!' 'Matrem
Marcelli, quaeso, monstres.' 'Ibi Iulia (nostin?):
interior sedet huic Octavia.' 'Di tibi multa,
60 di nato bona multa tuo.' 'Carum caput!' 'Omnes
unguibus insistunt visuri deinde, quod ante.'
'Leniter o!' 'Ne nos contundite!' 'State!' 'Procacis
hoc est et nimis audacis...' 'Bona, numquid ademi?'
'Ista quidem vis est.' 'Quidnam fert iste tumultus?'
65 'Parcite' sic Flaccus ridens, 'puerique puellaeque
(heu modo vos inlata sinat vis esse puellas!)
istis (omen habent) moniti iam parcite verbis.
Quis caecos timet Augusto redeunte tumultus?
Quisve mori per vim metuit te principe, Caesar?'
70 Dixerat et turbam simul eluctatus abibat,
atque aliquis 'Pulchre, recte: sapit' inquit 'homullus.'
Dum vespertinus redit, et simul undique turba

Here, from amongst the crowd a little Greek declaims: 'O people,
not otherwise does the son of Jupiter, to whom the lovely Hebe   35
joined herself in marriage by his father's will on high Olympus
(his shade hovers lightly in the regions of sadness: but he himself
up there among the carefree gods celebrates banquets);
just so, he returned the mightiest of avengers, O citizens, from the Hispanic land,
having seized the herd and bulls of Geryon: 40
he had robbed the three-bodied monster of his life ...' 'Ho there!
Stop it: that's enough!' 'No, he should go ahead and speak, with your consent,
Aulus, the huckster. It is honey-sweet to listen to those who speak well.'
'The hostess, I believe, likes the small Greek cloak.' 'He has had it!' 'By Hercules,
I could feel we stand before a fountain or a furnace: be quiet,   45
in silence: someone is saying something about Caesar's
ill-health.' 'The prince feels poorly (to use
his own word). See, suddenly the disease rages. All
press the doctors, breathless with fear, and pray to the gods ...'
'The triumphal bay, citizens, is *something* you pay for with death.   50
Now he returns to Rome, he who went for the prize of glory,
eager only for glory, and prodigal only of life ...'
'The little Greek is crazy.' 'What is this new crowd?' 'Why are you pushing
us away?' 'Here come the matrons.' 'Look, how they all have their heads
swathed in bands.' 'Is she a woman or a goddess?' 'It is Livia.' 'Surely   55
she is looking forward to the joy of hugging her tribune son.'
'But Augustus' sister keeps me captivated. How dutiful!' 'Please,
show me Marcellus' mother.' 'There is Julia (do you recognize her?);
next to her sits Octavia.' May the Gods grant many blessings to you,
and many to your son.' 'What a dear woman!' 'Everyone   60
stands on tiptoes, and so they then see nothing more than before.'
'Oh, gently!' 'Do not crush us!' 'Stay still!' 'This is the act of a man brash
and brazen over measure ...' 'Hey, my good woman, did I steal something from you?'
'This is violence, indeed.' 'What does this turmoil mean?'
'You boys and girls', Flaccus says, with a laugh,   65
'(alas! if you are still girls, despite the violence inflicted),
be warned and avoid these words of ill omen.
Who fears blind turmoil, while Augustus is on his way back?
Who is afraid of a violent death, while you are prince, Caesar?'
Having said this, he walks away, forcing his way through the crowd,   70
and someone comments, 'Well, right, this little man has sense.'
While the poet is returning home in the evening, and with him,
    on all sides, the crowd

(milia multa pedum resonant diversa per umbram:
ostia panduntur; deinceps dilabitur omnis
75 inque suas grex quisque domos, ut hirundinis alta
sub trabe clamosos nidus bibit ordine pullos:
cena Lares adolet, cellas et congius implet
Caesaris), hem! Secum meditatur multa poeta.
'Orbi igitur iam parta quies. Plebecula cenat
80 empta gravi pulmenta, modum legemque, labore.
Haec canerent sparsi Romana caede Philippi?
Quis non translatos alio tibi, Roma, penates
aut iam per vacuum vidisset civibus orbem
perpetuis equitare feros ululatibus hostes?
85 Qui fuit ille dies! Quartum, nisi fallor, ab illo
mox aderit lustrum, mihi nuper condidit aetas
octavum, capitique nives inspergit et acri
nescioquid glaciat sensim mihi flamine mentem.
Non sum qualis eram. Quam vellem paene per illam
90 militiam reddi, calidus te consule, Plance,
agminibus lentis properis et pellibus, armis
impiger et lituis! Verum quid sic queror, aut cur
ipsis sobrius adsisto potantibus unus?
I, puer, atque notae refer interioris ab horreis
95 Sulpiciis (cave det pro vino verba!) lagenam;
unguentumque petas. tarda nisi nocte tabernam
clausit, nil crassum minus et nil suavius illo est,
quod vico Scauri parat unguentarius imus.
Hunc Glycera stephanepolis prope tangit ... at hercle
100 ecquid in unguentis caelebs sertisve laborem?
Quamquam o!' Tum pueri, paulum cunctatus, ad aurem
'I, puer, et pulchrae, nosti quam forte, Neaerae
dic, veniat cithara (nempe est citharistria) sumpta.
Dic, properet: compto nihil est opus. Opperiar ... si
105 ianitor aut ... attende, puer ... si ianitor aut si
ipsa negat, noli nimius clamare: facesse.'
Post secum: 'Talem non est experta Neaera
illa prior; ditemque in paupertate iuventus
me caelo fulgens faciebat stella sereno.
110 Nunc vero ... nobis igitur negat illa?' 'Negavit.'
Quid faciat? Festo cenabis solus, Horati,
et solitas illas tecum meditabere nugas.

(many thousands of footsteps resound here and there in the shadows:
the doors open; then each group moves away, each into
its own home, just as under a high beam the nest 75
gradually swallows up the squeaking chicks:
the smell of dinner reaches the Lares, and Caesar's gallon fills
the pantries), oho! on the way the poet meditates many things to himself.
'So now the world is assured of peace. The populace enjoys
at dinner food purchased with great trouble, order and law.' 80
Was Philippi, bloodied with Roman carnage, to foretell this?
Who then would not have foreseen that your Penates would be moved
elsewhere, o Rome, and that through the world, deprived of its citizens,
savage enemies would ride with incessant howls?
What a day was that! If I am not mistaken, it will soon be 85
twenty years since then; and I have recently turned
forty; age has whitened my head like snow, and with an unknown
stinging breath gradually freezes my heart.
I am no longer the man I was. I would be half-tempted to go back to that
campaign, as fiery as under your consulship, Plancus,
with slow-moving columns and fast-pitched canvas 90
back to march at length, and quickly pitch my tents, full of energy for arms
and the sound of trumpets. But why do I complain like this,
or why do I stand by the drinkers, myself the only sober one?
'Go, my boy, and bring from Sulpicius' cellars a flask
of a label from far within (mind that he does not give you chat instead of wine) 95
and look for unguents. And if he has not closed his shop (it is a late hour),
there is none less greasy and sweeter than
what the perfumer at the end of Scaurus' road prepares.
Next to him is Glycera, the florist ... But, for heaven's sake,
why should a single person like me have the trouble of ointments and garlands? 100
If, however ...!' Then, after a brief hesitation, in the servants' ear:
'Go, my boy, and tell the beautiful Neaera – you know her, I think –
to come with her lyre (indeed, she is a lyre player).
Tell her to hurry: there is no need to dress up. I will wait ... If
the doorman or ... pay attention, boy ... if the doorman or if 105
she herself says no, do not make too much of a fuss: come away.'
Then to himself: 'She did not know me like this, Neaera,
earlier; and youth, a shining star in the clear sky, made me rich,
in my poverty.
But now ...' 'So, she says no?' 'Yes, she said no.' 110
What to do? On this feast day, you will dine alone, Horatius,
and brood to yourself your usual poetic trifles.

Nonne urguent Sosii semper maiora petentes?
Nonne librum Caesar tuus ὀγκωδέστερον optat?
115 Extruitur dum cena, iubet tabulas sibi ferri
atque aliis parat exiguum subscribere carmen.
Herculis (in mentem veniunt quae multa vagantem
perculerant) *ritu modo dictus*: scriptitat: *o plebs*.
Saepe stilum vertit, scalpit caput, exarat, haeret,
120 vixdum desierat suspirans *consule* vates
(consule quo demum vixisset!) scribere *Planco*,
ecce, fores pultare manus, dein stridere vestis
et positae paulum citharae vibrare fides et
in nodum religata comam prodire Neaera.
125 'Me tibi desse meo potuisti credere vati?
Quid muttis? Istum men exhorrere capillum?
Perpetuo gaudes aetatis flore poeta.'

Don't the Sosii insist on ever-increasing demands?
Doesn't your Caesar wish for a *weightier* book?
While the dinner is being set up, he has the writing-tablets brought in   115
and is about to add a short poem to the others.
'*Like Hercules*' (many things come into his mind, which struck him when
wandering around) '*he was reported but now*' – he goes on writing – '*o
   people of Rome*'.
He often turns his stylus, scratches his head, writes down, gets stuck.
The poet had just finished writing, with a sigh, *when Plancus*   120
was consul (the year in which he had really lived!),
when there is a hand knocking at the door,
a robe rustling, the strings of a lyre (resting briefly on the ground)
   vibrating, and,
finally, Neaera coming forward, her hair gathered in a knot.
'Did you think I could neglect you, my own bard?   125
What are you muttering? That I shudder at this hair of yours?
You, poet, enjoy the flower of eternal youth.'

Commentary

1–20 The character of Horace, who speaks to himself or to the accompanying *puer* (ll. 1–3; 11–20) and that of the narrator, who illustrates the context of the action, alternate here.

1–3 The incipit takes up, through direct quotation, translation and rewriting, Theocr. 15.44–5: ὦ θεοί, ὅσσος ὄχλος. πῶς καὶ πόκα τοῦτο περᾶσαι | χρὴ τὸ κακόν; μύρμακες ἀνάριθμοι καὶ ἄμετροι, 'My God, what a crowd! How are we ever to get through this lot? They are like ants – countless, innumerable.' Throughout the poem, Horatian material is employed, especially colloquial expressions: cf. *extrahar* (l. 1) with Hor. *Sat.* 2.5.94–5: (*eum*) *extrahe turba* | *oppositis umeris*; *Heia,* | *hoc age* (l. 1–2) with *Sat.* 1.1.18–19: *eia,* | *quid statis?*; 2.3.152: *ut vivas igitur, vigila: hoc age.*

2 Theocritus' μύρμακες ἀνάριθμοι καὶ ἄμετροι (l. 45) is translated on the basis of Erasmus, *Adagia* 232: *formicae numeroque modoque carentes*, which had in turn combined Horatian expressions: cf. *Epist.* 1.18.59: *extra numerum ... modumque*; 2.2.114; *Carm.* 1.28.1: *numeroque carentis harenae.*

3 Ἄνερ ... πατήσῃς is a quotation from Theocr. 15.52.

4–10 Horace, the narrator, explains, moves laboriously through the crowd humming *compressis ... labris* (cf. *Sat.* 1.4.137) the *Adoniazousai* (*Idyll* 15). *Amatum ... Adonin* (l. 6) translates the title of the *Idyll*, alluding to τριφίλητος, 'thrice-loved', and ἀγαπατός, 'darling', at Theocr. 15.86 and 149. The situation recalls Hor. *Sat.* 2.6.28–31, specifically echoing 30: *inprobus urget* and also *Epist.* 1.2.71: *nec tardum opperior nec praecedentibus insto*. The sounds in the squares are reproduced through alliteration (*per plena popello, per plateas pedibus*).

11–20 Horace, small and plump, manages to slip through the crowd: Theocritus is here interwoven with the Horatian life of Suetonius (p. 470 Rolfe), who paints a physical portrait of the poet, quoting a witty quip from Augustus: 'In person he was short and fat, as he is described with his own pen in his satires and by Augustus in the following letter: "Onysius has brought me your little volume .... But you seem to me to be afraid that your books may be bigger than you are yourself; but it is only stature that you lack, not girth. So you may write on a pint pot, that the circumference of your volume may be well rounded out, like that of your own belly."' (*vereri autem mihi videris ne maiores libelli tui sint, quam ipse es; sed tibi statura deest, corpusculum non deest. itaque licebit in sextariolo scribas, quo circuitus voluminis tui sit* ὀγκωδέστατος *, sicut est ventriculi tui*). *Triplex ... volumen* refers to the three books of the *Odes*, published in 23 BCE according to Pascoli.

16-18 These lines translate Theocr. 15.73-4: ὄχλος ἀλαθέως· | ὠθεῦνθ' ὥσπερ ὕες, 'It really is a mob; they are pushing and shoving like pigs', then (reversing the order of the verses) 61-2: ἐς Τροίαν πειρώμενοι ἦνθον Ἀχαιοί, | κάλλισται παίδων· πείρᾳ θην πάντα τελεῖται, 'The Greeks got into Troy by trying, my darlings; you can manage anything if you really try.'

19-20 These lines rewrite Theocr. 15.67-8: 'Give me your hand, Gorgo, and Eunoa take Eutychis': keep hold of her, so you do not get separated.' πλαναθῆς is found in Ahrens' edition and in those coeval with Pascoli (modern editions have πλαγχθῆς from papyrus discoveries). For the irony and the expression *latus tegere* (19), cf. Hor. *Sat.* 2.5.18-19: *utne tegam spurco Damae latus? haud ita Troiae | me gessi certans semper melioribus.*

21-33 The narrator introduces a long parenthesis: the similarity between the noises of the crowd and those of the countryside (crickets, grasshoppers, mosquitoes, dogs, frogs and the gurgling of water) perceived by a wayfarer, lying under an alder tree. The reader is thus transported into an idyllic space; noise and chaos give way to a serene nocturnal atmosphere pervaded by images and sounds typical of Pascoli's Italian poetry: compare the repetition of the liquids in *subtili murmure* (l. 30), *ranae rixis resonare* (l. 31), *longe latrare* (32), *liquidas ... bullas* (33), with the figures of sound in *Canti di Castelvecchio, La mia sera*, 1-6: 'Il giorno fu pieno di lampi; | ma ora verranno le stelle, | le tacite stelle. Nei campi | c'è un breve gre gre di ranelle. | Le tremule foglie dei pioppi | trascorre una gioia leggiera.'

This section has no correspondence in *Ode* 3.14, but takes up Hor. *Sat.* 1.5.14-19: *mali culices ranaeque palustres | avertunt somnos, absentem ut cantat amicam | multa prolutus vappa nauta atque viator | certatim. tandem fessus dormire viator | incipit, ac missae pastum retinacula mulae | nauta piger saxo religat stertitque supinus.*

27 Pascoli seems to recall Porphyrio's commentary on Hor. *Carm.* 1.9.1: *stet autem 'plenum sit' significat, ut Ennius* [*Ann.* 612 Skutsch] *'stant pulvere campi' et Vergilius* [*Aen.* 12.407-8] *'iam pulvere caelum | stare vident'.*

34-64 The focus shifts from Horace to the crowd commenting on the procession in honour of Augustus: we recognise, in the mass, a number of characters who do not appear in *Ode* 3.14. We find a pompous *Graeculus* poet (ll. 34-41 and 50-2), reminiscent of Juvenal 3.73-4; then there is Aulus, a shopkeeper (ll. 41-2), who intervenes to silence him, but is immediately rebuffed by a hostess (ll. 42-3). This is followed by three short speeches (ll. 44-7) attributable to different male characters. Finally (ll. 47-9), a man (*quidam*) reporting news of the *princeps*' health calls everyone to silence.

From v. 44 the voices become anonymous and increasingly agitated; in the chaotic clatter one can detect female voices protesting in ll. 62–4, interrupted by the vulgar apostrophe *Bona, numquid ademi?* (l. 63).

34–41   In Horace the comparison between Augustus and Hercules is brief and concentrated in the incipit *Herculis ritu*; the *Graeculus* develops it into an epic simile, which opens with a Vergilian form (cf. *Aen.* 4.667: *non aliter quam*) and takes up *Odyssey* 11.601–4: 'And after him I became aware of the mighty Heracles – his phantom; for he himself among the immortal gods takes his joy in the feast, and has for wife Hebe of the beautiful ankles, daughter of great Zeus and of Hera of the golden sandals.' The account of Hercules' fight with Geryon is inspired by Vergil, *Aen.* 8.201–4: *nam maximus ultor, | tergemini nece Geryonae spoliisque superbus, | Alcides aderat taurosque hac victor agebat | ingentis, vallemque boves amnemque tenebant.*

42–9   The members of the crowd are differentiated by the use of different linguistic registers: the epic tone of the *Graeculus* is interrupted by the colloquial tone of Aulus, a salesman, *prŏpola* (with -ŏ-, as in Greek προπώλης, although normally in Latin the first syllable is also long, cf. *TLL* 10.2057.13–4). The idea is taken from Theocr. 15.87–8, where a foreigner silences the Syracusans: παύσασθ', ὦ δύστανοι, ἀνάνυτα κωτίλλοισαι, | τρυγόνες, 'Hey, you wretched women, stop that endless chattering! You are like turtledoves'; but παύσασθε, translated as *desine*, is accompanied by the exclamation *Ohe | … iam satis est*, taken from Hor. *Sat.* 1.5.12. The invitation to be silent is repeated in l l. 45–6 with the more refined Ennianism *sileteque et tacete* (*Trag.* 14 Ribbeck).

47   *Vapide* (related to the root of *vappa*, 'wine that has gone flat': *OLD*[2] 2216) is used by Augustus according to Suetonius, *Aug.* 87.2: '*vapide se habere*' pro '*male*'.

50–3   Cf. *Carm.* 3.14.1–4: *Herculis ritu modo dictus, o plebs, | morte venalem petiisse laurum | Caesar Hispana repetit Penatis | victor ab ora,* is here combined with τι χρῆμα, which has an indefinite value (χρῆμα is pleonastic, cf. *LSJ* 2005, II.2) and also occurs in Theocr. 15.23.

54–9   The comments of the crowd, accompanying the appearance of the *matronae* (Octavia, Livia and Julia), wearing ritual bands, pick up *Carm.* 3.14.5–10: *unico gaudens mulier marito | prodeat iustis operata divis, | et soror cari ducis et decorae | supplice vitta | virginum matres iuvenumque nuper | sospitum*. Perhaps Pascoli had in mind the processions depicted on Augustus' *Ara Pacis*, which were already partially excavated, under the direction of the archaeologist Felice Barnabei, to whom the *Reditus* is dedicated.

60-1 The crowd rising in vain on tiptoe is a detail taken from Manzoni, *The Betrothed* 13 (transl. London 1844: 269): 'And everybody, standing on tiptoe, turned towards the part where the unexpected new arrival was announced. But everybody rising, they saw neither more nor less than if they had all remained standing as they were.'

62-4 Theocr. 15.52: ἄνερ φίλε, μή με πατήσῃς, quoted in Greek in the clause of l. 3, is here translated by *Ne nos contundite*. These verses concretise the interpretation provided in *Lyra*, in the note on *Carm*. 3.14.11-12: *male nominatis | ... verbis*: here Pascoli assumes that in the crowd a girl is protesting about the abuse she has suffered. He then imagines that someone else might intervene by saying *Quidnam fert iste tumultus?* (in his opinion *tumultus* would be a bad omen, a *verbum male nominatum*) and that another woman exclaims *Ista quidem vis est*, like Caesar struck by conspirators: cf. Suet. *Iulius* 82.1.

65-71 The first part of the poem ends with Horace jokingly attempting (*ridens*) to appease the harassed girls (*inlata . . . vis* of l. 66 relates to *ista . . . vis* of l. 64), reflecting on Augustus' role as peacemaker (ll. 65-9) and receiving the approbation of *aliquis* (l. 71).

Lines 65-7 recall *Carm*. 3.14.10-11: *vos, o pueri et puellae | iam virum expertae* and develop the interpretation given in *Lyra*: 'the words *iam virum expertae* will always seem strange and improper if one does not think that they are said cheerfully by the poet', while ll. 68-9 are inspired by ll. 13-16 of the Horatian ode: *hic dies vere mihi festus atras | exiget curas; ego nec tumultum | nec mori per vim metuam tenente | Caesare terras*, to emphasise the importance of the *pax Augusta*.

The anonymous passer-by's exclamations (l. 71) recall Hor. *ars*. 428: *clamabit enim 'pulchre, bene, recte'*, while *homullus* replaces *homūncĭō* (which does not fit into a hexameter), employed by Augustus to describe Horace: cf. Suet. *Vita Horati* (p. 468 Rolfe): *saepe eum . . . homuncionem lepidissimum appellat*.

72-8 The narrator compares the crowd's homecoming with the swallow's return to the nest. As in lines 21-33, here too the simile brings out the poet's true voice: 'the image that returns most frequently within Pascoli's familiar poetry is that of the home as a "nest", warm, closed, secret, . . . but teeming with complicit intimacies, instincts and visceral affections' (Barberi Squarotti 1968: 9).

In *cena Lares adolet* (l. 77), *adoleo* means 'to give out or emit a smell or odour, to smell', and not 'burn ritually', 'offer in sacrifice' or 'cremate', as one would expect: Pascoli found in Forcellini a lemma *adoleo*, explained as 'significat idem quod oleo, vel odorem spiro'.

While the crowd enjoys the dinner, thanks to Augustus' generosity (he had donated 400 sesterces each, cf. *Res Gestae* 15), Horace *meditatur multa* (l. 78): he not only reflects on, but composes poetry, according to the Augustan use of the verb: cf. l. 112: *meditabere nugas*.

79–110 This section too, albeit to a lesser extent, adopts the dialogic form: Horace's character alternates between internal monologue (vv. 79–93, 99–101 and 107–10) and dialogue with the slave (vv. 94–9, 102–6, 110), who utters only a lapidary phrase (*Negavit*, l. 110) to convey Neaera's refusal to attend the feast.

79–84 Horace reflects on the past of the civil wars, when the end of Rome seemed imminent: there are echoes of Vergil (*Aen.* 3.495: *vobis parta quies*; 4.21: *sparsos fraterna caede penates*) and Horace: cf. *Epod.* 16.11–14: 'A barbaric conqueror will tread on its ashes, his horseman will trample on the city with clattering hooves, and (the ultimate sacrilege!) he will scatter in his arrogance the bones of Romulus that are now sheltered from wind and sun', whose image of barbarians riding against Rome combines with Hor. *Carm.* 1.2.51–2: *neu sinas Medos equitare inultos | te duce, Caesare*.

85–93 The memory of the battle of Philippi (42 BCE, under the consulship of Plancus, cf. ll. 90 and 120) makes Horace regret his youth; he is now forty-one years old (Pascoli's age too). Horace's physical portrait depends on *Carm.* 3.14 (25: *albescens ... capillus*; 27–8: *calidus iuventa | consule Planco*), *Carm.* 4.13.11–12: *te ... | turpant ... capitis nives* and also 4.1.3–4: *non sum qualis eram bonae | sub regno Cinarae*. The indication of age echoes *Carm.* 2.4.22–24: *fuge suspicari | cuius octavum trepidavit aetas | claudere lustrum*. Like the rest of the Romans, who celebrate at home, thanks to Augustus' generosity, Horace organises his own dinner.

94–101 Horace gives instructions for the banquet: Pascoli (like Horace, cf. Woodman 2022: 244) combines the address to a slave boy with instructions reminiscent of the so-called shopping-list motif, frequent in Greek sympotic poetry and especially in epigrams. He amplifies *Carm.* 3.14.17–20: *i pete unguentum, puer, et coronas | et cadum Marsi memorem duelli, | Spartacum si qua potuit vagantem | fallere testa*.

The meaning of *notae ... interioris ... | ... lagenam* (ll. 94–5) is illustrated by Pascoli (1895: 55): he recalls that in *Carm.* 2.3.8 Horace defines an amphora as *interior* because those with the oldest wine remained at the back of the cellar. From Horace comes the mention of Sulpicius' shop (*Carm.* 4.12.18–19) and the *vicus* where items for the symposium are sold (*Epist.* 2.1.269–70 and *Sat.* 2.3.228). Finally, doubts about the necessity of a banquet for a *caelebs*

(l. 100) echo *Carm.* 3.8.1-3: *Martiis caelebs quid agam Kalendis,* | *quid velint flores et acerra turis* | *plena miraris* ...?

101-6 The request to the *puer* to invite Neaera elaborates *Carm.* 3.14.21-4: *dic et argutae properet Neaerae* | *murreum nodo cohibente crinem;* | *si per invisum mora ianitorem* | *fiet, abito.* Compared to the original, Pascoli emphasises Horace's uncertainty, first with the aposiopesis *Quamquam o!*, then with *cunctatus* (l. 101) and finally with suspension dots (ll. 104-5).

107-10 Horace reflects to himself on his past youth, with a rewriting of *Carm.* 3.14.25-8: *lenit albescens animos capillus* | *litium et rixae cupidos protervae;* | *non ego hoc ferrem calidus iuventa* | *consule Planco.* The image of youth as a *caelo fulgens* ... *stella sereno* (l. 109) transfers to a metaphorical level the nocturnal scene of *Epod.* 15.1-2: *nox erat et caelo fulgebat luna sereno* | *inter minora sidera.* The allusion is remarkable, because that *Epode* features the hetaera Neaera, who for Pascoli is the same as the one in *Carm.* 3.14, symbol of youth, as the etymology of the name would show (from νέα, cf. Pascoli 1895: 127). As Goffis (1978: 152) notes, Neaera, unlike Horace, has not aged, showing a lack of concern for temporal constraints typical of Pascoli's female figures.

111-27 The narrator describes Horace who, taking his cue from the events of the day, begins to compose *Ode* 3.14: as soon as he has finished, Neaera enters the scene and is the focus of the conclusion of the *Reditus*.

Horace meditating to himself (ll. 111-12) comes from *Sat.* 1.9.1-2: *ibam forte via Sacra* ... | *nescio quid meditans nugarum, totus in illis*; the claims of the greedy Sosii booksellers are inspired by *Ars* 345: *hic meret aera liber Sosiis*, and *Epist.* 1.20; Pascoli dedicates the poem *Sosii fratres bibliopolae* (1899) to their shop. Augustus' desire for a more substantial book is taken from Suetonius, *Vita Horati* (ll. 11-20): here Pascoli transforms the transmitted ὀγκωδέστατος ('weightiest') into the comparative ὀγκωδέστερον to fit the context (cf. also l. 113: *maiora petentes*), anticipating a conjecture of Leo (cf. Fraenkel 1957: 20).

The image of Horace writing is taken from *Sat.* 1.10.70-3: *et in versu faciendo* | *saepe caput scaberet vivos et roderet unguis.* | *saepe stilum vertas, iterum quae digna legi sint* | *scripturus.* The metaphor of ploughing to indicate writing was already classical: cf. Plat. *Phaedr.* 276c; Atta, *Tog.* 12-13 Ribbeck; Isid. *Etym.* 6.14.7. It is very frequent in Pascoli's poetry: cf. *Myricae, Il piccolo aratore* 1-4; *Sosii fratres* 2-4: *librarioli data verba* ... | *figebant calamis, et in albis nigra serebant* | *membranis; Catullocalvos* 71-3.

Neaera appears unexpectedly: *ecce* (l. 122) 'introduces the narration of an unexpected fact' (Pascoli 1911: 110). Her hair is inspired by *Carm.* 3.14.22: *nodo cohibere crinem* and 2.11.23–4: *in comptum* ... | ... *comam religata nodum*. She addresses Horace as *vates* (l. 125; cf. also 120) and as a *poeta*, who, as such, enjoys eternal youth. This is an Horatian theme: poetry defeats the *fuga temporum* (*Carm.* 3.30), and the immortal poet makes the man worthy of immortal praise (*Carm.* 4.8.28). The poem therefore ends, emphatically, with the word *poeta* (l. 127).

Index of Names

This index includes the names of early modern authors and of the ancient writers referred to as inspirations and precedents as well as of some of the historical figures they interacted with, as mentioned in the general introduction as well as in the introductory and commentary material to the selected texts.

Accius 2
Achilles Tatius 218
Alan of Lille 2
Alcuin 2
Ammianus 148
Apollodorus of Athens 122, 226
Apollonius of Rhodes 1
Apuleius 2, 293
Aratus 1, 189–92, 198–201, 204–6
Aristotle 69, 75, 83, 105, 106–7, 124, 283
Augustus (Caesar) / Gaius Iulius Caesar Octavianus 34, 64, 75, 121, 292, 313, 316–30
Ausonius 83, 188
Avienus 1, 199–200, 204, 206

Bacineto, Aurelio 34
Badoarius, Sebastianus 32
Barclay, John 4, 211–31
Bartholin, Thomas 256–7, 271
Below, Marie 285
Bembo, Pietro 106
Bering, Vitus 256–7, 277, 261, 263, 267
Boethius 2
Brahe, Sophie 282, 285
Brahe, Tycho 282, 283–5, 292
Brochmand, Rasmus Hansen 256, 258

Caesar (Gaius Julius) 155, 160
Caesius Bassus 2
Caetani, Daniele 27, 34
Calderini, Domizio 22

Callimachus 1
Cardano, Girolamo 106
Carnesecchi, Pietro 123–6, 134–5
Catullus 3, 4, 19, 38, 106–7, 117, 119–20, 123–6, 134–7, 151, 154, 164, 186, 199, 206, 266, 308, 311, 314
Celtis, Conrad 3–4
Chaula, Tommaso 30
Cicero 1, 2, 4, 30, 42, 75, 83, 102, 106, 116, 125, 126, 134–7, 154, 177, 189–92, 194, 198–201, 202, 204–5, 248, 253, 276, 294
de Cisneros, Francisco, Jiménez 60
Claudian 5, 83, 98, 294, 311
Columella 148
Costanzi, Antonio 16, 19, 22, 39
Crinito, Pietro 3

Dante Alighieri 64, 83, 99, 101
Diodorus Siculus 19, 116, 226
Dorat, Jean 4, 139–62
Dousa, Janus 4–5, 163–88
Duport, James 5, 233–54

Ennodius 83, 96
Erasmus of Rotterdam 4, 78, 83–4, 106, 324
Ernst, Heinrich 256, 266
Euripides 101, 122, 140, 191, 211

Faber, Johannes 256
Falcksen, Marcus Giöe 256, 257–8, 270

Filelfo, Francesco 175
Filomuso, Giovanna Francesco 16, 18
Filosseno, Marcello 23
Flaminio, Marcantonio 123–6, 134–5
de Fonseca y Ulloa, Alonso 59
Fracastoro, Girolamo 106
Fruterius, Lucas 167, 176

Galen 119
Gellius, Aulus 26
Germanicus 1, 189–206
Gesner, Johann Matthias 5, 293–310
van Giffen (Giphianus), Hubert 167, 174, 176–7
Giraldi, Lilio Gregorio 40
Grotius, Hugo 4, 189–209

Heinsius, Daniel 5, 253
Heinsius, Nicolaas 5
Heliodorus 212, 218
Hesiod 3, 52, 82, 135, 137
Hippocrates 106, 119
Homer 1, 3, 4, 137, 139, 161, 190, 204–5, 211, 218, 234, 249, 251–2, 282
Horace 4, 5, 18, 27, 34, 74, 80, 98, 105–7, 119–21, 122, 125, 135–8, 140, 144, 148–50, 151, 154–5, 157, 160–1, 164, 174–7, 186–8, 205, 251–4, 266, 270, 282, 288, 294, 307, 310, 311–30
Hrosvitha of Gandersheim 3–4
Huitfeldt, Arild 284
Hyginus 148

Jiménez *see* de Cisneros
Julian the Apostate 148
Juvenal 102, 114, 174–7, 187, 266, 325

Kochanowski, Jan 4, 189–209

Lambin, Denis 139, 167, 176, 189, 191
Lauremberg, Hans 256–8, 272, 285
Lernutius, Janus 167
Livy 56, 57, 117, 160–2, 194

Lucan 21, 39, 96, 99, 103, 118, 121, 149, 160, 186, 248, 266–7
Lucian 149–50, 293
Lucretius 1, 57, 118, 154, 160, 167, 176, 270

Manilius 1, 4, 154, 190
Mantuanus, Baptista 22, 148
Manutius, Aldus 3, 81–104
von Marschall called Greiff, Friedrich Gotthilf 293–307
Marsi, Paolo 3, 39–57
Martial 5, 10–11, 22, 26, 32, 76, 77, 82, 103–4, 135, 136, 148, 155, 174, 176, 177, 188, 234, 248, 250, 251, 266, 267, 271, 307
de' Massimi, Bernardo 28
Milton, John 234, 250–1, 253–4
Montano, Benito Arias 4
Morata, Olympia Fulvia 282
Muret, Marc-Antoine 4

de Nebrija, Antonio Elio 4, 59–80
Nigidius Figulus, Publius 18
van Nijevelt, Willem van Zuyle 178, 186
Nonnus 218

Octavian(us) *see* Augustus
Ogilby, John 234, 251
Ovid 3, 5, 7, 18, 19, 39, 40–1, 52–7, 64, 74–5, 80, 82, 98, 100, 102, 107, 117, 118, 119, 120, 121, 122, 125, 135, 136, 137, 148, 149, 155, 160, 161–2, 174, 211, 212, 213, 214, 220, 270, 283, 288, 289, 292

Palladio Sorano, Domizio 30, 40
Pascoli, Giovanni 5, 311–30
Perotti, Niccolò 3, 9–38
Persius 2, 60, 76, 177
Petrarch 2, 97, 139
Petronius 211–12
Phialtes 22
Philetas 1, 137

Index of Names

Pico, Giovanni 118
Pico della Mirandola, Giovanni 81, 97, 106
Pindar 140, 151, 154
Plautus 116, 154, 164, 187, 214, 254
Pliny the Elder 16, 211, 218, 308, 309
Pliny the Younger 293–310
Poliziano, Angelo 2, 3, 18
Pompeo Corniano, Giovanni 28, 32, 34
Ponticus, Ludovicus 16, 26
Pontoppidan, Erik Eriksen 257–59, 261, 266, 272, 282, 285
Propertius 4, 98, 107, 117, 125, 136–7, 138, 148, 149, 154, 155, 160, 186, 272

Quintilian 75, 80, 103, 294

de Ronsard, Pierre 139, 140, 144, 151, 154
Rosenkrantz, Holger 284, 285
Rosenkrantz, Jørgen 255, 256, 284
Rosing, Hans Clausen 257, 288

Sabellico, Marcantonio 16, 27, 30
Salmasius, Claudius 234, 250–1, 254
Sappho 74, 151, 314
Scaliger, Joseph Justus 4–5, 108, 117–18, 190, 250
Scaliger, Julius Caesar 4, 105–22, 186, 234, 250
Schumacher, Peder 257–8, 267, 292
van Schurman, Anna Maria 255, 256, 257, 259, 263, 266, 271, 282

Seneca 2, 3, 5, 100, 101, 155, 160, 211, 227, 248, 255–9, 261, 266, 270–1, 276, 282, 284, 288
Silius Italicus 23, 148, 149, 289
Smith, Jesper Lauridsen 257–8, 288
Sophocles 140, 191, 222
Statius 4, 10, 18, 27, 118, 154, 211–14, 218–19, 226, 227–32, 266, 271
Stobaeus 191
Strabo 1
Sulpicia 272

Terence 27, 71, 76, 135, 154, 186
Theocritus 5, 313–27
Theophrastus 106, 108, 233–4, 249
de Thoor, François 167
Thott, Birgitte 3, 5, 255–92
Tibullus 4, 98, 101, 121, 148, 155, 270, 271

Varro 2, 18, 41, 57, 77
Vergil 2, 3, 34, 40, 52–7, 75, 76, 80, 82–3, 96, 97, 98–9, 100, 102, 106, 116, 117, 118, 119, 120–1, 122, 135, 149, 154–5, 160, 161, 162, 174, 175, 189, 198–200, 205, 212, 219, 220, 234, 251–2, 272, 292, 307–10, 311, 312, 325, 326, 328
Vettori, Piero 3, 123–38
Vida, Marco Girolamo 105
Virgilio, Polidoro 28–30, 34

Zenodotus 1
de Zúñiga y Pimentel, Juan 59–60

www.ingramcontent.com/pod-product-compliance
Lightning Source LLC
Chambersburg PA
CBHW071800300426
44116CB00009B/1148